ICOMM:
Interpersonal Concepts and Competencies

ICOMM: Interpersonal Concepts and Competencies

Foundations of Interpersonal Communication

ROY BERKO, JOAN E. AITKEN,
AND ANDREW WOLVIN

ROWMAN & LITTLEFIELD PUBLISHERS, INC.
Lanham • Boulder • New York • Toronto • Plymouth, UK

Published by Rowman & Littlefield Publishers, Inc.
A wholly owned subsidiary of The Rowman & Littlefield Publishing Group, Inc.
4501 Forbes Boulevard, Suite 200, Lanham, Maryland 20706
http://www.rowmanlittlefield.com

Estover Road, Plymouth PL6 7PY, United Kingdom

British Library Cataloguing in Publication Information Available

Library of Congress Cataloging-in-Publication Data

Berko, Roy M.
  ICOMM : interpersonal concepts and competencies : foundations of interpersonal communication / Roy Berko, Joan E. Aitken, and Andrew Wolvin.
      p. cm.
  Includes bibliographical references and index.
  ISBN 978-0-7425-9962-8 (pbk. : alk. paper) — ISBN 978-0-7425-9963-5 (electronic)
  1. Interpersonal communication. 2. Interpersonal relations. 3. Communication. I. Wolvin, Andrew D. II. Aitken, Joan E. III. Title.
  BF637.C45B477 2010
  153.6—dc22

                                                                    2010001322

∞ ™ The paper used in this publication meets the minimum requirements of American National Standard for Information Sciences—Permanence of Paper for Printed Library Materials, ANSI/NISO Z39.48-1992.

Printed in the United States of America

Dedication

For most of the history of Western education the field now known as speech or communication mainly consisted of the study of public speaking, rhetoric, argumentation, debate, and speech analysis. In the late 1960s Dr. Gerald Phillips, a professor of speech at the Pennsylvania State University, and a group of his graduate students, started to use the research and theories of the social sciences (psychology, sociology, and anthropology) to examine what people did as communicators. Their work is credited as laying the foundation for the development of speech communication as a social science.

Phillips believed that people displayed their psychological underpinnings in the way they spoke and listened in their conversations, families, businesses, and organizations. He believed that these expressions were both verbal and nonverbal. He conjectured that by studying people's communication educators could improve what he called an individual's interpersonal and intrapersonal communication.

Phillips believed that the new field of communication would best be served by teaching not only concepts, but also competencies. He also believed that the best way for a person to learn was to experience the material. In addition, he believed that a person's culture is paramount in why he or she communicates the way that he or she does.

Gerald Phillips was my doctoral advisor. He was also my respected peer and friend. As one of the graduate students who studied with Phillips and taught one of the first courses in interpersonal communication, I owe much of my teaching abilities and educational philosophy to him. It is therefore both appropriate and with appreciation that *ICOMM: Interpersonal Concepts and Competencies* is dedicated to Gerald Phillips, the brilliant, controversial, exciting, and opinionated guru of so many of the leading lights in the field of communication.

Roy Berko

Contents

To the Students

As you use *ICOMM: Interpersonal Concepts and Competencies* you will become aware that this is not the usual textbook. The incorporation of activities and questionnaires within the textual material should allow you to use self-discovery to broaden your understandings and skills.

This text is written in a personal and friendly manner, stressing concepts that should be important in your daily life. Unlike many courses where students moan, "Why do I have to study this?" you will find that interpersonal communication is very important to you. Students who have been in our classes often say, "How come no one ever taught us this before?"

You spend more of your time on communicating than on any other activity outside of sleeping; and there is even evidence to indicate that you are doing self-talk through means of dreaming as you sleep. Your life will be enhanced and enriched by your learning the concepts and competencies taught in this text. You will be a better family member and employer or employee. You will be better able to understand why you say and do what you say and do. You will be better able to understand the people with whom you come in contact, no matter their culture.

For additional information please go to this book's companion site: http://onlineacademics.org/ICOMM/.

We hope you enjoy our journey together.

Roy, Joan, and Andy

Acknowledgments

This book would not have been possible without the editorial assistance of Eunice Berko.

Much of the philosophy of the materials presented comes from previous projects codeveloped with Lawrence Rosenfeld. His stamp of ideas is imprinted on this volume.

All of the graphics and cartoons are the handiwork of Bob Vojtko. We greatly appreciate his dedication and creativity.

Activities

CHAPTER 1

Foundations of Interpersonal Communication

Learning Outcomes

After reading this chapter, you should be able to:

- Define the characteristics of communication, intrapersonal communication, and interpersonal communication.
- List and explain the components of human communication.
- Identify and illustrate the linear, interactional, and transactional models of communication.
- List and explain the classifications of communicative noise and how to deal with them as they relate to interpersonal communication.
- Explain the basis for interpersonal communication including the roles of nurture and nature.
- Explain the role of culture in interpersonal communication.
- Compare some of the basic concepts of interpersonal communication.

A sign hanging on the bulletin board outside the office of a college communication professor read:

I know that you believe you understand what you think I said, but I am not sure you realize that what you heard is not what I mean.

One day, a student added, "Are you sure?"

The moral to the story is: Effective communication depends on a shared understanding of meaning.

Much like breathing, communication is one of your most basic activities. And if you are like most people, you take communication for granted, much like breathing, seldom pausing to ask yourself why it is important or what it really is, or what you need to do to be a competent communicator. Many of our educational institutions assume because you can speak, you can communicate, and because you can hear, you can listen. Students forget, or don't realize that speaking and listening are *learned* skills. Few schools teach students much about oral or nonverbal communication. Few teach the interpersonal skills of listening, question asking, speaking in a group, conversational skills, and direction giving. Studies show that some college students experience development problems including difficulty in communicating or processing words (language). In addition, some college students don't have the problem solving skills they need to succeed after college.[1] In spite of these observations, educational institutions fail to teach that:

Communication is meaningful in your life because it is how you know yourself. We talk to ourselves continuously, using labels to describe for ourselves who and what we are, and to determine what we should do, and why we should do it. Yet, you probably haven't been trained to listen to that voice or to pay attention to what your body is doing as you carry on your self-conversations.

Communication is the basis for human contact. Communicating is the way you share your ideas and feelings with others. You may tell others face-to-face, in writing, or by electronic means how you feel, what you know, what you want to know, and how the world appears to you. How proficient do you feel to do that sharing? How much do you hide because you don't know how to communicate your thoughts and feelings or the value of sharing?

Before considering the specific topic of this book—interpersonal communication—it is necessary to define and explain the broader area of *communication*.

LEARNING EXPERIENCE: Interested in learning how you perceive yourself as a communicator? If so, do Activity 1.1.

Communication Defined

Communication is a conscious or unconscious, intentional or unintentional process in which feelings and ideas are expressed as verbal and/or nonverbal messages, which are sent, received, and comprehended. Communication is dynamic, continuous, irreversible, interactive, and contextual.[2]

A person can be aware of sending a message, such as when you sit down with your best friend to discuss a serious problem. Thus, communication can be *conscious* and *intentional*. You plan what you want to say because you want to ensure that there is no doubt of the consequences of the situation. Or, you can react with an unintentional facial expression that you are unaware of, as when your boss tells you that he'd like you to work overtime, but you have a date and want to leave on time. Thus, communication can be *unconscious* and *unintentional*.

We call communication *dynamic* because it is in a constant state of flux, modification, or change. The individual's attitudes, values, and skills change, the context changes, and so do the messages. For example, if you and a friend are talking and she suggests your ideas are wrong, what started as a pleasant conversation can convert into a war of words.

Communication is *continuous* because it never stops. Whether asleep or awake, you are processing ideas and information through your dreams, thoughts, and expressions. Your brain remains active; you are communicating, if not to others then to

ACTIVITY 1.1
How Competently Do You Communicate?

Carefully consider the following list of communication skills. Your self-assessed communication competence is most accurate if you are able to think back over past situations in which you communicated with others and generalize from those situations to derive your answers. To further establish the validity of your self-analysis, it may be helpful to get feedback from people who know you well and with whom you communicate often. Then, based on the scales, indicate how often you use each skill and how satisfied you are with your ability.

Scale for How Often
5 = all or most of the time (91–100 percent of the time)
4 = often (71–90 percent)
3 = sometimes (31–70 percent)
2 = rarely (11–30 percent)
1 = never or almost never (0–10 percent)

Scale for How Satisfied
5 = very satisfied
4 = somewhat satisfied
3 = neither satisfied nor dissatisfied
2 = somewhat dissatisfied
1 = very dissatisfied

	How Often	*How Satisfied*
1. I listen effectively.	_____	_____
2. I use appropriate words for the situation.	_____	_____
3. I use appropriate pronunciation for the situation.	_____	_____
4. I use appropriate grammar for the situation.	_____	_____
5. I use effective eye contact.	_____	_____
6. I speak at a rate that is neither too slow nor too fast.	_____	_____
7. I speak fluently (avoiding "uh," "like, uh," "you know," awkward pauses, and silences).	_____	_____
8. My movements, such as gestures, enhance what I say.	_____	_____
9. I give appropriate spoken and unspoken feedback.	_____	_____
10. I use vocal variety when I speak (rather than speaking in a monotone voice).	_____	_____

(continued)

ACTIVITY 1.1 (*continued*)

11. I speak neither too loudly nor too softly.   _____ _____
12. I use appropriate facial expressions.   _____ _____
13. I understand my communication partner's
    main ideas.   _____ _____
14. I understand my communication partner's feelings.   _____ _____
15. I distinguish facts from opinions.   _____ _____
16. I distinguish between speaking to give someone
    information and speaking to persuade someone
    to think, feel, or act a particular way.   _____ _____
17. I recognize when my communication partner does
    not understand my message.   _____ _____
18. I express ideas clearly and concisely.   _____ _____
19. I express and defend my point of view.   _____ _____
20. I organize messages so others can understand them. _____ _____
21. I use questions and other forms of feedback to
    obtain and clarify messages.   _____ _____
22. I respond to questions and other forms of feedback
    to provide clarification.   _____ _____
23. I give understandable directions and instructions. _____ _____
24. I summarize messages in my own words.   _____ _____
25. I describe another's viewpoint.   _____ _____
26. I describe differences of opinion.   _____ _____
27. I express my feelings and opinions to others.   _____ _____
28. I initiate and maintain conversations.   _____ _____
29. I recognize and control my anxiety in
    communication situations.   _____ _____
30. I involve the other person in what I am saying.   _____ _____

                                            Total   _____ _____

Compare your totals with these ranges:

How Often:
135–150 = Communicate skillfully all or most of the time
105–134 = Often communicate skillfully
 75–104 = Sometimes communicate skillfully
 45–74 = Rarely communicate skillfully
 30–44 = Never or almost never communicate skillfully

How Satisfied:
135–150 = Very satisfied with my communication skills
105–134 = Somewhat satisfied with my communication skills
 75–104 = Neither satisfied nor dissatisfied with my communication skills
 45–74 = Somewhat dissatisfied with my communication skills
 30–44 = Very dissatisfied with my communication skills

Each item in the self-analysis describes a skill that is a component of communication competence. Your effective performance of these behaviors increases your potential for being a competent communicator.

Finally, even if you scored close to 150 on both parts of the self-quiz, you will find that there is still much to learn and put into practice! And, don't be discouraged if you scored lower than you would have liked. The purpose of this text and of your communication course is to help you develop the knowledge and skills you need to improve your competency as a communicator.

Source: These communication skills were determined by a task force of the National Communication Association and endorsed by the organization's Educational Policies Board to be minimal competencies for communicators. They are stated as NCA guidelines in the organization's publication, "Speaking and Listening Competencies for High School Graduates."

yourself. For example, as you take a test, you may conduct an internal dialogue as you review the material you studied and decide on an answer.

Communication is *irreversible*. When you say words, they are "out there" forever. You can't take back words of rage, a cutting remark, or a prejudiced smear. Apologies or denials cannot eradicate what has taken place. Remember when a friend let it slip that she didn't like your new car? The apology that followed her reading the hurt expression on your face didn't really erase the hurt. In a heated moment, a person may say "I want a divorce." No matter how many times the person says "I didn't mean it," the threat of a broken promise will remain in the other person's mind.

Communication is *interactive*. The communicators adapt as both people continually interact with each other. The words and actions of one person affect the responses of the other, which in turn affect the first person, and so on. You can think of communication as a cycle or spiral, which can carry the individuals in a positive—or negative—direction. For example, a soccer coach teaches you a new way of heading the ball by explaining the process and demonstrating it. You try it, ask some questions, he responds. This is an example of action-reaction.

Communication is *contextual*. Communication takes place in a setting, which not only is a location but which may have people who are participants in the action. In addition, the message sender has a purpose for communicating. The participants, the setting, and the purpose combine to make a context for the communication. A different combination of participants, settings, and purposes requires different communication strategies. For example, explaining to your friends about the great time you had on your spring break trip to Cancun, Mexico, is a different experience from trying to persuade the college's scholarship committee to extend your grant in spite of your slip in grades.

The Components of Human Communication

Although there are many ways to describe the act of communication, examining three models can illustrate the process. A model is a visual representation that tries to free action into a static drawing. Any model must necessarily be a simplification. Communication does not, for example, have the clear-cut beginning and end that a model suggests. Despite limitations, models can help you to see the components of communication from a perspective that will help you to analyze and understand the process.

THE LINEAR MODEL OF COMMUNICATION

In the **linear model of communication** (see Figure 1.1), a **source** (the person who sends the message) **encodes** (puts the message into the form he/she is going to use to send it) and sends a message to a **receiver** (the person who gets the message), through one or more of the **sensory channels** (seeing, hearing, touching, tasting, smelling). The receiver receives and attempts to **decode** (translate, understand) the message. To illustrate: José (the speaker) says, "Please put the book on the table when you are done with it." He then turns and walks from the room. Karon (the listener) has a stack of books in front of her, but she is not certain which one to place on the table. In this example, José is assuming that since he said something, this sending of a message is all there is to communicating. But this assumption ignores the important role of the receiver in responding to (and consequently affecting) the sender and/or the message. There are times, however, such as in sending an e-mail or leaving a message on an answering machine, that, despite its limitations, the only means of communication available is the linear model.

Figure 1.1. The Linear Model of Communication

THE INTERACTIONAL MODEL OF COMMUNICATION

In the **interactional model of communication** (Figure 1.2), a person (the source) uses the senses (channels) to send a message to another person, while that person (the receiver) simultaneously receives and makes sense of the message (decodes). To this point, it duplicates the linear model. The difference is that the receiver sends **feedback** (a verbal or nonverbal reaction to the original message). The original source then decodes the feedback and reacts by **adaptation**, altering the original message to ensure correct interpretation. Ideally, the process continues until the intent of the message is achieved. For example, Ryan says to Karon, "Please hand me the book." Karon looks at the pile of books in front of her and says, "Which one?" (*feedback*). Ryan responds, "The red one on the top of the pile" (*adaptation*). Karon hands the red book to Ryan (*feedback*) and Ryan says, "Thanks" (*feedback*).

Figure 1.2.   The Interactional Model of Communication

This view of communication accounts for the influence of the receiver's responses. It thus suggests a process that is somewhat circular: sending and receiving, sending and receiving, and so on.

THE TRANSACTIONAL MODEL OF COMMUNICATION

Theorists have suggested that communication may not be as simple a process of stimulus and response as the linear and interactional models suggest. This view supports the idea that communication is a transaction in which source and receiver play interchangeable roles throughout the act of communication. Figure 1.3 illustrates the **transactional model of communication**. In this model messages are processed simultaneously by the communicators. The first person (Communicator A) creates a message (encodes) and transmits the message to the other person. That person (Communicator B) responds through words and actions (feedback). Both aspects of communication can happen at the same time. For example, while Communicator A is talking, an expression on Communicator B's face sends feedback. Communication may occur at the conscious or unconscious levels, or a combination of these. We are seldom aware, for example, of the expression on our face as we listen to another person talk. So, messages are flying in both directions—verbally and nonverbally—from the sender and receiver.

Consider the simultaneous communication in this transaction:

Miguel (source) says, "I love you," *while*

Miguel (receiver) sees Latica walk away as he is speaking, *while*

Latica (source) walks away from Miguel, *while*

Figure 1.3.   The Transactional Model of Communication

Latica (receiver) says, "I love you," *while*

Miguel (source) stops, turns, frowns, and says, "I'm not sure you mean that," *while*

Latica (receiver) sees Miguel nod his head and walk toward her as she speaks, *while*

Miguel (receiver) hears her words, *while*

Miguel (source) nods his head and walks toward Latica as she speaks.

Throughout the encounter, both Miguel and Latica are simultaneously sending (encoding) and receiving (decoding or sense-making) both words (verbal) and body language and vocal elements (nonverbal). These messages can be sent and received at the same time as this model is multidirectional and circular.

LEARNING EXPERIENCE: Interested in learning whether you can recognize the basic aspects of how people communicate? If so, do Activity 1.2.

Communicative Noise

Messages are influenced not only by the interpretations of each communicator but also by **communicative noise**, which is any internal or external interference in the communication process.[3] The source of the interference can be distracting thoughts in the listener's head, the noise of a car driving by that makes it difficult to hear, a word the listener doesn't understand, a difference in making sense of the message, a slanted interpretation caused by one's cultural framework, or any other interference. Specifically, noise can be classified as environmental, physiological, semantic, syntactic, organizational, cultural, or psychological problems. Sometimes there is more than one cause for noise in a single communicative event.

ENVIRONMENTAL NOISE

Environmental noise is interference within the context of the communication, which prevents the communicators from understanding each other. Examples of environmental noise would be: You are in the kitchen running water and the sound muffles your friend's voice when he asks you a question from the adjoining room, or you are in class and several students behind you are talking so loud you can't hear the professor.

PHYSIOLOGICAL-IMPAIRMENT NOISE

Physiological-impairment noise is when a person's physical state causes misunderstanding. For example, persons who are deaf generally do not have the sensory capabilities to receive a message in the same way as do hearing people. Or, when you have laryngitis your verbal language-sending is temporarily impaired.

ACTIVITY 1.2
Elements and Characteristics
of Human Communication

Read the following dialogue and identify the elements and characteristics of human communication:

(Roberto and Sylvia are standing in line at a movie theater, waiting to purchase tickets.)

Roberto: "I'm really glad we got the chance to get out of the house tonight. The kids were driving me crazy."

Sylvia: "After spending all day at the hospital examining children, I was more than ready to relax."

Roberto: "Can you repeat that? I didn't hear you because of that motorcycle that just zoomed past."

Sylvia: "I said that I was ready to relax."

Roberto: "I agree, we both deserve a night out."

(A)   Which model of communication is being used?

(B)   Who is the sender?

(C)   Who is the receiver?

(D)   What is the channel of communication?

(E)   What is the encoding device?

(F)   Who are the participants?

(G)   What is the context?

(H)   What was the purpose of the transaction?

Answers:

(A)   Interactional model of communication

(B)   Roberto

(C)   Sylvia

(D)   speaking

(E)   English

(F)   Participants: Sylvia and Roberto

(G)   Context: standing in a public space, emotional stress on the part of both parties

(H)   Purpose: to express joint need for relaxation

SEMANTIC NOISE

Problems may also arise regarding the meaning of words, semantics, creating **semantic noise**. If you are from the United States and you watch a movie made in Australia, for example, you may have difficulty with their different use of the language. If you've used "texting" language with your grandmother, she probably didn't know what you meant. Just being in different ethnic, national, regional, or age groups causes us to use the same language differently, and thus experience semantic noise.

Examples of semantic noise are:

In many parts of the country's East Coast a U.S. midwesterner who goes into a store and asks for a *soda* will probably receive a soft drink (*pop* in the Midwest) rather than a mixture of ice cream, fruit flavoring, and soda water (a *soda* in the Midwest).

Clients often complain that doctors and lawyers fail to communicate clearly because they use "doctor-talk," confusing medical or legal jargon that the patient or client doesn't understand.

Computer experts employ such acronyms as LCD, GDSS, and CMC, forgetting that most people do not recognize the "alphabet soup" language common to computer techies.

SYNTACTICAL NOISE

Each language has a syntax, a customary way of putting words together in a grammatical form. If a person does not follow the structural rules of the language being spoken, **syntactical noise** can result. For example, a person intends to send an e-mail message that says: "What's the latest, dope?" but punctuates it, "What's the latest dope?" The comma misplacement makes the meaning totally different!

When one of the authors of this book began teaching in southwest Louisiana, she occasionally had trouble understanding her students. The problem was not their accent, but the way they put some words together. Because of the strong influence of the French language (Cajun) in that area, many popular expressions in English were constructed in the word order that would be used in French. That word order or syntax was confusing and created syntactical noise. For example, they might say "making groceries," which means "going grocery shopping," or "get down" which means "get out of a car." The difference in syntax can cause problems in understanding.

ORGANIZATIONAL NOISE

Because different people process differently, sometimes the arrangement of a message can cause **organizational noise**. In this case, the order of ideas fails to make sense to the listener. A friend who gives directions to his new apartment, but does not follow compass or landmark indicators in a first, second, third order could cause others to get lost when trying to follow the disorganized instructions.

CULTURAL NOISE

A person's cultural framework is an underpinning for communication, which can result in **cultural noise**. For example, for those who are members of the religious right, the belief that everyone should worship God in the same way, and be opposed to abortion and gay marriage, makes them see all those who do not pray in the same way or who do believe in abortion and gay marriage, as "wrong." Statements that illustrate cultural noise might be, "I am the father, and as long as you live in this house you will do as I say or you can just get out." or "We don't believe in interreligious marriages." These are examples of statements made by an individual whose cultural views set a clear pattern of rules and regulations.

PSYCHOLOGICAL NOISE

We sometimes find ourselves in situations where **psychological noise**—distractions resulting from our emotional state—cause communication problems. If you are upset, impatient, or stressed out, for example, you may have trouble concentrating, keeping an open mind, or processing communication effectively. Think of what happens when you are so angry that you "can't think straight." This is an example of psychological noise getting in the way of effective communication.

Some people have severe psychological problems that cause them to communicate in nontraditional or erratic ways. Those afflicted with schizophrenia (a disintegration of personality) may talk in riddles and rhymes, make up words, switch personalities, avoid communicative situations, or not communicate at all. Those who are communication phobic (have a fear of communicating) may not be able to carry on a coherent conversation out of terror of saying or doing the wrong thing.

DEALING WITH NOISE

Effective communicators find ways to adapt and respond appropriately to noise. While talking, you can turn off the television. When another person is upset, you may use extra patience in your communication. To deal with noise, you will need to be flexible. For instance, consider what happens if you request information and the other person does not respond. Environmental noise may have stopped the message from being received (the two people sitting behind you in class may talk while the instructor is giving a lecture), or the person may not have been paying attention because of psychological noise (being angry with you) or cultural noise (a female asking a direct question of a male who is from a culture where women do not directly converse with males who are not members of their family). Or a person may say, "I have difficulty hearing. Could you repeat what you said and speak up a little?" In this case, you must increase the volume level when you repeat the message. A response of "No comprendo!" to the question, "Where is the Grande Hotel?" may indicate that the person to whom you asked the question does not speak English. You may then want to switch to Spanish if you know the language, or show the person a brochure of the hotel. For example, a source should offer opportunities for feedback to make sure that a message has been received and understood. Rather than simply assuming that someone in another room has heard your message, word the statement so that it requires an answer: "The phone is for you. Are you going to answer it?" Another strategy that may help is to explain what you mean by defining words or concepts the other person may not understand. Rather than repeating exactly the same words in a message that has been misunderstood, you can change the terms or define them.

As a person whose intentions are to be a competent communicator, you must keep your eyes and ears open to anticipate a problem and, if one exists, adjust your communication accordingly.

Now that you have a basic understanding of the communication process, let's examine intrapersonal and interpersonal communication.

LEARNING EXPERIENCE: Interested in learning whether you can identify various types of communication noise? If so, do Activity 1.3.

The Basis for Communication

One of the questions that has challenged communication researchers is: Are your communication abilities and skills the result of nature or nurture? Are you born with the skills or do you learn them from your culture's agents, such as parents, school, peers, religious leaders, television and other forms of the media? The answer? Both nature and nurture influence you and your abilities to communicate.

We are each born with certain biological tools that allow us to communicate—a brain, sound-producing organs (mouth, tongue, larynx), and receiving apparatuses (ears, eyes). We also, according to ethnographers—researchers and theorists who study cultures—are born with need drives that must be satisfied. Some communication theorists think that these intrapersonal drives are the basis for our communication—what we think, what we express, what inspires us to act the way we do, and how we react to the way others express and use their drives.[4]

THE ETHNOGRAPHIC THEORY OF NEEDS

The **Ethnographic Theory of Needs** proposes that the basic drives that determine human behavior are feeling secure, protecting one's territory, finding pleasure, and ensuring survival of the species.[5] These drives are not manifested equally by every person. One person may have a pleasure need that is stronger than any of the other needs, whereas another may have strong needs for both security and territoriality.

Survival

A person who is threatened screams out for help; when a pebble flies against the windshield of your moving car, you probably duck or at least flinch. These are examples of

ACTIVITY 1.3

Which of the *noise factors* is displayed by each example?

(A) A child is trying to explain her trip to Vermont but has trouble putting her thoughts into a sequential order. _____

(B) A person from Puerto Rico has learned English but continues to structure sentences by Spanish grammar rules, which are different from American grammar rules. This makes it difficult for you to understand what she is saying. _____

(C) Rebecca's biology instructor is explaining a process Rebecca is to use in dissecting (cutting up) a frog. The instructor fails to define the terms she is using, and Rebecca doesn't understand what to do.
_____

(D) Your friend's father, who is a first-generation immigrant, insists that "nice girls don't do things like that" when she says she wants to move into her own apartment. He continues, "In my country a girl stays at home with her parents until she marries." _____

(E) Chang is sitting in the back of the class and a movie is being shown in the next room. The sound coming through the wall is so loud that Chang cannot hear the instructor's lecture. _____

(F) Patrick was almost hit by a car on the way to class. Patrick is so upset that while in class he has trouble concentrating. _____

Answers:
(A) organizational noise
(B) syntactical noise
(C) semantic noise
(D) cultural noise
(E) environmental noise
(F) psychological noise

attempts to ensure survival. These are *reflexive reactions*—inborn reactions—that you use to communicate your fear of a possible end to your survival.

You also may have *reflective reactions*, acting based on your environmental influences. Concern for the environment and economic stability show your regard for continuing life as you know it and protecting resources for future generations.

Your ability to communicate selectively gives you a distinct survival advantage. You can call for help, plead, explain your need for food, or try to convince attackers that their action is unwise. You can communicate about how humans reproduce, what causes people to die, and how you can attempt to alter conditions to prolong your life and those of your descendants. People have been able to communicate these ideas from person to person and thus to build on the experience of the past in developing intrapersonal understanding.

Pleasure-Seeking

We are basically *pleasure-seeking* and need-satisfying beings. A good part of your life is devoted to communicating your pleasure or lack of pleasure as you exploit your conquests, stress your influences, and reinforce your accomplishments. Awards are created, citations and grades given, to communicate to others that a person has succeeded, thus satisfying our intrapersonal needs.

People find different events pleasurable. Moreover, you may find pleasure in satisfying not only your own needs but also the needs of others, or in fulfilling long-term goals as well as immediate desires. What pleases one person may well torture another. One person happily goes to social events and walks up and introduces himself to others; another is petrified by interacting with strangers. You may be turned on by being a leader and running a meeting, while your friend thinks it an invitation to emotional suicide.

Communicatively, if given the opportunity, you choose to communicate in those situations in which you perceive you will get pleasure. You raise your hand to answer a question in class if you think you know the right answer. Unless forced to do so, if you fear public speaking, you will avoid putting yourself in the position of giving a speech. But a person who has received positive reactions from an audience is much more likely to try the experience again. You are constantly sending yourself intrapersonal messages relating to whether some experience was or was not pleasurable, or whether a perceived activity will render pleasure.

Security

You enter a classroom for the first meeting of the course. You see a setting that is unfamiliar, people you do not know, a professor who is an unknown entity. You may feel insecure. Your desire to participate and your comfort in this situation can be affected directly by the messages you send yourself such as "I hate this. I want out."

Because of your desire for security, you seek equilibrium, a balance. When security is absent, when you feel a lack of control, you may feel uneasy, overly cautious, and uncertain. Many phobias are based on the feeling that the spider or the snake will attack and you can't control the situation.

Your concept of yourself in situations of security or insecurity motivates your verbal and nonverbal communication. Fear causes the vocal pitch to rise, the body to shake, and the stomach to churn. You may find yourself afraid to speak, or speaking incessantly, or stammering. But as you become more comfortable in a situation, as you learn the rules of the game, you find yourself acting quite differently because you send yourself positive messages. The first day of class, for instance, you may not say a word. But later, as you acclimate yourself to the situation, you may feel relaxed enough to participate.

Territoriality

You intrapersonally define a particular *territory*, whether physical or perceptual, and then feel secure within that territory. You defend it from invasion and use it for protection. You mark your territory with ownership deeds, fences, signs, and numbers that specifically say, "This belongs to me." You feel secure when you are in our own territory, and often identify yourself by your hometown, your school, and your social groups, all of which are territorial markers.

You act differently in different territories. When friends come to visit, conditions may not be the same as when you go to visit them. The friend you invite over for dinner does not act the same at your house as when you go to his or her house for dinner. In the same way, there is a definite difference between playing an athletic game at home and playing it on the road. "Statistical analysis has proven that the home team has an advantage. Calculations have determined the numeric point advantage for teams playing in any sport in high school, college, or a professional league. A few examples of recent calculations provide the following: the National Basketball Association, 3.2; NCAA college basketball, 4.2; National Football League, 1.44; NCA college football, 1.94; and National Hockey League, 0.31."[6] The home team is familiar with the playing area and has the verbal and nonverbal backing of their supporters.

In addition to physical territory, you also have ideas and areas of expertise that you identify as yours. Inventors obtain patents to protect their inventions; writers copyright their books, you sign your class homework papers and put luggage tags on your baggage to show they are yours. These are attempts to establish territory and to communicate this to others.

Ideas and thoughts are also deemed territories. How do you like it when someone takes credit for an idea you presented? Teachers and parents sometimes get upset when their ideas are challenged by their children or their students. The child, the student, has invaded the knowledge territory of the person who is supposed to have the power, and that person feels a need to defend that territory.

The more insecure a person is within a territory, the greater is that person's intrapersonal fear of losing the territory. Thus, an invasion of someone else's territory is likely to invite a counterattack. Your cat, for example, nonverbally signifies irritation by arching her back and verbally hisses when a neighbor's cat enters your feline's territory. This parallels a human's yelling, getting ready to fight when someone enters that owner's territory.

Intrapersonal Communication

Now that you have an awareness of what communication is, let's probe into two specific types of communication, intrapersonal and interpersonal.

The basis for all of our communication is our intrapersonal communication. **Intrapersonal communication** is the active internal processing of messages. You become your own sender and receiver as you internally send messages to yourself and sometimes, even provide feedback to yourself. This may be done at the conscious or unconscious level. You may be aware you are "talking to yourself" or it may be below your level of awareness.

Intrapersonal communication takes the form of sense-making, interpreting of nonverbal messages, talking to yourself (such as when you are reading and mumbling the words), thinking and observing while you write, making gestures as you think, day-dreaming and participating in night time dreaming. An in-depth discussion of intrapersonal communication is presented in Chapter 2 of this book.

Interpersonal Communication

The concept of interpersonal communication was developed in the early 1950s.[7] Using concepts revealed in the social sciences such as the research and observations in the fields of psychology, sociology, and anthropology, the information was applied to communication. Since then, much research specifically related to interpersonal communication has been done.

Interpersonal communication is the interaction between two people who share a relationship. The basis for interpersonal transactions is the sending and receiving of messages in such a way that the messages are successfully encoded and decoded.

*In **intrapersonal communication** a person becomes his own sender and receiver as he sends messages to himself and sometimes even provides feedback to himself.*

Interpersonal skills have been identified by business executives as one of the three most important abilities that employees must have.[8] On the personal level, school, family, and relational communication are dependent on your being a competent interpersonal communicator. For example, interpersonal abilities affect academic success, roommate rapport, and social connectedness between college students. Think of the amount of face-to-face and electronic communication (e-mail, twitters, texting, cell phone usage) you do on a regular basis with peers, siblings, instructors, and salespeople.

The Role of Culture in Interpersonal Communication

The inseparable nature of communication and culture is perhaps most clearly manifested in the definition of culture. "**Culture** is the rules for living and functioning in society."[9] It is the deposit of knowledge, experience, beliefs, values, attitudes, meanings, hierarchies, religion, timing, roles, spatial relations, concepts of the universe, and material objects and possessions acquired by a group of people in the course of generations through individual and group striving. What this definition indicates is that people acquire their culture through various channels of communication and express their culture through these same channels.

In this book, the word "culture" encompasses all the cultures of each person, including his or her nationality, religion, race or ethnicity, sexual orientation, socioeconomic status, age, disabilities, and gender.

Now, more than ever before, your interpersonal relationships probably involve people from cultures different from your own. Some of those cultures might be as near as across the street, while others might be contacted only when you travel to other countries. Whether face-to-face or online, the world has shrunk. Shifting populations means more intercultural contacts. There are more women in the work place. People from different countries now work together. Racial integration has resulted in more and more contact with those from other races. As more and more gays and lesbians come out there is an awareness that 'they" are now part of "us."

Immigration statistics indicate that "whites, who currently make up around two-thirds of the US population, will become a minority (47%) by 2020."[10] The largest minority in the United States is currently Hispanic, whose proportion will double in the next decades to 29% in 2050.[11]

Regardless of the location and setting, people are now members of a "global village," interacting with new villagers whose perceptions and communication styles differ from those of the dominant culture. For example, you find that some people talk in whispers while others use loud voices. Why? Some people kiss acquaintances on the lips, some on the cheek, and some not at all. Why? Some people shake hands when they greet while others bow their heads or bodies. Why? In each case, the answer is that people's communication is affected by culture.

Whether or not the other person is from your own culture or from one that is alien to you, his or her cultural experiences greatly influence how she or he responds to you and your message. For example, if you were born into a nationality that does not display outward signs of emotion in public, such as the Japanese, you probably do not display outward signs of emotions in your interpersonal relationships. On the other hand Italian Americans and African Americans often display emotions in public as they communicate.

Note that throughout this text generalizations are presented regarding trends of various cultural groups. These are based, whenever possible, on research findings and expert observations. They are in no way intended to lead to the conclusion that all members of the cultural group noted conform to the generalized patterns.

CHARACTERISTICS OF CULTURE

Culture is learned. You are not born knowing your culture. You were not born knowing how to speak English or Spanish; or whether you should kiss on the mouth, the cheek, or not at all; or whether you greet someone with a handshake or a bow. You had to be taught these culture-based customs.

The messages and behaviors that a culture deems to be most important come from a variety of sources and are constantly being reinforced. Parents, schools, peers, the media, religious leaders, folktales, and even the art of a culture repeat the same message. If you were brought up in the United States, think for a moment of the many times and numerous ways you were "told" the importance of being popular and well liked. Your culture even supplied you with the specific behaviors needed to accomplish these two goals, such as using the "right" deodorant, using an antiperspirant at all, or respecting your elders. Being popular and well-liked are not universally important goals; thus, if you were brought up in another culture, these two stars to reach for might not be part of your constellation of needs.

Another culture-based characteristic has its roots deep in the communication process—people pass on culture between individuals, groups, and generations. Because we use symbols to convey ideas, patterns, values, and content of our culture, each person, regardless of individual culture, is born into a massive "library" of information and behaviors just waiting to be mastered. For example, North Americans can use spoken words as symbols and tell others about your being "number one." Your first generation Mexican American friend might be confused by this concept as he probably has been taught that the group is more important than the individual. "La familia" takes precedence over "yo."

In North American culture, a male is generally expected to be assertive or even aggressive ("If you don't stand up for your rights, others will walk all over you"). In many Asian cultures interpersonal harmony is stressed ("The nail that sticks up is the first to feel the blow of the hammer"). In North America some forms of touching in public are considered normal behavior. In many Asian cultures all touching in public is considered highly inappropriate.[12] There is an endless supply of examples, and each of them leads to the same conclusion: the content and communication patterns of a culture are subjective and transmissible. It accounts for why you and your acquaintances, fellow workers, and classmates each communicate in different verbal and nonverbal modes. You might encounter a major misunderstanding on a date with a person of Vietnamese descent, for example, if you attempt to hold hands in public. You might feel rejected when the person pulls away. Rejection is not the issue here. The nonverbal response of not touching, especially in public, may be a sign of cultural differences.

Although it may seem paradoxical, *culture is a dynamic system that changes over time; however, the deep structure of a culture resists change.* As cultures come in contact with each other they are bound to change. As Japan and the United States have more commerce, we observe Americans borrowing Japanese methods of quality control while the Japanese use American marketing practices. When Mexicans come to North America for work they often have to change their use of time. In their country people work hard and for long hours, but often treat themselves to a "siesta," an extended rest period during the middle of the day. Once in North America they often find that lunch is brief and that the work day ends much earlier. In both examples you can see how people can be forced to adapt to new cultures. However, you need also to remember that the deep structure of culture is less susceptible to change. The Japanese and Mexicans might alter their work environment, but it is doubtful if either of them is going to change their view of the family or their notion of obligation. Many first-generation immigrants cling strongly to the way "we did it in my country" and refuse or have difficulty adjusting their verbal and nonverbal communication patterns to fit their new environment.

ETHNOCENTRISM

Another concept regarding culture that is very important to all students of interpersonal communication: *members of a culture are often ethnocentric.* **Ethnocentrism** is a tendency to use a person's own culture and patterns of society as the basis of many decisions and judgments.[13]

LEARNING EXPERIENCE: Interested in finding out your ethnocentristic attitudes? If so, do Activity 1.4.

Feelings of "we are right" and "they are wrong," "I am right" and "he is wrong," traverse nearly every aspect of our interpersonal relationships with others. For example, how do you regard people who are different from you? You generally use the standards of your culture and apply them to each "foreign group." Male and female conflicts are sometimes the basis for the differences in their communication styles. Some people from the northern and eastern sections of the United States have attitudes about people who speak with southern accents and drawls, just as southerners have attitudes about "Yankees." And residents of the northeastern states often have beliefs about "flatlanders," those from states other than the favored few. The Civil War, though long over, still lives in the hearts of some as the "War of Northern Aggression," as can be illustrated by some people clinging to their Southern past through the nonverbal display of Dixie flags and emblems. Heterosexual males may be upset when they see gay males kissing, or fundamentalist Christians may have great disdain for a woman who has had an abortion.

While in one's own culture an idea may be normal, our judgments about other cultures can be arbitrary, prejudicial, incorrect, even immoral. It is truly a naive view

ACTIVITY 1.4
Generalized Ethnocentrism Scale

Using a scale of 5 (totally agree), 4 (agree), 3 (neither agree nor disagree), 2 (disagree), 1 (totally disagree), indicate the degree to which you agree with the following statements.

_____ 1. Most other cultures are backward compared to my culture.
_____ 2. My culture should be the role model for other cultures.
_____ 3. People from other cultures act strange when they come into my culture.
_____ 4. Lifestyles in other cultures are just as valid as those in my culture.
_____ 5. Other cultures should try to be more like my culture.
_____ 6. I am not interested in the values and customs of other cultures.
_____ 7. People in my culture could learn a lot from people in other cultures.
_____ 8. Most people from other cultures just don't know what is good for them.
_____ 9. I respect the values and customs of other cultures.
_____10. Other cultures are smart to look up to our culture.
_____11. Most people would be happier if they lived like people in my culture.
_____12. I have many friends from different cultures.
_____13. People in my culture have just about the best lifestyles of anywhere.
_____14. Lifestyles in other cultures are not as valid as those in my culture.
_____15. I am very interested in the values and customs of other cultures.
_____16. I apply my values when judging people who are different.
_____17. I see people who are similar to me as virtuous.
_____18. I do not cooperate with people who are different.
_____19. Most people in my culture just don't know what is good for them.
_____20. I do not trust people who are different.
_____21. I dislike interacting with people from different cultures.
_____22. I have little respect for the values and customs of other cultures.

To determine the ethnocentrism score complete the following four steps:

Step 1: Add the responses to scale items 4, 7, and 9.
Step 2: Add the responses to scale items 1, 2, 5, 8, 10, 11, 13, 14, 18, 20, 21, and 22.
Step 3: Subtract the sum of Step One from 18 (i.e., 18 minus Step One sum).
Step 4: Add the results of Step Two and Step Three. This sum is the generalized ethnocentrism score. Higher scores indicate higher ethnocentrism. The mean score is 32.5. Scores above 55 are considered high ethnocentrism. Reflect on your score. What skills do you need to develop to improve your intercultural communication?

Source: Neuliep, J. W. (2002, December). Assessing the reliability and validity of the Generalized Ethnocentrism Scale. _Journal of Intercultural Communication Research, 31_(4), 206.

of the world to believe and behave as if one culture, regardless of what it might be, has discovered the true, ultimate, and only set of norms. It is important as you encounter people from other cultures to avoid letting nearsighted views overshadow rationality.

LEARNING EXPERIENCE: The United States is a cultural salad. There are lots of ingredients, all of which retain some of their cultural identities. Interested in taking the "American Cultural Intelligence Test," which allows you to ascertain your knowledge of U.S. co-cultures? If so, do Activity 1.5.

Our culture also teaches each of us our ethical standards, which become a very important aspect of our interpersonal communication.

Ethics and Communication

Ethics is a study of what should serve as a framework for what is moral (acceptable) and immoral (unacceptable) behavior in a particular culture.[14]

Your morals are the values that have been instilled in you, that you have knowingly or unknowingly accepted, and that determine how you act. Ethical behavior is guided by such values as integrity, fairness, responsibility, equality, confidentiality, honesty, respect, and freedom.

Your **ethical value system** is the basis for your decision-making and your understanding of why you will or will not take a particular stand or action. It is the basis for your communication ethics.

"Potential ethical issues are inherent in any instance of communication between humans to the degree that the communication can be judged on a right-wrong dimension, involves possible significant influence on other humans, and to the degree that the communicator consciously chooses specific ends sought and communicative means to achieve those ends."[15] Therefore, communicators should give their listeners assistance in making wise decisions, and speakers' decisions about what to say should be based on moral principles. However, those who verbally attack others are often excellent speakers, but sometimes are considered to go beyond the ethical boundaries of a particular culture. For example, Michael Savage, "the radio talk show host who did a weekend TV show for the cable channel,"[16] was fired by MSNBC with the explanation that, "his comments were extremely inappropriate."[17] Savage had "referred to an unidentified caller to his show as a 'sodomite' and said he should 'get AIDS and die.'"[18] In May 2009 Britain's Home Secretary announced that Savage was banned from entry into the country "because the government believed his views provoke violence."[19] The Secretary went on to say, "I think it's important that people understand the sorts of values and sorts of standards that we have here, the fact that it's a privilege to come and the sort of things that mean you won't be welcome in this country."[20] As a spokesperson for GLAAD (Gay & Lesbian Alliance Against Defamation) stated regarding Savage, "This latest attack made the clearest case for why he has no place on any reputable news network."[21]

The use of questionable ethics is widespread, whether it be in politics, advertising, the media, or in any venue where individuals think it is their right to use information

ACTIVITY 1.5
American Cultural Test

Directions: Circle the correct answer for each question.

(1) "Chitlings" are a part of which of the following animals?
   A. Horse   B. Chicken   C. Pig   D. Cow   E. Sheep
(2) The Japanese American term "yonsei" means:
   A. A fourth-generation Japanese American
   B. A dish of fish and rice   C. Celebration of the New Year
   D. Love   E. A profitable business venture
(3) Chinese New Year is usually celebrated in which month?
   A. March   B. December   C. June   D. January   E. February
(4) Mexican Independence Day is celebrated on which of the following dates:
   A. April 17   B. September 16   C. October 10
   D. May 5   E. January 22
(5) What is the use/purpose of a C.I.B.?
   A. to provide free medical services
   B. to verify Native American ancestry
   C. to document immigrant numbers
   D. to create equal opportunities for women
   E. to ensure legal employment in the United States
(6) A kiva is:
   A. a Pueblo headdress   B. a rain God   C. a cornmeal grinding tool
   D. a sacred, ceremonial structure   E. an eagle staff
(7) What is the name of the African American celebration focusing on African cultural pride and celebrated during the month of December?
   A. Patois   B. Swahili   C. Imhotep   D. Natchez   E. Kwanzaa
(8) The Hebrew term "Shalom" means which of the following:
   A. Hello   B. Peace   C. Good-bye
   D. A, B, and C   E. Neither A, B, nor C
(9) The mythical homeland of the Aztec people is called:
   A. Michoacan   B. Neustra Senora de los Angeles de Porciuncula
   C. Aztlan   D. Teotihuacan   E. Quetzalcoatl
(10) What is the name of the traditional Filipino bamboo stick dance:
   A. Teatro   B. Pancit Palabok   C. Umoja   D. Sipapu   E. Tinkling
(11) The Spanish word "orale" is
   A. Used to curse at someone in a respectful way
   B. An expression equivalent to "cool!"
   C. A reference to fast eating
   D. The name of a spicy, chicken dish
   E. An expression to describe a "loud mouth"

(continued)

ACTIVITY 1.5 (*continued*)

(12) Which of the following is not the (English) name of a Native American tribe?

A. Arapaho   B. Tagalog   c. Pomo   D. Cahuilla   E. Potatomi

Answers:

1. C; 2. A; 3. E; 4. B; 5. B; 6. D; 7. E; 8. D; 9. C; 10 E; 11 B; 12. B

Grading scale:

9–12: You have a good grasp of cultural information of Americans from various cultures.

6–8: You need to find out more about Americans from various cultures.

5 and below: Your grasp of information about Americans from various cultures is weak.

Source: Intercultural Center, 1801 East Cotati Avenue, Rohnert Park, CA 94928, www. sonoma.edu/icc/americanculturetest/test.html. According to an office of the organization, this document is no longer on their website.

---

to reach their end purpose, no matter the ethical nature of that usage. For example, preachers of hate, even those who do it in the name of religion or national pride, attempt to manipulate public thought by using extreme language. "Their ultimate downfall is their lack of ethical values."[22]

Ethical communicators are generally defined as those who conform to society's moral code for communication. Although this definition seems plausible, it contains a major flaw: the words ring hollow because it is impossible to either list or gain acceptance for universal moral standards. Although some people claim they have the true answer, in reality there is no universal agreement on what exactly it means to be moral.

Accepting the limitations of culture and perspective, research in the communication field has isolated some specific traits of an ethical speaker in the United States. The premise of ethical speaking can be stated as, "You must understand that you are a moral agent, and when you communicate with others and make decisions that affect yourself and others, you have a moral responsibility because your actions have human consequences."[23] Specifically, the ethical communicator:[24]

- Communicates truthfully. Avoids telling only part of the story or any dishonesty, particularly falsehoods that can cause harm.
- Never uses the objective of honesty as an excuse to be abusive or hurtful.
- Is assertive, may be persuasive, but never coerces another person. It allows the individual to express his/her needs and wants without attacking or coercing others.
- Never invents stories or information without explaining the fabrication is for humor, to illustrate an idea, or make a point.

- Explains or gives credit to the source of information so the quality of the information can be accurately evaluated.
- Knows how to keep confidences.
- Owns up to biases, prejudices, and inappropriate behavior.
- Stops gossip and prejudicial comments.
- Avoids talking behind the back of another person, but instead confronts problems with others by using a content-based interaction.
- Avoids name-calling, personal attacks, or dredging up another person's past mistakes.
- Attacks the issue to be dealt with, rather than attacking the other person.
- Creates a positive interpersonal climate with the objective of supporting the needs of the individuals in the relational interaction.

Not only speakers but listeners need to operate within an ethical framework. To be an ethical receiver, you should listen carefully to the information presented and ask yourself whether the conclusions reached are expected, reasonable, and acceptable. In other words, can you, from the information presented, comfortably come to the conclusion that the sender makes sense? For example, if someone said to you, "one plus one equals five," you would reject the idea. Why? In the traditional number system, one plus one equals two. You expect the answer to the question to be two, not five. The answer given is neither reasonable nor expected, therefore, it is not acceptable. The same would apply to culturally prejudiced states such as racial, religious, or gender stereotypes.

Basic Concepts of Interpersonal Communication

As you study about interpersonal communication, keep some basic concepts in mind:

Communication takes place within a system. As we enter into communicative relationships with others, we set a pattern by which we will interact. For example, in a family, there are flow patterns of message sending and receiving: who speaks to whom, who controls the interactions, who has the power to praise and punish, who can encourage or stop the message flow. If you examine any relationship you are in, you will recognize patterns by which the communication flows.

A change in the system results in a change in the communication. If someone in the system changes roles (e.g., teenager leaves for college), or outside factors change the system (a grandparent gets ill and moves in), that changes the communicative system.

There may be resistance to changing the system because this may involve a shift in the power structure. If your boss, spouse, lover, or friend likes being in control and you are proposing a change, problems may arise. At the other extreme, there also may be situations in which the system requires an adjustment so that a person is forced to assume responsibility after having been dependent on someone else. Whatever happens, the communication system remains unchanged as long as the status quo is maintained.

Messages cannot be erased. Messages once sent and received cannot be erased. Suppose that, in the heat of an argument with a friend, you blurt out the one insult that you know will most hurt the other person. And, as soon as you complete the offending message, you want to plead, "I take it back, I didn't mean it!" Have you ever tried to retrieve an e-mail message you hastily sent to a friend who had offended you? No, it's not possible. There is no such thing as "taking it back." You and your partner may choose to behave as if the message were erased, but, in reality, you both know that it exists and continues to exist. One of the dangers of sending a text or e-mail message while you are feeling high levels of anxiety is that your emotional reaction may not be your rational reaction five minutes later.

Communication is proactive. Communication is a *proactive process*—that is, you respond to any message based on your total history. You select what portions to hear, amplify or ignore to suit your needs, and remember what you consider relevant based on your past experiences. Your culturally induced ideals and beliefs, and your previous experiences with the communicator are all in play as you send and receive messages.

The meaning of a given act of communication cannot be separated from the components of the communicative act. All communicative acts have three components: the **participants** (the people who are interacting), the **context** (physical and psychological surroundings) and the communicators' **purpose** (what the communicator wants to accomplish). If you change any of these components, you probably change the meaning and/or the effect of the message. For example, if you are planning on changing your college major from pre-med to theatre, stating this to your roommate is not the same as stating it to your parents, who really want you to be a doctor. Telling your parents face-to-face is not the same as sending them a text message. Making the statement at Thanksgiving dinner when the whole family is present is not the same as telling your parents privately.

Interpersonal communication is culture-oriented. The link between people and meaning is affected by each of the communicator's cultures. The participants' languages, attitudes, beliefs, and customs are all factors that affect the communication. What happens when you are talking to a classmate whose first language is not English? What happens when a male and female try to problem solve? Do African Americans and Euro-Americans have the same understandings of various life issues? Can someone who is homophobic competently communicate with a homosexual? Are members of religious conservative organizations capable of compatible communication with an atheist?

We teach others how to treat us. In developing a system, each person plays a role. If that role is accepted by the other person, then that becomes part of the system. If it is rejected, then it does not become a system rule. You may dislike the way another person treats you, but you say nothing, so you contribute to the pattern. You may wonder why a person acts that way, wish they would be different, but without objecting or expressing your needs, you set a path for future interactions. For example, a habitual verbal abuser at one point yelled obscenities and insults at a person, and that person didn't object or didn't feel that he had the power to defend himself. Therefore, the next time the abuser got angry, he or she repeated the action. The cycle is set! Only changing the system will disrupt the cycle. For example, the first time a person was confronted with harassment, he said, "I will not allow you to say things like that to me. The next time you raise your voice and swear at me, I'm out of here." If, the next time the person does attack, the receiver walks out, this sets the pattern for future interactions.

We communicate what and who we are. Every time we communicate, we tell a great deal about ourselves. We communicate information about who we are by the way we speak, the words we select, our accents, the values underpinning our communication, what we look and sound like. We give clues of our background by the pronunciation patterns we use, and the attitudes we express. As receivers, we form conclusions about senders and react to these conclusions based on our own culture—background, experiences, and beliefs.

We seek to persuade. When we communicate, we persuade. We may seek to persuade about ideas and actions, or we may simply need to persuade people to listen to what we say. Often when we communicate, we are trying to change people to believe what we believe, act the way we do, follow our advice, value what we value, or think what we think. Think of how often parent-child, boss-employee, husband-wife, or significant other interactions center on one person's trying to get the other person to take a particular action, act in a specific way, or change their point of view.

Meaning is in people, not in words. The meaning of a word only has that meaning by virtue of the meaning people give to that word. In communicating with others, we must be aware that what a particular symbol means to us is not necessarily what it means to them. A homeowner hearing the word *grass* may think of the *lawn*. A drug counselor probably thinks of *marijuana*. Unless some basis for understanding exists, ineffective communication may be the result. Thus, you must define terms and give examples, keeping your audience in mind and adjusting your messages accordingly.

We cannot not communicate. Communication exists even if people don't talk. Suppose you do not answer a question your instructor has asked. Or you sit quietly at the dinner table instead of joining in the conversation. In these cases, you are still sending messages, although your lips are silent. Much of our communicating is done below the verbal level. You may think that if you do not actively participate, you are not sending messages—but you are! In many instances your body is communicating nonverbally, and the very fact that you are not saying something may be interpreted as if you were telling the other person that you are not interested, don't care, or disagree.

People react to your actions. Sir Isaac Newton developed the law of motion that stated, "to every action there is an equal and opposite reaction."[25] The same principle holds true in human interaction. You are constantly demonstrating the **action-reaction principle**. People react to your actions. When you smile, others are likely to smile back; when you display anger, others tend to do the same. Try an experiment. The next time you walk down a hallway or a sidewalk, smile as others come toward you. You probably will find that the people you pass smile back, often saying *hello*. This is action-reaction in practice. Think back to the last time you had an argument. If you raised your voice, what did the other person do? No doubt that person also raised his or her voice. Again, action-reaction. Interestingly, raising of the voice to overshadow another person is not a universal tendency. Your Japanese roommate may lower her voice as you raise yours. Rather than trying to top you, a Euro-American custom, your roommate was probably taught to react by getting quieter in order to save face, not become the center of attention and to embarrass herself or you.

You do what you do because in the end you expect to achieve happiness. When you choose to enter into communication, you do so hoping to gain from the experience,

Communicatively, if given the opportunity, you choose to communicate in those situations in which you perceive you will get pleasure.

but certainly to be in no worse psychological shape than when you entered. It goes back to the desire for pleasure as described in the Ethnographic Theory of Needs. Consequently, many people try to avoid any situation in which they think they may get negative feedback or be unsuccessful in communicating their ideas.

You cannot always have the same understandings and feelings as others. As you communicate with another person, you must recognize that because of differences in your cultures, the only areas you share are those in which you have a common experiential background. As languages, values, beliefs, and ethics differ, so does the basis for understanding and agreeing with each other. A liberal has a different reaction to "universal health care" than does a conservative. Someone from Britain or Spain, where it is legal, may have a different reaction to legalization of gay marriage then a religious conservative from the United States

People would rather be praised than punished, and rather be punished than ignored.[26] People, based on the pleasure concept of the Ethnographic Theory of Needs, desire praise, to be affirmed. If you can't get that recognition you may revert to any action that gets attention. A child, for example, who can't attract his father's positive attention, may turn to negative acts in order to get some form of attention. This is often the story behind the actions of bullies and good kids gone bad. The teenage girl who can't get mom's attention will get lots of attention if she talks back, gets pregnant, or flunks a class or two.

Be curious, not furious.[27] When you react out of emotion, out of anger, you often close the door to competent communication. If, instead, you report the facts, ask questions to find out what is going on, you are much more likely to be able to navigate successfully through rough communicative waters. Before reacting, make sure you know to what you are reacting . . . the facts, not the perceived actuality.

Key Terms

communication
linear model of communication
source
encode
receiver
sensory channels
decode
interactional model of communication
feedback
adaptation
transactional model of communication
communicative noise
environmental noise
physiological-impairment noise
semantic noise

syntactical noise
organizational noise
cultural noise
psychological noise
interpersonal communication
participants
content
purpose
action-reaction principle
Ethnographic Theory of Needs
intrapersonal communication
interpersonal communication
culture
ethnocentrism
ethics

Competencies Check-Up

Interested in finding out what you learned in this chapter and how you use the information? If so, take this competencies check-up.

Directions: Indicate the extent that each statement applies to you:

1—Never   *2—Seldom*   *3—Sometimes*   *4—Often*   *5—Usually*

___1. I recognize that I send unintentional messages as part of a continuous communication process.

___2. I am careful about what I say because I know that communication is irreversible, and once I say something, I cannot take the message back.

___3. When communication is important, I consider the setting and minimize any noise that may cause interference.

_____ 4. I am sensitive to the effects of culture on communication and make an effort to avoid ethnocentric thoughts and behaviors.

_____ 5. I am an ethical and responsible interpersonal communicator.

_____ 6. When other people tell me personal information, I know how to keep confidences.

_____ 7. When upset, I never call people names, make personal attacks, or dredge up the past mistakes of others.

_____ 8. I listen carefully, sensitively, and ethnically.

_____ 9. I recognize that communication takes place within a system of people, and I take responsibility for the possible rippling effects of my communication.

_____10. I use a holistic approach to effectiveness, where I take into account the participants, context, and purpose of each communication act.

_____11. I teach others to treat me in a respectful way.

_____12. I know that I often communicate without meaning to communicate, so I give attention to using nonverbal communication effectively.

_____13. I frequently pass along praise to others.

_____14. I am curious, not judgmental, about other people.

_____15. This week, I motivated myself to actively work to improve my interpersonal communication skills.

Scoring: A total of 45 suggests that you perceive that you have the basic competencies for the foundation of interpersonal competency. A score over 60 suggests you have a solid foundation for interpersonal competency. Go back and look at any test items with a score of less than 3 and create a plan for changing that area to one of full competence over the course of this semester. Your instructor may want you to create a list of strategies for improvement based on your test results.

I-Can Plan!

You can take this course, learn the information for tests, pass the course, but never change the quality of your interpersonal communication or relationships. By taking an "I can change" attitude and developing and implementing a specific plan, you can develop your individual interpersonal communication competencies. Only *you* can motivate yourself to learn and apply the concepts in ways that improve your level of communication competence. Pick one and set up a plan to adjust your communication pattern(s).

Activities

1. Design a model of communication that differs from any of the three presented in this chapter. Be prepared to explain it to the members of your class.
2. Explain a time when you failed in your attempt to successfully communicate. List the sources of noise, using the classifications explained in this chapter, which apply to your situation. What might you have done differently?

3. Describe a context in which you find it difficult to communicate. Describe a context in which you find it easy to communicate. Why did you select each one? What implications for communication are involved in your choices?

4. Individually each student decides on what he or she would do in each of these situations. You will then be divided into small groups to discuss your answers and report back to the class as a whole on the trends in each group.

   a. You are taking an interpersonal communication course. The instructor requires three quoted references in a presentation you are going to make about interpersonal communication that you are to present in about five minutes. You know the material well enough to "wing it" but you did not have time to do the necessary research. Would you make up three references, not give the speech and get a failing grade, give the speech without the references and hope for the best, or take some other action? If you would take another action, what would it be? How does this fit into your ethical framework?

   b. You have just finished eating in a restaurant. You check the bill and realize that the waiter has made a $10 error in your favor. The waiter sees your reaction and asks if anything is wrong. How do you respond?

   c. You look up during a test and see that your best friend, who needs a passing grade in this class to get off academic probation, is using cheat notes. You think the instructor also saw the action. As you hand in your paper, the instructor says, "Remember, this class operates on the honor system. Is there anything you want to say to me?" How do you respond?

5. Your class will discuss: "Is it possible to be an ethical communicator?"

CHAPTER 2

The Self and Communication

Learning Outcomes

After reading this chapter, you should be able to:

* Define and explain intrapersonal communication.
* Explain how self-talk shapes our inner attitudes and behaviors.
* Apply memory techniques.
* Explain the role of values, attitudes, and beliefs in cognitive processing.
* Explain self-concept and the effect it has on intrapersonal and interpersonal communication.
* Differentiate between the idealized self, the real self, the should self, and the public self.
* Synthesize an understanding of yourself.
* Define and evaluate the causes of and strategies for dealing with communication apprehension.

* *You are studying for a final examination. As you go over the material you mumble the ideas you are going over, think of the concepts that have been taught, review your notes, and make comments to yourself as you try to recall information.*
* *A business woman did not assert herself during a discussion with her boss. Afterward, she thinks to herself, "I should have said that the plan he is proposing won't work because it is too expensive." The woman commits to going to her boss the next morning and tells him her beliefs.*
* *A boy tells his pet dog about the problems he had that day. The dog doesn't understand what his owner says, but the boy makes sense of his day's events and feels better because he "talks" to his dog. In actuality, he is self-talking.*
* *A college student goes online and "talks" to a stranger in an e-group about her latest conflict with her roommate. She tells the stranger about her conflict, not because she wants the person's advice, but because she needs to process her feelings and thoughts. She has discovered that by writing online, she can intrapersonally make sense of her ideas.*

- *A father writes a letter to his son in which he gives advice that the college student should not change his major. After writing several pages, the father decides not to send the letter. The father, in self-talking on paper, realizes that he would be interfering, but feels better because he has made sense of his own thoughts through the writing.*

Intrapersonal Communication—Defined

If someone asked you whether or not you talk to yourself, you would probably say, "no." In truth, as illustrated in the examples above, we all "talk" to ourselves. Almost all communication we do germinates from self-talk. We plan, evaluate, reevaluate, and visualize inside of our heads. This self-communication is called **intrapersonal communication**, which is systematic interfacing with the self.

Your mind is filled with images, feelings, memories, and sensations, not to mention words, that move at the rate of a speeding bullet. When you verbalize those thoughts by talking or writing, you give structure to your thinking. If you write an essay for a course assignment, for example, you may write multiple drafts as you formulate your ideas. In fact your own thoughts may not become clear to you until you have processed them, for example, by writing them down. This meaning-making, the

Your mind is filled with images, feelings, memories. When you verbalize those thoughts by talking or writing, you give structure to your thinking.

making sense of a situation or message, is the nature of intrapersonal communication. The more carefully you process the meaning of your intrapersonal communication the more effective your interpersonal communication will be. As you refine your messages as you are using cognition—thinking, reflecting, and mental processing.

We can also use self-talk to establish interpersonal conversations with others, real or imaginary. As the nonassertive business woman did in the example at the start of the chapter, you can talk and plan. You can also turn to others for "fantasy advice." You may, for example, turn to TV psychologist Dr. Phil for advice by asking yourself what he would say to you if you were a guest on his program. You might even turn to one of his books, find a passage, "hear" him speaking to you as you search for a solution to a problem. Thus, you are creating a **social reality**, a relationship outside of a social context and making it real through processing ideas internally.

If you are typical, you find that speaking comes fairly easily and naturally, so you don't think much about what you are doing. In fact, communication is *not* easy. Unless you take into consideration the factors present in all communication—*participants* (the originator of the message and the receiver of the message), the *setting* (where the communication takes place and emotional site of the participants), and the *purpose* (what is to be accomplished)—your attempts to communicate can be very ineffective. Processing your communication strategies and consideration of the factors takes place intrapersonally.

Self-Talk

Self-talk is communication to yourself in which you talk internally. Sometimes you are conscious of vocalizing within your head, but sometimes self-talk is silent thinking, an internal whisper of which you are scarcely aware. Self-talk can also trigger your nonverbal reactions. Even though it may be quiet, its impact can be enormous. "Your behavior, your feelings, your self-esteem, and even your level of stress are influenced by your inner speech."[1] "Self-talk shapes our inner attitudes, our attitudes shape our behavior, and of course our behavior—what we do—shapes the results we get."[2]

Think of the inner struggles you often have concerning whether you will believe something, will take a particular action, or will make a certain decision. Awake or asleep, whether you are aware of it or not, you continually communicate with yourself. Perhaps you blog or twitter, with no real audience. If you rehash a conversation in your mind and fantasize about what you should have said, that is intrapersonal communication. When you imagine a future situation, where you practice in your mind what you will say and what the other person might say, that too is an example of inner speech, where you communicate with yourself beyond traditional thinking or processing.

An important function of self-talk is to help you process who you are. This processing can result in positive or negative evaluations. One form of negative evaluation is the self-put-down. Self-put-downs have been referred to as acting like a vulture.[3] Consider for a moment the vulture, an unattractive bird with sharp claws and a pointy beak whose favorite activity is picking on the weak, the helpless, and, preferably, the dead. It dives into the flesh and picks away at it. The **psychological vulture** does much the same thing. It attacks a person's perceived weaknesses and eats at the person's self-worth.

What do you call yourself when you lock your keys in the car? What do you call yourself when you trip over the edge of the carpet? Every self-put-down—"Idiot!" "Failure!"—summons the vultures!

Put-downs may be either obvious or subtle. The obvious ones have a clear physical referent, like the keys dangling in the ignition of your locked car or the frayed edge of the carpet on which you tripped, and the words you applied to yourself because of your actions or perceived actions. The put-downs impose limitations on you that, though not obvious, are equally as destructive. Sample vultures include:

"I could never write an 'A' paper."

"I could never stick to a diet for more than a week."

"I just can't stop smoking."

Psychological vultures tend to nest in six areas. There are *intelligence* vultures ("I'm dumb," "I'm no good in math," "I'm no good at foreign languages"); *creativity* vultures ("I'm not imaginative," "I can't draw as well as Morgan," "I can't sing like Eric"); *family* vultures ("I'm the odd-ball in the family," "My brother is the favorite"); *relationship* vultures ("I'm no good at meeting people," "I can't make friends," "I'm shy"); *physical* vultures ("I'm too short/tall/fat/thin," "My nose is too big," "My teeth are crooked"); and *sexual* vultures ("I'm not sexy").

The results of self-put-downs are obvious: A person avoids the areas where the vultures lurk. Depending on the perceived vultures, she avoids such things as math classes, drawing, dates, singing, and going to social events. He wears large clothing to cover up his body or she makes excuses for not going to parties. A self put-down turns out to be a self-fulfilling prophecy in which what you predict to happen, will happen, what you expect to do wrong, will be done wrong. On the other hand, the **self-fulfilling prophecy** can be turned around so that it is positive. If you stop, kill off the vultures, and expect good things to happen, that may well happen.

LEARNING EXPERIENCE: Interested in finding out if you have any vultures? If so, do Activity 2.1.

Your self-talk can work for or against you. It's up to you. Tell yourself you're clumsy, or you aren't comfortable in social situations, and that is what you probably will be. You have a choice each time you think. You can think positively or negatively. You can recycle the negatives you listed in Activity 2.1 into something you can use. "I'm the odd one in the family" can be changed to "I'm the most creative person in our whole family." "I'm no good at meeting people" can be changed to "I'm getting better at meeting people now that I'm listening more and asking follow up questions." We can stop fearing our "weaknesses" and start seeing them as "needs" for which we can learn skills. Once we understand that our private thoughts are ours alone to determine, we can select to program our brains with empowering, confidence-building thoughts.

How do you use self-talk to kill off your vultures? A theory regarding changing your self-defeating self-talk encourages these strategies:[4]

• Pat yourself on the back by saying something good about yourself. You can surely think of something for which to compliment yourself.

- Pat someone else on the back by saying something good and true about her or him. Not only will you feel good about yourself for complimenting another person, but you'll also find that compliments beget compliments.
- Recognize your self-put-downs. This is hard, because you may utter self put-downs every day. To make sure you catch them, you may want to ask a friend for help. Be sure to identify both the obvious and the subtle ones (and don't argue when your friend points them out). This step is crucial: You can't cure what you don't recognize!
- Block each put-down. As you hear it coming out, put your hand over your mouth (literally, if you have to do so). Soon you'll feel a negative statement coming, and you'll be able to head it off before you say it.
- Turn the put-down around: Put it in the past tense and eliminate its evaluative component. For example, when you trip over the edge of the carpet, say, "I *used* to be *clumsy*, but I'm not anymore. I *tripped*, that's all, and that's human."

Another method to overcome negative self-talk is to (1) realize when you use negative inner speech; (2) rewrite the negatives into positives and review the positives periodically (recycled negatives); and (3) stop your negativity by allowing positive talk to flood your brain with such statements as "I'm an effective speaker," or "I'm a

---

ACTIVITY 2.1
My Vultures

List as many negative statements about yourself as you can for each statement. (Don't be concerned if you can't fill in all the blanks, but try and be honest!)

My *intelligence* (e.g., "I'm disorganized," "I'm no good in math.")

_____

My *creativity* (e.g., "I'm not imaginative," "I can't sing.")

_____

My *family* (e.g., "I'm the odd-ball in the family," "My brother is the favorite.")

_____

My *physicality* ("I'm too fat.")

_____

My *sexuality* ("I'm not handsome enough to attract anyone.")

_____

Me and my *relationships* ("I can't make friends," "Nobody likes me.")

_____

people person." Recycled negatives can be a way of turning your trash into treasures. Once you start focusing on the positives, the negatives go away. Negative self-talk can't survive if you don't feed it.[5]

Positive self-talk plus visualization is another effective device. This method has been used extensively with athletes to overcome negative self-talk and help improve skill levels. In one study, basketball players were divided into three groups for foul-shot practice. The first group used positive visualization (internally picturing that they were shooting and making their shots) and negative-message elimination but did not practice shooting. The second group only practiced shooting, and the third group did both positive visualization and practiced. Although all three groups improved, the third group improved the most, while the second group improved the least. Going by this experiment's findings it can be concluded that, "Positive self-talk really can turn your life around and make any life more successful."[6]

In addition to self-talk, one of the important aspects of intrapersonal communication is how we process information as we receive it.

Processing Intrapersonal Messages

Memory plays a major role in self-talk. Once you've processed the external world you need to store the information. Interestingly, research suggests that how you try to learn affects the degree of learning.

Effective self-talk can include various memory techniques including chunking, ordering, reordering, context organizing, and mnemonics, which help in processing and storing.[7]

CHUNKING

Chunking is the grouping of bits of information according to a mutual relationship. This allows you to condense information for easier recall. For example, while discussing a story in an American literature class, you could group the terms that describe each character so that later you remember each person's physical and emotional description rather than random details. Also, in conversation, as you and a friend talk about people you know in common, you can remember the names your friend tells you by placing the people in categories such as by "college major," "hometown," or "groups to which they belong."

ORDERING

Ordering is the arranging of bits of information into a systematic sequence. Thus, in chemistry class you can more easily remember a process by organizing it into a step-by-step progression. For example, first, get the equipment for the experiment; second, get the necessary chemicals; third, study the lab manual to determine the order in which the chemicals are mixed; fourth, mix the chemicals. Similarly, planning a trip with a friend, you can organize your ideas by each day of the trip or by what you are going to do at each place you visit.

REORDERING

Reordering is the changing of an existing system of organized information so that a new or different sequence is developed. Reordering is useful when you have difficulty remembering material in the sequence in which it is presented. For example, rather than remembering the causes of World War I by dates, you might remember them according to the causes in each country going from west to east (England, France, Germany, and Austria-Hungary).

LEARNING EXPERIENCE: Interested in finding out if you can chunk, order, and reorder? If so, do Activity 2.2.

ACTIVITY 2.2
Grouping Intrapersonal Messages

A. Chunk the following: Wheaties, Bananas, Peaches, Cheerios, Frosted Flakes, Pineapple, Shredded Wheat.
B. Chunk these: hammer, saw, screws, wood, bricks, chisel, screwdriver, nails, plaster board.
C. Order these: Christmas, Easter, Valentine's Day, Independence Day, Halloween, Labor Day.
D. Order these: France, Russia, Germany, England, Poland, India, Japan.
E. Reorder your answer for item D.
F. Reorder these alphabetically listed cities: Atlanta, Georgia; Baltimore, Maryland; Cleveland, Ohio; Dallas, Texas; Ft. Lauderdale, Florida; San Francisco, California.

Possible answers:
A. Fruits (bananas, peaches, pineapple, and strawberries) that are commonly put on cereals and cereals (Wheaties, Cheerios, Frosted Flakes, Shredded Wheat).
B. The list contains tools used in construction (hammer, saw, chisel, and screwdriver) and materials used in construction (screws, wood, bricks, nails, and plaster board).
C. Valentine's Day, Easter, Independence Day, Labor Day, Halloween, Christmas (chronological order).
D, E, and F. England, France, Germany, India, Japan, Poland, Russia orders the countries alphabetically. Other methods for ordering them include spatial—going from west to east (England, France, Germany, Poland, Russia, India, Japan) or east to west, and from the country with the largest population total to the smallest or vice versa.

CONTEXT ORGANIZING

Context organizing centers on the principle that some individuals find that putting information in a place, a context, allows them to remember it. A student once told one of the authors of this book that she remembered ideas by picturing where the instructor was standing in the room when he shared ideas and that she could "hear" them coming out of his mouth and recall them. Bad at recalling names? Take a visual picture of the person you meet in the setting in which you met. It also helps to repeat the person's name at least three times when you are introduced and during the ensuing conversation in order to set the image in your mind.

MNEMONICS

A **mnemonic** is an artificial memory aid that can be used to remember something important. If you have difficulty remembering the Great Lakes, for instance, the word HOMES can help you (*H*uron, *O*ntario, *M*ichigan, *E*rie, *S*uperior). In order to intrapersonally recall the three key ideas you want to express to your boss without using notes, for instance, you might develop a mnemonic device, such as PIP (*p*romise, *i*nterview, and *p*romotion).

Cognitive Processing

Each of us carries with us **values** (what you perceive to be of positive or negative worth), **attitudes** (your perspective and viewpoints), and **beliefs** (your convictions). Most people try to keep their actions parallel to their values, beliefs, and attitudes. If things are in balance, we feel good about ourselves and the world around us. If not, we may intrapersonally become confused and frustrated, which may cause us to act negatively toward ourselves or others, maybe even blaming them for what's wrong. This imbalance happens, for example, when you know that a certain action you are about to take is wrong based on your value system. Your "internal voice" cries out, "be careful, don't do that." It's like your personal Jiminy Cricket. Remember him sitting on Pinocchio's shoulder in the Disney movie and singing, "Let Your Conscience Be Your Guide." Before an event in which you perceive your value system is being challenged, you may have a sleepless night as you toss and turn with your internal voice speaking messages, or you dream about the negative things that are going to happen as a result of your taking the action. For example, you are planning on telling your friend that you can't go on vacation with him because you are short on money. That's not your real reason. You just don't think you can stand being with him for three weeks. You don't like to lie but for you this tale is a necessity.

The *imbalance* between your values, attitudes, and beliefs is called **cognitive dissonance.**[8] Cognitive dissonance often leads to what has become known as a **guilty conscience**—the real or perceived fear that we are going to get caught, get punished, or "found out." For example, an individual who believes cheating is wrong, yet does so on a test, may feel cognitive dissonance following the act, no matter the grade received.

If you become aware of cognitive dissonance before you act, and decide not to do the deed, you could chalk it up to your conscience warning you and saving you from a perceived disaster. If you brood about the action afterward, then you may need to accept the fact that you took the action, there is nothing you can do about it now, and go on from there, with the internal pledge of not doing it again. Your internal voice, through its self-talk technique, often continues to shout until you can put the imbalance to rest. Sometimes apologizing to someone is in order if your actions hurt the person.

Another dimension of intrapersonal communication is self-concept.

Self-Concept

Your understanding of yourself is your **self-concept**. "Self-concept is the guiding factor in a person's actions. How a human being views oneself will determine most of his or her actions and choices in life. Essentially a person is going to choose what he or she feels he or she is worth."[9] This means that your feelings about yourself will affect how well you communicate with others. If your self-concept includes **self-confidence**—a feeling of competence and self-assurance—this self-confidence can affect your interpersonal effectiveness positively.

SELF-ESTEEM

A humanist approach to the self contends that the sense of identity sets humans apart from others.[10] It is believed that we are each driven by our **self-esteem**, an awareness that we are distinct from others and that we express this awareness in either productive or nonproductive ways. By developing and promoting your individuality you constructively enact your drive for self-identity. In contrast, totally conforming to the views and desires of others is a destructive enactment of your drive for that self identity. For example, soldiers have been criticized and even tried in court for certain forms of conduct against civilians during times of war (e.g., the attack on the prisoners during the second Iraqi war). The accused soldiers claimed to be following orders from their superiors, but military tribunals considered their actions to be criminal. This is an instance where one's individuality is subsumed by the choice to conform to the demands of superiors, despite knowing right from wrong. Teens are noted for doing what the in-crowd does. They justify smoking, drinking, or drug use as acceptable actions because "everyone else is doing it."

Humans are capable of free choice and can be active in determining the course of their lives. The psychological concept of Choice Theory proposes that we live and act in the moment as people responsible for ourselves. Regardless of our personal history or emotional "baggage," we can make a choice to take care of our needs today and tomorrow. We can choose to accept the past as the past and be responsible for who we are now and tomorrow. Choice Theory contends that the only person's behavior you can control is your own.[11]

An especially important area where you make choices is in deciding how you see yourself. In other words, your level of self-esteem, which is the regard you have for yourself, and your own sense of self-worth, is not permanently fixed. Messages from others and our social interactions may influence what you think of yourself, but you are capable of altering your self-esteem.

In order to control the overall quality of your life, it is generally agreed in the Euro-American culture that it is particularly important to maintain a high level of self-esteem. Researchers have conducted many studies designed to assess the impact of self-esteem on peoples' attitudes and behaviors. They have found, for example that for African American students high self-esteem was a major contributor to their academic success.[12] Similarly, a broad sampling of college students revealed that low self-esteem and low self-worth can lead to academic and social difficulties.[13]

In other research, links have been found between low self-esteem and risky sex practices,[14] binge eating,[15] indecision about leaving violent relationships,[16] and young gay men's participating in unsafe sex practices.[17]

LEARNING EXPERIENCE: Interested in analyzing your general self-esteem? If so, do Activity 2.3.

The extent to which you think of yourself as a failure or a success, a good person or a bad one, depends largely on your notion of whom you would like to be. At least three images form your desired self-concept: the *idealized self*, the *real self*, and the *should self*. The extent to which you allow your real self to be displayed is your *public self*.

THE IDEALIZED SELF

Your **idealized self** is what you perceive yourself to be if you were "perfect." Elements of this image emerge when you say, "If I were _____, then everything would be great." It may be thought of as your fantasy self. When you feel overwhelmed by problems, you may temporarily invoke your idealized self. If you feel the need to be successful, you may dream that you can do anything and accomplish anything. And if you feel the need to be loved, you may dream of being attractive and desirable. Although the idealized self is not usually obtainable, it is the measuring stick for how you judge your own and others' successes or failures.

The idealized self that a person wants to be, like many goals, has roots deep in culture. For example, if your family has always stressed the necessity to be physically attractive, achieve high grades, and obtain a prestigious occupation, then your idealized self will encompass these goals because that becomes your image of what it means to be successful.

THE REAL SELF

The real self is what you think of yourself when you are being most honest about your interests, thoughts, emotions, and needs. If you like your real self, then you possess what is termed a positive self-image.

ACTIVITY 2.3
Analyzing Your General Self-Esteem

Indicate the extent to which you agree or disagree with each of these statements:

Write 1 if you strongly disagree with the statement.
Write 2 if you disagree with the statement.
Write 3 if you neither agree or disagree with the statement.
Write 4 if you agree with the statement.
Write 5 if you strongly agree with the statement.

_____1. I am generally satisfied with myself.
_____2. I feel that I have a number of worthy qualities.
_____3. I am able to do things as adequately as most people.
_____4. I think of myself in mostly positive ways.
_____5. I have few regrets about my life.
_____6. I wouldn't change much if I had the chance to live my life over again.
_____7. I feel like a useful person.

Add up your responses to the seven items. The higher your score, the higher your self-esteem. Scores of 21 and higher suggest positive self-esteem, while scores below 21 suggest lower self-esteem. Reflect on your score. Does it seem accurate? How would improving your self-esteem help you to be a more effective interpersonal communicator?

Source: Adapted from items presented in the "Tennessee Self-Concept Scale." Nashville, TN: Counselor Recordings and Tests, 1964.

For many people, the real self is dynamic and changing. Sometimes you like yourself and other times the vultures are in full attack. This accounts for why you may feel like you are in constant turmoil, searching for who and what you are, questioning your motives for doing and not doing certain things.

THE SHOULD SELF

Another component of self-concept is the **should self**, which contains all the "oughts" and "shoulds" that serve as your moral guidelines. These standards, against which you constantly measure yourself, come from your family, culture, school, friends, and the mass media. Your "shoulds" represent the moral standards of society; transgressing from them usually results in guilt or anger with yourself.

"Shoulds" result not merely from your socialization, but also from the unique demands you place on yourself. Getting *A*'s may not be a society-wide "should," but you may think that there is no alternative, that anything less than an *A* represents failure. You may be convinced that eating more than one scoop of ice cream is disgustingly self-indulgent, or that sleeping for more than eight hours is inexcusably lazy, or that watching television is a waste of time. Every "should" increases the likelihood that you will view yourself as bad.

The should self is another area where you need to be aware of cultural differences. For example, in cultures where religion determines a complete way of life, such as Hinduism, Islam, and Orthodox Judaism, the "should" list might include feelings of guilt for not spending more hours each day praying, for being a member of a group with an alternative lifestyle, or for performing a forbidden act, such as practicing birth control. Students from Asian backgrounds report feeling great pressure from their families that they *should* be excellent students or lose face and embarrass the family.

Believing that everyone should approve of you, when this approach is clearly impossible, and believing that everything you do should be perfect, another clear impossibility, guarantees that you will dislike yourself. On the other hand, understanding the basis for the *shoulds*, and how they can motivate you to achieve, can be a positive aspect of the should self.

LEARNING EXPERIENCE: Interested in identifying your "shoulds?" If so, do Activity 2.4.

THE PUBLIC SELF

The **public self** is the *you* you let others know. It is based on the concept that if others believe the right things about me, I can get them to like me; I can persuade them and generally get my way. It acknowledges that "if others believe the wrong things about me, I can be rejected and blocked from my goals. Not only actors and politicians shape their public selves, we all do."[18] It is often difficult to grasp the real versus the public self. The dating process is intended to allow people to spend time together to make this separation. This is why some relational counselors think that individuals should date for a minimum of one year before making a live-together or marriage commitment.[19] It takes time to know the real person you are involved with. If the process is hurried, you may likely find out things about the other person that the short dating process has not revealed; things you may not like.

THE THEORIES OF SELF-CONCEPT

Recognition of the importance of self-esteem and self-concept is not a new development. Mental health professionals have been interested in the study of the self for many years and have developed different theories about it. Communication theorists have examined the self and self-esteem based on observing and studying what people intrapersonally communicate to themselves about themselves and what is communicated to others.

ACTIVITY 2.4
Identifying My Should Statements

Read the following statements and indicate the extent to which you agree or disagree with each.

If you strongly agree, mark the statement 5
If you agree, mark the statement 4
If you neither agree nor disagree, mark the statement 3
If you disagree, mark the statement 2
If you strongly disagree, mark the statement 1

_____1. It is important that others approve of me.
_____2. I hate to fail at anything.
_____3. I want everyone to like me.
_____4. I avoid things I cannot do well.
_____5. I find it hard to go against what others think.
_____6. It upsets me to make mistakes.

Total your responses to items 1, 3, and 5:_____—this is your *everyone should approve of me* score. Total your responses to items 2, 4, and 6:_____—this is your *I should be perfect* score.

Scores of 12 and higher are high, indicating strong belief in the should statement; scores of 6 and below are low, indicating little if any belief in the should statement, and scores of 7 through 11 indicate moderate belief in the should statement. Think about your results. What do you need to do so that your beliefs support more successful interpersonal communication?

Source: Items are based on descriptions of several of the irrational beliefs discussed in Ellis, A., & Harper, R. (1977). *A new guide to rational living*. North Hollywood, CA: Wilshire Books.

A theory proposes that the self is composed of four different aspects: the spiritual, the material, the social, and the physical. The *spiritual* is what we are thinking and feeling, the *material* is represented by our possessions and physical surroundings, the *social* is represented by our interactions with others, and the *physical* is our physical being.[20] Much of your self-talk centers on how you perceive the four aspects. These factors strongly influence your self-esteem.

LEARNING EXPERIENCE: Interested in analyzing your specific self-esteem? If so, do Activity 2.5.

The public self is the you you let others know. It is based on the concept that if others believe the right things about me, I can get them to like me.

Another theory suggests that social interaction is key in determining our intrapersonal communication. The idea is that we are strongly influenced by our significant-others and even by media messages. How you intrapersonally integrate these messages into your thinking develops your self-thought. Over the years our self-talk grows and progresses according to messages we hear from important people. By way of example, most parents teach their personal values and attempt to develop a family spiritual system for their children. As the child matures he or she may develop a perception of being an individual different from the parents. The adolescent often tries to establish an even stronger sense of self-identity, which may cause family conflicts, especially if the teen's values are different from those of the parents. As an adult the person emphasizes even a stronger sense of independence. As you go through the various changes, your intrapersonal communication is influenced by your experiences. You may come to perceive yourself as having had different strengths and needs when you were growing up than the person you are today. You may feel that you show certain characteristics at home, somewhat different characteristics at work, and still different characteristics

---

ACTIVITY 2.5
Analyzing My Specific Self-Esteem

Indicate the degree to which each item is true or false for you.

If it is completely false, mark the item 1.
If it is mostly false, mark the item 2.
If it is partly false and partly true, mark the item 3.
If it is mostly true, mark the item 4.
If it is completely true, mark the item 5.

_____ 1. I am satisfied with my weight.
_____ 2. I am satisfied with my looks.
_____ 3. I am satisfied with my height.
_____ 4. I am satisfied with my moral behavior.
_____ 5. I am satisfied with the extent to which I am religious.
_____ 6. I am satisfied with my relationship with a supreme being.
_____ 7. I am satisfied with my family relationships.
_____ 8. I am satisfied with how well I understand my family.
_____ 9. I am satisfied with how I treat (treated) my parents.
_____10. I am satisfied with how sociable I am.
_____11. I am satisfied with the extent to which I try to please others.
_____12. I am satisfied with the way I treat other people.

Scoring:
Add items 1, 2, and 3:_____. This is your *physical self-esteem score.*
Add items 4, 5, and 6:_____. This is your *moral-ethical self-esteem score.*
Add items 7, 8, and 9:_____. This is your *family self-esteem score.*
Add items 10, 11, and 12:_____. This is your *social self-esteem score.*

Scores in any category between 12 and 15 indicate high self-esteem; scores between 3 and 6 indicate low self-esteem; and scores from 7 through 11 indicate moderate self-esteem.

Source: Adapted from items presented in "Tennessee Self-Concept Scale." Nashville, TN: Counselor Recordings and Tests, 1964.

when with friends. You are not just one person, but one person who shares different strengths and needs in different situations. Your self-talk affects your perceptions of your changes over time and in different contexts. You probably do not conceive of yourself as the same person today as you were five years ago, and you probably are not the same person today that you will perceive yourself to be five years from now.

Self-concept also seems to be situational. Who you are with one person in one place, may not be the same as who you are with someone else or in a different place. In one relationship you may take on the role of student, yet in another the role of friend. At work you may be the leader, and at home, the follower. Many of these role-plays are based on your intrapersonal perception of who you should or need to be with people in a specific environment.

It is important that you understand yourself and your perceptions of yourself. This is the basis of self-awareness, which, again, is the basis for much of your self-talk.

UNDERSTANDING YOUR SELF

Most people have only a general idea of who they are and what they really believe in. This explains why many of us don't understand why we think the thoughts we do and are intrapersonally motivated to act in particular ways. It is often of great personal value to attempt to discover the you who is within you, the you who carries on your self-talk, cognitively processes, and acts on her/his self-concept.

Before proceeding, complete these statements:

I am

I would like to be

I like to

I believe that

I have been

I wouldn't want to

The quality I possess that I am most proud of is

My biggest flaw is

Something that I would prefer others not know about me is

Once you are finished responding to these items, go back over your list of answers and write a two-sentence description of yourself based just on the answers to the statements.

It has been said that you are what you are based on your verb *to be*.[21] What you have done in the activity you just completed is to describe yourself based on your perceived verb *to be*. You have used your intrapersonally stored data to examine your past experiences (*I have been/ done*), present attitudes and actions (*I am*), and future expectations or hopes (*I would like to be/do*). If you were honest and revealed what you really think and feel, you have just gained a glimpse at your perceived self.

Another way of looking at yourself is through the model known as the **Johari window**,[22] which allows you to ascertain your willingness to disclose who you are and to allow others to disclose to you (see Figure 2.1). From an intrapersonal perspective, the Johari window helps you understand a great deal about yourself and some of the cultural underpinnings of your self-thinking.

This activity will help you chart your Johari window:[23]

Circle the number on the top line of the square in Figure 2.2, designated "receive feedback," that corresponds to your score on Part II of the activity. Circle the same number on the bottom line of the square. Connect the two circles with a straight line.

Then circle the number on the left side line of the square, designated "self-disclosure," that corresponds to your score on Part I of the activity. Circle the same number on the right side line of the square. Connect the two circles with a straight line.

You now have the four "panes" of your Johari window. Color in the four-sided figure in the upper left-hand side of the square as illustrated in Figure 2.3. Compare your pattern to those in the figure to ascertain your self-disclosure/receive-feedback style.

Style 1 people spend *little time disclosing or giving feedback*. They tend to be perceived as good listeners and fairly shy or quiet, sometimes labeled as introverts.

Style 2 people tend to be introverts who spend a *great deal of time listening and not much time revealing information about themselves*. After being with this type of

Figure 2.1. Johari Window Questionnaire

Directions:	PART I: Extent to which I am willing to self-disclose my

Before each item in Part I, place a number from 1 to 6 to indicate how much you are willing to reveal. A 1 indicates that you are willing to self-disclose nothing or almost nothing, and a 6 indicates that you are willing to reveal everything or almost everything. Use the values 2, 3, 4, and 5 to represent the points between these extremes.	____1. goals _____ 7. ideas
	____2. strengths _____ 8. beliefs
	____3. weaknesses _____ 9. fears
	____4. positive _____ and
	        feelings _____ insecurities
	____5. negative _____10. mistakes
	        feelings
	____6. values _____Total

Before each item in Part II, place a number from 1 to 6 to indicate how willing you are to receive feedback about what you self-disclose.
 	
A 1 indicates that you refuse or resist feedback, and a 6 indicates that you consistently encourage feedback. Use the values 2, 3, 4, and 5 to represent the points between these extremes.
	PART II: Extent to which I am willing to receive feedback about my
	____1. goals _____ 7. ideas
	____2. strengths _____ 8. beliefs
	____3. weaknesses _____ 9. fears
	____4. positive _____ and
	        feelings _____ insecurities
	____5. negative _____10. mistakes
	        feelings
	____6. values _____Total

Figure 2.2. Plotting Your Johari Window

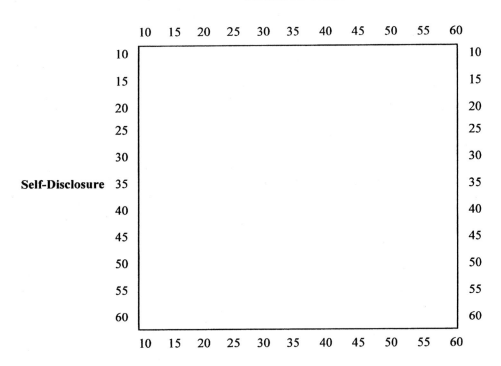

person for a while, they tend to know a great deal about you but you don't know much about them.

Style 3 people tend to be extroverts *who talk a great deal about themselves, but don't listen very much for information about the other person.* You tend to know a great deal about them, but they don't know much about you.

Style 4 people *like to both give and get information.* People who are very open and easily share themselves with others normally have a large free area and smaller blind, hidden, and unknown areas. Because these kinds of people share, they are known to themselves and to others. They are often referred to as extroverts, as they are outgoing and interactive.

A relationship between style 2 and 3 people seems ideal. One prefers to give information, while the other prefers to get information. Unfortunately, after a period of time there may be a parting of the ways as one or the other feels cheated in the relationship because there is a perception on the part of the style 2 person that they don't know a great deal about the style 3 person, and the style 3 person may perceive that they aren't being heard.

When style 1 and style 4 people get together, the style 1 person may be intimidated by the excessive probing and exposing of the style 4 person. The style 4 person, on the other hand, may think that the style 1 person is being standoffish and is not interested in developing a relationship because of the lack of sharing or probing.

Figure 2.3.   Johari Style Indicator

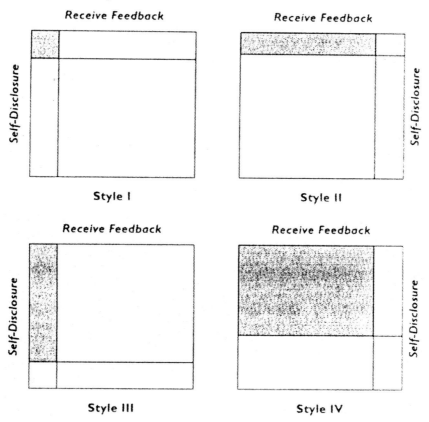

Style I

Style II

Style III

Style IV

If your four-sided figures are approximately the same size, you do not have a predominant self-disclosure/receive-feedback style.

What you hopefully gain from the Johari window exercise is an understanding of not only your perception of yourself, and how it affects your intrapersonal communication, but also how others may perceive you based on your willingness or unwillingness to both disclose and receive disclosure.

SELF-IDENTITY AND COMMUNICATION

One way of understanding the relationship between self-identity and communication with others is to view social interaction as if it were a drama being acted out. The Social Interaction Theory claims that the presentation of our self is actually a carefully conceived performance. People determine what goals they intend to achieve and then consider the "audience" with whom they will be interacting. The perceived demands of the audience shape the identity, or mask, worn for that communicative performance. In essence, people attempt to manage the impression they make on others by intrapersonally calculating how best to satisfy the norms and expectations others have for them. In other words, people manipulate their communication to get the desired effect. For example, think of situations in which you managed what you said based on to whom you were speaking. If, as a teenager, you wanted money, whom did you ask? What did you say? What appeals did you use? If you had gone to someone else for the cash, would you have used the same language, appeals, or approach?

Through communication with others, you refined your performances and expanded your repertoire of communication strategies. The better you learned to adjust your communication the more you fit in with others and achieved your communication goals. For example, suppose you were invited to a party where there were people you wanted to meet, and desired to make a good impression. You probably took great care in your personal grooming and selection of clothes. Once there you tried to listen carefully as others spoke, asked appropriate questions to keep the conversations going, answered queries about yourself that you thought would make a positive impression, used your best communication skills. As a result of presenting yourself in a way that fits the framework of what is demanded from those in this group, it was probably assumed you were a "nice person."

Occasionally, people mismanage the presentation of their identities by either misreading the situation, by unintentionally exposing parts of themselves not intended for public presentation, or by not knowing how to play the socialization game. The person whose social skills are lacking says the wrong thing, at the wrong time, to the wrong person. Often people who have weak social skills put their proverbial "foot in their mouth" because they just can't stop themselves from saying or doing inappropriate acts. These performances damage the view of others about the person, which may result in embarrassment, defensive behaviors, and/or attempts to repair the other's perception.

Communication Anxiety

Before reading ahead, complete the CAGC questionnaire in Box 2.1. It is designed to assess your feelings of comfort and discomfort while communicating. The first part focuses on your communicating in general. The remaining parts focus on your feelings about communicating in specific settings.

A form of stress specifically related to communication is called **communication anxiety**—the *fear* of engaging in communication interactions. Communication anxiety has been described as "shyness, Social Anxiety Disorder, or Social Phobia."[24] In this case, the individual's negative self-talk about communication reflects excessive worry, and can bring on such things as sleeplessness, headaches, and upset stomachs. The messages warn of unfavorable outcomes, and the person experiences a sense of impending doom. Other signs may include racing heart, palms sweating, dry mouth, vanishing words, cluttered thoughts, and the urge to escape from any communicative situation. It varies in its spectrum (see Figure 2.4).

It is estimated that between 80 and 93 percent of all people feel some communication anxiety and that 15 to 20 percent of all college students have high levels of communication anxiety.[25]

BOX 2.1
CAGC: Communication Apprehension in Generalized Contexts Questionnaire

Indicate the degree to which each of the following statements applies to you.

Circle 1 if you strongly agree.
Circle 2 if you agree.
Circle 3 if you are undecided.
Circle 4 if you disagree.
Circle 5 if you strongly disagree.

There are no right or wrong answers. Many of the statements resemble each other. Do not be concerned about this. Work quickly so that you record only your first impressions.

General

1 2 3 4 5   1. When communicating, I generally am calm and relaxed.
1 2 3 4 5   2. I find the prospect of speaking mildly pleasant.
1 2 3 4 5   3. In general, communication makes me uncomfortable.
1 2 3 4 5   4. I dislike using my body and voice expressively.
1 2 3 4 5   5. When communicating, I generally am tense and nervous.

Group Discussions

1 2 3 4 5   6. I am afraid to express myself in a group.
1 2 3 4 5   7. I dislike participating in group discussions.
1 2 3 4 5   8. I am tense and nervous while participating in group discussions.
1 2 3 4 5   9. Engaging in a group discussion with new people makes me tense and nervous.
1 2 3 4 5   10. I am calm and relaxed while participating in group discussions.

Meetings and Classes

1 2 3 4 5   11. I look forward to expressing my opinions at meetings and classes.
1 2 3 4 5   12. Generally, I am nervous when I have to participate in a meeting and class.
1 2 3 4 5   13. Usually I am calm and relaxed while participating in meetings and classes.
1 2 3 4 5   14. I am very calm and relaxed when I am called on to express an opinion at a meeting and class.
1 2 3 4 5   15. Communicating in meetings or classes generally makes me uncomfortable.

(continued)

BOX 2.1 (*continued*)

Interpersonal Conversations

1 2 3 4 5   16. While participating in a conversation with a new acquaintance I feel very nervous.

1 2 3 4 5   17. Generally, I am very relaxed while talking with one other person.

1 2 3 4 5   18. Ordinarily, I am very calm and relaxed in conversations.

1 2 3 4 5   19. I am relaxed while conversing with people who hold positions of authority.

1 2 3 4 5   20. I am afraid to speak up in conversations.

Scoring:

General

Total your scores for items 3, 4, 5 = Score A _____

Total your scores for items 1, 2 = Score B _____

$(18 - \_\_\_)$ + $\_\_\_$ =   _____

   Score A   Score B   Total

Group

Total your scores for items 6, 7, 8, 9 = Score C _____

Indicate your score for item 10 = Score D _____

$(24 - \_\_\_)$ + $\_\_\_$ =   _____

   Score C   Score D   Total

Meetings and Classes

Total your scores for items 12, 15 = Score E _____

Total your scores for items 11, 13, 14 = Score F _____

$(12 - \_\_\_)$ + $\_\_\_$ =   _____

   Score E   Score F   Total

Interpersonal Conversations

Total your scores for items 16, 20 = Score G _____

Total your scores for items 17, 18, 19 = Score H _____

$(12 - \_\_\_)$ + $\_\_\_$ =   _____

   Score G   Score H   Total

You'll learn how to interpret your scores as the chapter progresses.

Source: Printed with the permission of James C. McCroskey. For an in-depth discussion of this and other communication apprehension evaluation tools, see Richmond, V., & McCroskey, J. (1998). *Communication: Apprehension, avoidance, and effectiveness* (5th ed.). Needham Heights, MA: Allyn and Bacon. Retrieved from www.jamescmccroskey.com/.

Figure 2.4. A Spectrum of Shyness

Normal Shyness
You are jittery beginning a public speech, but afterward you are glad you did it. Your mind goes blank on a first date, but eventually you relax and find things to talk about. Your palms sweat in a job interview, but you ask and answer thoughtful questions.
Extreme Shyness
You clam up and your heart races when you know people are looking at you. You tremble when speaking up at a meeting, even if it is only to say your name. You avoid starting conversations for fear of saying something awkward.
Social Anxiety
You will do anything, even skip work, to avoid being introduced to new people. You have trouble swallowing in public, making it hard to dine out or go to parties. You feel you never make a good impression and that you are a social failure.
Severe Social Anxiety
You are free of nervousness only when alone and you can barely leave the house. You constantly worry about being embarrassed or humiliated by others.

Most people are understandably nervous when talking in important interpersonal contexts. Maybe you feel nervous when you must attend an important meeting at work or meet people you don't know or at a party. You may feel nervous about a class discussion because you don't think you are completely prepared or are afraid of the professor's evaluation. Whenever you convey ideas in these situations, you are opening yourself to judgment, so you may feel tense. An important idea to remember is that much of communication anxiety can be controlled.

"Shy people have inaccurate self-concepts."[26] They often believe that they are inadequate when they are not. "They tend to blame themselves for failure and credit others for success. They tend to erase themselves: They avoid eye contact, speak softly or less than others, and rarely take a strong position on a topic."[27] People who experience speech anxiety feel fearful and perform in an inadequate fashion.[28]

The messages that communicatively anxious people tell themselves are, "I lack the ability and/or confidence to share my true self with someone else," and, "I can't interact when I'd like to." Communication anxiety can be emotionally based and/or grows from a perceived lack of communication skills. Once a person accepts such labels of being "shy" or "communicatively apprehensive," his or her attitudes and actions reflect the label.

LEARNING EXPERIENCE: Interested in finding out if you have assigned yourself the title of "shy?" If so, do Activity 2.6.

PRIVATE AND PUBLIC COMMUNICATION ANXIETY

People differ in the context in which they are *communicatively anxious*—the extent to which they avoid interacting because they feel unable to communicate effectively or because they wish to escape being noticed. **Publicly anxious people** are strongly hesitant about communicating with others and display their anxiety through such outward signs as avoiding eye contact, blushing, perspiring, and speaking in a quavering voice when forced to communicate in public settings.

While some people are publicly anxious, others are privately anxious. **Privately anxious people** mentally resist active communication, but will participate—often by forcing themselves. They seldom display the outward physical reactions of stress, such as fingernail biting, sweaty palms, or dry mouth, but still feel discomfort. Famous people who have been reported as being privately shy include Abraham Lincoln, Eleanor Roosevelt, Thomas Jefferson, Donny Osmond, George Harrison, Gloria Estefan, Harrison Ford, Nicole Kidman, Tom Cruise, and Tom Hanks.[29] Each of these "shy" people gained success by learning to cope with their communication anxiety.

COMMUNICATION ANXIETY AND YOU

Up until now the discussion of communication anxiety has centered on people in general. Let's examine your scores on the first section of your CAGC to see how you

ACTIVITY 2.6
McCroskey Shyness Scale

The following fourteen statements refer to talking with other people.

If the statement describes you *very well*, circle, "YES."
If it *somewhat* describes you circle "yes."
If you a*re not sure whether it describes you or not*, or if you *do not understand the statement*, circle "?."
If the statement is a *poor* description of you, circle "no."
If the statement is a *very poor* description of you, circle "NO."

There are no right or wrong answers. Work quickly; record your first impression.

YES yes ? no NO   1. I am a shy person.
YES yes ? no NO   2. Other people think I talk a lot.
YES yes ? no NO   3. I am a very talkative person.
YES yes ? no NO   4. Other people think I am shy.
YES yes ? no NO   5. I talk a lot.
YES yes ? no NO   6. I tend to be very quiet in class.
YES yes ? no NO   7. I don't talk much.
YES yes ? no NO   8. I talk more than most people.
YES yes ? no NO   9. I am a quiet person.
YES yes ? no NO   10. I talk more in a small group (three to six people) than other people do.
YES yes ? no NO   11. Most people talk more than I do.
YES yes ? no NO   12. Other people think I am very quiet.
YES yes ? no NO   13. I talk more in class than most people do.
YES yes ? no NO   14. Most people are more shy than I am.

Scoring: YES = 1, yes = 2, ? = 3, no = 4, NO = 5

Score your responses as follows:

1. Add the scores for items 1, 4, 6, 7, 9, 11, and 12.
2. Add the scores for items 2, 3, 5, 8, 10, 13, and 14.
3. Complete this formula:

Shyness = 42 − (total from step 1) + (total from step 2) = _____

Evaluation: Scores 52 and above = high perceived shyness; scores 32 and below = low perceived shyness, scores between 33 and 51 = normal perceived shyness. As you think about this measure, what are the implications regarding your forming and developing new interpersonal relationships?

Source: McCroskey, J. C., & Richmond, V. P. (1982). Communication apprehension and shyness: Conceptual and operational distinctions. *Central States Speech Journal, 33,* 458–468. Printed with permission of the author.

label yourself. As you consider the results, remember that this is not an objective measure; rather, it reflects your *self*-perceptions. Also be aware that this anxiety is culture-sensitive. Research shows that certain groups, such as the Japanese, American Indians, and the Finns, because of cultural conditioning, tend to score quite high on the CAGC. According to a U.S. national sampling, a score of 14 or above in the General section of the questionnaire indicates that you perceive yourself as more apprehensive about communicating than the average person.[30]

Another way to look at communication anxiety is whether it is situational (only in certain contexts) or general (all the time). Once again examine your scores for the CAGC. If you think of yourself as a communicatively anxious person but scored lower than 14 on the General section, you may have been surprised. There is an explanation: You may be anxious in some contexts but not in others. Be aware that the public speaking element has been eliminated from this questionnaire, as we are discussing interpersonal in this text, so the public speaking score doesn't apply. Be aware of that when you evaluate your score. You might perceive yourself as being communicatively apprehensive, but that may only be in public speaking situations. Therefore, your score may reveal you are not apprehensive since you are perfectly comfortable in all situations other than public speaking.

If you received a score of over 16 for Group Discussion, or over 15 for Meetings and Classes, or over 13 for Interpersonal Conversations, you may have identified specifically where your anxiety lies. It is not uncommon for some people to display anxiety in only one context, whereas others display anxiety in several or all contexts.

THE CAUSES OF COMMUNICATION ANXIETY

In some cases, infants may be born with communication anxiety. Perhaps because of genetic reasons about 10 to 15 percent of children cry when they encounter the unfamiliar. Research suggests that these children will experience more communication apprehension than other people will.[31] Tests on potentially shy children progressing from two weeks of life to seven years indicated that at twenty-one months they clung to their caretakers in new situations and hesitated before interacting with new persons; at four years they remained quiet in the presence of an unknown adult, and at seven years they exhibited a greater degree of reaction to imagined threats than other children.[32] Biologically, shy children react more intensely to the stimuli around them than other children do, as exhibited by racing hearts, widening pupils, and vocal cord tenseness.

Social conditioning can also cause people to be communicatively apprehensive. Children may imitate or model such behaviors as observed in others. Apprehensive parents often have apprehensive children. If your parents were communicatively anxious, there is a 70 percent chance that you are anxious because you are imitating their patterns.[33] Another potential cause is perfectionism. If a person is worried about being evaluated because the individual or loved ones are critical, the perfectionist attitudes may make the individual afraid of the evaluation that comes in the communication process.[34] In addition, a person may be reinforced in anxiousness by the negative feedback received because of avoidance of communicative activities.

LISTENER APPREHENSION

It should be noted that communication apprehension, as it is generally understood, focuses on speaker or source apprehension. Receiver or listener apprehension, however, is also significant as a communication barrier. **Listener apprehension** has been conceptualized as "the fear of misinterpreting, inadequately processing, and/or not being able to adjust psychologically to messages sent by others."[35] It is possible that a listener can be anxious about the outcome of a communication. An example is the fear associated with getting a test report from a physician or being fearful in a class where one of your knowledge vultures has attacked such as, "I do terribly in science courses. I'm going to flunk this class." Either of these could stimulate a high level of listening apprehension. Listener apprehension can also stem from inexperience and/or unfamiliarity with the speaker, the situation, perfectionism, or the subject itself.

THE EFFECTS OF COMMUNICATION ANXIETY

For the person with communication anxiety, fear is powerful. The individual may feel like something terrible will happen during the upcoming communication event or that some disturbing outcome will result afterward. The person with communication apprehension often feels out of control, as if some foreign energy is in charge instead of the individual himself or herself. Communication apprehension can create a serious or even debilitating dilemma.

There are some demonstrated effects of communication anxiety.[36] In classroom situations, communicatively anxious students rarely volunteer, if at all.[37] They may drop classes that require oral communication or miss class when oral participation is necessary. These patterns can affect both learning and grades. Some anxious college students even fail to graduate with only one course to complete—a required course in speech communication.[38]

People with communication anxiety often choose college majors that require few, if any, oral presentations, such as research or technical fields. In the workplace, if they must participate orally—whether one-on-one, in a group, or in a public setting—they fail to do so, thus missing out on promotions and pay increases because they are handicapped by their fear.[39]

In interpersonal situations, people with communication anxiety talk very little about themselves and seem overly concerned that the other person understand and agree with them.[40] They also are nonassertive, tending to yield to the other person and submitting themselves to others' directions. Insofar as perceptions of communicatively anxious people are concerned, after interacting for only a short period of time with strangers, communicatively anxious people are perceived as less socially attractive, less trustworthy, and less satisfied than people who are not communicatively anxious.[41]

Finally, although they may have as much desire for social relationships as people who are not communicatively anxious, people who are afraid to communicate have fewer steady dates than those who are less anxious.[42]

DEALING WITH COMMUNICATION ANXIETY

If your scores on the CAGC indicated that you continuously are anxious in general, or in one or more communication contexts, you may be wondering what you can do.

First, unless it has reached the degree where it can be diagnosed as a *social phobia*, which is recognized as a mental illness,[43] be assured that communication anxiety is not an incurable illness.[44] Since, except for those born with the anxiety, communication apprehension is a title given to a person by significant others or the person himself or herself, the title can be removed.[45] The simplest way, of course, is for the person to declare that he or she doesn't want or need the title. This is very difficult for many to do, but aid is available to help rid those who want to rid themselves of the title but can't self-correct.

Second, recognize that knowing the factors that contribute to your communication anxiety and the extent of your reactions will help you to assess the seriousness of your situation and plan an appropriate course of action.

If your communication anxiety tends to be mild and infrequent, you can probably manage it by using short-term stress reducers. However, if you often feel communicatively anxious, if particular situations are always particularly stressful, and if you think of your anxiety as a serious handicap, you may want to seek a more permanent solution.

The success rate in teaching communicatively anxious people to cope with or alter their behavior is extremely high. But, like any attempt at changing personality or learning, the treatment or training will be effective only if the person truly wants help and diligently applies oneself. Options for coping are accepting the anxiety, developing a willingness to communicate, fantasizing positive visualization, gaining skill training, learning cognitive modification techniques, seeking a physician's help through drug therapy, and using systematic desensitization.

Skill Training

A lack of skills may be the cause of communication apprehension in some cases. The good news is that an individual can learn how to work collaboratively in a group, how to be a good conversationalist, how to ask questions, and other skills that will help them communicate interpersonally.

Learning the skills needed to be an effective communicator provides a sense of security, and pleasure can be anticipated. Many of these theories and skills are stressed in this book. Communicatively anxious people who wish to change may also search out a speech coach who, much like a personal trainer, deals with people who want to improve themselves. The coach will teach the skills needed for the communicatively anxious person to overcome the anxiety. Signing up for academic courses in the communication field may also help. People who are anxious about participating in groups in classes could benefit from a Small Groups class. Those who fear social interactions can take a Dale Carnegie course or enroll in a Social Psychology course.

Systematic Desensitization

Some people have difficulty with communication apprehension because they feel embarrassed or humiliated when communicating with new people and wondering what others think of them. Through **systematic desensitization**, individuals visualize or participate in communication situations while learning how to notice tension that creeps into their body and learning to release that tension.[46] The process is similar to taking allergy shots to desensitize the body against allergens. The people who are communicatively apprehensive are taught how to take small psychological steps in confronting and overcoming their apprehension by being exposed to and then confronting their fears. As many as 80 or 90 percent of the people treated professionally by this system report the complete elimination of their apprehension.[47] Again, such a program works only if the person wants to change and has the skills to modify his or her behavior. If the individual does not have the necessary abilities, then skill training must precede or follow systematic desensitization.

Cognitive Modification

Cognitive modification centers on the concept that people who are communicatively anxious need to find strategies for replacing negative thoughts with positive thoughts. The first step in this process is for people to learn how to recognize and identify when they are thinking negatively about their communication (e.g., the vultures). Then, they learn to replace negative statements with positive ones. Rather than saying, for example, "I really say stupid things," they can substitute "I can present clear ideas; it isn't that hard." The last stage of the training is to practice substituting positive statements for negative ones.

An aspect of cognitive modification is the use of affirmations. To do positive affirmations, select one or more that can counteract your weaknesses. When you are aware of your anxiety building up, repeat your affirmation. For example, when one of the authors of this book feels anxious, he intrapersonally states, "Cool it, you are okay." By stating this until he feels his body relax, he can overcome the anxiety. It even stopped him from stuttering when he was young. Some people paste their affirmation on their bathroom mirror and repeat it every morning to start the day right.

Here are a list of possible affirmations:

"I'm responsible for me. I'm not concerned about what others say."
"It's all right to meet my needs as I see fit."
"Nothing that bad can happen."
"If they don't like me, that's their problem, not mine."
"I am free to make mistakes."
"Shoulds, oughts, and musts are irrelevant."
"I can invent new ways to satisfy a need and choose the best option."

This process may sound very theoretical, but in reality, it works. The success of this technique is quite high.[48] The process can be taught by both communication coaches and cognitive mental health practitioners such as a counselor or psychologist.

Willingness to Communicate

Your personal communication apprehension may stem from a lack of willingness to communicate. Interpersonal communication is risky in that other people will analyze, evaluate, and respond to your communication. Thus, the person who is analytical and flexible about communication will probably be willing to take the risk of meeting and getting to know others. Those who are not willing to communicate follow the opposite path.

The willing communicator realizes that:

- *There is no such thing as a perfect communicator.* We all make mistakes.
- *You need to interact with others,* no matter what are perceived to be the negatives of that communication, such as being embarrassed.
- Most often, *the perceived fear of what will go wrong never happens* (deaths of people who attempt to interact with someone at a party or ask a professor a question in class, just don't happen, for example).
- *Accomplishing your communicative task is more important than your perceived fear of "what others might think."*
- You must assume that *if someone doesn't like what you say, or how you say it, it is that person's problem, not yours.* This attitude allows you to be immune to the personal negative self-doubts that are often present in communicative apprehensives.

Being willing to communicate may be the single most important characteristic of a person who is able to have a successful personal and professional life through interactions with other people.

Drug Therapy

"Pasted on bus shelters nationwide, a poster asks the passersby to imagine being allergic to people."[49] The purpose of those billboards was to alert individuals with social anxiety disorder that, in extreme cases, there may be some aid in dealing with the problem by using drug therapy as a support for psychological and speech communication assistance. Such drugs as Paxil and Paxil CR have been found to aid people who are communicatively apprehensive to manage their problems.[50] It does not solve the problem alone or "cure" the person. It "takes off the edge" and blocks emotional thoughts. The causes are still present. It also doesn't teach the necessary skills to be a competent communicator.

Positive Visualization

In **positive visualization**, a person prepares for an anticipated unpleasant experience by picturing the situation being carried out successfully. Based on the theory of the **self-fulfilling prophecy**, which states that if we anticipate a negative outcome, the odds of getting a negative outcome are likely, but anticipation of a positive outcome usually results in a positive experience. Once the individual develops the positive outcomes, the "mental film," he or she pictures it over and over before the event so that the expected outcome will be positive rather than negative. Positive visualization is a constructive form of the self-fulfilling prophecy.

Practice the concept of creating a positive visualization with this scene: Imagine that you fear meeting strangers. Before your next introduction, close your eyes and picture yourself being introduced, shaking hands, saying your name, listening to the other person's name, repeating the name, asking a question, hearing the answer, saying good-by, and feeling pleased about the whole experience. Envision this sequence repeatedly. If the example really fit you, you would probably be amazed to find that because you are prepared and are expecting positive results, the event will be much to your liking and less stressful than if you had predicted failure.

LEARNING EXPERIENCE: Interested in practicing positive visualization? If so, do Activity 2.7.

Accept the Anxiety

It may sound strange, but the act of accepting that you are anxious can help you to overcome it.[51] Your body is an amazing tool. When it doesn't like what is happening to it, it tries to protect you. That's why your body tightens up, causing you to take shallow breaths, feel light-headed or dizzy, and begin to shake. You may not like it, but that's your body's way of signaling fight or flight. Either you are going to run from the situation or stand and fight your way through it. Understanding this, accept that sometimes you will experience some anxiety. It is normal and it is natural. Accept that it will be there. In most cases, though you feel you are going to faint, that your voice is quivering, that you are in emotional meltdown, the person to whom you are speaking probably doesn't even notice these manifestations. Few listeners pay strict attention to every movement, stammer, or shake that the speaker exhibits. If you choose to use intrapersonal self-talk to convince yourself that you won't die, that you can get

---

ACTIVITY 2.7
Practicing Positive Visualization

Let's assume a friend has asked you to participate in a fund-raising drive for the Multiple Sclerosis Association. You agreed to help, think the drive is worthwhile, but you have realized you have other priorities and should have said, "No." You have decided to back out, but the person is a good friend. You think of what you are going to say and review it enough times until you feel comfortable with the language. The plea is prepared and you have rehearsed it. To further help you prepare and to help yourself relax, you are going to use positive visualization. Do the following: Close your eyes and visualize the friend. Picture yourself walking into the friend's apartment, saying "hello," and explaining the fact that you are overcommitted and must back out of your prior acceptance to help. Visualize yourself relaxed as you present your ideas. Next, see and hear the friend agreeing to your request. You are feeling positive about what you did and the outcome of your having acted assertively.

In the future, whenever you are preparing for what you perceive might be a stressful communicative situation, use a similar positive visualization exercise.

through the stress, that you are going to be okay, then you should be able to cope. If you choose to give yourself the message that you will do the best you can, and that you are not and can't be perfect, you are much more likely to be able to achieve your communicative goal.

Key Terms

intrapersonal communication
social reality
self-talk
psychological vulture
chunking
ordering
reordering
context organizing
mnemonics
values
attitudes
beliefs
cognitive dissonance
guilty conscience
self-concept
self-confidence

self-esteem
Choice Theory
idealized self
real self
should self
public self
Johari window
Social Interaction Theory
communication anxiety
publicly anxious people
privately anxious people
systematic desensitization
cognitive modification
listener apprehension
positive visualization
self-fulfilling prophecy

Competencies Check-Up

Interested in finding out what you learned in this chapter and how you use the information? If so, take this competencies check-up.

Directions: Indicate the extent that each statement applies to you:

1—Never   *2—Seldom*   *3—Sometimes*   *4—Often*   *5—Usually*

____1. I use positive self-talk to help me process who I am, and I avoid self-put-downs.

____2. I use positive visualization to help me achieve what I want.

____3. I use an array of memory strategies—chunking, ordering, reordering, context organizing, and mnemonics—to help me remember.

____4. I keep my communication actions consistent with my values, beliefs, and attitudes.

____5. I have a strong sense of self, self-confidence, and feelings of competence and effectiveness.

____6. My interpersonal communication is motivated by good self-esteem, and I express in positive, productive ways how I am unique and distinct from other people.

___ 7. I agree with the psychological concept of Choice Theory. Regardless of what has happened in my life, or what I have done in the past, I can choose behaviors that will help me meet my needs more effectively in the future because the only person's behavior I can control is my own.

___ 8. I like my real self and possess a positive self-image.

___ 9. Based on my Johari window, my style is consistent with my individual interpersonal communication goals.

___10. My CAGC is consistent with my individual interpersonal communication goals, and I seldom feel anxiety when I communicate.

___11. When I do feel communication apprehension, I employ specific coping strategies that help me control the apprehension so that I communicate effectively.

___12. I am willing to talk about myself, without dominating the conversation, and feel no particular need to have others agree with me.

___13. This week, I have actively worked to improve my interpersonal communication skills.

___14. I recognize that I need to interact with the people in my life, even strangers, regardless of what might be negatives related to that communication.

___15. I can ignore what others might think about me for the sake of communicating with others.

SCORING: A total of 45 suggests that you have perceive that you have the basic competencies for the foundation of interpersonal competency. A score over 60 suggests you have a solid foundation for intrapersonal competency. Go back and look at any test items with a score of less than 3 and create a plan for changing that area to one of full competence over the course of this semester. Your instructor may want you to create a list of strategies for improvement based on your test results.

I-Can Plan!

Only you can inspire yourself to become an effective intrapersonal communicator through positive self-talk, effective use of memory, strong self-esteem, and controlling communication apprehension. By taking an "I can change" attitude and developing and implementing a specific plan, you can further develop your individual intrapersonal communication competencies.

Activities

1. Are you in a relationship? If so, you may want to invite your partner, spouse, or lover to fill out a Johari window. Compare your styles and discuss the implications for the relationship.

2. Write out ten questions an interviewer could ask you. Using open-ended questions that will encourage a depth of response, come up with questions that should allow the interviewer to understand your personal history, beliefs, and future plans.

Phrase the questions so that they require more than a one- or two-word reply. Your instructor will then match you with another member of the class. You will interview each other using the questions that each of you has prepared. Then introduce each other in a two- to three-minute presentation to the class. After the class presentation, answer the following questions:

a. What did it feel like to reveal yourself to a stranger?

b. Did you conceal things about yourself during the interview? If so, why?

c. How did you feel and what did you do while your partner was introducing you to the class?

3. Bring to class a painting, poem, or piece of music you like. Share it with the class or a small group and indicate why you have positive feelings about it. What does your choice indicate about you?

4. Write out both sides of a debate for the following issues. Explain whether you believe pro or con and why.

a. The only person you can change is yourself.

b. In order to be successful in a relationship, you need to be able to change the other person.

c. People can change themselves if they want to, but most people are too lazy.

5. Fill out your Johari window. Get one of your friends to fill in the "Extent to which I am willing to receive feedback" part of the questionnaire as he perceived *you* are willing to receive feedback. Tell your friend to be completely honest. Compare the answers with yours. What did you learn about yourself from this activity?

6. Make a shield-like coat of arms out of a piece of cardboard large enough for the class to see. Draw or cut out and paste at least four pictures, symbols, or words on the coat of arms that represent you—your beliefs, attitudes, bodily image, hobbies, future plans, past successes, or failures. The class will be broken into groups. Each person is to explain his or her coat of arms and why you have selected these things to represent you.

CHAPTER 3

Listening as an Interpersonal Skill

Learning Outcomes

After reading this chapter, you should be able to:

- Explain the importance of listening in daily communication.
- Contrast hearing and listening.
- Define and state the role of steps in the listening process.
- List and explain some of the listening influencers.
- Define discriminative, comprehensive, therapeutic, critical, appreciative, and compassionate listening.
- Identify listening response styles.
- Analyze the basic concepts of intercultural listening.
- Identify and explain some of the techniques available for improving personal listening.
- Discuss listening apprehension, its causes, and approaches to dealing with it.

Consider a story from Center Harbor, Maine, where Walter Cronkite (at that time, television's leading news anchorman) piloted his boat toward the dock. Supposedly an excellent sailor, Cronkite noticed a group of people on land, who were waving to him and yelling "Hello Walter, Hello Walter." Cronkite was flattered by the yelling crowd, waved back and took a bow. Suddenly, Cronkite drove his boat aground. He suddenly realized the crowd was yelling "Low Water!," not "Hello Walter!"[1]

Like Cronkite, do you hear what you want or expect to hear, or do you hear the words actually spoken? There appears to be enough evidence to indicate that if you are typical, you probably use various strategies that look like listening, but don't quite qualify. Most people will at times feign attention, overreact emotionally, day-dream, or otherwise zone-out—all when they're supposedly listening.

If you are fairly typical, you have had little if any training as a listener. Most schools operate on the assumption that you don't know how to read or write when you come to school, so they teach you how to perform those skills. They also assume that

67

since you can talk and hear, you can communicate and listen. These assumptions are incorrect. Hearing is a biological process. Listening is a skill people learn.

How effective a listener do you think you are? How much of your time do you spend listening?

Most U.S. Americans spend more than half—as much as 80 percent of the day hearing—but actively listen only about half the time. Unfortunately, they understand and remember less than 25 percent of what they hear.[2] According to the father of the new generally accepted business theory that the "world is economically flat," few understand the importance and necessity of listening. He states, "Listening is a sign of respect. It is a sign that you actually value what the other person might have to say. If you just listen to someone first, it is amazing how much they will listen back to you."[3]

The Importance of Listening

Listening is an important skill that we use daily. How well you do in school, at work, and in your personal life may well depend on your ability to listen efficiently.

Success in college depends on effective listening. In fact, listening is the most used academic skill. "Students listen to the equivalent of a book a day; talk the equivalent of a book a week; read the equivalent of a book a month; and write the equivalent of a book a year."[4] In fact, effective listening skills may be more important to college students than aptitude or reading skills.[5]

As an educated person, you have an obligation to strive to be an effective listener. And to be a responsible listener, you must know what the process is about, what it takes to be an effective processor of messages, how to evaluate your own listening, and how to work toward improving your weaknesses while retaining your strengths.

The Listening Process

Many people assume that listening is just the same as hearing, but they are different. Hearing is the biological process of receiving sound, which is necessary for listening to be possible.

An additional aspect of hearing/listening concerns ear preference. Though they are unaware of it, "most people prefer to be addressed in their right ears in everyday settings."[6] Studies in ear preference indicate that each of the ears performs a different function.[7] The brain has two hemispheres (sides), which are used differently. The left side of the brain, for example, processes language. What you hear in your left ear is processed more in the right side of the brain, and what you hear in your right ear is processed more in the left side of the brain. This reverse of processing sides is called the *contralateral concept*, which means that sounds heard with the right ear are fed into the left side of the brain, which is the center of language and meaning. Left-ear sounds go to the right side of the brain, which is the center of emotions. Speech is therefore better processed with the right ear, while music, environmental sounds, and noises are better processed through the left ear. One of your authors experienced this phenomena when he had an operation on his right ear, which temporarily cut off the sound in that ear. He found that there was a delay in his thinking process as he fought to figure out the words he was hearing through his left ear. When the problem was cleared up, and he could again hear in his right ear, he noticed a remarkable difference in his cognitive processing.

Listening is a process that involves a message going through reception, perception, attention, the assignment of meaning, and feedback (a response by the listener to the message presented) (see Figure 3.1).

RECEPTION

The hearing process is based on a complex set of physical interactions between the ear and the brain. The initial step in the listening process is the **reception** of a stimulus or message, which includes both the auditory message and in some cases, the visual message. Proper care of the ears is important because auditory acuity enhances the ability to listen efficiently. It is estimated that "3.68% of the total population [of the United States] is hard of hearing and 0.3% of the total population is functionally deaf."[8] To keep these statistics from rising, people who work near loud machinery are now required to wear ear protectors. But the workplace is not the only source of

Figure 3.1. The Listening Process

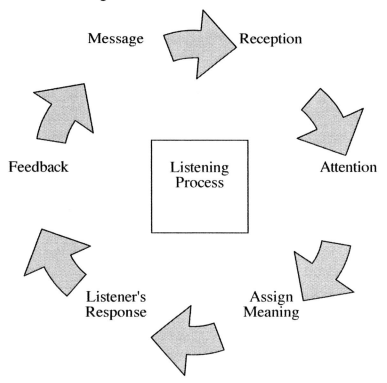

potential danger. Do you walk around with earphones connected to your blaring Ipod? Is your car radio or CD player so loud that the vehicle literally shakes from the sound? A person who listens to very loud music should be aware that they can damage their hearing mechanism. Indeed, the use of earphones to listen to music is considered the source of much hearing damage. An audiologist warns that, "As you enjoy the blaring music in your car, home, or your headsets, or at a concert, be aware that you can be permanently damaging one of your most important biological tools . . . your hearing mechanism."[9]

In addition to using the hearing mechanism, you listen through your visual system. You listen through the eyes to observe a person's facial expression, posture, movement, and appearance, which all provide important cues that may not be obvious merely by listening to the verbal part of the message.

Receiving the message through visual and auditory channels is but one part of the listening process. The listener also must attend to the message.

ATTENTION

Once the stimulus—the word and/or visual symbol—is received, the attention stage of the human processing system can take place.

The Role of Attention

In listening, **attention** represents the focus on one of the many stimuli around you at any given moment. In this phase, the other stimuli fade into the background, while you focus on what you see or hear from the other person. Typically, your attention comes and goes as you focus on the other person, the environment, and what is going on in your mind. Consider, for example, what happens when you go to a play. Perhaps the person in front of you is constantly whispering to the person next to him, there is a buzz in the sound system, and you are worried because you left your car in a no-parking zone. Your attention is being pulled in numerous directions. But if the production is interesting enough, you will focus on what is being portrayed and the other factors will be relegated to the back of your consciousness.

Your short-term memory enables you to focus attention. **Short-term memory** refers to the capacity for holding a small amount of information in mind in an active, readily available state for a short period of time. The duration of short-term memory is believed to be in the order of seconds. Estimates of short-term-memory capacity limits vary from about four to about nine items, depending on the experimental design used to estimate capacity.[10] Thus, your ability to focus attention is limited. In fact, teachers have observed that many students cannot handle much beyond a ten-minute time frame of active attention. The reasons for this are not yet fully understood, although experts have suggested that television viewing may have negative effects.[11] You've come to expect a seven- to ten-minute viewing format followed by a commercial break. This creates a pattern that encourages concentration in small spurts of time. On the other hand, the extensive use of video and hand-held electronic games may be increasing the ability to concentrate by those who are using the equipment.[12] In fact, in order to improve the listening abilities of those with ADD (Attention Deficit Disorder), researchers have suggested that electronic game players "improved in controlling their impulses and improved their concentration,"[13] thus improving their listening comprehension.

The Role of Concentration

One of the most difficult tasks you have to perform as a listener is concentration. Motivation plays an important role in activating your concentration. For example, wanting to listen to the other person will put you in a better frame of mind for concentrating than anticipating that she will be boring.

Your level of interest in the topic and the complexity of a message will affect your ability to concentrate. Ideally, you should be interested in everything you hear, but, realistically, that is not possible. Some messages are boring, but if you need to get the information, careful concentration is imperative. For example, you may not find the chemistry professor's ideas fascinating, but if you do not listen effectively, you probably will fail the next test. You also may find the information so difficult that you turn it off. Again, if it is imperative for you to understand the ideas, then you have to force yourself to figure out what you do not understand and find a way of grasping the meaning.

You can think three to four times faster than the normal conversation rate, which ranges between approximately 130 and 200 words per minute.[14] (You can realize approximately how many words the average person speaks in a minute by reading the following italicized text.) *And because we can receive messages much more quickly than the other person can talk, we tend to tune in and tune out throughout a message. The mind can absorb only so much material. Indeed, the brain operates much like a computer: it turns off, recycles itself, and turns back on to avoid information overload. It is no wonder, then, that our attention fluctuates even when we are actively involved as listeners. Think back to a class you attended. Do you recall gaps in your listening? This is a natural part of the listening process. When you turn off, the major danger is that you may daydream rather than quickly turn back to the message. But by taking notes and/or forcing yourself to paraphrase, you can help avoid this difficulty.* (You just read approximately one minute of spoken material.)

Research on *compressed speech* illustrates the great human capacity for efficient listening. In this technique, taped material is speeded up mechanically to more than three hundred words per minute. Incredibly, there is no loss of comprehension at this faster rate. Tests even reveal increased comprehension, much as the tests given to people who have been taught to speed-read show an increase in their retention of information.[15] Because of the rapid speeds, the test participants anticipated retention problems and thus forced themselves to listen more attentively and concentrate more fully than they would otherwise have done. So, if a person is using a rapid pace don't assume that your comprehension is going to decrease. The style may be helping you.

Concentration also requires the listener to control distractions. As a listener, you probably have a whole list of things that you have to attend to in addition to the message. Rather than attempting to dismiss them, try to control your concentration by mentally setting these other issues aside for the moment to give your full attention. Since the brain does not allow us to multitask, focus on more than one thing at a time, split attention means no attention on a single task. It takes mental and physical energy to do this, but believe it or not, if you really try to concentrate on the task at hand, you may well succeed.

The Role of Paraphrasing

Paraphrasing—making a summary of the ideas you have just received—will provide you with a concise restatement of what has been presented. Paraphrasing will help you figure out whether or not you understand the message. If you can't effectively paraphrase by writing or saying what the other person said, then you probably have failed to comprehend the message. Keep this in mind when you are listening to an instructor and taking notes. Try to paraphrase the material instead of writing down direct quotes. If you cannot do so, it is a clue that you should ask for clarification or make a note to look up that particular material later on. Many academic problems are caused because students don't realize what they haven't comprehended and don't know that they didn't understand or grasp the idea. Paraphrasing will help you realize if you did or did not gain the material.

Try verbally paraphrasing the next time you are involved in a demanding conversation, such as when you are receiving directions. Repeat back to the other person what you think she or he just said in order to check whether you both understood the same thing. One of the benefits of paraphrasing is that it eliminates the common complaint that you weren't listening. Giving people back the ideas they have just presented makes it impossible for them to support the claim that you were not paying attention.

LEARNING EXPERIENCE: Interested in evaluating your ability to effectively paraphrase? If so, do Activity 3.1.

PERCEPTION

After the message is received and attended to, the listener's perceptions come into play. Perceiving is an active process. During the act of **perception** you take the material received and attempt to evaluate what has been inputted. The act of perceiving might be compared to a chef straining ingredients in order to filter what she wants from what she is not interested in using; for example, separating pasta from the water in which it was cooked by passing it through a strainer. The strainer, like your **perceptual filter**, screens what you notice (perceive) and separates what makes sense from what doesn't. As you listen to information, your perceptual filter strains the information to which you are listening through your culture, experiences, mental and physical state, beliefs, attitudes, and values.

Another approach to this stage of listening refers to the perceptual screen through which you receive and evaluate in the sensory components of your brain and nervous system. This approach encourages you to listen emotionally, with all of your senses,

ACTIVITY 3.1
How Good Are You at
Recognizing Effective Paraphrasing?

Directions: Select what you consider to be the effective paraphrase of the sender's message.

1. *Speaker:* "Sometimes I think I'd like to drop out of school, but then I start to feel like a quitter."
    a. "Maybe it would be helpful to take a break and then you can always come back."
    b. "You're so close to finishing. Can't you just keep with it a little bit longer?"
    c. "It sounds like you have doubts about finishing school but that you don't like to think of yourself as a person who would quit something you started."
    d. "What do you think the consequences will be if you drop out?"
2. *Speaker:* "I really don't want to go to a party where I don't know anyone. I'll just sit by myself all night."
    a. "You're apprehensive about going someplace where you don't know anyone because you'll be alone."
    b. "It would really be good for you to put yourself in that kind of a situation."
    c. "I can really relate to what you're saying. I also feel awkward when I go to strange places."
    d. "Maybe you could just go for half an hour and then you can always leave if you're not having a good time."
3. *Speaker:* "I get really nervous when I talk with people I respect and who I fear might not respect me."
    a. "I've really found it useful to prepare my remarks in advance. Then I'm not nearly as nervous."
    b. "You really shouldn't feel nervous with people you respect because in many ways you are just as good as they are."
    c. "You feel uncomfortable when you talk with people who you think may not regard you in a positive way."
    d. "Why do you think you get so nervous about people you respect?"

Answers:
In the first situation, responses *a* and *b* offer advice, not a paraphrase, and response *d* poses a question that is not relevant since the speaker already indicates the consequence, "feel like a quitter." The only response that offers an effective paraphrase is *c*.

(continued)

ACTIVITY 3.1 (*continued*)

In the second situation, responses *b* and *d* offer advice, and response *c* expresses empathy, which may be helpful but, in this case, the feelings may not be accurately reflected (the speaker does not indicate feeling "awkward"). The only response that offers an effective paraphrase is *a*.

In the third situation, response *a* offers advice, response *b* tells the speaker that feeling nervous is foolish (so implies that she or he is stupid), and response *d* poses a question that the speaker already answered, people "might not respect me." The effective paraphrase is *c*.

Source: Based on a handout by an unidentified author entitled, "Listening," at the Speech Communication Association Convention, San Francisco, CA, 1989.

During the act of perception, the listener takes the material received and attempts to evaluate what has been input.

including intuition. It is an approach akin to eastern philosophies and often describes the listening approach of very global/right-brained people (a concept discussed later in this chapter.)

Selective perception is narrowing your focus to some specific information. An idea's distinctiveness or the satisfaction of your needs is often the basis for why you will pay attention to a particular stimulus. The louder, the more relevant, the more novel the stimuli, the more likely they are to be perceived by the listener.

THE ASSIGNMENT OF MEANING

Once you have paid attention to the material presented, the next stage in the listening process is to categorize the message so as to assign meanings to its verbal and nonverbal stimuli.

The Role of Assigning Meaning

The **assignment of meaning**—the process of putting the stimulus into some predetermined category—developed as you acquired your language system. You developed mental categories for interpreting the messages you receive. For instance, your categorizing system for the word *cheese* may include such factors as food, dairy products, taste, and nourishment, all of which help you to relate the word *cheese* to the context in which it is used.

The categorical assignment of meaning creates *schema*—scripts for processing information. The mental representations that you carry in your brain—*schemata*—are shaped by language categories and by the way your brain processes information. An individual's culture, background, family, education, and experience all serve as the framework for creating the schema that enable you, then, to deal with incoming information. The cognitive process draws on all of a person's schemata for the purpose of interpretation, and these schemata provide the mental links for understanding and creating meaning from the verbal and the nonverbal stimuli we receive. Understanding a discussion of some of the customs and traditions on a college campus, for example, may be difficult for freshmen because they lack the cognitive schema to relate to the information. As an upper class student, however, they have the data to process the information about the campus.

The Role of Global/Linear Thinking/Listening

We are unique in the way we listen and learn. Part of the differences among us is based on the way our brains work. One theory of thinking and listening contends that the human brain is divided into two hemispheres, and some people are prone to use one side of the brain more than the other. This **brain dominance** accounts for learning and listening in patterned ways.[16]

Note that throughout this text generalizations are presented regarding types of people and their actions and reactions. These are based, whenever possible, on research findings *and expert observations. They are in no way intended to lead to the conclusion that all members of a particular group conform to the generalized patterns. For example, in the following discussion not **all** linear or **all** global people follow the patterns described.*

A left-brained person uses the left hemisphere well and tends to be logical and linear. The individual will do well listening to information in a specific sequence, or may be persuaded through logic. Because they tend to take information at face value, abstractions and generalizations don't add much to their learning. Because they are so straight-line in their learning preferences, they are referred to as **linear learners/listeners**.

A person who is right-brained uses the right hemisphere well and tends to be more creative and visual. This person will listen well to information that is presented in concrete, visual, or spatial ways. This person would prefer seeing examples and considering applied information. Photographs or other visuals, focus on the intuitive, and exploration of ideas are interesting to the global listener. Because of their preference for a generalized rather than specific description, right-brain dominant persons are labeled as **global listeners/learners**. Many global learners find much of the traditional "read the textbook and listen to the lecture" method of teaching in U.S. schools and universities, a linear methodology, to be dull and frustrating.

Most people are a combination of global and linear learner/listeners. If you fall into this classification, you tend to be more flexible in how you listen and learn than those with extreme style patterns.

It is important for you to recognize your listening/learning style; it can make a difference in the way you approach the listening/learning environments. If you know that you need examples and your professor is not giving them, you should ask for them. If the professor is not drawing specific conclusions and not speaking in a structured format, and these are necessary for your understanding, then you must probe for information that will allow you to organize the ideas. Don't assume that the professor knows how you need to receive information; he or she often doesn't. Many classroom instructors teach based on their own listening/learning style, forgetting that all students don't learn that way. If you are a global listener/learner, this may account for why you had trouble with some math or science classes. On the other hand, if you are a linear listener/learner, literature and poetry classes may have been difficult for you.

LEARNING EXPERIENCE: Interested in finding out your learner/listener style based on the hemispheres of your brain? If so, complete Activity 3.2.

THE ROLE OF EVALUATION

One barrier to effective listening is our tendency to evaluate the stimuli received, regardless of whether they are relevant to the message. In fact, this tendency is thought to be the most persistent barrier to communication a person has to overcome.[17] Although assigning meaning to stimuli often requires a quick evaluation, listeners should attempt to avoid instant judgments based primarily on superficial factors. Sometimes,

ACTIVITY 3.2
Left/Right, Linear/Global Dominance

Answer all of these questions quickly; do not stop to analyze them. When you have no clear preference, choose the one that most closely represents your attitudes or behavior.

1. When I buy a new product, I
   _____A. usually read the directions and carefully follow them.
   _____B. refer to the directions, but really try and figure out how to assemble or operate the thing on my own.
2. Which of these words best describes the way I perceive myself in dealing with others?
   _____A. structured/rigid
   _____B. flexible/open-minded
3. Concerning hunches:
   _____A. I generally would not rely on hunches to help me make decisions.
   _____B. I have hunches and follow many of them.
4. I make decisions mainly based on
   _____A. what experts say will work.
   _____B. a willingness to try things that I think might work.
5. In traveling or going to a destination, I prefer
   _____A. to read and follow a map.
   _____B. get directions and map things out "my" way.
6. In school, I prefer
   _____A. geometry.
   _____B. algebra.
7. When I read a play or novel, I
   _____A. see the play or novel in my head as if it were a movie/TV show.
   _____B. read the words to obtain information.
8. When I want to remember directions, a name, or a news item, I
   _____A. visualize the information, or write notes that help me create a picture, maybe even draw the directions.
   _____B. write structured and detailed notes.
9. I prefer to be in the class of a teacher who
   _____A. has the class do activities and encourages class participation and discussions.
   _____B. primarily lectures.
10. In writing, speaking, and problem solving, I am
   _____A. usually creative, preferring to try new things.
   _____B. seldom creative, preferring traditional solutions.

(continued)

ACTIVITY 3.2 (*continued*)

Scoring and interpretation:
Give yourself one point for each question you answered "b" on items 1 to 5 and "a" on 6 to 10. This total is your score. To assess your degree of left- or right-brain preference, locate your final score on this continuum:

Left _____ Right

    1   2   3   4   5   6   7   8   9   10

The lower the score, the more left-brained tendency you have. People with a score of 1 or 2 are considered highly linear. Scores of 3 and possibly 4 show a left-brained tendency.

The higher the score, the more right-brained tendency you have. People with scores of 9 or 10 are considered highly global. Scores of 7 and possibly 6 indicate a right-brained tendency.

If you scored between 4 and 7 you have indicated you probably do not tend to favor either brain and are probably flexible in your learning and listening style.

Please bear in mind that neither preference is superior to the other. If you are extremely left- or right-dominant, it is possible to develop some of the traits associated with the other hemisphere, or you may already have them.

Source: Developed by Roy Berko, based on an concept of Paul Torrance and Bernice McCarthy and Rebecca Cutter. For an alternative questionnaire see: Connell, D. *Left brain/Right brain.* www2.scholastic.com/browse/article.jsp?id=3629.

if you feel you have too little information, or need to study the information, it may be better for you not to come to a conclusion.

A strategy useful to listeners in assigning meaning to messages is to differentiate factual statements (those based on observable phenomena or common acceptance) from opinions (inferences or judgments).

Likewise, it is helpful for the listener to sift through verbal obscurities and work for clarification of meanings. Unclear terms and phrases, euphemisms, and evasive language make interpretation difficult. The effective listener, however, asks questions and seeks clarification from others and the contextual cues in their messages.

As a listener you can also benefit from recognizing what your emotional biases are and how those biases affect your interpretation of messages. One way to discover such biases is to draw up a list of negative terms and phrases that serve as *red flags*, or positive words that trigger *green flags*, words that trigger particular emotional responses.

Recognition of such emotional barriers is a good first step toward compensating for the emotional reaction that make people turn off their listening. Anyone can have a strong reaction, for example, to certain words and concepts, such as *skinheads, gay rights, taxes, abortion,* and, yes, even *homework,* or to such positive terms or phrases as *vacation, rainbow,* or *winning the lottery.*

The assignment of meaning is a complex process involving categorizing, evaluating, filtering through verbal obscurity, and recognizing emotional biases.

RESPONSE

Once you have attached meaning to the message, you react emotionally or logically to the message. The response can be inside your head (internal) or directed outward (external). Scientists suspect that all stimuli are stored somewhere in your brain.

The Role of Questions

One area of response that can assist the listener in storing information in long-term memory, and at the same time provide meaningful feedback, is the asking of questions. This enables the listener to ensure that the message he or she has received and interpreted is consistent with what was intended.

To be effective, however, questions must be relevant to the topic of discussion. When asking questions, try to figure out what you don't understand. Most commonly, difficulties in perceiving information center on a lack of understanding of vocabulary, a need for clarifying examples, or a need for the material to be presented in a different format or order. For example, let's assume you are taking notes in class and can't paraphrase the instructor's ideas so that you can write them down. One of the mistakes students often make is not to say anything. If it is important for you to gain the information, you must probe for meaning. If an opportunity is available, such as when a teacher indicates that questions are welcome, use that invitation to your advantage. When asking for information, don't say, "I don't understand." The instructor won't be able to clarify; you haven't given him or her the clues needed to be of help. It is common in certain academic subjects for the vocabulary to be new and unusual. If you don't understand the terms being used ask, "Would you please define ____ (*fill in the term*)?" Or, if you vaguely understand but need something more, you could state, "Would you please give us several examples to illustrate ____ (*insert the specific topic*)?" This is often what is needed for global listeners to grasp the idea because they need examples they can picture, rather than terms. Or, if you don't understand the concept, you could inquire, "Could you restate the concept of ____ (*fill in the topic*) in a step-by-step process?" This is a technique needed by linear listeners, who need the structure to understand what may be confusing because it was not put in a patterned manner. In each case you are specifically centering on what needs to be done to help you gain the information. The same techniques work on the job and in other situations where gaining information is important.

The Role of Feedback

Good listeners are conscious of the role of feedback cues. Asking questions, nodding or shaking your head, smiling or frowning, verbalization such as "uh-huh" or "um?" are all forms of listener feedback. Feedback responses can be either verbal or nonverbal, and they should function to further enhance and/or reinforce the communication. If you are a member of a culture that does not encourage verbal or nonverbal feedback, this advice probably is of little value, but to most Euro-Americans the feedback clues are important.

Effective feedback should be easily perceptible to the other person. Listener feedback is a key responsibility, and will improve the communication process. Instead of entering into the listening process passively, assume an active role as a listening communicator. Both people have to take responsibility for any communication interaction. Take seriously your part in sending feedback that will support interpersonal goals, for this feedback plays a critical role in creating and maintaining the communication climate for interaction.

Listening Influencers

The process of listening, through which the listener receives, attends to, perceives, assigns meaning to, and responds to messages, is complex. To be effective, the listener must work to overcome barriers that may arise. Key influencers, for instance, the role of the interpersonal communicator, the role of the message, and the role of the channel, can facilitate or hinder the process.[18]

THE ROLE OF THE INTERPERSONAL COMMUNICATOR

Credibility is determined by whether a person is considered trustworthy, competent, and dynamic. This credibility—or lack of credibility—can lead the listener to accept or reject a message. Unfortunately, listeners are sometimes so in awe of a particular person that they may lose all objectivity in analyzing the person's message. For example, if you are listening to your supervisor whom you admire and who is expert on many things at work, you may overlook that she or he is not an expert on the specific subject in question.

The person's physical appearance, animation, and clothing can have an instantaneous effect on listener attention. A person who is dynamic and humorous may be able to get past the critical listening abilities of certain listeners. To be a discerning listener, it is important to listen to the message.

THE ROLE OF THE MESSAGE

Even interpersonal messages can benefit from a sense or organization for better understanding. Likewise, the tone and the treatment of the message can affect a person's listening abilities.

Listeners must apply the *sniff test* to what they hear. If it doesn't seem right, "smell right," if your suspicions are activated, be curious, probe more deeply before you accept an argument. If it appears to be too good to be true, it probably isn't true. Listeners must ascertain whether the message is appropriate for them, and whether they believe in the concepts presented.

THE ROLE OF THE CHANNEL

The communication channel also can influence listening ability. Some people are more auditory, and some are more visual in orientation. The interpersonal communicator who couples the message with clear visual aids may assist a listener in comprehending the material. For example, drawing a map while giving directions often helps the receiver to visualize the route.

Noise (any sort of interference) in the communication channel can diminish the effectiveness of the listener. Static on the telephone can interrupt good listening. If the lighting is poor or the room temperature is too cold, the listener can have difficulty attending to the other person's message. Control of or adjustment for the distraction may be necessary; for example, by moving closer so you can hear a soft-speaking person, or negotiating with the other person to move to a better environment, such as leaving the noisy coffee shop and sitting outside in a quiet park.

It should be recognized that listeners are influenced not only by a vast array of external factors but also internal ones. Receivers can be affected by their physical state (general health, age), experiences (background, life history, training), attitudes (predispositions), memory, and expectations. The listener's culture can also be influential. People from different cultures vary in their ways of attending to each other as indicated by their amount of eye contact, distance between each other, and amount of patience. For example, in some Hispanic cultures, it is perceived as bad manners to look directly into the eyes of another person, especially if he or she is an authority figure. This lack of eye contact may convey that the listener is not, in truth, listening when that is not the case. Some Arabic and Asian cultures stress standing very close to people while conversing, which makes some Euro-Americans uncomfortable, thus making concentration difficult.

The positive or negative attitude the listener carries into a listening situation, in conjunction with expectations of the experience, is important. A listener who goes to a job interview, for example, convinced beforehand that it will be a waste of time because "they aren't going to hire me," will probably carry that negative attitude into the session and not listen comprehensively.

The listener's positive or negative attitude extends to himself or herself as a listener. All interpersonal communicators have self-concepts. Most people have had very little praise or external reward for good listening but have probably heard lots of negative messages such as "Keep quiet and listen" and "Why don't you ever listen to me?" These negative messages, which are often received from a very early age, can create a negative attitude in listeners about their own listening abilities.

THE ROLE OF MEMORY AND TIME

Throughout the entire process of listening, memory plays an important role. The listener must be willing to hold the message received in short-term memory long enough to perceive, attend to, and assign meaning to it. This activity requires sufficient auditory and visual memory to maintain focus long enough to process the message. Taking notes, paraphrasing, and asking questions can often increase memory. When being introduced to someone, repeat the person's name three or more times in the conversation that follows to carve the name into your memory.

Purposes of Listening

We listen on a number of levels, for a variety of purposes. We listen to distinguish among sounds, gain ideas, discriminate among ideas, aid others, and appreciate sounds or symbols. Awareness of the purposes of listening often aids a listener to select the listening techniques that best fit the desired outcome. You may want to shift the way you listen for each of the various purposes of listening. Some purposes require deep concentration, others less intensity.

DISCRIMINATIVE LISTENING

In **discriminative listening**, you attempt to distinguish among auditory and visual stimuli. Through discrimination you can come to understand differences in verbal sounds (dialects, pronunciation) and nonverbal behavior (gestures, facial reactions). By understanding such differences, you gain sensitivity to the sights and sounds of your world. You can then determine, for example, whether a person is being sarcastic, cautious, negative, or uncooperative because you realize that the same set of words can be taken in a variety of ways.

Discriminative listening is also important when you come in contact with some of the nonhuman features of our everyday lives. You may listen, for instance, to household appliances to determine whether they are functioning properly. People in certain professions, such as doctors and repair persons, sometimes find discrimination to be their most important listening skill. On NPR's *Car Talk*, Tom and Ray Magliozzi often ask those calling in for car repair advice to imitate the sound that their vehicles are making. From listening to the sounds, applying discriminative listening, the car experts often can diagnose the problem.

COMPREHENSION LISTENING

In **comprehension listening**, the objective is to understand and remember what the other person tells you. Some techniques have been found to enhance listening comprehension. One strategy is to concentrate on getting the main points of a message rather than all the supporting details. That is, an employee listening to a supervisor should focus on the main point rather than on the elaboration and details.

Notetaking in Interpersonal Contexts

When taking notes in interpersonal contexts, you will want to carefully consider the context. When your physician gives you information about your recent tests, when your boss tells you about this year's objectives, or in other situations where you need to be sure you remember what is said, note-taking can be useful. Taking notes in a job interview or writing down information immediately after the interview may be a good idea. Taking notes while a friend tells you about a problem will seem strange, however, so you need to focus and remember without the aid of notes in many cases.

Relating one part of the message to another encourages the listener to connect one part of a message to another. Good radio and television talk-show hosts use this system when interviewing guests. Public Radio's award-winning interviewer Terri Gross is excellent at using *paraphrasing* (repeating ideas), *acknowledging* ("uh-huh" and "that's an interesting idea"), *internal summaries* (summarizing one topic before going on to the next), and *bridging* (indicating what topic or idea she'd like to talk about next by referring to a quote in a book or one just made by the interviewee). These are effective tools for individuals going into listening professions such as counseling, social work, police work, and reporting. Remembering the main points from interpersonal encounters may require the development of a number of memory techniques.

Using comprehensive and discriminative listening as the foundation, people listen for special purposes: to provide a therapeutic setting for a person to talk through a problem, critically evaluate a persuasive message, or appreciate aspects of a particular message.

THERAPEUTIC LISTENING

Listening at the therapeutic level is important for those in such fields as psychology, social work, speech therapy, and counseling. **Therapeutic listening** is the process of probing in order to help the other person think through a problem or situation.

Therapeutic listening is not restricted to professional counselors. In daily life people often need a listener when dealing with a problem. As a listener you can help a friend or colleague talk through a situation. To be effective in this role, you must have empathy for the other person—the ability to understand that person's problem from their perspective by momentarily putting yourself into his or her shoes and attempting to see the world as the other person sees it. This is difficult for many people to do, as there is a tendency to want to solve the other person's problem and rid them of pain or to tell the listener's personal experiences or beliefs. You will want to listen from the viewpoint of the other person.

How can a person learn to be an effective therapeutic listener? The empathic training given to hotline volunteers includes teaching them to *resist the temptation* to jump in with statements such as "The same thing happened to me" or "If I were you,

I would. . . ."[19] In addition, remember that there is nothing wrong with silence. Often you want the other person to keep talking. Listen patiently. The person in pain may need time to feel the pain and get in touch with her or his thoughts and feelings. You can help the other person generate a list of possible alternatives from which he or she may choose and feel commitment to carrying them out. Another technique is *not* to diminish the person's feeling of pain. They feel pain; they know it. Saying, "that's no big problem," doesn't help diminish the hurt.

CRITICAL LISTENING

Critical listening is the process of carefully analyzing and judging a message. When you listen to a car salesperson, or if you are considering the pros and cons of a certain graduate program, for example, you need to look past the excitement of the communication and clearly evaluate the message.

An understanding of both the tools of persuasion and the process of logic and reasoning can enable you to use critical listening in interpersonal contexts.

Consider the personal appeal of the other person. The interpersonal communicator's credibility stems from the position held (e.g., sports celebrity), expertise, trustworthiness, and dynamism. You as a critical listener need to recognize how much this credibility is influencing how the message is being understood and analyzed.

Consider the person's arguments and evidence. In the Western logic system of reasoning to conclusions, the most critical test of accuracy is the proof given in developing the argument. The question in this reasoning system becomes: Does the interpersonal communicator present a logical argument supported by substantive and relevant data?

Consider motivational appeals. How is the interpersonal communicator attempting to get the listener involved in the message? Which appeals to your needs are utilized to get you to respond to a persuasive message?

Consider assumptions. Does the interpersonal communicator assume that something is a fact before it has been established as such? Just because someone says, "It is readily apparent that . . ." doesn't make it so. Be careful of phrases like, "They say" and "Everybody knows." Who is "they?" Does everybody really know? What gives a person the right to speak for "everybody"?

Consider what is NOT said. In some cases, the interpersonal communicator implies, rather than states, his or her ideas, so you are forced to read between the lines to supply the message. "You know what I mean" is a remark to which you should be alert. What do you really know from what was said?

You, as a critical listener, should be aware of these factors and assess the merits of a particular message. Sales pitches, coworker suggestions, and persuasive briefings all require critical analysis.

APPRECIATIVE LISTENING

Appreciative listening takes place when you simply enjoy listening to a message, such as when you and a friend catch up on the news of the day. Appreciation is about enjoyment and a highly individual matter. Some people want to learn more about everything. Others feel, however, that the more they know about something, the more they lose their ability to appreciate all but the best.

COMPASSIONATE LISTENING

"**Compassionate listening** is a tool for conflict resolution, reconciliation, and the prevention of violence. The objectives of compassionate listening are to deepen our understanding of the perspectives and suffering of people on all sides of a disagreement or conflict, and to build bridges between them."[20]

Compassionate listening is difficult because you need to be open-minded and not pass judgment. The compassionate listener avoids evaluation and does not probe for truth. The compassionate listener uses reflective listening and nonadversarial questioning to attempt to heal individuals in conflict and generate amicable solutions to conflict.

This is a tool that is used in such instances as the Arab-Israeli conflict, differences of opinion between adversaries in a lawsuit, and couples entering into divorce proceedings. Developed by an international peacemaker and founder of the US/USSR Reconciliation program, the approach employs the philosophy of Buddhism, which encourages listening to the sufferings of all sides, relating the sufferings of all sides to one another, and bringing all sides together so that they may hear one another.[21] Also referred to as "The Skill of Tracking," compassionate listening requires that the listener track the messages using a series of statements that attempt to identify what the interpersonal communicator is sensing by paraphrasing answers to these statements:[22]

The issue is . . .
You thought/think . . .
You wanted/want . . .
You felt/are feeling . . .
You needed/are needing . . .
Your experience was/is . . .

What then happens is the interpersonal communicator will agree or disagree and then go more deeply into the subject. The basic purpose is to understand the other person's thoughts and feelings.

As one practitioner explains it, "There's something about the respectful silence and attention of the listener that brings out feelings that need comfort or affirmation."[23]

The concept encompasses seeking first to understand with no external agenda and without blaming or shaming. It strives for balancing caring for ourselves with caring for others by acknowledging the needs of the other ("I wish I could . . ."), respecting our own needs (" . . . but I can't."), and respecting our abilities and limitations. It incorporates the Jewish mystical tradition of kindness, which includes empathy, strength, and boundary setting.[24] Compassionate listening is often difficult for many Euro-Americans because it requires attentive silence, but the process can be learned.[25]

Listening Response Styles

You tend to have a listening style with which you are most comfortable. These preferences have been honed by modeling after those with whom you have come in contact (e.g., parents, teachers), what you have been taught to do (e.g., classes, workshops), what you have observed (e.g., television interviews), and how others have reacted to you (e.g., social interaction). Each of these response styles has some advantages and disadvantages, and each is useful in particular situations. Effective listeners know the various response styles, and though you may favor one style over another, you need to adjust your style according to the participants, setting, and purpose of the listening. The four response styles are active, recommending, information-seeking, and critical.

ACTIVE RESPONSE STYLE

If your general response style is active, you are probably nonjudgmental as you listen. Listeners who display an **active response style of listening** figure out key ideas while creating mutual understanding. Active listeners also demonstrate a good grasp of paraphrasing because their feedback reflects the content plus the feelings of the communicator.[26]

The primary advantages of this response style for your communication partner are support and concern. With your support and concern, she or he can feel safe to explore whatever is on her or his mind, whether to clarify thoughts, feelings, or ideas. The primary advantage of active listening for you is that you come to know and understand another person in more depth than is usual in most relationships. Also, you feel the pleasure that comes from helping someone.

Although active listening has several important advantages, it has some drawbacks. First, to listen actively you must put aside your own prejudices and concerns—something that is quite difficult. Second, active listening requires time, and you may not have the time to spare. Third, active listening requires a great deal of skill. Focusing your attention exclusively on the other person, recognizing the main themes in the messages you receive, insightfully detecting the emotions being expressed, and communicating your understanding clearly and supportively are difficult tasks requiring a great deal of proficiency. And fourth, given the skill and time required to listen actively, it is apparent that this response style demands a great deal of energy to perform well.

RECOMMENDATION RESPONSE STYLE

If your general receiving pattern is a **recommending response style of listening**, you are probably an advice giver who wants to tell your friend what to or not to do. You may decide you know the answer to solve your friend's problem. This kind of recommendation response style is pretty typical of U.S. Americans. Euro-American men, in particular, often hear another's talk about a problem as a request for a solution, while, Euro-American women hear talk about a problem as a request to talk about the problem itself.[27] Unfortunately, although a popular response style for Euro-Americans, it may not be the most helpful. What may be a useful recommendation for you may not work for your communication partner. Also, by providing your own solution, instead of having your partner generate his or her own, you make it possible for your partner to avoid responsibility for the decision. And if your recommendation fails to work, you may lose a friend!

Before you make a recommendation, be as sure as possible that it is correct, that your communication partner is seeking your recommendation, and that you won't be blamed if the recommendation doesn't work.

People may seem to want advice, but what they really need is to talk about how they feel and what they think.

INFORMATION-SEEKING RESPONSE STYLE

If you ask for additional information when you want to clarify your understanding, you are using the **information-seeking listening response style**. Questions can relate to the content of what someone says—for example, if your roommate asks you to "keep the place cleaner," you could ask, "what does 'cleaner' really mean?"—or the feelings communicated—for example, "how do you feel about the room not being as clean as you would like?" Questions often are useful for getting others to think about their problems and to see them more clearly, and to understand better how they feel about them—your roommate may not be sure what "cleaner" means until you talk about it, and may not realize how annoyed he or she feels about your not picking up your clothes and putting them in the laundry bag until the feelings are expressed verbally. Or, the request may be irrelevant to cleaning because a totally different issue is the real concern.

An information-seeking response style is usually positive, but if you overuse it, your communication partner may feel grilled or that you aren't dealing specifically with the problem and how she or he feels.

For a response style to be effective, avoid seeking information just to satisfy your own curiosity. The other person might be confused as to your purpose (e.g., a question such as "Did you grow up in a house that was super clean?" may be of interest to you, but not relate to the conversation at hand). Also, your partner may become angry (e.g., "What does it matter how clean my home was?").

In addition to not asking questions just to satisfy your curiosity, don't ask questions that are disguised criticisms. Questions that look like traps are not helpful and may even make matters worse—your partner still has a problem, and now, added to that, you both have a damaged relationship. For example, saying, "Don't you think it's overly compulsive to want to clean the room more than once a week?" is not really asking a question; rather, it is a critical statement in disguise.

Not every culture considers it appropriate to answer a request for additional information. In fact, you may be considered rude for probing. For example, in some Asian cultures, a person may agree in order to save face. Sometimes, the agreement is to prevent the other person from becoming embarrassed. In some Asian and Latin cultures, the interpersonal communicator is expected to tell the other person what he or she wants to hear. This response is never intended to be dishonest, but to be protective and increase harmony.

CRITICAL RESPONSE STYLE

The **critical response style of listening** is one where you decide to pass judgment about what the other person says.

Negative judgments that are purely critical, such as, "You were wrong to call him," and "You asked for it!" are rarely helpful, although there is a slight chance that the person criticized may be motivated to consider changing (e.g., she may decide to "stop calling him"). Less critical responses may be taken as constructive criticism, as responses meant to help and not necessarily to hurt. Like purely critical responses, however, less critical responses are prone to get a defensive reaction. Your communication partner may feel attacked, and the usual response is for the attacked person to attack back.

A critical response works best when your partner asks for your evaluation. Invited criticism is more likely to be listened to than uninvited criticism. Also, your critical response should be genuinely constructive and not designed as a put-down. Too often the phrase "I'm only telling you this for your own good" is not true.

LEARNING EXPERIENCE: Interested in finding out your listening response style? If so, do Activity 3.3.

Intercultural Listening

Since not all ethnic, gender, or sexual orientation groups speak or listen in the same manner, intercultural listening is affected by language, thought and reasoning processes and listening expectation.

Please be aware that throughout this text generalizations are presented regarding trends of various cultural groups. These principles are based, whenever possible, on research findings and expert observations. The concepts are in no way intended to lead to the conclusion that all members of the cultural group noted conform to the generalized patterns. With this in mind, let's briefly examine some perceived differences in intercultural listening.

Obviously, if people speak different languages, they will have problems, as the common basis for their understanding each other will be missing. The participants' ways of reaching conclusions differ, as will their abilities to understand each other's viewpoints. Someone who has strong religious views and literally believes what appears in the Bible or the Koran, will probably perceive the message of an atheist with a questioning listening attitude. In certain cultures, such factors as the ages of the communicators, the gender of the participants, and their sexual orientation may aid or hinder listening processes.

ACTIVITY 3.3
Your Listening Response Style

How do you typically respond to others' statements and actions? To determine your style, circle the letter that best describes your first response to the person in each situation. The goal is to tell how you would actually respond, not what the right response would be or how you would like to respond. Each is a school-related example. Put yourself into the situation, whether or not you have actually had the experience.

1. "I think I'm doing all right, but I don't know where I stand in the course. I'm not sure what my instructor expects of me, and she doesn't tell me how I'm doing. I'm trying my best, but I wish I knew where I stood."
    a. "Has your teacher ever given you any indication of what she thinks of your work?"
    b. "If I were you, I'd discuss it with her."
    c. "Perhaps others are also in the same position, so you shouldn't let it bother you."
    d. "It seems that not knowing if you're satisfying your teacher's requirements leaves you feeling unsure. You'd like to know just what she expects from you."
2. "The policy in the Chemistry Department is supposed to be to hire lab assistants from people in the advanced chemistry classes. And now I find that this person from a beginning class is getting hired. I wanted that job; I've been working hard for it. I know I could be a terrific assistant if I had a chance."
    a. "You shouldn't complain—they probably hired the best person to be an assistant."
    b. "Getting ahead is very important to you, even if it means hard work, and you feel cheated that someone else got the job as lab assistant."
    c. "What else besides being a lab assistant can you do to show them you're really capable?"
    d. "You should take some more chemistry classes to help you advance."
3. "I'm really tired of this. I'm taking more classes than anyone I know, and then, on the same day, three of my profs tell me that there's another assignment due on top of what's already due. I've got so many people asking me to do things that I just can't keep up, and it bothers me. I like my teachers, and my classes are interesting, but I could use a vacation."
    a. "With so many teachers asking you to do extra assignments, it's difficult for you to accomplish all of it, and the pressure gets you down."
    b. "Are all these requests from your teachers required work?"
    c. "You seem to have too much work. Why don't you talk it over with your teachers?"
    d. "You're probably overworked because you're not organized."

(continued)

ACTIVITY 3.3 (*continued*)

4. "My professor tells the class that he would appreciate getting term projects as soon as possible to help him with grading. So I work like mad to get it completed and on his desk early. What's my reward for helping him out? Nothing! No thanks, no nothing. In fact, I think my project will sit on his desk until all the projects are handed in."
   a. "How often do professors do this to you?"
   b. "You ought to tell him how you feel."
   c. "You feel like he's taking advantage of you and that you're being treated unfairly."
   d. "You shouldn't get so angry."
5. "He used to be one of the guys until he was made the team's coach. Now, it's like he's not my friend anymore. I don't mind being told about my mistakes, but he doesn't have to do it in front of the rest of the team. Whenever I get the chance, he's going to get his!"
   a. "To be told about your mistakes in front of the rest of the team is embarrassing, especially by a person you once considered a friend."
   b. "If you didn't make so many mistakes, the coach would not have to tell you about them."
   c. "Why don't you talk it over with a few other people on the team and then go talk to him about this situation?"
   d. "How often does he criticize you in front of the others?"

Listed below are the possible responses for each of the five situations. If you circled answer *a* in situation number 1, circle 1a below (in the "information-seeking response" category). If you circled answer *b*, circle 1b below (in the "recommendation response" category). Do this for your five responses.

Active response: 1d, 2b, 3a, 4c, 5a
Recommendation response: 1b, 2d, 3c, 4b, 5c
Information-seeking response: 1a, 2c, 3b, 4a, 5d
Critical response: 1c, 2a, 3d, 4d, 5b

Underline the category (or categories) in which you have the most circled answers. This (or these) is your general listening response style.

Source: Adapted from Burley-Allen, M. (1982). *Listening: The forgotten skill.* New York: John Wiley, pp. 85–89.

Euro-Americans, for example, often speak from the standpoint of "helping" the listener to understand the message, thus defining terms, giving examples, and repeating ideas. This, it is felt, helps in decoding the message. This is not the pattern in many other cultures. For example, Asians start listening with the assumption that it is their responsibility as a listener to understand. If the Euro-American doesn't understand, they have traditionally been taught to ask questions in order to achieve understanding.[28] Asians tend not to ask. To do so would be to lose face and embarrass the other person. Therefore, Euro-American professors are often surprised that some Asian students don't ask questions when they don't understand. Collectivist cultures (e.g., Native Americans, Japan, Korea, and China) place a higher value on listening than do individualistic cultures (e.g., United States and Canada).[29]

In the Chinese culture, the general listening concept is "When you listen, you use your ears, eyes and heart to determine the meaning. The eyes are actually more important than the ears. You have to learn to listen to the content, but you have to know what the people mean."[30]

A male who has been brought up to believe that he is entitled to dominate women, based on religious or ethnic tradition, will listen to a woman with a different attitude than those males who believe in gender equality.

Individuals from cultures where conflict is encouraged, and speaking one's mind is an accepted pattern of communication (e.g., Israel), may listen with the view of collecting information to develop a counterattack, or not truly listen to an entire message.

Since many Muslims view future planning as a futile and potentially sinful act, open-minded listening between Muslims and Westerners may be very difficult.[31]

In some cultures, such as many in Asia, good listening means being a silent communicator in order to receive messages. People in Japan, for instance, typically spend less time talking on the job than do Euro-Americans, stressing instead the listening aspect of communication. In addition, some cultures stress concentration, resulting in longer attention spans. Buddhism, for instance, has a notion called "being mindful." Being mindful is when you are experiencing, enjoying, and living the moment. Training to have long attention spans starts in childhood. To those raised in a typical Euro-American environment, these listening-enhancing concepts are not generally part of their background.[32]

Cultures have been identified as low context and high context.[33] In *low context cultures* such as the United States and Canada, communicators expect to give and receive a great deal of information, since these cultures perceive that most message information is contained in words. In *high context cultures* such as Japan and Saudi Arabia, more of the information is situated in the communicators themselves and in the communication setting, so fewer words are necessary. In high context cultures, it is the responsibility of the listener to understand; in low context, it is the speaker who is responsible for making sure the listener comprehends all.

An investigation into the listening style of the Navajos, a Native American tribe, demonstrates cultural effects. The Navajo processing style, which is at the heart of the Navajo culture, has five components: observe, think, understand, feel, and act. This is in contrast to the "Anglo [Euro-American] process of act, observe/think/clarify, understand."[34] Anglos tend to learn from examining components in relationship to the whole. Native Americans spend much more time watching and listening and less time talking.[35] In an academic learning situation, this may result in "Anglo teachers seeing Native Americans as inattentive, laconic and dull-witted, while students see their teachers as directive and bossy."[36]

Many more examples can be added here, as entire books have been written about differences between cultures. The bottom line in understanding the listening process is that as the participants, setting and purpose change, so do the requirements to alter the way you listen.

Listening Apprehension

Some people are apprehensive about speaking, others may be apprehensive about listening, and still others are apprehensive in both situations. **Listener apprehension**, "the fear of misinterpreting, inadequately processing, and/or not being able to adjust psychologically to messages sent by others,"[37] is a major concern for many people. It may be a short-term fear, such as the anxiety associated with knowing you are going to

Listener anxiety makes a person less able to interact effectively, less willing to communicate, and less confident about communication abilities.

receive a negative evaluation, or the fear of the person who is going to talk to you, or of what she or he might say. For example, in the context of physician-patient interaction, the difference in power roles between you as a patient and the doctor as the expert may interfere with your ability to calmly and accurately listen to your physician. You also might be afraid of what the doctor might say, so you dread listening.

Listener apprehension may also be a long-term disability. There are individuals who have lived their entire lives being told they are bad listeners and have come to believe it. There are others who have a hearing disability and fear that in listening situations they will miss the core of the message.

Listener anxiety makes a person less able to interact effectively, less willing to communicate, and less confident about communication abilities. Further, if we are emotional about the content of the message, that may shake our confidence and increase our listener apprehension.

Part of what you may be worried about is how you will respond in a listening situation, whether you will be able to adapt to what you hear, and if you can respond appropriately.

In a study of employment interviews, the people with high apprehension did less thinking about or preparing for the scheduled meeting, thus doing more poorly in responding to questions. They gave fewer examples, displayed more uncertainty, and exhibited more nervousness.[38]

If you experience listening apprehension, what can you do? Here are some suggestions:

Relax. Realize that worrying isn't going to make you a better listener, so if you can't avoid the situation, then you must force yourself to participate and accept that you will do the best job you can.

Take notes. If appropriate, have a writing instrument and paper to take notes. It forces you to listen and allows you to know if you understand or not. If you are restricted from taking notes, ask questions to clarify what has been said in an attempt to make sure you understand and have idea clarity.

Paraphrase. Repeat back the ideas as you listen, so that you can assure yourself that you are receiving the message and you are letting the other person know that you are listening and understanding.

Prepare. Prepare ideas and arguments in advance if you know you are going to be evaluated or will need to defend yourself or your ideas. If there has been an agenda, memo, or outline of what will be discussed, such as for a meeting or an interview, go over the material and be ready to listen. If at work, have the ideas researched. In a classroom situation, read and prepare the assignment. Write notes to use during the discussion. This way you won't have to worry about remembering what you want to say or not having anything of value to say.

Improving Your Listening

Effective listening is a skill you can learn. Although listening is a complex process, you can take steps to improve your overall interpersonal communication through better listening.

LEARNING EXPERIENCE: Interested in self-evaluating your listening so you can determine what adjustments you need to make to be a better listener? If so, do Activity 3.4.

Here are some suggestions that should help you to develop greater listening skills:

Recognize joint communication responsibility. If possible, as listener, repeat the major ideas so that the communicator can check to be sure you have grasped his or her meaning.

Reserve judgment. As a listener, you should not assess communicators before you have comprehended the entire message.

Be a tolerant listener. You may find yourself beginning to act before you have totally understood what is being said. This pattern is especially true for global listeners, who intuitively act on perceived information. If that is your pattern, recognize it and put the listening skills you've been taught in this chapter into action.

Avoid egospeak. **Egospeak** is the "art of boosting our own ego by speaking only about what we want to talk about, and not giving a hoot in hell about what the [other] person is speaking about."[39] When you jump into a conversation and speak your piece or listen only to the beginning of another's sentence before saying, "Yes, but . . . ," you are engaging in egospeak. As a result, you do not receive the whole message because you are so busy thinking of what you want to say or saying it. Although egospeak is a very natural human pattern, allowing it to be activated can easily become a real barrier to communication.

Several techniques can be used to control egospeaking. First, monitor your body. Individuals who are about to interrupt have a tendency to lean forward as if to jump into the conversation, and poise an arm and hand so that they can thrust them forward to cut in. If you feel your body taking these actions, be aware that you are about to egospeak—and don't. Slide back, relax the arm, focus on the communicator. Try paraphrasing. Be aware that if you can't summarize, you didn't listen long enough to gain the message.

Use engaging nonverbals. Sit up and lean forward to be engaged. An effective listener learns when it is necessary to listen in a totally active way and when it is possible to relax. An analogy can explain the concept. When you're driving a car with an automatic transmission, the car shifts gears when it needs more or less power. Unfortunately, people don't come equipped with automatic transmissions; we have to shift gears for ourselves. When you need to concentrate, you shift into your active listening position—feet on the floor, posture erect, looking directly at the other person—in order to pick up verbal and nonverbal clues. Once you feel that you understand the point being made (a test for this would be the ability to paraphrase what has been said), you may want to shift your posture to a more comfortable position. When a new subject arises, or when you hear transitional words or phrases such as *therefore* or *in summary,* then you shift back into your active listening position.

Control distractions. All of us are surrounded by noise. Such factors as the sound of machinery, people talking, and music playing can interfere with efficient listening. If the message is important to you, try to adjust the interference or control it. If possible, turn off the machinery or move away from it. Tell someone who is speaking to you while you are talking on the telephone that you cannot listen to both people at

ACTIVITY 3.4
Willingness to Listen Measure

Directions: The following twenty-four statements refer to listening. Please indicate the degree to which each statement applies to you by marking whether you:

Strongly Disagree = 1; Disagree = 2; are Neutral = 3; Agree = 4; Strongly Agree = 5

_____ 1. I dislike listening to boring people.

_____ 2. Generally, I can listen to a boring person.

_____ 3. I am bored and tired while listening to a boring conversation.

_____ 4. I will listen when the content of a conversation is boring.

_____ 5. Listening to boring people about boring content makes me tired, sleepy, and bored.

_____ 6. I am willing to listen to boring people about boring content.

_____ 7. Generally, I am unwilling to listen when there is noise during a conversation.

_____ 8. Usually, I am willing to listen when there is noise during a conversation.

_____ 9. I am accepting and willing to listen to communicators who do not adapt to me.

_____10. I am unwilling to listen to communicators who do not do some adaptation to me.

_____11. Being preoccupied with other things makes me less willing to listen to the other person.

_____12. I am willing to listen to the other person even if I have other things on my mind.

_____13. While being occupied with other things on my mind, I am unwilling to listen to people talk.

_____14. I have a willingness to listen to other people, even if other important things are on my mind.

_____15. Generally, I will not listen to a communicator who is disorganized.

_____16. Generally, I will try to listen to a communicator who is disorganized.

_____17. While listening to a non-immediate, non-responsive communicator, I feel relaxed with the person.

_____18. While listening to a non-immediate, non-responsive communicator, I feel distant and cold toward that person.

_____19. I can listen to a non-immediate, non-responsive communicator.

(continued)

ACTIVITY 3.4 (continued)

_____20. I am unwilling to listen to a non-immediate, non-responsive speaker.
_____21. I am willing to listen to a person with views different from mine.
_____22. I am unwilling to listen to a person with views different from mine.
_____23. I am willing to listen to a person who is not clear about what he or she wants to say.
_____24. I am unwilling to listen to a person who is not clear, not credible, and abstract.

SCORING:

Scores can range from 24 to 120. To compute the score on this instrument complete the following steps:

Step 1: Add scores for items 2, 4, 6, 8, 9, 12, 14, 16, 17, 19, 21, and 23
Step 2: Add scores for items 1, 3, 5, 7, 10, 11, 13, 15, 18, 20, 22, and 24
Step 3: Total score = 72 - Total from Step 1 + Total from Step 2.

Scores above 89 indicate a high willingness to listen. Scores below 59 indicate a low willingness to listen. Scores between 59 and 89 indicate a moderate willingness to listen.

Source: Adapted from Richmond, V. P., & Hickson, M., III. (2001). *Going public: A practical guide to public talk.* Boston: Allyn & Bacon.

the same time. Remember that there is little point in continuing the communication if you cannot hear the other person.

Key Terms

hearing
listening
reception
attention
short-term memory
paraphrasing
perception
perceptual filter
selective perception
assignment of meaning
brain dominance
linear learners/listeners
global listeners/learners

discriminative listening
comprehension listening
therapeutic listening
critical listening
appreciative listening
compassionate listening
active response style of listening
recommending response style of listening
information-seeking listening response style
critical response style of listening
listener apprehension
egospeak

Competencies Check-Up

Interested in finding out what you learned in this chapter and how you use the information? If so, take this competencies check-up.

Directions: Indicate the extent that each statement applies to you:

1—Never   *2—Seldom*   *3—Sometimes*   *4—Often*   *5—Usually*

____ 1. I work to listen carefully because I know that effective listening can affect my academic success, employment achievement, and personal happiness.

____ 2. I recognize that listening is a process that involves my attention to a message through reception, perception, attention, the assignment of meaning, and feedback processes.

____ 3. As soon as I catch myself daydreaming, I admit to the other person that I need part of the message repeated, and I refocus on the listening process.

____ 4. I concentrate on messages and use the extra thinking time to make connections and contemplate the message I'm hearing.

____ 5. I frequently paraphrase to check my understanding while listening.

____ 6. I listen emotionally, with all of my senses, including intuition, as well as logic.

____ 7. I know and understand my personal listening/learning style and brain dominance. I ask for other people to provide messages that adapt to my processing, and I listen with a variety of adaptive strategies.

____ 8. When listening, I am sensitive to high context and low context cultural influences.

____ 9. I temper my tendency to evaluate the stimuli I receive and look for relevance. In fact, I actively work to stay open-minded and avoid critical and judgmental tendencies, which can be the most serious and persistent barrier to communication.

____10. I frequently use a strategy of assigning meaning to messages by differentiating factual statements (those based on observable phenomena or common acceptance) from opinions (inferences or judgments made by the speaker).

____11. I carefully reflect on and recognize my emotional biases and how those biases affect my interpretation of messages. Further, I reflect on the various internal and external factors that affect my listening.

____12. To engage my long-term memory and provide meaningful feedback, I ask questions.

____13. When asking questions, I try to figure out what I don't understand. I own up to problems, tell the other person when I don't understand information, need clarification through examples, or need material to be presented in a different format or order.

____14. Where appropriate, I use an active response style by showing support and concern, using eye contact, leaning forward, putting aside my biases, and showing my interest through clear feedback, asking questions, nodding or shaking my head, smiling or frowning, taking notes, and using verbalization such as "uh-huh" or "hmmm."

___15. I use an appropriate style of listening according to my purpose and the expectations of the context (discriminative listening, comprehension listening, therapeutic listening, critical listening, appreciative listening).

Scoring: An ideal score is 75. A total of 45 suggests that you have basic listening competencies in your interpersonal communication. Evaluate your test results and how you can improve your listening skills.

I-Can Plan!

Mull over the content of this chapter, your test results, and what you need to do to improve your listening skills. Be sure to consider your culture's influence on your communication as you design an appropriate proposal for strengthening your communication skills. Be sure to take note of any items with a score of less than 3 because these areas may need important skill improvement. Then, put your plan into action.

Activities

1. Each student in the class is to prepare a story that will take about two minutes to read (approximately three hundred words) or bring in a story from the newspaper or magazine that the class is unlikely to have read. Each of you will prepare four questions to test whether the class members listened and comprehended the material read. On the day the presentations are to be made, five students will be selected to read their stories and give their listening comprehension tests. The answers are read and students are asked to evaluate their own papers.

2. Analyze your own listening. Name one listening behavior you have that does not match the characteristics of a good listener as described in this chapter. Consider how you can change this listening behavior to be more effective.

3. Make a list of your "red flags." Go back and review these terms. Why do you think they incite you? If class time is available, your instructor will divide the class into groups of four to six students. Discuss your "red flags" and what implications they have for your communication.

4. a. Indicate whether you thoroughly agree (TA), agree (A), disagree (D), or thoroughly disagree (TD) with each of these statements:
   (1) Prayer should be allowed in the public schools.
   (2) We should have started the war in Iraq in 2003.
   (3) Homosexual marriages should be legally sanctioned.
   (4) College students should not have required courses outside of their major area of concentration.
   (5) All guns should be outlawed.
   (6) The phrase "under God" should not be included in the pledge to the flag of the United States.

b. Your class is divided into groups of four to six students. Your task is to get everyone in the group to accept one of the attitudes (TA, A, D, or TD) for each of the preceding statements. You must paraphrase during the entire discussion. You may not give your opinion until you have summarized the statement of the person who preceded you. One member of the group acts as referee and says, "Foul" if anyone speaks without summarizing. (If time does not allow for a discussion of all four questions, your instructor will randomly select one for discussion.)

c. Now make a list of the positive aspects of paraphrasing as a listening technique, then the frustrations it causes.

5. Go online to www.listen.org, which is the website of the International Listening Association. Find an article that you think your class will find interesting. You will be assigned a date to present a summary of the article to your class.

CHAPTER 4

Verbal Language

Learning Outcomes

After reading this chapter, you should be able to:

- Define language.
- Evaluate theories about human language.
- Analyze the process of learning and using symbols.
- Explain the characteristics of language.
- Define and explain denotative and connotative words.
- Clarify two-valued orientation.
- Apply functions of language, such as cognitive, identification, phatic, and rhetorical.
- Explain language distortion.
- Explain the roles of ambiguity, vagueness, inferences, and message adjustment in relation to language distortion.
- Explain cultural-negative language.
- Explain the concept that people use different languages.
- Define and contrast standard versus nonstandard dialects, and relate the effects of speaking a nonstandard dialect.
- Analyze slang as it relates to standard dialects.
- Compare and contrast Standard American English, Ebonics/Black English, Spanglish, Asian-American Dialect, Native American Languages.
- Be aware of the English-only movement.
- Relate the effects of speaking a dialect or nonstandard language.
- Analyze the effects of using verbal language.
- Compare the similarities and differences between male and female communication.

The four-year old came running down the stairs screaming, "The sink is overfloating!" It sure looked to him like the overflowing sink was, indeed, overfloating. This is the same kid who once asked, as his parents drove past a house that had things for sale on the front lawn, "What's that?" His mother replied, "It's a rummage sale." The boy looked and asked, "Why would anyone want to buy other people's rubbish?" Cute, yes, but the kid was displaying a very important language concept, "meaning is in the mind of the beholder."

Before you went to school you succeeded in accomplishing the most complex feat you will ever accomplish: You mastered the basics of **verbal language**, the ability to communicate using the words and grammatical system of a particular society. You discovered how to use words the way people around you used them. You learned to create sentences that fit the rules for how sentences should be created in your culture's language. If you were brought up where U.S. American English was spoken, you learned to say "put the pen on the table," and not "the pen on the table put." You learned to say "dog" and not "bird" when you pointed at a four-legged, furry animal that barked. You learned meanings for words like "love," "good," and "right" that are too subtle for dictionaries to fully explain.

If you were fairly typical, by age four you had learned enough basic vocabulary to survive for the rest of your life.[1] You knew how to use language to satisfy your need to understand the world, to express yourself, and to form relationships—all without the aid of formal schooling!

What is so engrossing about the way in which you learned to talk is that while so much of the learning process is universal, there is also a great deal of it that is culture specific. Language represents the experiences within a geographic or cultural community. Through social interaction your culture teaches you both the symbol (a sound or written marks) and what that symbol stands for. You hear the sound symbol "dog" and you have a cultural picture in your head of what the symbol means. Members of different cultures will usually have different sounds and/or marks, and they also may have different pictures in their heads for what the symbols mean. "Dog" in some parts of the world, such as China and Korea, may be considered food—quite a different word picture than the same symbol when used in U.S. American culture. What pictures do you think form in heads throughout the world for words such as "freedom," "gay rights," and "God"? The equivalence of these terms in another language, in another culture, may have different pictures, different connotations. Does the word "freedom" mean the same in the United States as it does in Iran? Does the word "God" mean the same thing to a Christian as it does to an agnostic? Some languages do not have a word that stands for "gay" or "homosexual." For example, in (Asian) Indian languages, the idea is expressed as, "man to man sex." That limits the broad meaning of the sexual orientation term to simply a sexual act, not a lifestyle. Cultures differ, and so do the words they use and the meanings they give to words.

Note that throughout this text, generalizations are presented regarding trends of various cultural groups. These are based, whenever possible, on research findings and expert observations. They are in no way intended to lead to the conclusion that all members of the cultural group noted conform to the generalized patterns.

The value system of speech communication teaches each generation assumptions as to what is right and wrong, what is to be respected, and what is to be rejected. Language creates a **social reality** because it affects the way people view the world, and in turn creates rules and values about how to live and act in a culture.

Self-perception and self-esteem are affected by the link between language and behavior. Your attitudes come in part from your language. In fact, anti-hate laws and affirmative action plans, which cause people to use different language, change the way people act and believe.

Historically in the United States, the role of women, African Americans, gays, and Native Americans, among others, were prescribed through the language used to put people in certain categories, and these people were treated according to the terms used to describe them. It has taken the passage of laws, court dictates, and the work of many people to grant equal rights to certain groups. It took an acceptance of a different type of language, different descriptors, to allow some people to vote, sit any place in a bus, hold certain jobs, or even get married. Even today, some of those rights are granted or denied because of the "names" applied to specific people or groups of people and the meanings those names connote. Interestingly, in the battle over same-sex marriage, *marriage* is defined as a unique legal status conferred by and recognized by governments to two people, while a *civil union* is a status that provides legal protection to couples at the state law level, but omits federal protections.[2] The implications of word choice can be illustrated by use of the statistic of a 2004 MSNBC poll in which 54 percent *favored* civil unions, while 59 percent *opposed* same-sex marriage.[3]

Language—Defined

What is **language**? It is "communication of thoughts and feelings through a system of arbitrary signals, such as voice sounds, gestures, or written symbols." Such a system includes rules for combining its components, such as words.[4]

Not only the word, but the interpersonal communication channel also affects how we interpret words. If a friend tells you about the latest news, you may "hear" your friend's words differently via texting than you would face-to-face. The short and abbreviated messages in a text give different meanings than your friend's warm tone of voice, forward-leaning posture indicating intensity, and rapid speech indicating excitement.

It is interesting that when the word *language* is used, it is usually assumed that it is a single thing. In fact, each of us has four categories of any language that we use. There is written, spoken, listening, and reading language. They are often not the same. We may say something that we can't write because we don't know how to spell it. You might be reading a book and come across a word you don't recognize. If the word was spoken to you, you might understand it. Research shows that "Of all the time spent in communicative activities, adults devote 45% of their energies to listening, 30% to speaking, 16% to reading and 9% to writing."[5] Thus, you may or may not understand the message if it is sent in the language form for which you have the weakest vocabulary.

Origins of Human Language

Where language comes from remains one of human evolution's enduring puzzles. One study suggests that "long before early humans spoke, they jabbered away with their hands."[6] **Gestural Theory** contends that "speech was an ingenious innovation but not quite the freakish marvel that linguists have often made it out to be."[7] A theorist proposes that only fifty thousand years ago, our ancestors "could make voluntary movements of the hands and face that could at least serve as a platform upon which to build a language."[8] Before you buy this as the explanation of the start of language, know that this view is not universally accepted since there is no fossil record to prove Gestural Theory.

Some anthropologists believe that two hundred thousand years ago important changes took place in humans, giving us a finer degree of control over mouth and throat muscles. This control gave our ancestors new abilities for producing sounds, which would be used in language.[9]

Other scientists believe that early nonverbal signs (facial expressions, hand gestures) and vocalics (sound through cries and grunts) were the first stage of language development.[10]

Still other scientists believe that primate grooming behavior started the process of language development.[11] Another theory is that chewing behavior was the beginning of using the mouth to create sounds for language. A computer neuroscientist proposes that speech is based on mental reflexes.[12]

However it started, "once speech caught on, it gave Homo sapiens a decisive advantage over less verbal rivals including Homo erectus and the Neanderthals, whose lines eventually died out."[13] As one researcher puts it, "We talked them out of existence."[14]

Verbal language has continued to evolve as an oral and written code. For example, Standard American English is in a constant state of flux. In 2008 the *New Oxford American Dictionary* declared that "hypermiling" was the new word of the year. It is a term used to explain how to save gas while driving.[15] Some new words added to the most recent Merriam-Webster dictionary include *spyware, avian influenza, supersize, drama queen,* and *sandwich generation.* "To be added to the dictionary, a word must be found in five different sources over five years."[16]

Using Symbols

What is the process of attaching meaning to symbols? An example can show how we use symbols. If someone holds up a large, spherical object made of plastic or leather, filled with air, weighing about a pound, you may say "ball." The type of ball that comes to mind depends on many factors in your experience. Even if it is a little dark, if you are on a soccer field, the context tells you this is a soccer ball. If the ball feels heavier, is orange, and has a different surface, you might say "Why did you bring a basketball?"

You instantly take in all kinds of information to attach meaning. In learning language, you figured out the complex process of creating ideas. In this description of the ball, ideas come to mind. The words *soccer* or *basketball* immediately bring ideas to mind so you have a clearer picture of the ball because those words are symbols. A symbol represents something else. A person who didn't speak English would use a different symbol to represent a soccer ball, such as *fútbol, fodbold, pilka noza,* or *balón de futbol.*

Processing Symbols

Another question now emerges: how do we remember what we have been exposed to in our environment? In the human brain, the area that allows us to communicate selectively is the cortex. It is the center for memory and other activities necessary for communicating. The primary language areas of most human brains are probably in the left cortex because only rarely does damage to the right hemisphere, for example when one has a stroke, cause language disorders.[17]

The cybernetic process functions much like a computer. You use your brain and senses to select what to pay attention to in your environment, make sense of the stimuli, and store information in your memory bank. The cybernetic process is schematized in Figure 4.1.

If we go back to the soccer ball example, you learned the words *soccer ball* (*input*), which you keep in your cortex (*stored*). When you see the soccer ball (*stimulus*) you automatically find the information in your memory (*search*), and use the appropriate symbol (*recall*), so you say the words "soccer ball" (*output*).

We use our senses (*taste, smell, sight, sound, touch*), which are tested against stored material (*symbols, images*); and the output (*feedback*) represents the symbol or image. The major difference between human and machine communication is that human communication is imperfect. You can program a computer to send and receive the messages exactly the way you intended, but this is not the case with human beings. The human factor means that each person will interpret communication a little differently, attaching slightly different meanings to symbols, using an imperfect memory with individual experiences. It is possible to get so upset, for example, that you block messages from coming forth. But when the emotional pressure is removed, the normal flow returns. That is why some test trainers suggest that while taking a test or under stress you should "turn off" every so often and then return to the work. Stress relievers such as a diversion, square breathing,[18] or music can help.

Figure 4.1. Cybernetic Process

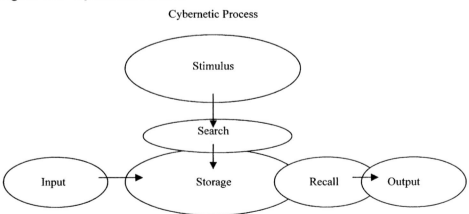

Learning Symbols

Four views of how we acquire our unique language along with our beliefs, values, and attitudes are the Language-Explosion Theory, Significant-Other Theory, the Language Instinct Theory, and the Social Construct of Reality Theory.

LANGUAGE-EXPLOSION THEORY

The **Language-Explosion Theory** proposes that your language develops from the key person(s) in your early life. Your primary caregivers—such as your mother, father, babysitter—talked to you as an infant. That interaction became the basis of what you learned about using language. For the neglected child with little early interaction, language development is often deficient. For the normally developing child who has a rich environment full of human interaction, an explosion of language occurs.

Whatever the child's primary influence, his or her circles of influence quickly expand to include the communication patterns of many other people. The child's neighborhood, area of the country in which he or she lives, and schools attended all influence overall ability to communicate, as does exposure to the media.

SIGNIFICANT-OTHER THEORY

When you are young, your influences comprise all of the sources around you. The **Significant-Other Theory** proposes that the most important person in your early development, such as your mother, becomes the key influence in your language development. This theory looks less at the rich social interaction and more at the influence of a primary caregiver in language development. A child's identity is based on the communication with the significant other.[19]

Perhaps you have a friend who talks like his father, seems to have the same mannerisms, favorite words, a similar vocal style, and even thinks like his dad. Your friend typifies the Significant-Other Theory because his language and communication was primarily influenced by his father. Thus if you respect someone, you are likely to respond to the feedback of that person, which is a powerful developmental force.

You are constantly coming into contact with people who have the potential to be significant others in your life. If you think about who you are today and compare your present language, beliefs, values, and attitudes with those you held five years ago, you will probably find some noticeable differences. These very likely were brought about by your acceptance of someone else's influence. No one can change you except you, but the significant others in your life can alert you to new concepts and help lay the foundation for the changes that come when you accept them.

LEARNING EXPERIENCE: Interested in finding out about the significant others who affected your language development? If so, do Activity 4.1.

ACTIVITY 4.1
My Language Development

A. Who are five people or things that influenced your language development?
B. Examine your list, then circle the name of the person who or thing which was the most influential.
C. List at least five specific things the person/thing taught you.

What did you learn about yourself and your language learning process from this activity?

LANGUAGE INSTINCT THEORY

A neuroscientist[20] proposed a **Language Instinct Theory** that furthered the understanding of linguistic development. His theory argues that language is a human instinct, wired into our brains by evolution much as spiders spin webs. Thus, language is a biological adaptation to communicate information. Infants are born with linguistic skills, skills that have developed as the brain forms in the fetus in the womb. Bombarded by sounds, the unborn child listens.[21] He disputed the notion, proposed by others, that a child is born with a "blank slate."[22] If this is true, then more of the language system may be in place at birth than linguists previously had realized.

SOCIAL CONSTRUCT OF REALITY THEORY

The power of language in human communication is profound. The **Social Construct of Reality Theory**[23] captures this significance. This theory suggests that our words and language shape the way we view the world. Thus communication frames our society. Recent history, for example, has transformed "bums in the street," to "beggars," and then to "homeless people." These language changes reflect the change in society's social attitudes toward the "less fortunate" and the social construction of reality about how to deal with and view these individuals. As the language changed, the society's perceptions of the people being referred to changed as well.

The **Sapir-Whorf Hypothesis** reinforces the concept of social reality in that it states that the language we use guides how we see and interpret the environment and helps shape our ideas. In other words, a people's language serves as a key to understanding their culture.[24] To understand a person's verbal communication is to understand how that person sees the world, how that person thinks—the reality in which that person's culture lives.

Many examples support the Sapir-Whorf Hypothesis. For one, although many people use only one word for snow, Alaskan native people use many different words for snow.[25] The Masai of Africa have seventeen terms for cattle. Arabic has over six

A people's language serves as a key to understanding their culture.

thousand words relating to what most Americans call a *camel*. And U.S. Americans have a wide vocabulary for distinguishing types and models of cars. This reflects the importance of snow for Eskimos, cattle for the Masai, camels for Arabs, and cars for U.S. Americans. The point isn't that Americans cannot see the distinctions in snow that Eskimos see, but that they do not see them because such subtleties about snow aren't important to them. The vocabulary you use reflects your interests and concerns, the way you look at the world, and the distinctions among objects, people, and events that are important to you.

Grammar, too, serves as evidence for the Sapir-Whorf Hypothesis. How you think about something is reflected in and affected by the grammar you use. In English, for example, you would say, "the white wine" (the specific, white, comes first, and the general, wine, follows), while in French you would say, "le vin blanc" (the general, *wine*, comes first, and the specific, *white*, follows).[26] As with differences in vocabulary, differences in grammar do not necessarily reflect inabilities to think differently, but rather preferences for what is important to a particular language community.

We can observe an extension of the Sapir-Whorf Hypothesis by looking at the language patterns of some of the many cocultures in the United States. These groups have evolved an **argot**, a jargon or slang, which is a special vocabulary that mirrors their experiences, experiences that are often different from those of the mainstream culture. An understanding of these unique vocabulary systems is important because you might hear private words and phrases that sound foreign and alien to you. Secondly, these specialized vocabularies, as noted by the Sapir-Whorf Hypothesis, can offer insight into the experiences of these cocultures.

Members of the male gay coculture, because they may live two lives—one among the dominant heterosexual culture and one among members of their own homosexual coculture—have developed a rather extensive argot. A fellow gay is often referred to as "a member of the family." In this case, "family" means the brotherhood of homosexual men. A bisexual may be labeled as "AC/DC," much like electrical alternating and direct ("straight") current. In asking whether a fellow gay has come out to society the question is asked, "Have you told your story?" "Coming out" signifies no longer hiding a person's sexual preference.[27]

Street gangs have acquired a rich vocabulary that reflects their experiences. "Claim" or "turf" is an area that each gang maintains as belonging to them. Again, these are "logical" words to describe the idea or action: "claim," a marking off of territory, "turf," a piece of territory. "Signs" are hand signals used to communicate to other gang members. Based on the bridge between the argot and the implied meaning, what do you think gangs mean by "homeboy," "buster," and "claimer"? A "homeboy" is a member of the same gang, a "buster" is someone who doesn't stand up for the gang, and a "claimer" is someone who wants to be a member of the gang but has not yet proven himself or herself.

The argot of African Americans mirrors that culture's environment, perceptions, and values. *Please remember, as we discuss this subject, that examples are based on research findings and expert observations that were appropriate at the publication date of this text. They are in no way intended to lead to the conclusion that all members of the cultural group conform to the generalized speech pattern, nor may they be current when students read this material.*

In African American argot, "Feel draft" expresses some thoughts of racism in white people. A person who attempts to emulate or to please white people may be referred to as a "Tom" or an "Oreo." "Tom" often refers to the subservient slave, Uncle Tom, in *Uncle Tom's Cabin*, and "Oreo" refers to the cookie—white on the inside, although dark on the outside. "The man," referring to anyone who has power, harks back to slavery days when "the man" or "master" had all the power.[28] Though the African American argot, like all argot, changes over time, a conversation containing Ebonic argot at the time this book was published could be: "You gots to git those Benjamins so you kin git dat bling-bling fo yo ride." In Standard American English the same idea would be: "You need to get money so that you can get expensive accessories for your car."[29] Another example is, Ebonic argot: "Why you all up in my grill yo?" Standard American English: "Why are you invading my personal space?"[30]

There are many cocultures in any society that have extensive argot, each of which is composed of a vast number of words. Argots also are regional. For example, African

Americans in Los Angeles might well have different terms than African Americans in San Diego, even though the two cities are only 120 miles apart. Also, argots are subject to change. A term that is used one month may be discarded the next. In fact, because most cocultures feel alienated from the dominant culture, they are constantly changing their argot.

In addition to argots, studies have linked ethnic identification with ethnic language use. For example, Mexican Americans who were strong ethnic identifiers were found to be frequent users of Spanish language media. Strong support for the relationship between language use and ethnic identification was found in a study of Welsh-speaking individuals living in England whose language maintenance was found to be a function of ethnic identification.

Today there are an estimated six to seven thousand languages spoken on the planet, but predictions are that within the next one hundred years most will be gone.[31] It is estimated that the entire population of the Earth will speak between 250 and 600 languages. This may facilitate communication between groups of people, but it also means the loss of aspects of the cultural identity of the people whose language disappears. A researcher states, "Language is the DNA of a culture . . . a lost language is a lost culture."[32]

Yiddish, for example, a language that was used extensively by eastern European Jews, has basically been eliminated due to the Holocaust and the founding of the State of Israel. The extermination of eastern European Jews who used the language eliminated its users. When Israel was founded Hebrew became the official language of the country. This was another blow to Yiddish's usage.[33] Languages threatened with possible elimination include 153 aboriginal languages in Australia, 23 languages in Siberia and adjacent areas, 40 indigenous languages in the southwestern United States, and 113 in South America.[34]

Characteristics of Language

The study of the sounds, structure, and rules of human language is linguistics. **Linguistics** is the study of the common elements in all languages. What are the common characteristics of all languages?

Language is symbolic. Words have no meaning in themselves, but are assigned meaning by people. For example, let's examine the words "pizza" and "Coke." If words were not symbols but things, you could eat the word "pizza" and drink the word "Coke." There is nothing pizza-like about the word "pizza," and nothing liquid-like about the word "Coke." If there were a logical connection between a symbol and what it symbolized, wouldn't it seem silly for the word "big" to have fewer letters than the word "small"? Why would "ten," "diez," and "dix" all mean the same thing (and why would none of the three have ten letters)?

Although the connection between a word and what it symbolizes is arbitrary, people often act as if words had some inherent meaning. For example, a professor placed a "cookie" on each desk in his class. After his students came into the room, saw the cookies, ate them, and thanked him, he told them the cookies were actually dog biscuits. Many students got sick! The reality of the good cookie was overshadowed by the two symbols "dog" and "biscuits." The students substituted the words for the reality.[35]

If the connection between a symbol and the object, idea, or event that it refers to were simple, communicating would be rather easy. Every time you said the word "car" it would mean the same thing to you as it meant to the person with whom you were talking. But because the relationship between a word and what it symbolizes is arbitrary, meanings are in the people who use the words, not in the words themselves. No meaning is inherent in any symbol. People attach a specific, personal meaning to every word they use. For example, for you, the word "car" may mean a beige 2001 Volvo S60, even though the same word could refer to a blue 2010 Prius. For someone else, car might mean a different specific automobile, such as the one she owns, or all autos of a particular make, such as a Toyota. And if the person is from a nonmotorized culture, the word "car" might be a funny-sounding word without meaning.

Just because meanings are in people, not in words, does not imply that communication is impossible. No, you daily talk to people. You are reading this book right now. How is this possible? Even though each of us has his or her own language dictionary, people with a common language also share a dictionary. This common dictionary is what makes it possible to communicate. You can speak to others and read this book because of societal shared language and meanings.

Language is dynamic. In addition to shared meanings and individual meanings, new words with new meanings and old words with new meanings constantly are created. As already illustrated, dictionaries continue to add new words and drop out-of-date terms as the vocabulary of people within a particular culture changes. *Languages are rule-governed.* Rules that govern how words can be arranged are called **syntactic rules**. Remember when, in your early years of school your teacher said, "In English, the noun comes first and then the verb and then the object"? For example, syntactic rules that guide English dictate the syntax, "Did you wash the car?" whereas syntactic rules that guide German would have the sentence read, "Did you the car wash?" Which is right? Neither. The syntax of the languages are just different, not right or wrong. This does not mean that you can make up sentence structures as you speak. If you are speaking a language, you need to know the grammatical structure and follow it or the people you are talking to will not understand or think that you are not fluent in that language.

Languages that are alphabetically based recognize the differences between vowels and consonants. Alphabet-based languages use vowels and consonants. The sounds of *a*, *e*, *i*, *o*, *u* (vowels) sound different to English-speakers than consonants. In some pictorial languages, such as Chinese, the word is composed of ideas about the word.

Languages have categorical order to them, such as verbs and nouns. The sentence, "Ian saw the car," designates the noun (*car*) and the verb (saw).

Languages contain denotative and connotative words and meanings. Because you interpret symbols, you assign meaning to them according to your *frame of reference*—your background, experiences, and perceptions. Since each of your frames of reference are so different, your interpretation may be very far from the intent of the sender. Many symbols are hard to define. Symbols can carry both denotative and connotative meanings.

Denotative words are commonly identified as those words that have explicit meanings that can clearly be stated in a dictionary.

However, that definition is not always easy to ascertain. An examination of any dictionary will confirm that many words have several definitions.

The word "team," has several denotations in addition to "an athletic group." It refers to a clique, assemblage, association, band or collection of people, crew, or an organization. Individuals unfamiliar with English may be unaware of any given word's multiple denotations. Assuming that only one denotation exists, a word may be used incorrectly in varying contexts. For example, a denotation for "got" is "obtained." A new English speaker who knew this denotative connection could say, "I obtained up this morning at 7 A.M." The speaker failed to recognize that not all denotations are interchangeable.

Connotative words are those that refer to the attitudes or feelings people have for the word or what it symbolizes. Words like, "pretty" and "wonderful" are classified as connotative words since there is no universal definition of exactly what is meant by "pretty" or what is "wonderful." Connotative words are generally more abstract than denotative words and carry much individual personal meaning.

What are your connotations for the word "car"? Is it something good or bad? Fast or slow? A plaything or a necessity? If you have had good experiences with cars—no accidents and few repairs—you are likely to have positive associations with the symbol. The opposite would be true if you had a series of negative experiences.

The connotations you have for a word are more likely to determine your response than the denotations, probably because you learned the connotative meanings for many words before you learned their denotations. For example, as a child you may have learned that "unpaid bills" are "bad" before you understood what unpaid bills were. The process of reacting first and learning the denotation second is a hard habit to break.

Because connotations are more subtle and varied than denotations, new English speakers have a great deal of difficulty mastering this aspect of language. Words such as "love," "hate," and "democracy" have a great number of connotations. For example, you may "love chocolate," "love your partner," "love your mother," "love going to the movies," and "love the way your car drives." The word "love" is the same, but the connotations are seemingly different. Grasping the subtlety of these differences requires familiarity with a culture's language.

One device used for measuring connotative meaning—the attitudes and feelings you have toward a concept or term—is called the **semantic differential**, a tool that measures a person's reactions to an object or concept by marking spaces between a pair of adjectives, one positive and one negative, with each space representing an attitude position.

LEARNING EXPERIENCE: Interested in determining your ability to use the semantic differential? If so, do Activity 4.2.

Languages determine how we categorize people and things. Semantics refers to the word choices used to develop messages. Those choices can follow many patterns, which may help or hinder in dealing with the world around you. So, for example,

---

ACTIVITY 4.2
Semantic Differential

Rate the concept *my high school education* on the following scales by circling the number that best reflects your feelings. The endpoints 1 and 7 are defined by the adjectives. The numbers between them represent less extreme positions. For example, on the first scale, 1 = bad, 2 = somewhat bad, 3 = slightly bad, 4 = neither good nor bad, 5 = slightly good, 6 = somewhat good, and 7 = good.

bad	1	2	3	4	5	6	7	good
not satisfying	1	2	3	4	5	6	7	satisfying
boring	1	2	3	4	5	6	7	exciting
tense	1	2	3	4	5	6	7	relaxed

You can get a sense of your semantic differential, whether your connotations for the concept *my high school education* are positive or negative simply by adding your responses to the four scales and comparing your sum with the highest score possible, 28, and the lowest score possible, 4. If your sum is close to 28, your connotations are positive. On the other hand, if your score is close to 4, your connotations are negative.

---

instead of approaching the world with an either/or, **two-valued orientation**, we can remember that life is multidimensional and that meanings vary as the backgrounds and experiences of the communicators differ.

Instructors who say, "Alex is a good student" or, "Manuel is a poor student" reflect a two-valued orientation because such statements do not allow for other dimensions of a student's performance. Perhaps, for example, Alex is strong in some subjects but weak in others. Or maybe Manuel has not been motivated to work in school but does have considerable academic ability. The use of a two-valued system eliminates the possibility for the unknown or other possibilities.

LEARNING EXPERIENCE: Interested in testing your two-valued orientation? If so, complete Activity 4.3.

Language Distortion

Effective language use is difficult, in part because language causes distortion. **Language distortion** can be caused by uncertainty, doubt, mental leaps, and message problems.

Ambiguity occurs when vagueness about a word's meaning makes it open for misinterpretation. If you say the word *dog*, do you mean an animal, a guy who causes trouble, harassment, an unattractive person, or something else? All these definitions are appropriate depending on the context. Fortunately, ambiguity can often be overcome

ACTIVITY 4.3
Two-Valued Orientation,
Separating Fact from Inference

Read the following story, assuming that all the information is accurate and true. Then, for each statement, indicate T (true), F (false), or ? (don't know).

A certain West Coast university scientist chartered a ship for exploration purposes. When a large white bird was sighted, the scientist asked permission to kill it. He stated that white albatrosses are usually found only off the coast of Australia. He wanted the bird as a specimen for the university museum. The crew protested against the killing of the bird, calling the scientist's attention to the old sea superstition that bad luck followed the killing of a white albatross. Nevertheless the captain granted permission to kill the bird, and the bird was killed. These mishaps happened after the bird was killed: The net cables fouled up three times, a rib was broken when Jackie Larson, a scientific aide, fell down a hatch ladder, and the scientist became seasick for the first time in his life.

1. The scientist had never been seasick before.   T F ?
2. The purpose of the voyage was primarily pleasure and sightseeing. T F ?
3. The scientist asked the captain for permission to kill the bird.   T F ?
4. Jackie Larson broke his rib.   T F ?
5. The white albatross was sighted near Australia.   T F ?

Key
1. T—The story specifies that "The scientist became seasick for the first time in his life."
2. F—The story specifies that "A . . . scientist chartered a ship for exploration purposes."
3. ?—We do not know whom the scientist asked.
4. ?—We do not know if Jackie Larson broke a rib or if it was the ship's rib. In addition, we don't know if Jackie Larson is a male or a female.
5. ?—We do not know where the ship was when the sighting was made.

Statements 3, 4, and 5 are inferences because they are not based on observations, but only suggested by them. Statements 1 and 2 are facts because they are based on observation.

What did you learn about your ability to separate fact from inference from doing this activity?

if the listener refers to the word's context to determine whether it describes an over-indulging dinner guest or the purchaser of a Harley cycle, or if the sender defines the term when used.

Vagueness results from words or sentences lacking clarity. Use of words such as *they*, *he*, and *things like that* are vague unless we specifically know who or what is being referred to by the speaker. Although any word might be misinterpreted, connotative words are apt to be the most unclear.

Doublespeak is an imprecise use of language designed to be confusing, elusive, intentionally misleading, or cagey.[36] Doublespeak is a negative approach to communication, using words intentionally to hurt, exploit, or wound other people. Doublespeak is often used in power and control communication. It can be a weapon of power, exploitation, manipulation, and oppression.

According to an expert on doublespeak, as a result of the language of members of the Bush administration, "The distortion of words is becoming increasingly overt."[37] As examples, he suggests that a phrase such as "bringing freedom to . . . " refers not to bringing any real freedoms, but to taking whatever is wanted, without opposition. "War on Terror" is a war *of* terror. "Diplomacy" refers to threats and intimidation preceding an already decided upon military strike, while "collateral damage" is actually the intentional killing of innocent civilians, and "freedom fighters" is the name given to terrorists.[38]

Inferences result when we interpret beyond available information, or jump to conclusions without using all of the information available. Because communicating is a creative process, inferences are an inevitable part of processing information. If you do not have enough material, you just might complete an idea with what seems logical to you, what you have experienced in the past, or what you hope or fear is the potential outcome. Read the following sentence quickly:

> The cow jump over
> over thee noon.

Did you see "jump," or did you read it as "jumped"? What about the first and the second "over," or "thee" and "noon"? Many people simply see the first couple of words and, based on their past experience, instinctively infer the nursery rhyme statement "The cow jumped over the moon."

CULTURAL-NEGATIVE LANGUAGE

Cultural-negative language expresses stereotyped attitudes or feelings of superiority of one culture over another. The cultural conflicts can be, for example, male/female (sexist language) or caucasian/negroid (racist language). Whereas sexist language in the United States has traditionally divided the world into "superior" males and "inferior" females, culture-negative language usually divides the world into "superior" and "inferior" groups. All the same sexist assertions about women have been made for so called inferior cultural groups. For example, _____ (fill in any group) are less

Cultural-negative language expresses stereotyped attitude or feelings of superiority of one culture over another.

intelligent and more emotional than _____ (fill in any group). As with the word "male," connotations of the word "white" are positive—clean, pure, innocent, and bright—and connotations of the word "black" are negative—dirty, dark, decaying, and sinister, as are those for "yellow"—chicken, afraid, and sickly.

The same applies to heterosexual and homosexual stereotypes. For the general population those things related to heterosexuality are positive, those related to homosexuality are negative. Calling someone a "fag," "homo," or "lesbo" is considered by many to be an insult. On the other hand, "macho," and "stud" are positively viewed describers by many.

It is generally perceived as being callous and ignorant to use words such as "Hymie," "Kike," "Dago," "Wop," "Jap," "Spic," "Chink," "Chinaman," "Kraut," and "Polack" when referring to people from specific ethnic backgrounds. These types of words are a sign of verbal bigotry. It is also insensitive not to respect the wishes of members of a particular group who prefer words such as "Chinese" for "Oriental," "Sioux" for "Indian," and "African American" for "negro" or "Black."

Cultural-negative language fails to make important distinctions among individuals who may have only one characteristic in common. Members of a racial, ethnic, gender, sexual orientation group may differ more from each other than they do from members of other groups. To be a competent interpersonal communicator, you should eliminate from your communication remarks that encompass entire groups of people. Avoid abstractions and be concrete: refer to your own experience and to the particular limitations of your own experience.

The Languages People Use

Language has structure, just like chemical compounds. There are a certain number of vowels and consonants, just as there are a certain number of elements. Letters are combined much as elements are put together to form something new. It makes sense, therefore, that language is studied by linguists, who are social scientists who study language structure, just as a chemist studies how to put together elements.

"Systematic and rule-governed differences exist between languages,"[39] reports one linguist. "Each language is a collection of similar dialects [a social or regional variation of a language]. Dialects, like languages, differ from each other in terms of pronunciation, vocabulary, grammar, and prosody [accent or tone.]"[40] A **dialect** is the regional use of a language. If a dialect is used over a long time, it may develop into a separate language, just as Italian, French, and Spanish were once dialects of Latin.

Many factors prompt differences in language, such as social class, ethnicity, social groups, age, gender, religious affiliation, and location. Philadelphia's "hoagie" is a "bomber" in upstate New York, and "a wedge" in New York City. A "soda" in Kansas City is called a "pop" in Cleveland and a "coke" in Atlanta, no matter what brand or taste or soft drink is being requested.

In spite of differences, the dialects of the English language have more similarities than differences. Yes, the English call a "flashlight" a "torch" and a "traffic circle" a "roundabout" and an "umbrella" is a "bumbershoot." They also "queue up" rather than "get in line." But there are more terms that are the same than there are different. For this reason, speakers of varying English dialects can communicate with relative ease, though at some times, their ways of pronunciation (**accent**) may create difficulty.

Even in the United States there are differences in pronunciation. If you meet a person born and raised in New York City and someone born and raised in Mississippi, you could probably identify who is from where by their accents.

Each speaker of a language speaks some dialect of it, or a combination of dialects. No one dialect is best, although some are considered **standard dialects** (high prestige) and some are considered **nonstandard dialects** (low prestige). The high prestige standard dialects are those used by people in a society who are in power, better educated, the keepers of official records, and writers of science and literature.[41] "Powerful groups have held nonstandard speech against its speakers because it was a way of bonding their own social identity and of manifesting their social status."[42]

STANDARD AMERICAN ENGLISH

Standard American English is the dialect linguists consider representative of the U.S. American public. Standard American English is the form you hear on the national news, and is typical of well-articulated speech most typical in the middle and Western states. An accent may be positive, negative, or neutral.

Out-of-the-mainstream pronunciation often is used as a source of humor. Entertainers Rosie O'Donnell, Rosie Perez, Barbra Streisand, and Fran Drescher, for example, have made their accents a focal point of their careers.

Although there may not be one "best" way of pronunciation, some standards of American pronunciation are generally accepted. The words *pitcher* and *picture* do not have the same meaning and are not pronounced the same way. Such words as "hunderd" (*hundred*), "liberry" (*library*), "secatary" (*secretary*), and "alls" (*all*) linguistically do not exist. Words ending with *ing*, such as *going* and *coming* are not generally pronounced "goin" and "comin." Saying "jeet yit?" is not a substitute for *Did you eat yet? Many* isn't "minnie," and *didn't* is not "dint."

Standard American English form and grammar is the same as what you see published in quality national magazines and newspapers, such as *US News and World Report* and *USA Today*. The *New York Times* is another example of standard use, and you will notice that although New Yorkers tend to have their own pronunciation patterns, these do not carry over into their grammatical usage or word selection in publications.

In addition to dialects and accents, slang plays a role in language.

SLANG

"There are, at the very least, a quarter of a million distinct English words, excluding inflections, and words from technical and regional vocabulary."[43] No one can be sure exactly how many slang words the English language has, but estimates are that the average Euro American has about twenty-thousand words in his/her vocabulary and about 10 percent (two thousand) are slang.[44]

Argot is specialized language used by particular groups. **Slang** is typically related to a certain activity or incident. The words are less formal and open to misunderstanding because the words are understood by people of a certain group, age, or region. Groups create their own language within a language. Peers recognize each other through its use. It's a way of belonging. In fact, almost any group that wishes to bond together develops argot or slang. Think bikers, theatre people, sports fans, or gangs, who all have "in" words they use to converse with each other.

Types of Slang

Because of the prevalence of computers in our society, we now *reset* a problem, or *couch surf*, for example, as these words enter our language. The *Online Slang Dictionary* (onlineslangdictionary.com) updates slang terms used in the United States on a daily basis. For example, on July 1, 2009, it added "chomo" (child molester), "crunk" (extremely fun, exciting, wild), "MILF" (an attractive older woman), "jonesing," (to feel withdrawal symptoms, especially from drugs), and "emo" (emotional and melodramatic music) to their lexicon of slang.

Inarticulates

Inarticulates are vocalized pauses between words with meaning. Terms like "um," "er," and "like," fill in spaces and appear on the average once every ten words, and actually do have a purpose beyond being distractions.[45] "Pauses in speech point to thinking, not as has been previously thought, a lack in thinking, a gap between thoughts, some psychic anxiety, or embarrassments. Pauses are part of a cycle of thinking and speaking. It takes place when we try and think and talk at the same time. We can't think and talk at the same time."[46] In spite of this finding, inarticulates become conversational mannerisms that can distract from the substance of the message and from your credibility as a speaker.

NONSTANDARD AMERICAN LANGUAGES AND DIALECTS

People in the United States speak many variations of language. They may speak a variation of English (such as Black English or Ebonics), combinations (such as Chinese or English), or different languages (such as Russian or Korean). Any discussion of dialects must recognize that there are many languages, dialects, and argots. Some get a lot of respect and some don't get any. "In some cases, the respect given to the dialect is in the same amount that is given to the people who speak it."[47]

Please remember, as we embark on the topic of languages that reflect various segments of U.S. culture, that generalizations are presented. These are based, whenever possible, on research findings and expert observations. They are in no way intended to lead to the conclusion that all members of the cultural group noted conform to the generalized patterns. Your own ethnocentricities could play a part in how you approach this material.

Ebonics (Black English)

Any discussion of African Americans in this country speaking a language other than Standard American English is fraught with political and social overtones in both the white and Black communities. Some will contend that what is referred to as Ebonics is just bad English. Some will contend that it is a slang form of English. Others will contend that there is no such thing as Ebonics.

Since research by major linguists contends that there is such a language form as Ebonics, it will be discussed here. This does not mean you must accept this concept.

Ebonics, also known as **Black English**, is the primary language of many African Americans in the United States.[48] Ebonics is a term introduced by Black linguists in the mid-1970s, and refers not only to a particular grammar and syntax, but also to paralinguistic (i.e., noises such as laughing and crying) and gestural (movement) features of African American communication.[49] "This is not street talk; it is not broken English; and it is not slang."[50] It is "a private vocabulary of Black people which serves the users as a powerful medium."[51] "Moreover, Black English is not a regional dialect. It reflects a common national culture of the American black community. The grammar used by many Black adults in Los Angeles in their home setting is virtually the same as that used by adolescent groups in New York. Listening to TV shows that feature black characters enforces this concept.

Linguists disagree about the historical development of Ebonics. One theory holds that, "Black English is rooted in a historical past that spans Africa, the Caribbean, the Creole heritage, the South, and now the northern U.S. cities."[52] Another proposes that "Africans came to the United States with no knowledge of English and developed the dialect [language]."[53] Still another version is that "It is a Creole language formed out of mainstream American English and native African languages evolving from largely West African pidgin forms."[54]

Whatever its roots, linguists cite characteristics of Black English that differentiate it from Standard English. "Ebonics is characterized by a systematic grammar, for example, the frequent use of the habitual tense [e.g., "I be sick."—"I have been and still am sick."]"[55] This is not present in Standard American English, but is part of the syntactic system of both French and Spanish.

In addition, there are "particular sound patterns [e.g., "wif" rather than "with"], and in some cases, words that deviate in their meanings from standard English [e.g., "the man"]. These elements are thought to have some linguistic basis in West African languages, particularly those belonging to the Niger-Congo language family."[56]

The interactional pattern of *call and response* is a distinctive vocal way of African American expression, which originated in places of worship. "The spontaneous reactions and supportive statements of encouragement involve the speaker and listeners in a dynamic interactional dialogue."[57] "This stands in contrast to the traditional Euro-American speaker/audience setting in which the speaker or expert dispenses wisdom and the audience listens attentively and reacts only at appropriately defined moments."[58]

Another tendency among some African Americans is "the form of thinking and problem solving that they have acquired from their cultural and life experiences. This characteristic is a strong reliance on internal cues and reactions as a means of problem solving. This is in contrast to the enforced reliance on external cues that is required for most problem solutions in a classroom setting."[59] It is very subjective and has been called "intuition"[60] This, according to some psychological research, makes the African American child, in the school setting, "particularly vulnerable to his emotional reaction interfering with his learning." However, from an interpersonal perspective, "reliance on intuition makes African-American children particularly adept in social relations because such a facility relies heavily on empathy."[61] This carries over into adulthood as well, with African Americans displaying strong empathetic interpersonal reactions. "So long as the setting is an interpersonal setting, the child [and adult] is comfortable and efficient. When the learning situation is devoid of human involvement, then frequently, the African-American child experiences difficulty."[62]

This socialization pattern, which often includes loud and emotional outbursts, is often misunderstood by Euro-Americans, who may perceive the loudness and physical reactions as being out of control and threatening. It can also account for why African American children, especially males, are often perceived as discipline problems in the classroom.

One Black linguist contended that "African American modes of communication and expression are grounded in African World View—a view which she claimed emphasizes rhythm, analogy, metaphor, and intuition."[63] Other Black linguists have maintained that "Ebonics is based on an African perspective which, they say, differs radically from Euro-Western views of nature and reality."[64] This contention reenforces the Sapir-Whorf Hypothesis that the language we use creates our worldview.

"The distinctiveness of African American speech style has been problematic for group members [with mainstream speakers and in commerce]. On the one hand, speech that marks the individual as a member of the group can be important for in-group acceptance."[65] The other is that "children don't learn standard dialect so that they will be able to assimilate and demonstrate marketable skills in mainstream society."[66] Based on the latter viewpoint, some Black community leaders have encouraged African Americans to use **code switching**, so they speak the most appropriate dialect in a given context.

Spanglish

A significant group of Americans speaks **Spanglish**.[67] Spanglish is a combination of Spanish and English words. This practice of combining languages is common among many immigrant groups, who blend their language of origin with U.S. English. Yinglish (Yiddish and English) is another example.

Sometimes the combination comes from a lack of the specific word in one language or the other, sometimes because of product development in the United States, sometimes for slang or convenience.

"There are many people out there that speak English, Spanish and Spanglish. It is a language that, to this day, academics [distrust], that politicians only recently have begun to take it more into consideration. But poets, novelists and essayists have realized that it is the key to the soul of a large portion of the population."[68]

Spanglish can be word combinations from *hasta la bye-bye* (so long) to *lonche* (a quick lunch rather than a leisurely one), the description of a group of *los teenagers*, and the almost universally used *no problema*.

The use of Spanglish is widespread. A sign in Springfield, Massachusetts, warns young Latinos: "No Hangear"—don't hang out on this corner. On a street in a Hispanic neighborhood phrases can be heard like, "Backupear" (back up a car), "yarda" (yard), and "pregneada" (pregnant).[69]

As an author of a book on Spanglish states, "Spanish actually is becoming a major force in this country. But it's not surviving in an uncontaminated, pure way. And in that sense, Spanglish is similar to previous patterns of linguist assimilation but very different in that Spanish remains alive and strong and is creating this mixture that is unique and is defining the way Latinos describe themselves, feel, think. I think Spanglish is more than a way of communication; I think it's a way of thinking, a new way of being for us almost 40 million people in the U.S."[70]

Since Spanglish does not have a unique semantic and syntactic system, it is not considered, as is Ebonics, to be a language.

A linguist who speaks Spanglish said, "Among Latinos, Spanglish conversations often flow easily from Spanish into several sentences of English and back again. It's unconscious. I couldn't even tell you minutes later if I said something in Spanglish, Spanish, or English."[71]

With the Hispanic population in the United States now surpassing African Americans as the most populous minority, emphasis on the need to speak Spanish, as well as English, is becoming accepted more and more in certain parts of the country. Many jobs require that employees be **bilingual**, fluent in two languages, in order to be employed. Most commonly, these languages are English and Spanish.

Asian-American Dialect

The U.S. population has a growing number of people from the Pacific Rim. New residents from Cambodia, China, Korea, Philippines, Taiwan, and Vietnam, for example, bring unique languages that combine with English in words, style, structure, and accent. Besides their native language, many use a type of language which, for the lack of a more definitive term, is called **Asian-American Dialect**, which may differ greatly according to the individual cultural background of the person.

Some people think of Asian Americans as one single homogeneous group. Actually they are one of the most diverse groups. In reality, "an Asian or Pacific Islander is a person having origins in any of the original peoples of the Far East, Southeast Asia, the Indian subcontinent, or the Pacific Islands. This area includes, for example, China, India, Japan, Korea, the Philippine Islands, and Samoa."[72]

Asians have values that don't fit easily into the Euro-American culture. For example, in contrast to the individualism and straightforward talk of many Euro-Americans, an important value that Chinese hold is the concept of "face." It basically means, "I am not going to do anything to embarrass anyone else."[73] In acting on "face," individuals who disagree with someone will not argue person to person. They will get an intermediary, who will mediate between two people, so the disagreement can be resolved to avoid direct conflict.[74] This can confuse Euro-Americans, who want to "settle this here and now!"

Euro-American teachers and professors are often frustrated when Chinese, and other Asian students, won't ask or answer questions in class, even when encouraged to do so. The base reason for this is the concept of face. The student does not want to embarrass the professor as the teacher may not know the answer, and the Asian student doesn't want to embarrass the other Asians in the classroom who will "lose face" if one of their own shows ignorance. (Asians are group- rather than individual-oriented and, therefore, what one does reflects on the others.)

"Japanese-Americans have a very important value of visibility. It may be more accurate to say invisibility. For example, they do not want to draw attention to themselves. Which means they would refrain from playing loud music, driving luxury cars, living in a big house in Beverly Hills. They will work hard and fit in with everyone else. Basically becoming unnoticeable."[75] This carries over into their communication, where loud talk, laughing in public, and showing emotions to others is not acceptable.

A Korean value is the concept of *Kibun*, which means "to feel."[76] This concept is very similar to the Chinese value of "face," and results in not wanting to upset others. When asked for directions, for example, they will often give them even if they don't know where the location is. They don't want to upset their guests.

Trying to recreate Standard English sounds is often difficult for many Asians as their languages do not contain some of the sounds of English. For example, there is no equivalent of the "l" sound in Japanese. Therefore, the word "plastic" becomes "prastic" and "laugh" becomes "raff."

Some Asian-Pacificers also have difficulty in what Euro-Americans would call logical arguments, as "English is a language whose relative preciseness encourages not just argumentation and debate, but detailed analysis, Western logic, and thorough explanations."[77] The pictographic languages, those which use icons rather than individual alphabetical symbols, such as Chinese and Japanese, are ones where "precision is [often] cumbersome and inelegant. Ordinary speech is vague and depends heavily on the cooperative imagination and sympathy of the listener."[78]

Native American Languages

There is considerable controversy about how to discuss native peoples in the United States. "**Native American languages** do not belong to a single Amerindian family, but 25–30 small ones; they are usually discussed together because of the small numbers of natives speaking most of these languages and how little is known about many of them. There are around 25 million native speakers of the more than 800 surviving Amerind languages. The vast majority of these speakers live in Central and South America, where language use is vigorous. In Canada and the United States, only about half a million native speakers of an Amerind tongue remain."[79]

Because of the differences between the Indian nations and languages, it is difficult to look at Native Americans as a group. We can generalize, however, that Native American communications contain: "(a) reticence with regard to interaction with strangers, (b) the acceptance of obligations, (c) razzing, (d) attaining harmony in face-to-face interactions, (e) modesty and doing one's part, (f) taking on familial relations, (g) permissible and required silence, and (h) a unique style of public speaking."[80] The use of silence may result in some Native Americans' being mistakenly labeled as communication apprehensive.

The idea of harmony pervades many tribes' belief systems. "Rhetoric in such a universe has as its primary function not in discovery but in use, and its uses are carefully prescribed, sanctioned by ancestral tradition, and functional in maintaining the world as it ought to be."[81] The approach is to talk it out and solve problems, while discussing problems with everyone of the family or group.[82]

"*Razzing* is a collective form of storytelling in which participants take some episode, humorous or not, from a present or past experience and relate it humorously to the others in attendance. The story, which is often lengthy, is then characteristically embellished and altered by others who are present."[83] This communication works to determine cultural competency, identify in-group and out-group members, and as a form of instruction.[84]

A difficulty some Native Americans encounter in speaking with Standard English speakers centers on the use of narration. Traditionally, Native Americans have relied on razzing and telling historical or experiential stories to clarify their points. Often the tales only allude to the point being made rather than directly relating to the specific issue. It is called the *spiral structure of argument.* This is similar to the narrative communication patterns of many Hispanics and Arabs and may seem imprecise and abstract to many interpersonal communicators.

The Effects of Speaking Nonstandard English

Nearly one in five people living in the United States speak a language at home other than English.[85] There are those who believe that anyone living in the United States should speak English and only English. These people tend to believe that a country is defined by the language it uses, that it is a waste of taxpayer money to have information printed in more than one language, and without laws requiring the use of English immigrants will not learn to speak the "language of the country."

Just as languages other than English have always been a part of our history and culture, debate over establishing a national language dates back to the country's beginnings. John Adams proposed to the Continental Congress in 1780 that an official academy be created to "purify, develop, and dictate usage of" English. His proposal was rejected as undemocratic and a threat to individual liberty.[86]

The controversy has raged on. "The movement to make English the official language of the United States gained momentum at both the state and federal levels in the mid-1990s. In 1995 alone, more than five bills designating English as the official language of the United States were introduced in the U.S. Congress." None of these passed.[87]

Though there has been no change on the federal level, as of the publication of this book, 28 states had made English the official language of that jurisdiction.[88]

Some cities have also attempted to pass such legislation.

Generally the more conservative members of the United States population think that the government should adopt English as the national language and require everyone to use it. In 2009, voters in Nashville, Tennessee, considered a proposal that would have limited local government to conduct its business in English. The proposal was defeated.[89]

There is evidence that using Standard American English will increase success in K–12 schooling, college, and at work.[90] Failure to speak Standard American English increases the likelihood of dropping out of school and being offered less pay.[91]

PERSON-FIRST LANGUAGE

Throughout this book we encourage you to show rhetorical sensitivity toward each person in the specific interpersonal communication context. One way to emphasize the uniqueness of each individual is to use **person-first language**.[92] In person-first language, when referring to someone, you put the descriptor after the person.

In person-first language, you would not say someone is a "disabled person." There is nothing disabled about the individual's personhood. We know a man with schizophrenia, for example, who resents it when people refer to him as "the schizophrenic guy" or "the schizo." The man explains: "Schizophrenia is just one part of me. I'm a man first, who happens to have schizophrenia." By seeing disabilities as a fact of life instead of a problem, careful language can avoid a negative label as a definition for a person. Although 6 million of us were born with some condition with disabling effects, the vast majority will have such a condition before we die.[93]

Further, many people with disabilities would like others to stop using terms associated with disabilities as insults. There is a movement to simply remove certain words from our language through lack of use. For example, no interpersonal communicator should call someone a "retard" or "idiot." These terms were originally used to describe a certain type of brain processing. For many people, having developmental delays is no reason to be ostracized or made fun of, including "innocent" remarks that throw insults to others. For effective communicators, a source's intention is not nearly as important as the way the receiver perceives the comment. Think about the slight yet powerful differences in perceptions in the list below.

"My boss gets around in a wheelchair" emphasizes ability better than "My boss is crippled." Does the term "crippled" make you cringe?

"My cousin John is a pretty typical tenth-grader and his twin brother Chris has developmental delays" sounds more matter-of-fact than "My cousin John is normal, but his twin Chris is retarded." Does "retarded" make you cringe? After all, is anyone "normal?"

Although originally intended for improving language-use regarding people with disabilities, using specific person-first language helps clarify and personalize your words through rhetorical sensitivity.

Using Verbal Language

Since language is symbolic, it is necessary to be as clear and precise as possible when using words. You need to consider the other person's frame of reference and whether or not he/she will share your interpretation of the language used. If not, it is important to adjust your vocabulary level and word choice to fit the listener(s). For example, you need to be careful not to use technical terms that are beyond your listener's experience.

"Sticks and stones will break my bones, but words will never hurt me," may not be totally true. Words can, according to the findings, "cause physical harm."[94] In investigating emotionally abused women, it was reported that they showed strikingly similar illnesses "to those affecting physically abused women."[95] As a result of these findings, health-care providers are being encouraged to determine whether psychologically fragile women suffer from sexual or physical abuse.[96]

Male/Masculine—
Female/Feminine Communication

"Some people become angry at the mere suggestion that women and men are different."[97] For example, "[In 2005] Harvard University president Lawrence Summers suffered condemnation and jeopardized his job for suggesting that the under-representation of women in engineering and some scientific fields may be due to in part to inherent differences in the intellectual abilities of the sexes."[98] Those who took Summers's side contended that "among people who do the research, it's not so controversial. As one female researcher says, 'I know it's not politically correct to say this and I've been torn for years between my politics and what science is telling us. But I believe that women actually perceive the world differently than men.'"[99] According to a neuropsychiatrist, "Advances in neuro-imaging and neuro-endrocrinology have begun supplying exciting new insights into how women and men use their brains differently."[100] On the other hand, a prominent psychologist, "examined decades of studies that compared the emotional and behavioral lives of men and women and concluded that most differences between the genders center on the area of the brain devoted to emotions and memory. Because they [women] have 'mirror neurons' they are also better at observing emotions in others."[101] But another states, "Nurture plays such a huge role in human behavior that focusing on biology is next to meaningless."[102]

This controversy has directly affected the field of communication. In the early 1990s, research in the area seemed to strongly indicate that there were vast gender communication differences. However, a set of communication scholars has investigated the research background of one of these early works that "makes quantitative claims based on thin sources, generalizes from small and unrepresentative study samples, and overlooks studies that support other explanations of differences in conversational styles."[103] The investigators contend that "the best evidence on gender and communication suggests that men and women are far more alike than different."[104]

While scholars accept that there are many similarities, there also appears to be enough evidence beyond that of the initial writings in the field that indicates that differences between male and female communication do exist—enough so that the different tendencies deserve to be discussed.[105]

In this discussion of male and female tendencies, please be aware that the statements are assertions based on research findings. This means that any individual male or female may not follow the patterns described. Testing looks for norm patterns, patterns of the general members of the group. You, for example, may fall outside of the statistical sample description for the particular gender or sex being described.

SEX AND GENDER

"*Sex* refers to one's biological or physical self [male/female] while *gender* refers to one's psychological, social, and interactive characteristics [masculine/feminine]."[106]

From the sexual perspective, biological research has "produced a body of findings which paints a remarkably consistent picture of sexual asymmetry. The sexes are different because the brain, the chief administrative and emotional organ of life, is differently constructed in men and in women. It processes information in a different way, which results in different perceptions, priorities and behavior."[107]

These biological underpinnings can have a profound effect on communicating. For example, scientists suggest that the gender differences in the brain may account for some communication differences. A woman's ability to use both sides of the brain more rapidly than men may prompt her to make idea links and emotional responses more efficiently. Men may mistakenly view the women's rapid brain skill as "flighty" because men are unable to make the same kinds of links.[108]

Parallel to this view are findings about gender. This research shows that "gender is socially constructed. Because of the lessons we learn about ourselves and our world, people may develop differently. As children and later as adults, females and males, no matter the culture, often are treated differently, so it is hardly surprising that our ways of knowing and ways of being are distinct. In the Euro-American culture, from infancy on, males generally learn [perceived] masculine traits—independence, self-absorption, competition, aggression."[109] "Men value power, competency, efficiency, and achievement. They are more interested in objects and things than people and feelings."[110] "Females learn feminine traits—dependence, other-absorption, nurturance, sensitivity."[111] However, recognize that there are some children who learn reverse gender roles.

Another factor to keep in mind is that the terms *men's traits* and *women's traits* really refer to "masculine traits" and "feminine traits." In fact, it has been suggested that discussion of male and female communication should refer to "mannish tendencies" and "womanish tendencies."[112]

Remember that gender tendencies are not sexual descriptors. Someone whose gestures, walk, voice pitch, and language better fit the stereotype of what a member of the opposite sex uses does not make the user sexually that gender. These patterns may not be the same in the other gender.

Interested in finding out how you perceive yourself on a masculine/feminine scale? If so, do Activity 4.4.

HOW MEN AND WOMEN COMMUNICATE SIMILARLY/DIFFERENTLY

Accepting that males and females generally communicate in somewhat the same patterns, it can also be reasoned that cross-cultural differences may also exist. "Men use speech to report, to compete, to gain attention, and to maintain their positions in a social hierarchy. Women use speech to gain rapport, maintain relationships, and reflect a sense of community."[113] Women often use language to connect with others, while men are more inclined to use language to enhance their independence and status.

Some communication differences probably have developed because of the way boys and girls have been raised in U.S. society. Today, by participating more in competitive sports and going to the highest levels in organizations, women are learning

ACTIVITY 4.4
Bem Sex-Role Inventory

Indicate the degree to which each statement is true of you.

Write 1 if the statement is never or almost never true of you.
Write 2 if it is usually not true of you.
Write 3 if it is sometimes but infrequently true of you.
Write 4 if it is occasionally true of you.
Write 5 if it is usually true of you.
Write 6 if it is always or almost always true of you.

_____ 1. I am self-reliant.
_____ 2. I am cheerful.
_____ 3. I am independent.
_____ 4. I am affectionate.
_____ 5. I have a strong personality.
_____ 6. I am sympathetic.
_____ 7. I act as a leader.
_____ 8. I am eager to soothe hurt feelings.
_____ 9. I am analytical.
_____10. I am warm.

The odd-numbered items represent a stereotypical "masculine" personality and the even-numbered items represent a stereotypical "feminine" personality. Add your responses to the odd items to obtain your "masculine" score. Then add your responses to the even items to obtain your "feminine" score. Total scores above twenty-two in either category are considered high and scores below twenty-two are considered low.

If you scored high on masculine and low on feminine, you would be classified by this instrument as having those personality characteristics that research shows are indicative of a person called "masculine." If you scored low on masculine and high on feminine, you would be classified by this instrument as "feminine." High scores on both lead to classification as "androgynous," a balance of both masculine and feminine personality characteristics, and low scores on both lead to classification as "undifferentiated." These classifications exist apart from your biological-sex categorization. Both males and females fall into all four personality categories.

Source: Adapted from Bem, S. L. (1974). The measurement of psychological androgyny. *Journal of Consulting and Clinical Psychology, 42,* 155–162. The original inventory developed by Bem contains sixty items, twenty masculine, twenty feminine, and twenty neutral (neither masculine nor feminine exclusively).

how to communicate when they are part of a team instead of only the traditional focus on one friend, or a small group. Girls traditionally have not been expected to boast about their successes. Girls tend to express their preferences as suggestions. Boys say, "Gimme that!" and "Get out of here!" Girls say, "Can we do this?" and "How about doing that?" By age three, communication tends to differ between boys and girls.[114]

Both male and female communication styles are both valid, and each can work well in certain situations. The problems come when people are misunderstood because of their communication styles. Because of today's increasing role of women in leadership positions, some of these patterns of boy and girl communication have changed, but there is still not a complete elimination of general cultural masculine and feminine role stereotypes.

Do you see gender patterns related to communication? Which of these do you think tends to be true, false, or questionable? *As stated earlier, please be aware that the "answers" are assertions based on generalized research findings. This means that any individual, male or female, may not follow the patterns described.*

1. Women use more words to make their point.	True	False	?
2. Men are more competitive in their speaking.	True	False	?
3. Men tend to be more task oriented.	True	False	?
4. Women are more supportive conversationalists.	True	False	?
5. Men are more direct in their communication.	True	False	?
6. Women disclose more personal information to others than men do.	True	False	?
7. Women have larger vocabularies for describing emotions and aesthetics.	True	False	?

1. Questionable. "The myth is that women use many more words per day than men." Recent research, using an electronically activated recorder (EAR), says the "data fail to reveal a reliable sex difference in daily word use. Women and men both use on the average about 16,000 words per day, with very large individual differences around this mean."[115]

2. Yes, *men tend to use a more competitive style in communication.* Men do tend to interrupt more than women do. Indeed, research on male-female communication patterns found that 96 percent of the interruptions and 100 percent of the overlaps in mixed pairs in daily conversations were performed by men.[116]

3. Yes, *most men are more task oriented in their communication and women are more likely to be maintenance oriented.* Traditionally, men have tended to expect results and women have been more cooperative and process-oriented. Women characteristically use tentative phrases such as "I guess" and turn direct statements into indirect ones. For example, a woman may say, "Don't you think it would be better to send that report first?" A man will typically say, "Send the report."[117] Men will say, "What's next on the agenda?" and "What's the bottom line?" Women tend to ask, "You haven't spoken; what do you think?" or "How does everyone feel about this?"

4. Yes, *women tend to use more supportive communication.* They ask more questions and work harder than men do to keep the conversational ball rolling. Generally,

women ask questions three times as often as men do. Women often feel that it is their role to make sure that the conversation goes well, and they assume that if it is not proceeding well, they have to remedy the situation.

5. Yes, *women tend to use less direct communication than men.* A man may ask a woman, "Will you please go to the store?" He wants something; he thinks that he has the status to ask for it and get it. But a woman asking a man may say, "Gee, I really need a few things from the store, but I'm so tired." Often she speaks this way because she thinks she is in a low-status position that does not include the right to make a request.[118] A man may describe the manner in which a woman makes a request as "beating around the bush," and he may ask, "Why, if you want something, don't you just ask for it?" Women also tend to use more **tag questions**—questions added onto the end of statements, such as "That movie was terrific, *don't you think?*" The intent is to get the partner to enter the conversation. Men sometimes construe the tag question as continuing what has already been discussed.

6. Yes, *women often tell more personal information than men do.* Women use vocabulary that is concerned about people, showing concern about emotions.

7. Yes, *women use a wide variety of words to describe emotions and aesthetics.* Women tend to have a larger repertoire of words to describe what they are feeling. Women also have broader vocabularies that can finitely separate aesthetics such as colors. Men, for example, will describe the color as red; women describe specific shadings such as ruby, magenta, or rose.

Other factors also seem to be present in masculine-feminine patterns:

- *A woman may feel disrespected if a man rejects her suggestion.* She may even stop trusting him.[119] But "when a woman resists a man's solutions, he feels his competence is being questioned. As a result he feels mistrusted, unappreciated, and stops caring. His willingness to listen understandably lessens."[120]
- *Women complain that men don't listen.* One difference is that men tend to be less responsive nonverbally, so they don't seem to listen when in fact they do. Second, men tend to go straight to the solutions, whereas women often want to talk and vent. So, women may feel like men's solution-orientation is a lack of listening, when it's really a different response orientation.[121]
- *"Men are more interested in visual stimulation, physical details. Women are more interested in tactile sensations, emotional overtones, and intimacy."*[122]
- *Men prefer to talk about actions rather than emotions.*[123] Over lunch, the guys may throw around a football, while women talk about their lives.
- *Men tend to pull away and silently think about what's bothering them, while women want to talk about it.*[124]
- *Men tend to want a kind of love that is accepting, trusting, and appreciative; women primarily need a kind of love that is caring, understanding, and respectful.*[125]

Whose communication patterns are right? For the past decade, some people have believed that men need to change since it is perceived that women are more effective communicators and more sensitive to human needs. In fact, a review of communication books leads to the conclusion that feminine patterns of being supportive, talking through issues, and not interrupting are positive; however, the task orientation, the directness, and the lack of tentativeness of males also gain points. Some communication theorists think that one approach to a "best" interpersonal communication can use both approaches and that the most effective communicators are androgynous. Effectiveness means flexibility and adaptation to the situation. For example, a person may behave both emphatically and objectively, and both assertively and cooperatively, which increases the person's adaptability—one of the qualities of the competent communicator. Therefore, the overall thinking in regard to effective communication seems to indicate that a person who has more **androgenic communication** qualities, a combination of masculine and feminine communication qualities, and who uses the communication style that works best in a particular situation, is going to be most effective.

Key Terms

verbal language

social reality

language

Gestural Theory

cybernetic process

Language-Explosion Theory

Significant-Other Theory

Language Instinct Theory

Social Construct of Reality Theory

Sapir-Whorf Hypothesis

argot

linguistics

syntactic rules

denotative words

connotative words

semantic differential

two-valued orientation

language distortion

vagueness

doublespeak

inferences

cultural-negative language

dialect

accent

standard dialects

nonstandard dialects

Standard American English

slang

inarticulates

Ebonics/Black English

code switching

Spanglish

bilingual

Asian-American Dialect

Native American languages

person-first language

tag questions

androgenic communication

Competencies Check-Up

Interested in finding out what you learned in this chapter and how you use the information? If so, take this competencies check-up.

Directions: Indicate the extent that each statement applies to you:

1—Never   *2—Seldom*   *3—Sometimes*   *4—Often*   *5—Usually*

____1. I reflect on the connection between language, self-perception, and self-esteem, attitudes, and behavior.

___ 2. I adapt my language to the appropriate style for writing, speaking, listening, and reading.

___ 3. I use descriptive, precise, and concrete language to increase my clarity.

___ 4. I strive to use suitable grammar, and use argot only when appropriate, and use clear pronunciation, so that my language use contributes to an ease of understanding.

___ 5. I am patient and respectful toward people who use my language as a second language. When speaking, I articulate clearly and say things in multiple ways to increase the chances of understanding.

___ 6. I check perceptions, ask about connotative meanings, and request clarification of words that may be unclear or unfamiliar to me.

___ 7. I guard against language distortion such as ambiguity, vagueness, and double-speak by using lucid and precise language.

___ 8. I am careful about my use of inference.

___ 9. I refrain from biased language, culturally negative language, stereotyping, callous, belittling, or tasteless labels.

___10. I am patient and never make fun of people who have a language dialect different from my own.

___11. I strive to use standard pronunciation in general U.S. American communication contexts.

___12. I am careful to use slang appropriately and carefully.

___13. I avoid inarticulates.

___14. I am culturally sensitive regarding gender, ethnicity, and other factors in my use of language.

___15. I use language in ways that are memorable.

Scoring: If your score is above 45, you probably have basic competencies in your verbal communication. Do you have some low items that suggest an area where you need to do some work?

I-Can Plan!

Think about the chapter information and how effectively you use verbal language. Write out a specific chart of strategies you can follow to implement new skills. Then take action to improve.

Activities

1. List the pros and cons of this idea: "Accepting Black English as a language is a sell-out to street slang and abandons good sense and kids' futures." You may want to go beyond the discussion in this chapter or your opinion, and conduct research on the topic.

2. State your position regarding this statement: "Every person in the United States should be required to speak Standard American English in order to obtain citizenship." Be prepared to defend your stand.

3. Give an example of doublespeak from your personal experience or the media. What do you think the person was trying to hide or manipulate?

4. Write down one phrase or expression that has meaning only for a select group. It may be an ethnic expression or an in-group reference. The other students then read the expression and try to figure out what it means.

5. What are five words that have different meanings in different contexts? List all the possible definitions for each word.

6. Identify someone who speaks a nonstandard dialect. Write down some examples of her or his pronunciation and language selections. Share the information with the class. (You are trying to learn about nonstandard dialects, not belittle the user.)

7. Your class will conduct a debate on the proposition: "English should be the official language of the United States."

CHAPTER 5

Nonverbal Communication

Learning Outcomes

After reading this chapter, you should be able to:

• Describe the value of nonverbal communication.
• Identify the sources of nonverbal messages.
• Analyze the influence of emotions on nonverbal communication.
• Illustrate the characteristics of nonverbal communication.
• Compare independent and dependent interaction of verbal and nonverbal communication.
• Apply categories of nonverbal communication.
• Attempt to evaluate nonverbal communication within a cultural framework.
• Explain how people send and receive messages nonverbally.

The cocktail party was almost over when Tina came to say goodbye. "Are you leaving alone?" said the surprised hostess. Tina shook her head.

"See that tall blond guy near the kitchen? He'll take me home."

"You mean Jim?"

"I guess so. We haven't been introduced."

"Then how do you know he'll take you home?" the hostess demanded.

"We've made eye contact. We haven't said a word, but we've been communicating for the last ten minutes."

"Across a crowded room? Honestly, Tina . . ."

But Tina wasn't listening to the hostess. She was looking at Jim, as he stood talking to another man. While the hostess watched, Tina caught Jim's eye, smiled, glanced at the clock and then at the door. A moment later, as Tina pecked the hostess on the cheek and sauntered toward the door, Jim smiled, clapped his friend on the shoulder and turned away. He and Tina reached the front door at virtually the same moment.

Do you believe that while communicating with another person your *words* carry the majority of the meaning of the message? Do you believe that you make the majority of decisions about people by what they say? If you answered *yes* to both of these questions, you are mistaken. There has long been an awareness that it is possible to communicate a great deal without using verbal language. We are also aware that nonverbal acts are symbolic acts closely connected to any talk in progress. They don't merely reveal information, they *represent* meaning. Nonverbal communication is a major force in our lives. Nonverbal expressions of happiness, surprise, anger, disgust/contempt, and sadness appear to be used and understood the world over.[1]

To illustrate the concept of message sending, think back to the last time you walked into a room filled with strangers. Before a word was spoken, a great deal of information was exchanged. How did you decide to whom you would speak? What clues did you look for and how did you interpret them? Which actions and characteristics did you focus on?

Place a check next to any of the items on this list that you might have looked for or reacted to when you were in that room filled with strangers:

_____Body shape, whether she or he was fat or thin, muscular or flabby, short or tall.
_____The clothing the person was wearing, whether it was clean or dirty, in or out of style.
_____Whether the person had tattoos.
_____Jewelry, such as a wedding band or piercings.
_____Eye contact, such as whether the other person looked at you and how long eye contact was sustained.
_____Facial expression, whether the person was smiling, frowning, or looking bored or puzzled.
_____Distance, the space between you and the other person, such as how close you could get before the other person backed up or broke eye contact.
_____Voice, such as whether the person's voice was nasal, throaty, or resonant.
_____Body movements, such as the person's gestures and stance.
_____Touch, such as whether the person was touching others, or how he/she responded to the touch of others.

If you checked any of the listed items, you were using nonverbal cues and clues.

Nonverbal Communication—Defined

"To most people, **nonverbal communication** refers to communication effected by means other than words (assuming words are the verbal element)."[2] People interpret body communication, perhaps without knowing they are doing so, and often without even knowing what it means.

LEARNING EXPERIENCE: Interested in finding out what you know about nonverbal communication? If so, do Activity 5.1.

ACTIVITY 5.1
What Do You Know about
Nonverbal Communication?

Take this true and false test to find out what you know about some basic concepts of nonverbal communication. If you think the answer is *true* put the letter "T" on the line provided. If you think the answer is *false* put the letter "F" on the line provided.

_____1. People from all societies use time in the same way. For example, all societies agree on what "to be on time" means.

_____2. The person with the most power in a group is the one who looks most often at others.

_____3. In the Euro-American culture men touch men more than women touch women.

_____4. If the communication signals you receive are contradictory, you should pay more attention to the verbal than the nonverbal.

_____5. Most people feel comfortable when a person with whom they are involved in conversation stands about one foot away from them.

_____6. African American males and Euro-American males display the same duration of eye contact when speaking to members of their cultural group.

_____7. Slow, deliberate speaking conveys power.

_____8. Extended silence is a sign of breakdown and stress in communication.

Key:
According to research in the field of nonverbal communication here are the correct answers:

1. False. Time is culturally based.
2. False. High-power people receive, not give the most frequent eye contact, though people in power feel that if they need to show authority they can visually invade the territory of a subordinate.
3. False. Euro-American women touch each other more frequently. Men in the Euro-American culture have generally been conditioned to touch other men only under specific conditions.
4. False. Nonverbal tends to be more accurate.
5. False. Space distance is a cultural matter. In some societies, such as the Euro-American, people generally feel comfortable if someone is more than three feet away from them.
6. False. Euro-Americans normally retain eye-contact of between three and ten seconds when speaking to someone. African Americans often retain eye contract for longer periods of time in conversation.

(*continued*)

ACTIVITY 5.1 (*continued*)

7. False. Fast tempo is more dominant and more persuasive.
8. False. Complete agreement and harmony may also be accompanied by extended silences.

Scoring: Scores of 6 or over indicate you are aware of the basic principles of nonverbal communication. A group of college freshmen and sophomores given this quiz scored an average grade of 4.

Source: Some of this exercise is based on Burgoon, J. K., Buller, D. B., & Woodall, W. G. (1996). *Nonverbal communication: The unspoken dialogue* (2nd ed.). New York: McGraw-Hill.

Remember, as you read this chapter, that research generalizations and expert observation about cultural groups cannot be applied to every culture, every individual, or in every context. These generalizations are designed to make you more alert to interpreting the communication around you. For example, not all Euro-Americans want three feet of space between themselves and another person as they speak. Some want more, some less space; however, since research shows that the average Euro-American does want a 3-foot bubble of space around them in personal interactions, the generalization is stated.

Characteristics of Nonverbal Communication

"The figure most cited to support the claim that nonverbal communication is more important than verbal messages is the estimate that 93 percent of all meaning in a social situation comes from nonverbal information, while only 7 percent comes from verbal information."[3] The figure is deceiving, however. It is based on two 1976 studies that compared vocal cues with facial cues.[4] Other studies have not supported the 93 percent, but it is agreed that both children and adults rely more on nonverbal cues than on verbal cues in determining social meaning.[5]

Normally we consider how nonverbal signals operate together in a **cluster**, an interactive grouping. When you interpret a message, for example, you consider the person's vocal elements, facial expression, clothing, and gestures *together* as a package, leading to meaning.

Also important in observing nonverbal actions is **congruency**, whether the present actions are parallel to or different from past actions. For example, think of a female you know well. What are her nonverbal signs when she is happy? If she came into the room and displayed that set of nonverbal actions, you would likely assume that she was happy. There is congruency, past actions parallel to present actions. On the other hand, if she displayed a different set of signs, and when asked if she was happy,

Like the variation of words, nonverbal communication can have many meanings depending on the people involved, the context, and culture.

and said, "Yes," you probably would not believe her verbal message. There is a lack of congruency, the past actions don't parallel to the present actions.

Like the variation of words, nonverbal communication can have many different meanings depending on the people involved, the context, and culture. A jiggling foot could mean a person is nervous or that the person jiggles her foot as a habit. A quick rub across the nose may mean the person is lying, or it may mean an itchy nose. A very jittery person could signify that the individual is lying or simply that they are communicatively apprehensive and find the setting uncomfortable.

Often we use nonverbal communication to manage conversations, without even realizing it. When you are ready to leave, you may look at your watch, which your partner interprets as a "wrap it up" signal. If your partner doesn't get the message, you may position yourself toward the door, stand up, or even make a move toward the door. Often we use our body and voice this way to create signals about engaging or disengaging in communication. We may be unaware of the way we are sending signals. When you think a class should be over, you may put away your computer or notes. When the professor sees everyone packed up, the professor knows the students have turned off their classroom listening ears. Students may not actively think, "I'm going to put away my things in hopes of ending the lecture," but their behaviors send a message.

When a woman with a speech problem writes out her order at Burger King, the clerk smiles, nods, maintains a relaxed posture, and looks back and forth between the customer and her paper. The message appears to be that the cashier is glad to wait on the customer. In another case, an impatient cashier has tense muscles, taps her finger on the counter, crosses her arms. The message seems to be that she doesn't want to wait on this customer. She may be signaling that she wants the interaction to end.

The Basis for Nonverbal Communication

Your school and family spend years teaching you how to use words through vocabulary, spelling, syntax, and grammar. However, if you are typical, you received little, if any, instruction on how to use nonverbal communication.

NEUROLOGICAL PROGRAMS

Innate neurological programs are automatic nonverbal reactions to stimuli with which you were born. These nonverbal "automatic responses" are **reflexive reactions** caused by neurological need drives. For example, we blink our eyes automatically when we hear a loud noise (survival drive) or when a pebble hits the windshield of the car we are driving (survival and territorial drive). Your stomach muscles tighten and your hands sweat when you feel insecure (security drive). When someone gets too close you may step back (territorial drive).

That humans are born with some nonverbal tendencies, is illustrated by the fact that "people born blind move their hands when they talk, although they've never seen anyone do it."[6]

CULTURAL INFLUENCES

Reflective reactions are the nonverbals you use because you were taught them by your family, friends, and culture. In this case, you *reflect* back the nonverbal communication of people you observe in your life.

As we discuss the influence of culture on nonverbal signs, note that generalizations are presented. These are based, whenever possible, on research findings and expert observations. They are in no way intended to lead to the conclusion that all members of the cultural group noted conform to the generalized patterns.

As you were growing up, you noticed the nonverbal actions of your family and important people around you. These vocal, bodily, time, and contextual cues were grounded in the culture, including nationality, ethnicity, gender, and similar influences. As a research anthropologist indicates, "The important thing to remember is that culture is very persistent. In this country, we've noted the existence of culture patterns that determine [physical] distance between people in the third and fourth generations of some families, despite their prolonged contact with people of very different cultural heritages."[7] Cultural influences may be easy to identify. Typically, Italians and Israelis use their hands when they speak. In contrast, the Japanese and British tend to use hand gestures less often.

"He didn't look at me once. I know he's guilty. Never trust a person who doesn't look you in the eye."

"Americans smile at strangers. I don't know what to think of that."

"Americans seem cold. They seem to get upset when you stand close to them."

These statements were made by an American police officer, a Russian engineer, and a Jordanian teacher about interactions they had with someone from a culture other than their own. Their comments demonstrate how people can misinterpret nonverbal communication that has different patterns than their own."[8]

"Universal emotions, such as happiness, fear, sadness, are expressed in a similar nonverbal way throughout the world. There are, however, nonverbal differences across cultures that may be a source of confusion for foreigners."[9]

When a person knows multiples languages, the individual is likely to use hand gestures appropriate for the language currently used. Fiorello LaGuardia, New York City's mayor in the 1930s and early 1940s, carried on his political campaigns in English, Italian, and Yiddish—the languages of the major voting blocs in the city at that time. LaGuardia used one set of gestures for speaking English, another for Italian, and still another for Yiddish.

The meaning of nonverbal behaviors can vary based on a person's idiosyncrasies, their culture, and the context. An Arabic male, for example, commonly strokes his chin to show appreciation for a woman, whereas a Portuguese man does it by pulling his ear. But in Italy a similar kind of ear tugging is a deliberate insult.

An individual's nonverbal communication is influenced by an **action chain**, which is a behavioral sequence of standard steps for reaching a goal. When steps are missed or go out of order, the participants have to start all over again. These action chains vary according to cultural influences. Euro-Americans engaged in business dealings with Arabs, for example, should understand and adhere to that culture's action chains of hospitality in order to be successful. The first meeting with an Arab businessperson is often devoted to fact-finding and creating a relationship. No commitments are implied or made, but the initial session is usually lengthy and thorough. Based on the pattern of working quickly so as not to waste time, Euro-Americans often find the Arab process tedious. The next meeting is usually taken up with additional rituals. It is not unusual, then, for a business deal to take a long time to complete.[10]

The communication patterns used in gestures also vary according to culture. The thumb-and-forefinger-in-a-circle gesture means "okay" in the United States. In France or Belgium, however, the gesture means the recipient is worth zero. The same finger gesture in Greece and Turkey is a sexual invitation. Similarly, an index finger tapping to the temple with the other fingers curled against the palm usually means "you're smart" in the United States, whereas it communicates "You're stupid" in most of Europe."[11]

People communicate by their use of space, which is affected by culture. Arabs, South Americans, and Eastern Europeans generally favor being close to their conversational partners. This closeness may make some Euro-Americans feel uncomfortable. The same discomfort may be felt by many Germans and Scandinavians, who prefer distance between themselves and the other conversant.

Nonverbal Communication and Emotions

If you think about a time when you were trying to talk but felt very upset, you may remember your voice or hands quivering, your body becoming tense, or voices being raised. The physiology of emotions affects the way people interact nonverbally. Many people who are nervous about social interactions report that their throats tighten and their stomach muscles contract when they are at a social event. Under tension, the pitch of the voice may also rise because vocal chords tighten.

If you are upset, a person may seem closer and larger because of your heightened emotions. To a frightened child, an adult can seem like a giant. Because of this emotional distortion, in dealing with crying or hysterical children, adults should kneel to talk with them. By the same token, police interrogators and trial lawyers know that moving in close to an interviewee may cause the person to become upset and say something they wouldn't normally say.

Outside influences can change your nonverbal communication. If you are extremely tired, for example, your voice and body may not show its usual energy. If a person drinks too much alcohol, speech may become slurred, inhibitions reduced, and bodily movements change. A person under the influence of alcohol or drugs does not walk, talk, or have the same bodily controls as when that person is sober. This has resulted in the development of drunk-driver-walking-a-straight-line and touching-the-nose tests, with the assumption being that a sober person can perform these acts, while a drunk person normally can't.

The Relationship between Words and Nonverbal Cues

Nonverbal cues are used with words in four possible ways. Nonverbal actions can substitute for words, complement words, conflict with words, and accent words.

THE SUBSTITUTING RELATIONSHIP

A mother standing on the wedding dance floor caught her adult son's eye across the room. The mother raised a finger and wiggled it toward her while striking a dance pose. The son shook his head from side-to-side. This communication is a case where nonverbal actions totally substitute for words. The mother asked her son to dance, and the son said "no" without uttering a word. Substitution is when two people use means other than words to communicate, thus creating a **substituting relationship**. In this case, their distance apart, the noisy wedding reception, the crowded dance floor between them, and the desire for a private exchange prompted the mother and son to have their conversation without words.

THE COMPLEMENTING RELATIONSHIP

While explaining to the workmen the way she wanted the wall repaired, the woman climbed on a ladder and said: "Paint to this point [she used her finger to show the stopping point], then add a wood strip here [she ran her hand along the wall where the wood strip should go]. In this communication the words and nonverbal cues work together to make each more effective, and thus showed a **complementing relationship**. Complementing is a typical way we use nonverbal actions to clarify and emphasize our words.

THE CONFLICTING RELATIONSHIP

When actions conflict with verbal messages, thus forming a **conflicting relationship** between the verbal and nonverbal, as a receiver you should rely more on the nonverbal aspect of communication. Nonverbal clues are often more difficult to fake than verbal ones. When you were young, you might have been surprised to find that your parents knew when you were not telling the truth. There you stood, looking at the floor, twisting your hands, with a flushed face, as you insisted, "I didn't do it." The father of the modern psychology movement said, "He that has eyes to see and ears to hear may convince himself that no mortal can keep a secret. If his lips are silent he chatters with his fingertips; betrayal oozes out of him at every pore."[12]

Lie detectors read the body's nonverbal reactions by measuring changes in blood pressure, respiration, and skin response—in other words, by attempting to detect a conflicting relationship between the verbal and nonverbal. This is accomplished by measuring body temperature, perspiration, or checking heart rate on an electrocardiograph machine. "Most psychologists agree that there is little evidence that polygraph tests can accurately detect lies."[13] The estimate of about 61 percent, led the National Research Council to conclude that regarding national security "the machines are simply too inaccurate."[14] However, a new approach, the functional magnetic resonance imaging machine (fMRI) is promising. The fMRI scans the brain and could well morph into a forensic tool far more potent than the flawed polygraph test.[15]

THE ACCENTING RELATIONSHIP

After two minutes in time out, the mother told her toddler to come to her. "Look at me please," the mother said gently. When the child didn't look, the mother gently held her child's face and moved it toward her face while repeating, "Look at me please." Pounding your finger on the table as you say, "Do it now," emphasizes or accents the words. These are both examples of **accenting relationships**. Accents are a type of exclamation mark, italics, or ALL CAPS nonverbal cue that goes with the words.

Concepts of Nonverbal Communication

Some basic concepts of nonverbal communication are:

For emotional content, nonverbal communication is more accurate and easier communication than words. Whereas words are best for conveying specific ideas, nonverbal communication may be best for conveying feelings and emotions. For example, the emotions felt at a funeral of a loved one are communicated more concisely and effec-

Substitution is when someone uses nonverbal communication instead of spoken words to communicate thoughts or feelings.

tively by crying and hand patting than are attempts to put those emotions into words. *Culture influences the way people communicate emotions.* In many cultures, outward signs of emotion are accepted as natural. People from the Middle East, for example, in Israel, are expressive and animated. In other cultures, nonverbal restraint is valued. For the Japanese, external signs are often considered a mark of rudeness and an invasion of privacy. The same is true in the British Isles. Think about what the implications are of the British expression, "Keep a stiff upper lip."

Nonverbal communication conveys meaning naturally. We cannot easily control nonverbal actions. Because nonverbal behaviors are, for the most part, performed without thought, they are relatively free of distortion or deception, especially in comparison to the more easily controlled verbal messages. It is difficult to bring nonverbal behaviors under conscious control. For example, this is true of a flushing face, stammering, or jaw clenching when a person is nervous or embarrassed. The behavior is automatic, an unconscious reflex.

Nonverbal acts work better than words when you want to soften communication. If you think something you might say is likely to elicit a rebuke or embarrassment, you run less risk of these reactions if you avoid using words. For example, if you want to know whether your date likes you, and are unwilling to ask directly, gently taking hold of the other person's hand and gauging the response (pulling away or allowing the hand-holding) may provide you with the information you need.

Nonverbal behaviors indicate how you should interpret the verbal messages you receive. Consider the difference between someone saying, "I think I understand the directions to your apartment," in a confident tone of voice and someone saying the same thing in a hesitant tone, accompanied by head-scratching and raised eyebrows. In the first situation you might feel pleased with your direction-giving; in the second one you probably should consider how to restate your message to make it clearer. The key to interpreting the meaning of words is to look at what is "said" nonverbally. Vocal pitch, softness of tone, posture, eye contact, facial expression, movement, gestures, and clothing are some of the nonverbal cues that give communication meaning.

As with all communication, the concepts just expressed must be put into a cultural context. There are cultures that rely heavily on verbal language and others that put more stock in nonverbal messages. Anthropological studies show that cultures can be classified and placed on a continuum according to the emphasis they put on verbal versus nonverbal messages as tools for carrying meaning.[16] At one end of the continuum are German, French, Scandinavian, North American, and English societies, which tend to believe that verbal messages are extremely important. Japanese, Chinese, and Koreans, on the other hand, believe that most meaning is found in a physical context. People know what is being felt without having to talk. The Korean language contains the word *nunch'i,* which means "communicating through the eyes."[17]

Classifications of Nonverbal Communication

Nonverbal communication can be classified or grouped according to similarities. The generally accepted divisions are: kinesics, space, paravocalics, time, smell, and taste and their subdivisions.[18]

KINESICS—BODY COMMUNICATION

Kinesics is the study of the use of the body to communicate. You communicate through the gestures you use, the way you move and stand, the expressions on your face, the glint in your eyes, and the way you combine these variables to open or close channels.

Specifics studied in the area of kinesics are the face, eyes, gestures, posture, walk, stance, artifacts, and physical characteristics.

The Face

"The 80 muscles of the face can create more than 7,000 expressions."[19] These expressions range from communicating our internal states, such as anger or fear, to carrying messages to others of whether you want to interrupt what they are saying, or are interested and want them to continue to speak. The face sends information about our personality, interests, responsiveness, and emotional states. What we think about another person is often based on that person's facial expressions as we observe or interact with them.

We have more data about the face than about any other physical nonverbal communication tool.[20] What has been determined is that facial expressions are very complex. Facial expressions are movements of such brief duration that if you don't watch carefully, you miss the message. An upturn of the corners of the mouth, nasal cavity expansions, an eyebrow arching, a dropping jaw, or open mouth are so subtle that they are often overlooked and the message is missed.

The Eyes

Raising an eyebrow, squinting, or a long slow blink are nonverbal cues that can give meaning. The eye, unlike other organs of the body, is an extension of the brain.[21] Of all our features, our eyes are the most revealing. Often they communicate without our even knowing it. For example, when the pupils of our eyes are dilated, we may appear friendlier, warmer, and more attractive. Sayings such as, "Look at the sparkle in her eye," and "He couldn't look me straight in the eye," have meaning.

Something that seems simple—eye blinks—can convey meaning. For example, nervousness is often cued by the slowness or rapidity of eye blinks. The normal blink rate for someone speaking is thirty-one to fifty blinks per minute. During the first presidential debate of 1996 between President Clinton and his Republican opponent, Bob Dole, polls indicated that Mr. Dole was considered to be very nervous. A review of the videotapes of the debate indicated that he had averaged 147 blinks per minute, about three times the normal rate.[22]

Pupilometrics is a theory of nonverbal communication, which suggests that eyes dilate when they are focused on a pleasurable object, and contract when focused on those which are not pleasurable.[23] Enlarged pupils can signify interest and contracted pupils can reflect boredom. Thus, aware teachers often watch the pupils of their students' eyes to ascertain their interest in a particular lesson.

Like other types of nonverbal communication, the use of eyes is often related to cultural expectations. Euro-Americans often complain when they think non-Euro-Americans stare at them too intensely or hold a glance too long. This discomfort with extended eye contact is because Euro-Americans tend to be comfortable with a gaze of between three to ten seconds. A gaze that lasts longer than ten seconds may make a Euro-American feel uncomfortable. A gaze that lasts less than three seconds may indicate disinterest or uncertainty. Gazes of over ten seconds may indicate strong emotional feelings, such as rage or sexual attraction.

With enough distance between people, however, a long eye gaze may be acceptable. Try this experiment. As you walk down a corridor, notice that you can look at someone for a long period of time until you or the other person suddenly feel uncomfortable and glance away. If you are Euro-American, this usually happens at a distance of about ten feet.

Like people of many Western cultures, when U.S. Americans feel emotional or want to hide their inner feelings, they often will avoid eye contact. Thus the child who has eaten forbidden candy will not look at a questioning parent during the interrogation. Remember when you were told, "Look me in the eye and say that"?

Because of the powerful messages that come through the eyes, some people seek to hide their eyes. "Since people can't control the responses of their eyes," reported one source, "many Arabs wear dark glasses, even indoors."[24] This is especially true if they are negotiating.

Certain groups of Native Americans also feel uncomfortable with unbroken eye contact. So strong is that orientation that Navajos tell a folktale about a terrible monster called He-Who-Kills-With-His-Eyes. The legend teaches the Navajo child that a stare is literally an evil eye and implies a sexual and aggressive assault.[25] Communication between Black and Native Americans and white Americans is yet another area where cultural differences show. "In North America, people of African American and First Nations origin usually prefer to make far less eye contact than Caucasians do."[26]

In Euro-American society, gender also affects eye contact usage. Women tend to look more often at their communication partners, look at one another more, hold eye contact longer, and appear to value eye contact more than men do.[27]

Eye movements, which have been studied extensively by neurolinguistic psychologists, indicate that each of us has patterns of eye shifts that reflect whether a person is thinking in past, present, or future tenses and is "seeing" the information in either pictures or words.[28] A study of *eye accessing cues* indicates "whether a person is thinking in images, sounds, self-talk, or through their feelings, their eyes move in patterns."[29] According to *Neurolinguistic Psychology* (NLP) research, about 90 percent of people will look up for visual accessing, down for linguistic accessing, to the left for past experiences, to the right for future perceptions, and straight ahead for present-tense thinking.[30] "Some NLP experts consider eye movements to be an aid to accessing inner speech since the eye movements stimulate different parts of the brain."[31] If this is true, then the advice that you should maintain good eye contact when speaking to someone, makes "a person unable to make the accessing movements"[32] and "can interfere with and slow down the normal thinking style."[33] In academia, teachers often make the mistake of misinterpreting students' actions. For example, a professor asks a question and you struggle to visualize the answer, eyes moving up or down, and to the left or right (depending on if you are looking for past-learned ideas or inventing new material). The teacher states, "Well, you won't find the answer on the ceiling." The teacher is wrong. The answer may be found by glancing up and to the left if your normal eye glance pattern for past tense and picturing concepts is up[34] (see Figure 5.1)

A student who knows his or her eye-shift pattern may be able to access previous learning by moving his or her eyes in the direction of his or her past tense triggering, and looking up or down depending on whether he or she is trying to access images or words.

LEARNING EXPERIENCE: Interested in finding out your eye accessing patterns? If so, do Activity 5.2.

Gestures

Gestures include posture, walk, stance, hand movements, body shifts, and head nods, which can give clues about a person's status, mood, ethnic and cultural affiliation, and self-perception. Nods of the head and body shifts can encourage or discourage conversation. Other movements may show internal feelings. For example, people who are bored often tap their fingers on a table or bounce a crossed leg.

Why do people gesture when they talk? One study suggested that not only does talking with your hands as you speak help you get your point across, but, "helps you to think too."[35] Another study indicates that, "Gesturing may make thinking a little easier by easing the burden on verbal communication."[36]

You probably gesture while you communicate. Gestures are sometimes dependent on speech and sometimes independent of speech. **Speech-independent gestures** are not tied to speech (e.g., you give someone encouragement with a "thumbs up" gesture

Figure 5.1. Eye Accessing Cues

ACTIVITY 5.2
Eye Accessing Patterns Activity

This activity is best done by forming a dyad in which one person observes the other as each answers the questions posed. You can do it yourself by concentrating on your eye shift patterns as you answer each question. Some people find using a mirror aids them. Be aware that in some cases, individuals do not display or cannot identify their eye shifts. There are many reasons for this, including inhibitions, being unwilling to relax enough to access the words or images, or the quickness of the eye shift.

1) Picture the outside of the home in which you grew up.
    Did your eyes shift to:
    the right____ the left____
    up toward the ceiling____ down toward the floor____
2) Picture the outside of the high school building that you attended.
    Did your eyes shift to:
    the right____ the left____
    up toward the ceiling____ down toward the floor____

You can continue to do this activity by picturing things from your past . . . your first car, the face of your first girl or boyfriend, and so forth.

If you looked up to the left in reciting your answers you looked to the left for past tense. That is the pattern of most people. If you looked to the right then your pattern is to find past experiences by glancing to the right. If you looked up to see the buildings then you visualize by looking upward. This means to picture something you will glance upward and to access numbers and words you will look downward. If, on the other hand, you looked down to see the pictures then this is your visualization pattern and your linear pattern is to look upward.

without saying a word). These gestures are referred to as emblems.[37] **Speech-related gestures** are directly tied to, or accompany, speech (e.g., you nod your head while saying, "Yes.").[38] These gestures are illustrators, affect displays, regulators, and adaptors.

Adaptors are movements that accompany boredom, show internal feelings, or regulate a situation. Consider the typical situation in which you are waiting on a street corner for someone who is late: you stand with your arms across your chest, fingers tapping on upper arms, foot tapping the pavement, checking your watch every few seconds. You are displaying a cluster of nonverbal adaptive signs.

Affect displays are facial gestures that show emotions and feelings such as sadness or happiness. Pouting, winking, and raising or lowering the eyelids and eyebrows are examples of affect displays. Different individuals and people from various cultures tend to use facial expressions in different ways. For example, many Euro-American males frequently try to mask and internalize their facial expressions because they have been taught that to show emotion is not manly; however, Italian males tend to express their emotions outwardly.[39]

Emblems are nonverbal acts that have a direct verbal translation or dictionary definition, which usually consist of a word or two.[40] Sign language of the deaf, gestures used by behind-the-scenes television personnel, and signals between two underwater swimmers are all examples of the use of emblems, as is holding up three fingers to illustrate the number 3 or holding up your arms and waving your hand from side-to-side to indicate "hello." It is important to realize that not all emblems are universal. In fact, they tend to be *culture-specific*, meaning that an emblem's meaning in one culture may not be the same as in another. For example, in Hong Kong, signaling a waiter for the check is done by making a writing motion with both hands. Extending the index finger and motioning toward yourself, as is done for calling a waiter in many parts of the United States, is used only for calling animals in many parts of the world.[41]

Illustrators are kinesic acts accompanying speech that are used to aid in the description of what is being said.[42] They are used to sketch a path, point to an object, or show spatial relationships. Saying, "*Ian, please stand up* (point at Ian and bring your hand upward), *go out the door* (point at the door), *turn to the left* (point to the left), *and walk straight ahead* (point straight ahead)" is an example of a cluster of illustrators.

Regulators are nonverbal acts that maintain and control the back-and-forth nature of speaking and listening between two or more people. Nods of the head, eye movements, and body shifts are all regulators used to encourage or discourage conversation. Imagine, for example, an interaction between a department manager and an employee who has asked for a raise. The manager glances at her watch, her fingers fidget with the telephone, and she glances through some materials on the desk. The manager's regulator signs indicate that for her the transaction is completed. An unobservant employee may miss these regulating signs.

Touch

When a person physically puts one part of the body against another person's body, the person is communicating through **touch**. A pat on the back, a poke in the ribs, and intimate lovemaking are examples of how people communicate by touch. Touch may be done with or without permission.

Pats, pinches, strokes, slaps, punches, shakes, and kisses convey meaning through your skin. When a physician touches your body to ascertain sensitivity and possible illness, communication takes place. You shake hands to satisfy social and business welcoming needs. You intimately touch through kisses and use sexually arousing touch in the act of lovemaking. The messages that touch communicates depend on how, where, and by whom you are touched.

Touch can have a profound effect on a person. Many people find that when they are upset, they rub their hands together or stroke a part of their body such as the arm.

You can reassure others by touching them on the shoulder or patting them on the hand. "Touched and massaged babies gain weight much faster than babies who are not massaged. They are more active, alert, responsive, better able to tolerate noise, and emotionally are more in control."[43] The touched baby is being sent a message which evokes security and is pleasurable.

Most people—except those who have been abused, raped, or brought up in a low-touch or no-touch family or society—associate appropriate touching with positive messages. Those whose bodies have been invaded without permission, however, as in the case of sexual abuse, often pull back or feel uncomfortable being touched. In fact, touch avoidance is one of the signs psychological counselors sometimes use to identify those who have been physically or sexually molested.[44]

A woman had extremely long, flowing hair, nearly down to her knees. Another woman kept thinking "There's something about her I don't like. I just don't know what it is." After interacting together, the second woman realized what she didn't like. When the first woman moved, her hair moved, and would often touch the person she talked to. The second woman was uncomfortable being touched by the other woman's hair. People from different cultures regard touch in different ways. Some cultures avoid touching, while others encourage it. The same is true within families. For example, in the United States, which is a moderate-touch society, "it is not unusual for an adult to pat the head of a small child who has been introduced by his or her parents. In Malaysia and other Asian Pacific countries, touching anyone's head—especially a child's—is improper and considered an indignity because the head is regarded as the home of the soul."[45] In France, two people may greet with a kiss on the cheeks. In Japan, a mother and adult child may seldom if ever touch, but instead bow to each other. Two business people in the United States may shake hands when they meet.

Another difference may exist when touching someone of the same sex. Though heterosexual men in the United States or England rarely touch other men, except in times of great emotion (such as athletic game victories), or for shaking hands when meeting someone, arm linking between two men is common in many Arabic and Latin countries.[46] To illustrate the inconsistency in U.S. American males regarding same-sex touch behavior, one of your authors asked one of his students, the star of the basketball team at the college at which he teaches, what the coach normally does when the star player is taken out near the end of a game in which he has done extremely well. The response was, "When I come back to the bench, he slaps me on the butt." The instructor said, "And, if when I passed back an exam on which you got an A, how would you react if I slapped you on the butt?" (The class broke out into laughter.) The student blushed and said, "No way, that's not the same." Think about it. Why isn't it the same?

Women in the Euro-American culture tend to engage in more intimate same-sex touch than do men. Female pairs are more likely than male pairs to exchange hugs, kisses, and touches on the arm or back, and to do so for longer durations.[47] Men touch one another using only narrowly circumscribed behaviors such as handshaking, or in instances of extreme emotion (e.g., athletic accomplishments), in such actions as giving high fives, body bumping, hugging, butt slapping, or kissing. The acceptability of showing physical affection by women may be one of the reasons lesbians may be less discriminated against than gay men.[48] People tend to react less to physical displays between two women than between two men. This is not true in some other countries, where men holding hands or kissing is an acceptable action. In the United States, when men touch, kiss, or hug each other, attention is often drawn to the activity, and since it is not generally part of the heterosexual cultural norm, it is perceived by some in negative ways.

An action chain sequence can take place when two people touch. If you have ever wondered why someone with whom you'd like to be intimate pulls away or gets rigid when you or the other person is touched, it may well be that you have jumped forward in the sequence too quickly. For a person brought up in a moderate-to-low-touch society, there is an appropriate time to not touch, then to touch, to kiss, and then to fondle. If one person feels he or she is at the "no" touch stage, and the partner acts at the fondle stage, strong negative verbal and physical reactions may follow.

"Individuals differ dramatically in the degree to which they like or dislike being touched."[49] How much a person shies away from being handled is called **touch avoidance**. People in the Euro-American culture, no matter the gender, who are avoiders tend to have less overall intimacy, are less open, less expressive, and have somewhat lower self-esteem.[50] In addition, touch avoiders judge people who touch them less favorably than do touch approachers.[51] Further, people who like to touch and be touched by others are not only more communicative, but generally, also tend to be more self-confident.[52]

LEARNING EXPERIENCE: Interested in finding out your level of touch usage or avoidance? If so, do Activity 5.3.

Touch is most useful for communicating intimacy, involvement, warmth, reassurance, and comfort. In fact, there is therapeutic power in touch, which nurses and other health-care professionals employ to help their patients emotionally as well as physically. The therapeutic benefits of touch may derive in part from the effect that touch has on a recipient's willingness to talk. Because touch implies reassurance and caring, it encourages self-disclosure.

Touch helps to persuade people. For example, requests to sign a petition received almost twice as many positive reactions when touch was involved—even when it was "accidental," as when fingers touched when a piece of paper was passed.[53]

Touch can also communicate power. When a supervisor touches an employee, that may indicate a power play, an attempt to show who is in control and who can invade the other person's territory. Generally, the person who initiates the touch is perceived as more powerful, more dominant, and of higher status than the one who is touched. In interviews, for example, while an initial greeting handshake is mutual and customary, the handshake that ends the interview is the prerogative of the interviewer, the person with more power in the situation. The interviewer may or may not offer to shake hands, but the lower status interviewee may be perceived as "pushy" if he or she makes the offer.

An interesting study regarding touch indicates that "a firm handshake is key to landing a job."[54] The researcher recommends, "Good handshakes involve a firm,

ACTIVITY 5.3
Assessing Your Touch Avoidance

Read the following statements concerning touch and indicate the extent to which you agree with each statement.

If you strongly agree, mark the statement 1.
If you agree, mark the statement 2.
If you are undecided, mark the statement 3.
If you disagree, mark the statement 4.
If you strongly disagree, mark the statement 5.

_____1. I often put my arms around friends of the same sex.
_____2. I like it when members of the opposite sex touch me.
_____3. I like to touch friends of the same sex as I am.
_____4. I find it enjoyable when my companion and I embrace.
_____5. Touching a friend of the same sex does not make me uncomfortable.
_____6. Intimate touching with members of the opposite sex is pleasurable.

SCORING:
Add your responses to items 1, 3, and 5. This is your same-sex touch avoidance score. _____
Add your responses to items 2, 4, and 6. This is your opposite-sex touch avoidance score. _____
Add the two sums together to obtain your total touch avoidance score. _____

Same-sex and opposite-sex scores of 14 and 15, and a total score of 27 and above, indicate a high propensity to avoid touch. Same-sex and opposite-sex scores of 3 and 4, and a total score of 9 and below, indicate a high propensity to touch. Same-sex and opposite-sex scores between 5 and 13, and a total score between 10 and 26, indicate neither a high nor low propensity to touch.

Source: This instrument is adapted from the eighteen-item questionnaire developed by Andersen and Leibowitz. For the complete instrument, see Andersen, P. A., & Leibowitz, K. (1978). The development and nature of touch avoidance. *Environmental psychology and nonverbal behavior* (3rd ed.), pp. 89–106.

complete grip, eye contact and vigorous up-and-down movement."[55] This was true for women as well as men.

Whether your expectations about touch are violated depends on several considerations: Where is the touch? How long does it last? How much pressure or intensity is used? What is your relationship with the person touching you? What are the circumstances—for example, are other people watching? What is your cultural background?

Reactions to being touched in the wrong place or by someone you don't like can range from politely ignoring the gesture to starting a fight. If someone offers a limp handshake, you probably won't respond visibly, although you may form a particular impression of the person. If a male punches another male on the arm, however, the one who was punched will likely respond with a punch of his own, a verbal attack, or a smile.

Posture, Walk, and Stance

Does a person's posture, walk, and the way the person stands, say something about him or her? It most decidedly does.[56] Posture, walk, and stance can give impressions about status, mood, ethnic and cultural affiliation, and self-perception.

Detectives and airline-security personnel are trained to pick out suspicious people by the way they walk. Walking even follows cultural patterns: Europeans coming to the United States, especially New York City, often ask why people are in such a hurry, an impression that comes from the quick pace at which those from the Big Apple tend to walk. Men tend to walk differently than women. "Men and women are built differently and walk differently from each other and casual observers use this information as clues in making a range of social judgments."[57] Researchers also determined that gay subjects tended to have more gender-incongruent body types than their straight counterparts (hourglass figures for men, tubular bodies for women) and body motions (hip-swaying for men, shoulder-swaggering for women) than their straight counterparts.[58]

Your walk may give away information about how you feel and whom you are. When someone enters a room, you may instantly form conclusions about that person. Some people walk with confidence, and stand with head high, shoulders back, jaw set. Others walk slowly with a stance of sloping shoulders, eyes down, withdrawing into their bodies. This posture may indicate a lack of confidence.

Artifacts

Artifacts are those things which adorn the body. These objects send messages to others about us, as well as saying something about ourselves and our selection of these items. A person's clothing, makeup, eyeglasses, and jewelry, carry distinct messages.

Clothing is a substitute body, telling an observer something about who you are. Because you have made a choice about what to wear, it follows that this is the image you want to portray, this is the attitude you want to present about the type of person you are, and this is the way you want others to perceive you.

Clothing—how much, how little or much, and what kind—reflects an individual's culture. For Orthodox Jewish women, the custom is to cover the body from neck to feet, while the men wear head coverings (usually a skull cap called a yarmulke or a wide brimmed black hat and a black suit with a white shirt). In the Arab world, the burka, robes, and veils are part of the attire for many women and are expressions of the cultural value of modesty. There are, of course, individuals in those cultures who choose not to wear "traditional" garb. Some Arabic women, for example, stress their independence by wearing Western-style clothing and no veil. However, removal of usually required garments can lead to severe penalties in countries like Iran.

Certain accessories communicate specific messages. Wedding bands, tattoos, and religious symbols convey messages. Jewelry also may be used to communicate social status and economic level, such as a Timex versus a Rolex watch. A college student with a book bag slung over the shoulder conveys an image of normality, while that same person toting a leather briefcase most probably would be seen as different, atypical.

Some junior and senior high schools, thinking that clothing can incite distractions and lead to undesirable actions, have dress codes that bar bare-midriffs for females and t-shirts with inciting wording. Black trench coats were banned in many schools after it became known that the two students who went on a shooting rampage at Columbine High School in Littleton, Colorado, wore such coats.

People working in corporations are generally expected to wear certain clothing that parallels the individual corporate culture. The clothing you wear to a job interview may be the deciding factor on whether or not you get hired. "A job interview is like any other ceremony that requires a costume."[59] For women a navy, black, or gray suit with a color-coordinated blouse and a skirt long enough to allow for comfortable sitting is recommended. Jewelry should be minimal and tasteful. Shoes should be conservative. For men, a gray or blue suit, white or color-coordinated long sleeve shirt and red or blue patterned or striped tie, dark socks, and polished dress shoes, is the way to go. Conservative haircuts and natural hair colors are preferred. Leave home the exposed body piercings. Don't forget to turn off your cell phone and do not text while at the interview.[60]

Originally started in California's Silicon Valley, at such companies as Apple Computers, was the idea that the company's employees are modern and forward-thinking and their dress should reflect that attitude. In 1992 the Levi Strauss corporation launched its casual dress campaign. In order to promote sales of casual clothing, the company sent a "Guide to Casual Business Wear" to thirty thousand human resource managers across the nation. The estimate is that 87 percent of all companies in America have adopted "dress down" policies in which employees can wear some sort of casual clothing on designated days of the week or month.[61] Although business casual is accepted by many firms, not every company follows the trend.

Companies dealing in foreign markets know that the business suit, which originally rose in nineteenth-century Europe as a costume to make managerial workers stand out from production workers, is still very much the correct business garb. In countries like Japan, England, and Germany, casual is definitely not the *in* thing.

In the United States, adorning the body with tattoos and body piercing is a fairly recent trend for the general society, especially among the young. However, "Tattoos and body piercings (e.g., eyebrows, lip, navel) have been used at various times in history. Traditional Polynesian cultures (e.g., Samoa, Tonga, Maori of New Zealand) have used tattoos and piercings as indicators of class, status and roles."[62] "Traditional tattoos, for example, in Hawaii, have been used to take pride in the rich history that represents past ancestors."[63]

PHYSICAL CHARACTERISTICS

We are sometimes drawn to or repulsed by people according to how they appear physically. Your **physical characteristics**, how much you weigh, your height, skin color, and age communicate.

Attractiveness

Attractiveness is in the eye of the beholder. In spite of that, prejudice against unattractive people is deeply ingrained in Euro-American society. This attitude may, in part, be the result of the emphasis on attractiveness projected by the advertising industry in their advertisements, and the depiction of what makes for attractive people, whether men, women, or children. Interestingly enough, being too attractive may also cause problems.

Each culture determines attractiveness for that particular culture. Judges at international beauty contests have difficulty judging who the winner is, for instance, because of the vast physical differences between the contestants and the lack of a universal definition for beauty. And, though thinness for women might be the in-beauty thing in white Euro-American culture, that is not necessarily true with African Americans. In a study of U.S. teenage girls, white girls painted attractiveness as "5' 7", between 100 and 110 pounds, with blue eyes and long flowing hair."[64] The Black girls in the study named full hips and large thighs as signs of attractiveness.[65]

The physical appearance of jury members may affect whether or not they are selected to serve. The physical appearance of the plaintiff and defendant may affect a jury's decision. In one study, participants in an automobile-negligence trial heard tape-recorded testimony. The first set of jurors was shown photographs of an attractive male plaintiff and an unattractive male defendant; the second set of jurors saw the reverse. A third panel saw no pictures but heard the testimony. The results: the attractive plaintiff received a 49 percent positive vote from the first jury, the unattractive plaintiff got only a 17 percent positive vote from the second jury, and 41 percent of the third group, which did not see any pictures, ruled for the plaintiff.[66]

Even salary can be affected by attractiveness. A study indicates that male attorneys who are attractive earn more money than their counterparts who are plain-looking.[67]

Interestingly, being too attractive can cause problems. A movie star, noted for her beautiful body and facial beauty, indicates that she has missed out on parts because directors find her to be too attractive and too modern.[68] A concept referred to as the *Prom Queen Syndrome*, further explains the negative side of being beautiful. Very attractive women who are winners of beauty pageants often find themselves without dates. The average male is afraid to ask them out as the guy is sure that no one "that beautiful" will accept a date with an ordinary male. Some gay men complain about not being perceived as "date material" because their attractiveness makes them untouchable.[69]

Height

Men often are judged purely by their physical presence. "Size can affect a man's life. Short men are discriminated against."[70] Men under 5 feet 6 inches are considered short. People regard them as having less power. Short men are referred to as *submissive* and *weak*, while tall men garner such titles as *mature* and *respected*. Even elementary students are aware of height prejudice.[71]

What are the implications? Short men need to be better prepared, be aware that they must exceed in grades and talent, sell themselves during job interviews. Success is not impossible; for example, President James Madison was 5 feet 4 inches; warrior Attila the Hun, 5 feet; actor Elijah Wood is 5 feet 5 inches; Hollywood sex symbol Tom Cruise is 5 feet 7 inches[72] (shorter than the average male American), and, of course, there was the diminutive Napoleon.

"In the U.S. culture, there is a bias against short stature, and a glorification of those taller in stature. The result of this prejudice is discrimination against short people in a variety of areas, including politics, business, dating and sports."[73] The business world favors the tall male over the short. For example, "one study found a positive relationship between newly hired MBAs' height and starting salaries. Tall men (6 feet 2 inches and above) received a starting salary 12.4% higher than graduates of the same school who were less than 6 feet, even when the shorter applicant was a man of higher intelligence."[74] Researchers also found that "each extra inch of a man's height commanded an additional $789 dollars annually."[75]

Height prejudice exists in dating. Studies have shown that women favor tall men over short men. For example, "when women were asked to evaluate photographs of men all of them found the tall and average men significantly more attractive than shorter men."[76]

In politics, the same rule tends to hold true. "Of all presidential elections, the taller person won the popular vote 65 percent of the time and won the electoral college vote 59 percent.[77] Predictably, in the 2008 presidential election, Barack Obama, who is 6 feet 2 inches, beat his much shorter opponent.[78]

Although Euro-American society tends to show a preference for taller men, "tall women often are labeled 'ungainly'; short business women, in fact, may have an advantage in not acquiring whatever threatening overtones may attend to increasing height."[79]

However, shorter women also may be perceived as not being as proficient as taller women. The forty-year-old, five feet one, size 2, audiologist daughter of one of the authors of this book relates that when her patients call many ask to make appointments with "the little girl doctor," while the average sized female clinic employees were not referred to by their stature.

PROXEMICS—SPATIAL COMMUNICATION

Proxemics is the study of how individuals use space to communicate. Space can include the distance people stand from each other, the perception of territory, how many people make a space feel crowded, and similar spatial considerations.

Just as restaurants and libraries "tell you" what their purpose is by their formality, comfort and privacy, how you choose to decorate your office, room, or home communicates a great deal about who you are. For example, viewing slides of upper-middle-class homes, students accurately inferred the personality of the owners. Decorating schemes gave important clues to the owners' intellectualism, politeness, maturity, optimism, family orientation, and sense of adventure. The exterior of the homes gave clues to the owners' artistic interests, graciousness, privacy, and desire for quiet.

LEARNING EXPERIENCE: Interested in understanding how space sends messages? If so, do Activity 5.4.

Another aspect of the physical environment is climate—typically ignored since no one can do much about it. Researchers have found that temperature, humidity, and atmospheric pressure all affect how we feel and, therefore, how we interact with others. For example, when barometric pressure falls (when the sky turns cloudy and it rains or snows), our bodies retain water, adding as much as an inch to our waistlines. The retained water may be a cause for increased irritability, not because of the extra inch, but because the water increases pressure on the brain. The good news is that high pressure days (bright and clear) have the opposite effect. This could explain, in part, why people seem cheerier and more talkative when the weather is nice, and sadder and quieter when the weather is rainy or cloudy, especially for several days in a row. People who get depressed on overcast days may have SAD (Sun Affect Disorder). Special sun-like lighting has been developed to aid those people to cope with overcast days.

Space and Culture

Although people typically assume that everyone uses space the same way, national, cultural, and ethnic influences affect the way people view communication through the use of space. In fact, "cultures can be distinguished by the distances at which members interact and how frequently members touch."[80] It has been proposed that there are **contact cultures**—those characterized by tactile modes of communication (e.g., Latin Americans, Mediterraneans, French, Arabs, Israelis, Spanish, Eastern Europeans, Latin Americans). People from these cultures tend to touch, have a great deal of physical contact, face one another more directly in conversation, and look each other in the eye more. **Noncontact cultures** (Euro-Americans, Germans, English, Chinese, Japanese, Swedes) tend to be more standoffish, not touching or having a great deal of physical contact.[81]

Space Distances

The bubble of space you have around you as your safe territory is influenced by your culture. Studies related to Euro-Americans' use of space as communicators have revealed that there are four classifications that explain their spatial needs: intimate, personal, social, and public.[82]

Intimate space distance covers a space varying from direct physical contact with another person to a distance of eighteen inches. It is used for your most private activities—caressing, making love, and sharing intimate ideas and emotions. You can often get clues about a relationship by noticing whether the other person allows you to use his or her intimate space. For example, if you have been on a hand-holding/physically

ACTIVITY 5.4
Does Space Send Messages?

Think of a fast food restaurant you have frequented. Describe the restaurant by stating your reactions to the colors, furnishings, lighting. For example, if you describe the fast-food restaurant as uncomfortable, specify why. Is it the hard plastic chairs, the bright lighting, the lack of soundproofing, the colors, the sounds?

Fast-Food Restaurant
1. Comfort
2. Desirability of staying in the environment for an extended time
3. Emotional level
4. Attractiveness
5. Personnel (i.e., waitstaff)

Now do the same for a fine dining restaurant

Fine Dining Restaurant
1. Comfort
2. Desirability of staying in the environment for an extended time
3. Emotional level
4. Attractiveness
5. Personnel (i.e., waitstaff)

A. Given your analyses of each environment, compare them with respect to the purpose of each.

B. Does each environment communicate its purpose clearly?

C. What did you learn about settings and your emotional reactions in those settings?

touching basis with someone, and suddenly he or she will not let you near, or pulls away when you get very close, based on congruency patterns, a change in the relationship may have occurred. If the other person suddenly encourages close body proximity, this may also indicate a change in attitude.

Personal space distance, eighteen inches to four feet, is sometimes called the *comfort bubble*. Most Euro-Americans feel most comfortable keeping this distance when talking with others, and invasion of this personal territory will cause them to back away. If you are backed into a corner, sitting in a chair, or somehow trapped, you will lean away, pull in, and tense up. To avoid invasion of your territory, you might place a leg on the rung of a chair or on a stair. You can even arrange your furniture so that your territory cannot be invaded. For example, businesspeople may place their desks so that employees must sit on one side and the boss on the other. In contrast, interviewers have reported a completely different atmosphere when talking to job applicants if the two chairs are placed facing each other about three to four feet apart with no table or desk acting as a barrier instead of on opposite sides of the desk.

Social space distance covers a four-foot to twelve-foot zone that is used during business transactions and casual social exchanges. Also part of social distance is the standing-seated interaction, in which the person in control stands and the other person sits. Standing-seated positions occur in teacher-pupil and police officer–arrestee transactions.

Public space distance may dictate a separation of as little as twelve feet, but it is usually more than twenty-five. It is used by teachers in lecture rooms and speakers at public gatherings as well as by public figures who wish to place a barrier between themselves and their audiences.

Small-Group Environment

The environment of a small group is affected by how members use personal space. For example, a long, large, rectangular formal table will prompt a different type of interaction than a small, round, worktable. **Small-group ecology**, which includes the placement of chairs, the placement of the person conducting a meeting, and the setting for a small-group encounter, clearly influences the group's operation. If, for example, people are seated in a circle, they will probably feel more comfortable and interact more than they would if they were sitting in straight rows. They will be able to see each other's nonverbal reactions, and because there is no inhibiting physical distance, they may lose their self-consciousness as they become members of the group. Classrooms in which students sit in circles or in a "U" with the teacher in the open end of the "U" are more interactive than classrooms in which the students are seated in straight rows.[83]

Want to be an active class communicator? In the traditional academic classroom, with the instructor in the front center of the six seats in the front row–six seats in each row arrangement, the majority of communication tends to come from the center four seats in the front row, the center three seats behind those, the two center seats behind those and the single seats in the middle of the next two rows. Those seats are called the *zone of participation*.[84]

PARAVOCALICS—VOCAL COMMUNICATION

Paravocalics are the vocal elements beyond the words themselves. Vocal quality communicates nonverbally to the listening ear. These sound elements communicate about you, what you say, and what you feel:

Pause—stopping, hesitation, length of pause
Pitch—highness or lowness of tone, such as soprano or bass
Rate—how fast you talk
Stress—emphasis or intensity of sounds all have particular meanings
Volume—how loudly you talk

These paravocalic tools are often referred to as vocal cues. Vocal cues offer clues to determine the sex, age, and status of a speaker. You can also make some pretty accurate judgments about the emotions and feelings of the people with whom you communicate by their paralinguistic presentation. If you are very angry, the pitch of your voice may go up. And when you are very, very angry, you sometimes say words slowly and distinctly, pausing after each word for special effect.

Your voice is crucial in persuasion.[85] A faster rate of speech, more intonation, greater volume, and a less halting manner seem to be related to successful persuasion. If a person sounds assured, the receiver credits him or her with a higher degree of credibility. Television news anchors, for example, work to cultivate an assured broadcast voice.

Silence—not speaking or making nonverbal vocal sounds, such as "um," when you are interacting with another person—is highly varied in meaning. Silence may communicate anger, attentive listening, grief, depression, respect, awe, or the message "leave me alone."

Many cultures feel comfortable with the absence of noise and talk, and are not compelled to fill every moment with words as most North and South Americans feel obliged to do. An African proverb states, "Silence is also speech."[86] Differences of cultural use of silence is illustrated by: "In response to the question, 'Will you marry me?' silence in English would be interpreted as uncertainty; in Japanese it would be interpreted as acceptance."[87] In addition, those from Eastern cultures "do not feel uncomfortable with the absence of noise or talk and are not compelled to fill every pause when they are around other people."[88] In fact, Buddhism teaches that "what is real is, and when it is spoken it becomes unreal."[89] There are numerous Asian sayings that reflect their cultural bias toward quietness, such as, "It is the duck that squawks that gets shot," "Numerous words show scanty wares," "A flower does not speak," and "The mouth is to eat with, not to speak with."[90] In other cultures silence has meaning as well. In "Finland, Sweden, Denmark and Norway, silence conveys interest and consideration. In fact, your silence tells the other person that you want them to continue talking."[91] Even members of cocultures living in the United States differ in their use of silence. Many Native Americans, for example, believe that silence, not speaking, is a sign of a remarkable person. From silence, it is believed, one derives "the cornerstone of character, the virtues of self control, patience, and dignity."[92]

Listeners respond to a person's vocal cues. Perceptions of vocal cues, combined with other verbal and nonverbal stimuli, mold the conceptions we use as bases for communicating.

LEARNING EXPERIENCE: Interested in developing your vocal perception abilities? If so, do Activity 5.5.

ACTIVITY 5.5
Using Vocal Cues to Regulate Conversations

Read the dialogue and note the vocal cues used to regulate the conversation in these ways: (1) to maintain the role as speaker; (2) to get the other person to speak; (3) to take over as speaker; and (4) to get the other person to continue speaking. The conversation, between a communication student and her instructor, takes place after class in the instructor's office.

Student: I . . . well . . . had a little trouble understanding today's lecture on the voice. I . . .

Instructor: What specifically did you have trouble with?

Student: (*Leans forward and points at the instructor as if to speak.*)

Instructor: (*Raising the pitch of his voice and speaking quickly.*) If you would ask questions in class, maybe you wouldn't have this problem.

Student: B-b-b-but, I have trouble asking questions in front of the other students.

Instructor: I used to have the same problem when I was a student. (*Leans back in chair, looks at student for several moments.*)

Student: Gee, I would never have guessed that.

Instructor: (*Lowering his pitch and speaking slowly.*) As I was saying, I used to have that problem until I realized that I needed to ask whenever I had a question, if I wanted to know the information.

Student: I think I see what you mean.

Instructor: Hmmmmmm.

Student: But sometimes it's just hard for me.

Instructor: (*Pitch rising as he speaks.*) But, you do what you need to do. (*Pause.*)

Student: I guess you're right.

Instructor: Uh-huh.

Student: (*Pitch lowering, rate decreasing, and final two words stretched.*) I'm just going to have to do it.

Instructor: If you give it a try, I'll work with you on it.

Your analysis of the dialogue may have revealed:

Student: I . . . well . . . (**vocalized pause used to maintain his role as speaker**) had a little trouble understanding today's lecture on the voice. I . . .

Instructor: (**interrupts to take over as speaker**) What specifically did you have trouble with?

Student: (*Leans forward and points at the instructor as if to speak.*) (**attempt to take over as speaker**)

Instructor: (*Raising the pitch of his voice and speaking quickly.*) (**rising intonation to maintain his role as speaker**) If you would ask questions in class, maybe you wouldn't have this problem.

Student: B-b-b-but **(stutter-start to take over as speaker)**, I have trouble asking questions in front of the other students.

Instructor: I used to have the same problem when I was a student. (*Leans back in chair, looks at student for several moments.*) **(silence to get other person to speak)**

Student: Gee, I would never have guessed that. **(relinquishes speaker role)**

Instructor: (*Lowering his pitch as he speaks slowly.*) **(falling intonation to maintain his role as speaker)** As I was saying, I used to have that problem until I realized that if I didn't understand something, and didn't ask, I would never get the information I needed.

Student: I think I see what you mean. **(relinquishes role)**

Instructor: Hmmmmmm. **(vocal encourager to get other person to continue speaking)**

Student: But sometimes it's just hard for me. **(relinquishes role)**

Instructor: (*Pitch rising as he speaks.*) **(rising intonation to maintain his role as speaker)** But, you have to do it. (*Pause.*) **(silence to get the other person to speak)**

Student: I guess you're right. **(relinquishes role)**

Instructor: Uh-huh. **(vocal encourager to get other person to continue speaking)**

Student: (*Pitch lowering, rate decreasing, and final two words stretched.*) **(falling intonation and stretching final words to get the other person to speak)** I'm just going to have to do it.

Instructor: If you give it a try, I'll work with you on it. **(Finality)**

TIME AS COMMUNICATION

Time communicates. Classes or work start at a specific time. What happens if you are late? You are going to a theatrical production. You expect the play to start on time. You have a doctor's appointment. How do you react if the doctor is extremely late in treating you? How do you feel when a friend is continually late?

The use of time centers on your particular society. Each of us is born into and raised in a particular time world—an environment with its own rhythm.[93] Only within certain societies, for example, is precise time of great significance. Some cultures relate to time as a *circular time phenomenon* in which there is no pressure or anxiety about the future. Existence follows the cycle of the seasons of planting and harvesting, the daily rising and setting of the sun, birth and death. In **circular time**, there is no pressing need to achieve or create newness, or to produce more than is needed to survive. Additionally, there is no fear of death. Such societies have successfully integrated the past and future into a peaceful sense of the present. Many Native Americans, as well as those who believe in reincarnation, have been raised using circular time.

Some cultures operate on **linear time**, focused primarily on the future. These societies focus on the accurate and technical information needed to fulfill impending demands. In most of Western Europe, North America, and Japan, punctuality is a part of good manners. Tardiness can be a sign that a person wants to avoid something or that the activity or person to be met is not important enough to warrant the effort to be on time. Procrastinators are not valued in linear time societies. Late papers at school lose grade points. People who arrive late at a meeting irritate those who made the effort to be there on time. Individuals who are late to the theatre may have to wait to be seated, if they are admitted at all. Employees can get fired for being late to work or turning in late reports.

Time can be analyzed according to its technical, formal, and informal uses. **Technical time** is precise time, as in the way some scientists look at how things happen in milliseconds. Few of us continually come in contact with this usage. On the other hand, **formal time** is the way in which a culture defines its time, and it plays a daily role in most of our lives. It refers to centuries, years, months, weeks, days, hours, and minutes. As a student you may think in terms of semesters or terms or class periods. As an athlete or sports viewer you know that games are divided into quarters, innings, or periods and that those time limits can affect the outcome of matches.

Informal time refers to a rather flexible use of time such as "soon," or "right away." These terms often cause communicative difficulty because they are arbitrary and mean different things to different people. For example, how long is "pretty soon"?

LEARNING EXPERIENCE: Interested in finding out about your use of time? If so, do Activity 5.6.

Use of time is often crucial to U.S. business. Throughout a person's career, punctuality can be used as a measure of effectiveness. A person who arrives late for a job interview probably will not receive the job because of the bias against people who cannot plan properly. There's a negative sense of entitlement generated by people who think they don't have to be on time. Employees who arrive late or leave early may be reprimanded and even dismissed.

Some cultures, such as among gays or Hispanics, often are amused by their use of time and even have names that refer to the habitual lateness such as *gay-late* and *mañana time*.

A married Hispanic student related that she became very aware of varying cultures' use of time when, at her wedding, all of the Euro-American guests arrived at the announced 1 P.M. ceremony time. She actually had planned for the vows to be taken around 2, which was when all of her Hispanic friends and relatives arrived.

In a **monochronic culture**, where time has a single meaning and promptness is valued, one has to wonder why some people are late. These people clearly communicate negatively through inappropriate use of time, so why do they do it? Chronic lateness is often deeply rooted in a person's psyche. Compulsive tardiness is often rewarding on some level. A key emotional conflict for the chronically late person may involve his or her need to feel special. The person may believe he or she is better than other people and doesn't have to play by the rules. Such a person may not gain enough recognition in other ways; people must be special in some way, so the person is special by being late.

ACTIVITY 5.6
The Psychological Time Test

Instructions: For each statement indicate whether the statement is TRUE (T) for your general attitude and behavior or FALSE (F) for your general attitude and behavior. If a statement appears more than once, answer it the same way as you did the first time it appeared.

_____ 1. Meeting tomorrow's deadlines and doing other necessary work comes before tonight's partying.

_____ 2. I meet my obligations to friends and authorities on time.

_____ 3. I complete projects on time by making steady progress.

_____ 4. I am able to resist temptations when I know there is work to be done.

_____ 5. I keep working at a difficult, uninteresting task if it will help me get ahead.

_____ 6. If things don't get done on time, I don't worry about it.

_____ 7. I think that it's useless to plan too far ahead because things hardly ever come out the way you planned anyway.

_____ 8. I try to live one day at a time.

_____ 9. I live to make better what *is* rather than to be concerned about what *will be*.

_____10. It seems to me that it doesn't make sense to worry about the future, since fate determines whatever will be, will be.

_____11. I believe that getting together with friends to party is one of life's important pleasures.

_____12. I do things impulsively, making decisions on the spur of the moment.

_____13. I take risks to put excitement in my life.

_____14. I get drunk at parties or at bars.

_____15. It's fun to gamble.

_____16. Thinking about the future is pleasant to me.

_____17. When I want to achieve something, I set goals and consider specific means for reaching those goals.

_____18. It seems to me that my career path is pretty well laid out.

_____19. It upsets me to be late for appointments.

_____20. I meet my obligations to friends and authorities on time.

_____21. I get irritated at people who keep me waiting when we've agreed to meet at a given time.

_____22. It makes sense to me to invest a substantial part of my income in insurance premiums.

(*continued*)

ACTIVITY 5.6 (*continued*)

_____23. I believe that by doing things now I save time and stress in the future.

_____24. I believe that accomplishing something now, and being assured of having that done and achieved, is better than assuming that things will be easier and better if I wait to achieve the task.

_____25. I believe that it is important to save for my future even if I have to deny myself something I want now.

_____26. I believe a person's day should be planned each morning.

_____27. I make lists of things I must do.

_____28. When I want to achieve something, I set goals and consider specific means for reaching those goals.

_____29. I believe that by doing things now I save time and stress in the future.

The psychological time test measures seven different factors. If you selected *True* for all or most of the questions within any given factor, then you are probably high on that factor. If you selected *False* for all or most of the questions within any give factor, then you are probably low on that factor. You may be high in more than one area. Here is the identification for each factor:

Questions 1–5: *A future, work motivation, perseverance orientation.* People who score high in this section tend to have a strong work ethic and are committed to completing a task despite difficulties and temptations. The more future oriented a person is, the greater that person's income is likely to be.

Questions 6–10: *A present, fatalistic, worry-free orientation.* People who score high on this factor live one day at a time, not necessarily to enjoy the day but to avoid planning for the next day and to avoid the anxiety about a future that seems determined by fate rather than by anything they can do themselves. "A child with parents in unskilled and semiskilled occupations is often socialized in a way that promotes a present-orientation."

Questions 11–15: *A present, hedonistic, pleasure-seeking, partying orientation.* These people seek to enjoy the present, take risks, and engage in a variety of impulsive actions. Teenagers and those who still desire to be teenagers and avoid responsibility score particularly high on this factor. This factor is more likely to be male- rather than female-oriented.

Questions 16–18: *A future, goal-seeking, and planning orientation.* These people derive special pleasure from planning and achieving a variety of goals. A child of parents who are professionals learns future-oriented values and strategies designed to promote achievement. The future-oriented person who works for tomorrow's goals will frequently look down on the present-oriented person who avoids planning for tomorrow and focuses on enjoying today as lazy and poorly motivated.

Questions 19–21: *A time sensitivity orientation.* People who score high on this factor are especially sensitive to time and its role in social obligations. People who score high in this section tend to be from societies and families that stress strong time-sensitivity, for example, the Japanese, the Swiss, the Germans, and Euro-Americans whose families carefully hold to a clock-orientation.

Questions 22–25: *A future, pragmatic, action orientation.* These people do what they have to do to achieve the future they want. They take practical actions for future gain. (See comments in "Future, Goal Seeking and Planning Orientation" section for an explanation of individuals who score high in this section.)

Questions 26–29: *A future, often obsessive, daily planning orientation.* People who score high on this factor make daily "to do" lists, and devote great attention to specific details and goal setting/achieving.

What did you learn about yourself from doing this exercise?

Source: Test was constructed by Gonzalez, A., & Zimbardo, P. G. (1985, March). Time perspective. *Psychology Today, 19,* 20–26.

Other reasons for being late in a monochronic culture include needs for perfectionism, punishment, power, or to express hostility.[94] To explain, if you are a perfectionist and are afraid to fail, by not doing things on time you can blame the lateness, not yourself, for the bad grade or poor evaluation. Wanting to punish yourself or the people you work with can result in putting off a task. You can get a lot of negative attention for procrastinating, thus satisfying your desire to be put down. By doing things late you control others. The group can't get its work done or the dinner can't proceed if you don't turn in your part of the project or are late to the meal. By being late you can show disdain for others, thus demonstrating your hostility.

SMELL AS COMMUNICATION

The sense of smell communicates and is well connected to arousing memories. Research reveals that "scents can have positive effects on mood, stress reduction, sleep enhancement, self-confidence, and physical and cognitive performance."[95] "Despite the tendency of humans to underestimate the role of smell in our every day lives, for most mammals, smell is the most important sense."[96] Our sense of smell is very selective and helps us reach conclusions. We are attracted by the scents of certain colognes and repulsed by others. Some people find certain body odors offensive. This is especially true in a country such as the United States, where we have been taught by advertisers and medical people to wash off natural odors, use antibacterial products, and replace them by neutral, fragrance-free, or substitute smells. Not all cultures require daily bathing, and in these cases, the using deodorants and the regular washing of clothing are not the norm.

Odors may influence what we think without our awareness of the influence. Several phenomena provide insight into how smell serves as a nonverbal communication tool: smell blindness, smell adaptation, smell memory, smell overload, and smell discrimination.

Smell blindness occurs when a person is unable to detect smells. It parallels color blindness or deafness because it is a physiological blockage. It accounts for the fact that some people do not smell their own or others' body odors or detect the differences in the odors of various foods. Because smell and taste are so closely aligned, this can explain why people who are smell-blind may also have taste-identification difficulties. People with smell blindness are termed *hypo-olfactic*. Those with a high sensitivity for odors are termed *hyper-olfactic*. Hyper-olfactic individuals often have allergies to airborne smells and find walking down the soap and detergent aisle in the supermarket to be sneeze inducing.

Smell adaptation occurs when we gradually lose the distinctiveness of a particular smell through repeated contact with a specific odor. When you walk into a bakery, you may be aware of the wonderful odors. The clerk, however, may have become so used to the odors that she is not aware of them. The speed at which the odor message is adapted to depends on the strength of the odor and the length of time a person is in contact with it.

If as a child your grandmother baked your favorite dessert, walking into someone's home years later and smelling that same odor may cause you to flash back to memories of your grandmother. This ability to recall previous situations when encountering a particular smell is **smell memory**. Smelling a crayon may trigger flashbacks to experiences you had in kindergarten, the odors of a dentist's office may cause your teeth to ache, or passing a perfume counter with samples of a cologne a former lover wore may trigger intrapersonal smell memories.

Have you ever entered an elevator and been bombarded by the heavy dose of perfume of another passenger or walked past a full garbage can on a hot day? These are both examples of smell overload. **Smell overload** takes place when an exceptionally large number of odors or one extremely strong odor overpowers you. Walking down a detergent aisle in a supermarket or standing in a small room with several people who are smoking can trigger smell overload.

The ability to identify people, places, and things on the basis of their smell is **smell discrimination**. Although the human sense of smell is feeble compared to that of many animals, it is still very acute. We can recognize thousands of different smells, and we are able to detect odors even in infinitesimal quantities.[97] You may have been able to distinguish someone who comes up behind you undetected by the smell of her or his hair. The identification takes place through smell discrimination, which allows us to tell the difference between cinnamon and garlic, bananas and oranges, and one person and another.

Want to improve your memory and therefore your test grades by using the sense of smell? "Research suggests that your ability to recall information may be improved by inhaling an odor you breathed while absorbing information."[98] Try this. Put an odor on a piece of cloth and smell it occasionally as you study. Bring the smell saturated cloth with you to your next test and see if you have memory flashback.

AESTHETICS AS COMMUNICATION

Aesthetics is the study of communication of a message or mood through color or music. Music, for example, can heighten a person's attention or induce boredom, thereby creating a nonverbal language that can change or stimulate various activities.[99] As you stroll through the supermarket, you may not even be aware that this principle is in force. During a nine-week test, the music in one supermarket was randomly played at a slow 60 beats a minute on some days and at 108 beats a minute on others. Not surprisingly, on slow-tempo days the store's gross receipts were 38.2 percent higher, as people wandered slowly around the store.[100]

Effects of music can be observed in many situations. For example, when you are driving a car, the type of music on the radio affects your driving, alertness, and concentration. And the music in an elevator is almost never loud and pulsating because such strong sounds would be too emotionally stressful for a small contained area. A study on the impact of rock music tested more than twenty thousand songs for their effect on muscle strength. (This sort of activity is part of a science called **Behavioral Kinesiology**[101] which holds that particular kinds of food, clothes, thoughts, and music strengthen or weaken the muscles of the body.) According to a behavioral kinesiological study, "listening to rock music frequently causes all the muscles in the body to go weak."[102] This relationship may account for the drugged and dreamlike feelings of some people who attend rock concerts. It is theorized that some rock music has a stopped quality that is not present in other types of music. That is, the beat is stopped at the end of each bar or measure. Because the music stops and then must start again, you subconsciously come to a physical halt at the end of each measure; this may tire you out.

Other studies indicate that the effect of music is also based on tempo, rhythm, and instrumentation. Music can heighten your attention or induce boredom, thereby creating a nonverbal language that can change or stimulate various activities.[103] These effects suggest that music can serve as a type of drug in regulating behavior. Music has been credited with easing pain as exemplified by a type of music therapy used in hospice work with dying patients. Do you listen to music as you study? It might aid, but the wrong music might lull you to sleep. Be careful that the music doesn't have words that you start to sing as you attempt to read or a beat that distracts you.

The colors around us can influence communication. Hospitals are experimenting with using various colors for their rooms in hopes that the colors may help sick people to get well or ease pain. Hospitals also are painting large pieces of equipment, such as x-ray machines, the same color as the background walls so they do not appear as frightening to patients. Prisons are using pale pink shades because it is the most calming of colors. Similarly, bright colors are being added to classrooms to make students feel alert, but not in such amounts that the colors become overpowering.

A study of soccer teams suggested that teams in black received more penalties. A study of Olympic athletes finds those wearing red have an advantage over other competitors.[104] The study suggests that red correlates to male dominance and testosterone levels. It is interesting that the Chinese have long used red to pay homage to the wise spirits.

TASTE AS COMMUNICATION

Taste communicates. Research in the field has identified classifications of taste, the role of culture on taste, the role of food deprivation, food preferences, taste expectations, color, and textures as sources that encourage or discourage eating and drinking.[105]

We receive taste signals—bitter, salty, sour, and sweet—much as we do smells. We come in physical contact with the object that brings about the sense reaction within us. These sense reactions are located not on our tongue, but in various regions of our mouth and throat. The taste buds of the mouth are the most common tasters.

Some people have a poor sense of taste, or the ability to taste may change over the years. **Taste blindness** is the inability to taste. People with this inability are *hypogustoric*. This can either be a defect in their senses at birth, or the destruction of the tasters through accidents or illnesses. This can be long- or short-term.

Some people have extremely sensitive tasting abilities. These individuals are *hypergustoric*. They react very strongly to the slightest taste and may find slightly spicy foods to be very offensive.

Another phenomenon associated with taste as a communicator is taste adaptation. **Taste adaptation** takes place when you become used to a taste to the degree that you can eat a substance and not taste it. If you eat a lot of very spicy foods you may become insensitive to the tang.

Using Nonverbal Communication

A question arises as to why, if nonverbal communication is such an important aspect of communication, most people aren't aware of it or don't pay much overt attention to its powers. If nonverbal communication is so important, why aren't people better informed and more careful about their use of nonverbal communication? One reason is that most people have not been taught that actions communicate as clearly as words, so they don't look for nonverbal components. Schools don't generally teach courses in the subject, and what we do learn tends to be through subtle cultural communication. You may have been told that if you didn't look someone in the eye as you spoke, they might not believe you, or that you should stand up straight and walk with pride, or that you are judged by what you wear. These messages actually do say, "Pay attention to the nonverbals," but most of us don't tie that to the fact that nonverbal communication is carrying messages.

Increasing your awareness about the way we communicate nonverbally can help you improve your communication skills. Also, be aware of your body "speaking" to you in nonverbals.

Key Terms

nonverbal communication
cluster
congruency
innate neurological programs
reflexive reactions
reflective reactions
action chain
substituting relationship
complementing relationship
conflicting relationship
accenting relationship
kinesics
pupilometrics
gestures
speech-independent gestures
speech-related gestures
adaptors
affect displays
emblems
illustrators
regulators
touch
touch avoidance
artifacts

physical characteristics
proxemics
contact cultures
noncontact cultures
intimate space distance
personal space distance
social space distance
public space distance
small-group ecology
paravocalics
circular time
linear time
technical time
formal time
informal time
monochronic culture
smell blindness
smell adaptation
smell discrimination
aesthetics
Behavioral Kinesiology
taste blindness
taste adaptation

Competencies Check-Up

Interested in finding out what you learned in this chapter and how you use the information? If so, take this competencies check-up.

Directions: Indicate the extent that each statement applies to you:

1—Never   2—Seldom   3—Sometimes   4—Often   5—Usually

___1. I pay attention to and interpret meaning of nonverbal messages based on their context (the setting and purpose of the communication) and verbal communication (words) they accompany.

_____ 2. I recognize that both children and adults rely more on nonverbal cues than on verbal cues in determining social meaning, so I pay attention to nonverbal details.

_____ 3. I understand that people use nonverbal communication to encourage and discourage conversations and transactions.

_____ 4. I realize that the effect of culture is very persistent, and nonverbal messages must be interpreted within the cultural context.

_____ 5. I appreciate that emotions have a direct effect on the size of people's personal territory and their resulting nonverbal responses. When people are insecure, I give them space.

_____ 6. I know that people under stress often find that others loom larger and closer than they actually are. When I talk to an upset child, for example, I kneel to talk.

_____ 7. I pay attention to how well nonverbal messages substitute for, complement, conflict with, or accent the verbal (word) message. Further, I pay attention to vocalics, use of time, smell, aesthetics, the sense of taste, and other less obvious aspects of nonverbal communication.

_____ 8. Because of their particular effectiveness, I use nonverbals to communicate emotions and feelings, and express messages in a less confrontational manner.

_____ 9. Because of the expressiveness of the face, I interpret nonverbal communication expressed through the face, including the eyes.

_____10. I pay attention to emblems, illustrators, affect displays, regulators, and adaptors.

_____11. Other than shaking hands, I avoid touch in work contexts. I only use touch appropriately and never use touch as a power move. I am sensitive to potential cultural taboos, follow the permission-to-touch sequence, and respond appropriately to the reaction of others about being touched.

_____12. I give attention to artifacts so they project my self appropriately, and I interpret the artifacts of others as part of the interpersonal communication process.

_____13. I use my clothing and personal attractiveness to help convey my self in the way I desire, while considering the influence of context and culture on what is appropriate.

_____14. My spatial communication skills—including proxemics, use of distance, and comfort bubble—are high. In addition, I am highly sensitive to whether I am communicating with people of contact or noncontact cultures.

_____15. I use small-group ecology to communicate effectively.

Scoring: If your score is above 45, you probably have basic competencies in nonverbal aspects of your interpersonal communication. Evaluate your test results and figure out ways to improve how you communicate nonverbally.

I-Can Plan!

As you think about the chapter content and your test responses, create a concrete method for improving your nonverbal communication. Plan your action, and then act on your plan.

Activities

1. Research one of these topics or people and be prepared to give a two-minute speech on what you have learned regarding the topic and nonverbal communication: Neurolinguistic Programming, Ray Birdwhistell, Albert Mehrabian, Edward Hall, pupilometrics, biorhythms, Muzak, behavioral kinesiology.
2. Give examples of your own recent use of substituting, complementing, conflicting, and accenting.
3. At a family gathering, carefully observe the nonverbal patterns of each person. Can you find any similarities between their patterns and your own?
4. Identify a culture-specific nonverbal trait you have observed and describe the trait to the class.
5. Make a list of five emblems—gestures with a clear dictionary definition—you have observed made by you, members of your family, or within your culture. Be prepared to demonstrate them. Evaluate your explanations of what they mean compared to what others think.
6. Conduct a conversation with someone. As you speak, slowly move closer to him or her. Continue to move in on the person gradually. Observe his or her reaction. Did the person back up? Cross his or her arms? Make a report to the class about the results of this experiment.

CHAPTER 6

The Principles of Relational Communication

Learning Outcomes

After reading this chapter, you should be able to:

- Explain how relationships are at the very heart of our social and psychological existence.
- List and explain the forms of relationships.
- Clarify why communication plays a key role in all types of relationships.
- Define culture and explain that all aspects of people's relationships are a result of their culture.
- Apply principles of good communication—expression and acceptance—in an interpersonal relationship.
- Explain relational goals, structure, and rules.
- Distinguish relationship structures according to dominant versus submissive and loving versus hostile behavior.
- Compare and contrast complementary, symmetrical, and parallel relationships.
- Be able to explain the concept that all relationships have a structure.
- Be able to explain the difference between "like" and "love."
- Explain that men and women establish intimacy differently.
- Explain and illustrate how people use the economic model of costs and rewards in analyzing their relationships.

As the airplane reached about the half way point on its flight from Albany, New York, to Cleveland, Ohio, the pilot came on the intercom and said, "Passengers, we'd like you to shift your attention to Row 9, seats B and C. Eric has something he'd like to say to Lisa." At that moment, a portable tape recorder was switched on by a passenger seated in Row 9, seat A, Eric slipped into the aisle, and as the piano sound filled the cabin he sang words from the song "With You," from the musical Pippin, *which included such phrases as, "But all my days are twice as fair, If I could share my days with you," "But nights are warm beyond compare, If I could share my nights with you," and, "And I will need no memories there, If I could share my life with you."*

Eric dropped to one knee, pulled a velvet box from his pocket, removed an engagement ring and asked Lisa to marry him.

The passengers broke into applause.[1]

Relationships—Defined

Relationships are at the very heart of our social and psychological existence. What would your life be like without your relatives and friends? Many of our emotional highs and lows center on our relationships. Most of us, unfortunately, know little about how our relationships form and operate. Have you ever asked yourself, "Why am I friends with ___?" or looked across the room at a party as your significant other entertains, and asked yourself, "Why are we together?" After breaking up with someone you've been dating, or getting mad at a "so-called" friend, have you ever thought, "Why did I ever want that person in my life?" Most of us just assume relationships "are" and don't give much thought to how we got into them, are staying in them, or how to enhance or fix a relationship.

When you say that you have a "relationship" with another person, what do you mean? For our discussion let's say a **relationship** is a connection, association, or involvement, an emotional or other connection between people. Usually, it is perceived that relationships are more than casual contact. For example, though in a general sense you have a relationship with the Starbuck's salesperson from whom you buy your mocha cappuccino, it's no more than a surface level connection, unless he asks you on a date, and then the level of connection changes. What about that cute woman who sits three rows away from you in biology class? Again, you may say "hi" each day but you know little about each other, maybe not even her name. The same for the mail guy at work. So, what really makes a relationship?

Please remember, as we discuss relationships, that generalizations are presented. Although the principles are based on research and expert observation, no concepts can apply to every person in every context. The intent is to examine how interpersonal relationships conform to generalized patterns.

In the context of interpersonal connectedness, to use the word *relationship*, three conditions are usually present: (1) you and the other person need to be aware of each other and take each other into account, (2) there needs to be some exchange of influence, and (3) there needs to be some agreement about what the nature of the relationship is—impersonal or personal, formal or informal—and what appropriate behaviors should be given the nature of the relationship.

Although many of your relationships may contain common characteristics, each one is unique as each relationship involves a different set of people. You communicate differently depending on whether you are with a parent, a sibling, a lover, a friend, a boss, or a fellow employee.

In addition, *relationships, like all aspects of life, are constantly in a state of flux,* continually changing. Think back to any relationship you've been involved in. For example, is that best friend you have now the same person s/he was in junior high school? Is your relationship with a parent or a peer the same now as it was ten years ago? Interestingly, if you say "yes," the relationship may be in a state of stagnation. In some cases the desire of one party to take the relationship to another level, such as getting engaged rather than just dating, may be a cause of conflict. It is our inability to accept change in relationships that can cause problems in our personal connections.

People come into our lives for a reason, a season, or sometimes, forever.[2] We meet people or we seek out people who become part of our lives for various reasons. You may work with or go to school with someone. You may turn to an online dating service to find that "special" someone. Whatever, there is a reason, intentionally or not, that people come into your life. How long do they stay? Sometimes it's a quick get together and they are gone. Sometimes its as long as the committee continues to meet or as long as the semester lasts. In rare instances, the contact turns into a long-term relationship, lasting forever (however long that is).

Relationships come in a variety of forms, from the work-on-a-project type to the live-together-forever type. Relationships can be classified as (1) role relationships, (2) acquaintances, (3) friends, (4) good friends, and (5) intimate relationships. These five types of relationships are distinguishable by their communication. For example, you speak more personally with good friends than friends, and your interconnectedness is more complex with good friends. That is to say, the components of a role relationship are less complex than those of an acquaintance relationship, which are less complex than those of a friend relationship, and so on. An intimate partner relationship is the most complex. It has the most perplexing goals, structure, and rules. In fact, you can often track a relationship by what is talked about, what kind of nonverbal activities take place during interactions (e.g., holding hands, kissing), the length of time you spend interacting, the statements of expectations for each other (think back to junior high when that special someone asked you to go steady, or if you are married or living together, the point at which the agreement was made to take the relationship to that level of intimacy), and the amount of self-revealing you each do.

Role relationships are characterized by your interacting with others in light of the roles (such as the positions, functions, or jobs) you and the other person play. You may be an employee communicating with a boss, a customer talking with a salesperson, a student interacting with a professor, or a patient describing an ailment to a doctor. In each of these situations, behavior is dictated by the roles of the participants. In most instances role relationships involve very little individuality. For example, enacting the role of "student" is usually limited to performing stereotyped "student behaviors" without doing anything distinctive. In fact, doing something distinctive, such as challenging the authority of the professor, or socializing with the instructor, changes the relationship.

Acquaintances are people in your life, for either short or long periods of time with whom you share a common experience or context. You may know this person from work, school, religious organizations, sports teams, or clubs. Most of your communication with an acquaintance focuses on the common experience you share. For example, you and a person in your psychology class may discuss the tests, professor, assignments, and even other students. Although you may talk about your opinions (such as what you think the professor does well) and attitudes (such as what you dislike about the

Relationships can be classified as (1) role relationships, (2) acquaintances, (3) friends, (4) good friends, and (5) intimate relationships.

term paper assignment), rarely will you talk about anything extremely personal. If you do, the person moves from the rank of acquaintance to that of friend.

Friends are much more than acquaintances—you know more about your friends than your acquaintances, your friends know more about you than their relational acquaintances, and you feel comfortable with friends. You share more personal information with friends than acquaintances, and usually talk about a larger range of topics. Whereas the conversation with the class acquaintance may be limited to class concerns, there is no such automatic limitation on conversational topics with friends. The list of taboo and permitted topics is the result of complex negotiations, which take place over time. You learn, after a while, which topics are of mutual interest and which incite negative reactions.

Good friends are much more than friends—you know more about your good friends than your friends, and, likewise, they know much more about you. You are usually more open and honest with good friends because you believe they will be accepting of what you say and do. This mutual acceptance encourages more spontaneous behavior, as well as more mutual dependency than with acquaintances or friends.

People with whom you have an *intimate relationship* are like good friends with significant additions. Intimate relationships, such as when people are married or in long-term partnerships, have the most intricate set of rules about what may or may not be discussed, and what behaviors may or may not be tolerated. For example, a good friend may not care whether you have other good friends, but your intimate partner may not take kindly to your having additional intimate partners. Similarly, while there is usually no problem discussing past good friends with a current good friend, the topic of former intimate partners may be taboo with your present intimate partner.

In addition to the emotional, intellectual, and spiritual commonality, an intimate relationship may include sexual intimacy. The hallmarks of an intimate partner relationship are commitment and long duration, neither of which are present in a brief encounter, no matter how intense. Intimate relationships may have a sexual component, not present in other relationships.

Communication plays a key role in all five types of relationships. The verbal and nonverbal messages you send others, and the messages they send you, help establish, maintain, and change these relationships. The movement from one relationship level to another is influenced and mirrored by each partner's communication. Changes in communication as you move from a role relationship to an intimate relationship include (see Figure 6.1): an increase in open and honest self-disclosure; a decrease in stress-related behaviors; an increase in feeling relaxed; an increase in spontaneous behavior; an increase in the number of positive comments you receive from the other person; an increase in talk about the plans for the relationship; an increase in eye contact, smiling, laughing, and touching; and an increase in the number of different topics you talk about and the depth to which you discuss them.

Culture and Relationships

Culture, as in all aspects of who you are and how you communicate, plays a major role in relationships. While there are many similarities in how relationships are perceived across cultures, there are also numerous differences. In Japan, for example, individuals interact most frequently with members of the same sex; there is little social interaction

Figure 6.1. Five Types of Relationship

Complexity Spontaneity	↑	Intimate Relationships
Self-disclosure Topics of Discussion	↑	Good Friend Relationships
Depth of Discussion Comfort	↑	Friend Relationships
Positive Comments about Ourselves Talk about the Future	↑	Acquaintance Relationships
Eye Contact Smiling Laughing Touching	↑	Role Relationships

between opposite-sex individuals.[3] The Arab culture, for religious reasons, is another culture that fosters same-sex relationships and clearly limits and defines opposite-sex contact. In the Mexican culture there is a blending of different generations that is not nearly so prevalent in the more generation-segregated United States. There are also cultures that keep intimate relationships to a minimum. A German axiom makes this point clearly: "A friend to everyone is a friend to no one." The opposite view may be found in many African cultures, where a large number of close relationships is encouraged. In the Maasai culture, for example, there is a belief that everyone is interconnected. For example, a Maasai is brought up with the concept that "The child has no owner." This value is a clear indication that everyone is linked to everyone else.[4]

As people from various cultures integrate into the United States population, they carry with them their cultural patterns. Thus conflict between individuals may occur when an attempt at relational bonding takes place. The assumption on the part of some people is that because all people are living in the same country, they all follow the same relational patterns. That idea is wrong because culture is deeply ingrained and does not automatically eliminate itself when a person from one culture physically moves into another culture. Sometimes people who move to a new culture adopt some ways of the new culture and keep some ways of their old culture, and thus never feel totally at home in either culture.

Positive Relationships

There are some general concepts that have been identified to describe positive relationships from a Euro-American perspective. These include:

A good relationship allows freedom of expression and reflects acceptance of the idea that the feelings of both people are important. We should remember, however, that any alliance experiences times of uncertainty and anxiety. The persons may change as individuals, what appeared to be acceptable behaviors and attitudes may no longer be so, and can be the cause for relational cessation.

We also must recognize that *we cannot achieve happiness through someone else. If it is to be found, it must be found within ourselves.* Unfortunately, it is the desire to find happiness through someone else that may cause you to try changing people you supposedly love, when in fact your love should allow them to be themselves and do what they feel is best for themselves. A psychologist once proposed the general idea that having other people in your life is like having dessert.[5] It's nice to have them, but they aren't really necessary to complete a meal. In regard to relationships, this means that you, as a person, must realize that you are, in and of yourself, a full course meal, and that others can enhance you, but aren't necessary to make you a complete person.

Love is the ability and willingness to allow those that you care for to be what they choose for themselves without any insistence that they satisfy you. Unfortunately, this idea is easier to present as a concept than to live as a reality. Most of us spend a great deal of our time trying to alter the people we supposedly love.

Each person is totally responsible for his or her own happiness. Happiness is a choice each individual makes, not something anyone else can affect. Often people select a

Love is the ability and willingness to allow those that you care for to be what they are without insistence that they satisfy you.

partner, then set out to change that person in ways that will "make them happy." A person doesn't change unless s/he wants to do so. It is not wise to go into a relationship thinking "He isn't perfect, but I can change him." Unless a person wants to change, he or she isn't a candidate for a rehabilitation program.

Communication is the key to creating and maintaining positive relationships. Research shows that couples who are happily married argue no less vigorously for their own positions than do those who are not happily married. But happily married couples come to agreement fairly readily, through either one partner giving in to the other without resentment, or by working out compromise. Unhappily married people tend to get caught in a situation that centers on cross-complaining. Neither partner is willing to give in to resolve a dispute; each must continue to have his or her own way.

An approach to successful relational communication centers on six guidelines:

When you are speaking, get into the habit of using "I" messages instead of "you" messages. Indicate what you are feeling and thinking or how you are reacting to the situation rather than accusing the other person. Say "I feel . . . " or "I think . . . " rather than "You did . . . " or "You make me. . . ." Report facts to back up your contentions. Rather than saying, "You are always late" try "I get upset when you tell me you will be here at 2:00 and you arrive at 2:45."

If you have a problem with the way your partner does dishes, for example, that's *your* problem, not his or hers. First, you may want to think of the consequences of complaining, which could result in your partner no longer doing dishes. Second, don't blame the other person with a statement like this: "What's the matter with you. You didn't rinse the dishes like you should have." Instead you can use an I-message like: "When I emptied the dishwasher, I noticed food, milk rings, and chocolate stuck to the dishes. I think they'd be clean if the really dirty dishes and glasses were rinsed first." An I-message will allow you to express yourself *and* deal with the other person's behavior.

It is difficult to argue with an "I" message, You aren't accusing the other person, so it is unlikely that s/he can get defensive and counterattack. This is especially true if you state facts from your perspective and avoid the accusatory "you" word and generalizations.

Respond to what the other person has said. When you go off on a tangent without first having replied to the original statement, you are catching the other person unaware.

In the dishwashing example, your partner might say: "I agree, if you'd rinse your dishes as soon as you finish eating, the food wouldn't stick to them." There's no need to "go off" on the other person ("You want cleaner dishes, then you wash them!") or going off on a tangent ("The dishes are nothing compared to the mess you leave in your car."). Instead, stick with the subject. Attack the problem, not the other person.

Give the other person freedom of speech. If you want to have the opportunity to state your view, you must also be willing to hear out the other person. By doing so you may even gain some insights into the other person's actions.

Again, using the dishwashing tale, the other person may not be aware of the problem. Upon being told of your concern, s/he might say, "You always empty the dishwasher. I didn't realize the dishes weren't clean."

After being aware of the issue, there may be a logical explanation such as. "Hmm, that's interesting. I switched the brand of soap I was buying in order to save money. I'm doing the dishes the same way, so we need to go back to the better soap. Thanks for letting me know about the problem. With all the illnesses going around, we don't need spoiled food on our plates."

If you are in a relationship, set aside talking time. We often get so busy that we forget to talk to each other. Don't talk only when there is stress or disagreement. Remember that people are not mind-readers. Don't assume the other person knows what you are thinking. Phrases such as "you should have known," are of little value. Unless you let the other person know what you are thinking and feeling, they probably won't know. No one is a mind reader, though you may assume that because you are an important person in someone's life they should know what you are thinking or feeling, they usually don't know.

Having private time for the two of you—just to talk about your day or whatever—does much to help a relationship. A couple who takes a walk has a chance to talk without interruptions from the telephone, children, dogs, or the blare of the television. Interestingly, walking, according to psychologists, is a good activity because it places the participants in a good interaction position . . . side-by-side, rather than face-to-face.[6] According to the theory, face-to-face interactions are more confrontational, especially for men. Looking at each other eye-to-eye is more likely to incite conflict.[7]

Do not put labels on either yourself or the other person. Name-calling can be destructive and doesn't solve issues. Stating the issue and discussing it can possibly solve it or, at least, get it out into the open. If the issue is trying to get the dishes clean, calling your partner a slob or stating, "You are just like your mother, she never could do anything right, either," will probably incite conflict and not solve the problem.

We teach others how to treat us. People learn how you want to be treated and dealt with by following your lead. If they act or react in a particular way, and you don't object to that treatment, the assumption is that what they did or said is acceptable to you. The next time a similar situation comes up, they will remember your past actions, or lack of actions, and repeat their previous pattern. For example, if someone verbally or physically attacks you, and you don't say or do something to indicate that you won't accept that kind of behavior, the assumption will be made that that negative type of treatment is acceptable to you. On the other hand, if you object, indicate you will not be spoken to or treated in that way, you have alerted the other person that his/her behavior is not acceptable. At times it is not only necessary to state your negative reaction to someone's actions, but also to set parameters, including actions that you will take if the behavior is repeated. For example, if someone yells at you, you can say, "I don't appreciate being yelled at. If you do that again, I will leave the room." If you make a threat, make sure you are ready and able to take the action threatened. Threats not carried out only encourage the person to continue to take the undesirable action. It is easier to eliminate negative patterns of interaction the first time they happen than try to adjust behavior later. Once a pattern is set, it is hard to break.

Anytime you think, "I don't like the way I'm being treated or spoken to," you owe it to yourself to take some action to stop your being a victim. Watch out for specific communication patterns that cause conflict in intimate relationships.

Teasing can also be destructive. Teasing can start out as fun, but often has an underlying message behind it that is not humor. When people get angry, humor can become the source of attack and conflict.

Psychological manipulation also can result in relational trouble. Such activities as trying to make a person measure up to preset expectations, making an individual prove how much he or she loves you, and forcing someone with whom you have a relationship to follow your wishes can result in conflicts that are not reconcilable.

Another problem occurs when you attempt to make your partner fuse with you or vice versa. **Relational fusion** takes place when one partner defines, or attempts to define, reality for the other. In other words, the controller dictates what is good, right, and acceptable for the partner. If the partner, at first, allows that to happen, the pattern for the future can be set. Then, when the defined partner wants to break the pattern, abuse may result. You teach others how to treat you. If you allow others to verbally or physically abuse you, and you don't take action to stop the abuse, a cycle is set in motion.

People who are unhappy in their relationships tend to talk *at* each other, *past* each other, or *through* each other, but rarely *with* or *to* each other. Just because you're talking doesn't mean you are communicating. Though couples may spend time talking with each other, many lack the skills needed to get their messages across effectively, to express their feelings, or to resolve conflicts without emotionally or physically hurting each other or provoking anger.

The Framework for Interaction in Relationships

Relationships are complex. To understand them means breaking them down into their component parts and looking at each part separately. That sounds like an academic and not "real world" activity. However, even though you probably don't consciously analyze your relationships because they "just happen," your decision to stay in or leave a relationship is based on your evaluation of whether the relationship is of any value to you.

Each of your relationships has goals, structure, and rules that form the context within which you and the other person interact and make decisions about whether to remain in the relationship, and the nature of the relationship if you do continue it. Your communication both reflects and determines each of the three relational dimensions.

LEARNING EXPERIENCE: Interested in finding out about your relational needs and wants ? If so, do Activity 6.1.

With your answer in mind, let's look at the basis for the descriptions you chose to include or avoid. These include your goals for the structure and sense of commitment regarding the relationship.

Relational Goals

Relationships form because of some relational goal, some relational outcome that each person wishes to achieve. The goals may be such things as overcoming loneliness, changing another's attitude or behavior, completing a project, killing time, releasing tension, being entertained, helping someone, fulfilling a family responsibility, or becoming intimate with someone. There are as many goals as there are individuals, cultures, and relationships.

The differences among the advertisements you wrote reflect the differences in your goals for each relationship. Although the general goal for each—"a work relationship," "a friend relationship," or "a loving relationship"—is prescribed, you meet your specific needs and desires by seeking particular characteristics in a partner in a relationship.

ACTIVITY 6.1
Placing a Personal Ad

Assume you have relational vacancies in your life. Write three personal ads for people to fill these vacancies. Specify the exact characteristics you want in the other individual as well as the personal qualities you have to offer. (If you need help with this activity look at personal ads in local papers or online to serve as models.

1. Advertise for a person with whom you wish to establish a work or school relationship. (What do you want? What do you offer?)

2. Advertise for a person with whom you wish to establish a friendship. (What do you want? What do you offer?)

3. Advertise for a person with whom you wish to establish a loving and caring/ intimate relationship. (What do you want? What do you offer?)

How do your advertisements differ from each other? Do your descriptions relate to each relationship's goal, such as "to have fun," "to get a job done," or "to keep from being bored"? Do they refer to whether you are the person in the relationship who plays the role of "the leader," or the subordinate one, "the follower?" Do some characterizing words focus on the amount of love and affection or hate and hostility you want in the particular relationship? Did you concern yourself with some of the rules that make each relationship unique, such as "to date each other exclusively," or "to have a 50–50 partnership in the business"? Did you use such words as *commitment* or *intimacy*?

What did you learn about yourself and the qualities you possess and which you desire in a relationship?

LEARNING EXPERIENCE: Interested in finding out what your goals are for specific relationships? If so, do Activity 6.2.

The goals of our relationships are affected by **dialectical tension**, our intrapersonal and interpersonal conflicts over our wants and needs. Sometimes we want to be closer to a partner and share everything, while at other times we want more privacy. Sometimes we want to be close physically to another person, and at other times we want our own space. Sometimes we want to be dependent on the other, while other

---

ACTIVITY 6.2
Relational Goals

Select three relationships in which you are currently involved: (a) an acquaintance relationship, (b) a friend relationship, and (c) a good friend relationship.

1. What are your goals for each relationship?
   (a)

   (b)

   (c)

2. Are the goals the same? Why not?

---

times we want the other person to back off and let us be independent. Sometimes we want to be spontaneous, while at other times we like to have everything planned out. "Surprise!" will go over well one day, but over badly another day.

Our interpersonal relational goals are always pushing us toward or pulling us away from people. The problem comes, for example, when you want to go out with friends (be more independent) and your partner wants your help (be more dependent). People who can't recognize and adjust to conflicting goals, and deal with them in constructive ways, are going to be frustrated in their communication and in their relationships.[8]

Your goals for love, friendship, and work relationships usually seek different outcomes. On the other hand, there also may be some similarities. Assume, for example, that you seek a person with whom to share an intimate relationship who is kind and considerate, a friend who likes the theatre and physically challenging experiences, and a work partner who is financially responsible and well educated. Each set of characteristics reveals different relationship goals: to share a long-term intimate relationship, to provide companionship, and to complete some task efficiently. A person seeking a work partner who focuses exclusively on intelligence, experience, and a willingness to work hard reveals different goals from one seeking a partner who is easygoing and flexible. Someone seeking a friend who is a good listener has a different goal from someone who seeks a person with whom to share weekends of mountain climbing. Seeking a partner for an intimate relationship who is quiet and considerate displays different goals than looking for someone wild, exciting, and willing to take risks. If you have ever looked through the personals in a newspaper or gone on-line to a dating or mating service, you may have glanced at an ad and thought, "Why would anyone be looking for those characteristics?" or "That sounds like a keeper."

How did you make your choices? As you read the announcement you decided that the person did or did not fit your goals. If you were negative toward what the person wrote, it doesn't mean that the person isn't of value, but that he or she doesn't fit your values, wants, needs, goals. Although most people seek a relational partner who is quite similar to themselves, some differences can add interest. If you are not good at planning, you may enjoy a partner who has that skill because it creates a type of balance. The very quality you love in good times may be what drives you crazy about the other person in challenging times.

Your needs and wants may be influenced by your culture as not all cultures have the same goals for their relationships nor do they apply the same list of traits when seeking partners to fulfill those goals. For example, in Indian and Arabic cultures, or among people who were raised in those cultures, a male generally would be interested in a subservient woman. In Scandinavia, on the other hand, many women would be repelled by a male who would want to control them and define their lifestyle or even their clothing choices.

Intimate Relationships

Intimate relationships are the most complex and involved. In the United States, 45 to 50 percent of first marriages end in divorce.[9] The highest percentage of divorces are for those under twenty years of age to those twenty-four years of age.[10] In spite of these statistics, people continue to get married. In fact, a major political and moral battle is raging over a person's right to be in a recognized intimate legal and spiritual relationship. The attempt by political bodies, religious groups, and gay/lesbian organizations to define marriage, considered by many to be the highest form of intimate relationship, illustrates the importance of these types of relationships.

Intimate relationships provide stimulation (an escape from loneliness and boredom) and an opportunity to share experiences (whether a beautiful sunset or a horrible test grade). Intimate relationships frequently present a nonthreatening arena in which to try out new ideas and behaviors, and often increases enjoyment of certain activities, as sharing time with your companion is usually more satisfying than being with strangers. Intimate relationships also provide an opportunity for self-disclosure, the self-revealing communication that strips away the front you present to others and displays the person you really are. Accompanying the rewards, however, are potential costs, the greatest of which is rejection by the other person.

Regardless of the particular goals you have for an intimate relationship, you should bear several things in mind. First, people rarely set out to form an intimate relationship in a rational and intellectual way. Their conscious aim often is something other than to become involved. People seldom enter a classroom with a specific plan for leaving with a commitment, although many individuals have met in a class and eventually lived together or gotten married.

Most relationships are not formed with the primary goal of achieving intimacy. Usually, relationships form as accompaniments to everyday activities. For instance, you like to jog, so you meet people who share the same interest; you may not think about extending the relationship beyond your noontime run. Or a class project may require you to work with another student; your only goal may be to fulfill the assignment.

Nonetheless, in the back of your mind at certain times during your lifetime, your specific goal may be to find someone with whom you can follow a path toward intimacy—a person with whom to share your innermost thoughts and feelings and, possibly even your love. For example, teenage girls often want "a boyfriend" and set out to achieve that goal. As people in the U.S. American culture reach their mid-twenties, they may think it is "time" to find a mate. Women in their mid-to-late thirties who want children may perceive that their biological clocks are ticking and set out on a path to find someone to father their children (assuming they want a person, rather than going to a sperm bank). If this is the case, the goal—to seek out and develop an *intimate* relationship—is conscious, not a by-product of other relationships with different goals. Interestingly, in some cultures, such as some Indian, Arabic, or Orthodox Jewish groups, prearranged marriages eliminate the search for such relationships as they are arranged by the parents or a matchmaker.

LEARNING EXPERIENCE: Interested in further probing into your goals for being in a relationship? If so, do Activity 6.3.

The Structure of Relationships

The characteristics you want in a partner often reflect how you expect to interact with her or him and the **relational structure**, the patterns of how the relationship works. For some people, the patterns of interaction in work, friendship, and loving relationships might be similar, even if the goals are different. For example, you might want to be the person who controls what happens, whether the goal is to complete a project with a school mate or to see a movie with a friend.

A relationship may be like a slow dance. Two people move together in a coordinated display. The partners may glide about smoothly, anticipating each other's movements and responding with grace, or they may appear awkward and out of step. Or, the relationship may be like a wrestling match—each partner trying to outmaneuver the other or defeat him or her. Relationships are distinguished by the structure of their communication—how their talk is organized and coordinated—much as dancers are distinguished by their choreography or wrestlers by their strength and strategies.

Three possible relationship structures have been identified. These structures can be classified as complementary, symmetrical, and parallel relationships.

In a **complementary relationship**, one partner's behavior complements or completes the other's—the behaviors seem to go together. The relationship is based on differences (for example, one partner may be dominant while the other is submissive). When they come together, they form a stable relationship in which both participants are happy with their own role and accepting of their partner's role. Each partner has

---

**ACTIVITY 6.3
My Relational Goals**

Select a relationship in which you are now involved (for example, a work relationship, a friendship, an intimate relationship, a family member). Complete these statements regarding that relationship.

1. I am in this relationship in order to . . .

2. I stay in this relationship with this person because . . .

3. This relationship will continue until . . .

4. This relationship will end once . . .

What have you discovered about your goals for this relationship?

---

particular duties and obligations, whether one works and earns the family income while the other manages the home, or one washes the dishes while the other dries. The partners work better in combination than alone. If the combination is acceptable to both parties, and their actions work well together, then a complementary set of actions takes place. This illustrates that not only can opposites attract, but they can form a positive and productive relationship if they understand and cooperatively use each other's strengths. For example, one of the authors of this book and his wife have different styles of decision making. He works rapidly, she works slowly. They have worked out a system regarding purchasing of major items. After they both agree that the item should be purchased, he goes out and finds several products that he finds acceptable, he brings home the literature or the samples and then she takes her time making up her mind which of those she prefers. If none are acceptable, he goes out again. This system is used for selecting art work, wall paint colors, appliances, even the purchase of their home. This system slows down his urge to "get it done quickly" with the possibility of purchasing something that is undesirable, and her tendency to wait and wait until the purchase is made.

In a **symmetrical relationship** the partners contribute equally to their relationship, thus creating a balance. Whereas the partners in a complementary relationship create a whole from their two separate parts, partners in a symmetrical relationship maintain their individual identities. In the ideal symmetrical relationship, power is equally distributed, independence is stressed, and both partners are either submissive or dominant. Though ideal, there are few truly symmetrical relationships. Though there may be equal sharing in some areas it is nearly impossible for two people in a relationship to share all responsibilities equally. This disparity leads to a hybrid type of relationship referred to as a parallel relationship.

In the **parallel relationship** complementary and symmetrical aspects are combined. One partner may be dominant and the other submissive at times; other times, the partners may reverse roles; and sometimes, both partners may be dominant or both may be submissive. In general, the parallel structure allows contributions to the relationship to vary from time to time and topic to topic. What happens is that one person performs certain tasks, the other person performs others. For example, in a marriage, one person handles the household maintenance, the other the couple's social scheduling and family maintenance. Financial decisions, a major cause of marital conflict, is taken care of by having a joint account for household expenses. For example, if both partners bring in income, the total household expenses are figured out, each person puts into the general fund the percentage of his/her income in relationship to the total costs. This becomes "our" money. The remainder of each person's income becomes "my" money so each partner has his or her own account for personal wants. Both are happy with their "roles" so the couples are acting symmetrically with little conflict. This approach sounds theoretical, but marriage experts report very good success in eliminating financial conflict and equal power distribution with this approach.[11]

Relational Rules

Relational rules, the regulations that govern actions in a relationship, are necessary for you to make predictions about another person's behavior. If you don't know the rules governing your interaction, you can't predict whether the person to whom you nod and say hello will, in return, ignore you, hit you, or start screaming. But because most people share the same rule for greeting behavior, you can predict a reciprocal response: a nod and hello will get you a nod and hello in return. Rules and customs organize the world for you, add predictability, and reduce uncertainty.

Most people like to reduce the uncertainty of relationships because they want to be able to predict what the other person will do. Like all rules, some may be more important than others in particular relationships and in particular societies, and some may even be broken. The five general relational rules found in democratic but not autocratic cultures tend to be:

1. You should respect the other's privacy.
2. You should look the other person in the eye during conversations.
3. You should not divulge something that is said in confidence.
4. You should not criticize the other person publicly.
5. You should seek to repay debts, favors, or compliments, no matter how small.

Several specific *relational structure rules*, the format for the structure of particular relationships, such as loving, friendship, and work relationships, have been determined. Specific rules in democratic, but not necessary in autocratic cultures are:[12]

1. You should stand up for the other person in her or his absence.
2. You should share news of success with her or him.
3. You should show emotional support.
4. You should trust and confide in each other.
5. You should volunteer your help in time of need.
6. You should strive to make the other person happy when you are with her or him.
7. You should not nag the other person.

To what extent do the relational and structural rules found in relationships around the world exist in your own relationships? Are there differences in how the rules apply to your good friend, friend, and acquaintance relationships? You may find that the relational rule "you should respect the other's privacy" is very important in your good friend, friend, and acquaintance relationships, but that "you should not criticize the other person publicly," while also important in all relationships, is most important in your good friend relationship and only moderately important in your acquaintance relationship. Similarly, you may find that the structural rule, "you should volunteer your help in time of need" is very important in all relationships, but that "you should trust and confide in each other" is only important in your good friend relationship. For some people, asking for help shows more commitment to a relationship than providing help. The feeling of indebtedness affects relationships. What do the differences and similarities in how these rules apply to your different types of relationships reveal about your relationships as well as your relationship rules?

The differences and similarities you find among relationships in terms of their rules are determined, in part, by your cultural values. Rules are influenced and modified by each culture; therefore, people from other cultures would not necessarily answer the same way. For example, the rule concerning privacy is a perfect illustration of how different cultures can respond differently to the same message. Some cultures don't even have a word or definition for the concept of "trespassing." In relationships in these societies, invasion of someone's personal territory is simply not a matter of consideration, it just happens. People touch and get close to others with no thought of doing something that would make the other uncomfortable. Privacy is not valued. In cultures such as those of the Arabs, Greeks, and Mexicans, which have a strong group orientation, seclusion is not usually part of an individual's set of needs when dealing with members of their own group.

There is a definite contrast when compared to customs found in French, English, German, and North American cultures.[13] In the latter, privacy and personal space are valued. Think of what is being said by the U.S. American proverb "A man's [or woman's] home is his [her] castle" in contrast to the Mexican proverb "Mi casa es su casa" ("My house is your house").

A friendship may evolve into a love relationship. If it does, new rules arise, mostly concerned with self-disclosure and the expression of emotion. If the love relationship culminates in marriage or a living-together commitment, the number of rules increases dramatically to virtually all forms of interaction, both with the partner and with people outside the relationship. Rules may develop about who can dance with whom at a party (relatives may be okay, but not people one dated in the past), who can have lunch with whom, and even whom a person can talk with on the phone. Parents, for example, may restrict a teenager's phone or texting or e-mail time. The multitude of rules arises from an attempt to keep the communication orderly and predictable, but the very number of rules points to a high probability of conflict and friction between spouses or relational partners. It is interesting that people who get married after living together often report a major change in their relationship. The difference? The rules change.

Unique rules, as well as universal rules, govern interaction in a work relationship. Rules, which may be encoded in the organization's policies or for which there is an unspoken set of guidelines, are often in place. For example, intimacy rules such as those protecting an employee from sexual harassment, or regulations concerning not dating other employees, or bosses not dating those they supervise may be clearly stated. But task-maintenance rules, such as "Both people should accept a fair share of the workload" and "Workers should cooperate" may be understandings.

Rules also exist for topics that should and should not be discussed. For example, in both platonic and intimate relationships, talking about the current or future state of the relationship may be considered taboo because partners fear that such talk might destroy the relationship. Thus, you might want to talk about making a lifelong commitment, but avoid the topic because you fear scaring away a potential partner. For example, though it is often the subject of jokes, males sometimes do exhibit **commitment phobia**, the fear of dedicating himself to a single person.[14] Someone with commitment phobia might fear the end of youth or may just be afraid of a long-term vow. They are not likely to identify themselves as having commitment issues, but the results tend to be the same, "his or her partner is left hurt and rejected."[15] Women also appear to exhibit commitment phobia, as dramatized in the movie, *The Runaway Bride*. There have been reported cases of "real" women who have what appears to be commitment phobia.[16]

To further complicate matters, how rules apply to particular situations may be unclear. For example, you may know, in general, rules about intimacy, but be unaware about the rules governing the first kiss or having sexual intercourse. When should it happen? Should it happen? What should you say, if anything? Do you know each other well enough to talk before having an intimate experience? How can you avoid looking like a sex pervert or the most desperate person around?

You may not consciously apply the general rules, but you probably resort to them anyway because they create a structure that makes beginning an interaction moderately predictable and not unpleasant. As a relationship grows, however, more rules need to be negotiated. Whether you and your partner sit down face-to-face and discuss existing rules or ones that need to be created, or whether you proceed in a less formal way, such as trying some action and assuming, if there is no objection, then that's the "new" rule, the task cannot be avoided.

LEARNING EXPERIENCE: Interested in finding out what rules guide your relationships? If so, do Activity 6.4.

ACTIVITY 6.4
Your Relationship Rules

Select either an important family relationship or an important nonfamily relationship. Answer each of the following questions.

1. What are two rules that you have for each person? (e.g., "Don't take my things without asking." "Call me if you are going to be late.")

2. What are two of the other person's rules for you?

3. What are two shared rules that give the relationship excitement?

4. What are two shared rules that give the relationship stability?

5. What are two shared rules that give the relationship personal and mutual benefits?

6. Write two positive and two negative statements about how you feel about the rules. (Are some hard to follow? Are they negotiable?)

7. How do you ensure that the other person follows the rules?

8. What does the other person do to make sure you follow the rules?

What did you learn about yourself and the other person as it relates to relational rules?

The Systems Approach to Relationships

All relationships have a structure, a **system of relational operation**. Each person has a role he or she plays and rules by which the relationship will operate. The rules for a relationship develop gradually. In fact, much of the maintenance stage of a relationship centers on forming a system of operation and then adjusting the operational rules for maintaining the relationship. Think of a couple or family you know. What are the do's and don't rules of that relationship? These do's and don'ts define the relationship and how it operates.

A system that is operating to the general satisfaction of the participants is a **functional relational system**. As long as no one changes the system and each member of the relationship maintains his or her assigned role, the structure is working. But if someone wants alterations, wants to do things that are not normally done, then the system becomes a **dysfunctional relational system**. In a healthy relational system, when conflicts do arise, the partners are capable of working out the problems without destroying the relationship or building up bad feelings. They are capable of recalibrating the system, restructuring and reconstituting how the relationship operates. They have learned such skills as fighting fair, positive conflict resolution, have adopted a problem-solving pattern, and have respect for each other to the degree that the relationship is more important than winning an argument. They accept that conflicts will happen, but there is usually a way to confront those issues for the sake of the relationship.

In contrast, in a **dysfunctional relational system**, one in which its members are confused about the roles they are to play, where "I" is more important than the "we," where one partner feels he or she must be in control, where jealousy and distrust exist, where weak communication skills are present, recalibration is often impossible.

It is often possible to understand a relationship by investigating the pronouns the participants use to describe the component parts of the system. Phrases such as "*my* house," versus "*our* house," may be a clue to the connectedness or separateness of the relationship.

This does not mean to suggest that unhealthy relational systems are not operational. Some people learn to live with physical or emotional abuse, live on the brink of financial disaster, or give in to the inconsistent behavior of alcoholics and drug users.

The need to reestablish a system is not necessarily disastrous. In fact, most relationships go through adjustments on a regular basis. As a system is being **recalibrated**—restructured—growth can take place. People learn to assume new roles, develop new respect for each other, or make a new team effort. On the other hand, chaos may result as people fight for new role identities, defend their emotional territories, or feel compelled to make changes not to their liking.

Besides the goals, structure, language, and rules that establish the framework for a relationship, relationships have quality and resources.

A relationship's quality can be classified by such terms as "goodness" or "badness." If asked, you could probably rank any of your relationships along a continuum from good to bad, from high quality to low. Similarly, you could probably also describe your relationships with respect to the resources, or benefits, they provide.

Qualities that are important for understanding any relationship are love/like, commitment, and intimacy.

LOVE/LIKE

The **Theory of Love/Like**[17] describes a very important, but little understood aspect of relationships. The theory proposes that **love** is an *emotional feeling* of relational bonding. The reason for loving someone takes no explanation, no reasoning. It just is. It is an ephemeral feeling. It is an intrapersonal reaction which is explained with the words, "I love him/her/it." It may be a feeling toward a lover, child, life partner, pet, or anything to which you have an emotional attachment. In its truest sense, love is unconditional. You love the object of your emotion without boundaries, for as long as the feeling exists. Whether the "puppy" love of tweens, the "I can't live without you" love of teenagers, or the love that inspires a couple to get married or have a commitment ceremony, it isn't based on "I will love you as long as you satisfy some need or want I have." For all intents and purposes, it is unconditional.

On the other hand, **like** is a *rational evaluation of a person* which is conditional. There are actions that the other person may take, statements that may be said, ideas expressed or acted out, which make the relational bonding conditional. The breaking of a trust, acting in an unacceptable way, not fulfilling some ethical or moral rule, or displaying infidelity, may cause a breach in relational bonding.

Understanding the Theory of Love/Like allows for individuals to work through many conflicts that might otherwise lead to a total fracturing of a relational bond. A father, for example, after his teenage son is suspended from school because of breaking some academic rule, may say, "I will always love you, but I don't like you very much right now." A mother might say to a daughter, "Homosexuality is against my religious belief, and since you came out to me I don't like your lesbian lifestyle, but it has no effect on my continued love for you." Accepting the language of the Theory of Love/Like allows a person to be able to explain the emotionally unexplainable, and not act irrationally. It helped a student to answer the question she posed regarding how it was possible to continue to love the person to whom she had been engaged. He had had an affair with one of her friends. Therefore, she broke the engagement. She stated, "I hate him, how can I still love him?" After the discussion, she smilingly stated, "I get it. I can still love him, I just don't like him. And, since I don't want to be in a relationship with someone I don't like, I'm okay with these feelings. I don't want to have anything to do with him." She related several weeks later that she was sleeping better, and not daydreaming about her ex during classes. Yes, being able to place ideas and feelings into language is often a breakthrough to understanding the thoughts and feelings.

COMMITMENT

Commitment, as it relates to relationships, is a popular word to toss into magazine articles and sprinkle into conversations. It appears to imply a great deal about a relationship, such as: "She's afraid of committing herself to anything," and "He has trouble even saying the word commitment," or "If you're not committed to completing the project, why did you agree to do it in the first place?"

Commitment, a pledge to become involved in, or to the continuation of, a relationship or project, includes your intentions, your perception of the other's intentions, and to what you are committed. In general, you link your commitment with the perceived connection to the other person or the other person's connection to you. If you think your partner is less committed than you, you are likely to decrease commitment;

similarly, if you think the other person is more highly committed, you might increase your commitment. A relationship is unstable if the levels of commitment are unequal. For example, if you see your relationship as a long-term involvement to which you're highly committed, a problem may arise if your partner sees it as a casual pastime involving little commitment.

The meaning of the phrase "commitment to a relationship" is vague, but each person who is involved in a relationship to which he or she is committed has a definition and explanation of why they are committed to the other person. The reasons may be clear or may be below the person's level of awareness. For example, you may commit yourself to continuing the relationship even if you and your partner are separated by geographical distance, or you may commit yourself to increasing the intimacy of your relationship, or you may commit yourself to working together to increase business sales. Often, however, you haven't voiced your reason, to yourself or to others. It is often wise to ask yourself why you are committed to the relationship to determine whether you really are interested in continuing it.

LEARNING EXPERIENCE: Interested in finding out your level of commitment to a relationship with either a good friend or an intimate partner? If so, do Activity 6.5.

INTIMACY

Intimacy is an umbrella term that includes, among other things, emotional closeness and intellectual sharing. Essentially, intimacy is a quality of a relationship based on detailed knowledge and deep understanding of the other person. Consider these questions with respect to one of your relationships:

1. How much do you really know about each other?
2. To what degree are your life and the other person's life intertwined and interdependent?
3. Do you trust each other?

Each of these questions relates to one aspect of intimacy and underscores the difficulty of defining precisely what intimacy is.

Intimacy is an expectation you have for a relationship, an anticipation that you and your partner will come to know each other more and more deeply, more and more personally—that you will continue to share intimate experiences.

Intimacy and intimate experiences are not identical. Although any relationship may include an intimate experience—sexual activity or a moment of important personal sharing, for example—it is only in intimate relationships that continued intimate experiences can be expected.

The intimacy of a relationship may be determined by examining three factors. First, what is the breadth and depth of the information you and your partner know about each other? Breadth refers to the number of topics you discuss and depth

ACTIVITY 6.5
Commitment Probe

Think of a relationship you have with either a good friend or intimate partner.

With the selected relationship in mind, mark each statement using this scale:

Mark 1 if the statement is definitely false.
Mark 2 if it is mostly false.
Mark 3 if it is neither true nor false.
Mark 4 if it is mostly true.
Mark 5 if it is definitely true.

_____1. It is likely that my partner and I will be together six months from now.
_____2. I am not attracted to other potential partners.
_____3. A potential partner would have to be truly outstanding for me to pursue a new relationship.
_____4. It is likely that this relationship will be permanent.
_____5. My partner is likely to continue this relationship.
_____   Total your five responses. This is your commitment score.

A relationship identified as "casual dating" has an average commitment score of 13, one identified as "exclusively involved" has an average score of 17, and a marriage relationship has an average score of 21. Where does your friendship or intimate relationship fit along this continuum?

Commitment can be an important factor for long term success in a relationship. Although the term commitment is often applied to relationships on a path toward intimacy—such as dating relationships—it is equally important in long-term work relationships, particularly partnerships. Scores below 16 indicate a weak or unstable work partnership, one likely to break up if an attractive offer comes along from outside the relationship. The higher the commitment score, the more stable the relationship and the higher the probability that it will continue.

What did you learn about your commitment to the relationship you just examined?

Source: Adapted from Lund, M. (1985). The development of investment and commitment scales for predicting continuity of personal relationships. *Journal of Social and Personal Relationships, 2,* 3–23.

pertains to how important and personal the information is. As breadth and depth increase, so does intimacy.

The breadth and depth of the information we share with our partners often reflects our cultural background. In many cultures people are expected to know what someone else is thinking and feeling. Hence, in cultures such as the Japanese, expressions of intimacy are very different from those used in the United States.[18] There is often difficulty when someone from a **revealing culture**,[19] such as in North America where *self*-image, *self*-esteem, and *self*-awareness are important and the word "I" appears with great regularity, attempts to get highly personal with someone from a **nonrevealing culture**,[20] a culture in which personal issues are not discussed. In the Chinese culture, for example, thoughts of the self are suspended to the degree that there is no specific symbol for selfish. (The closest symbol for selfishness is two different symbols that mean "I" placed together.)

Learning all you can about another person's openness, based on his or her cultural background, helps you decide how much information you should disclose and how much you should expect the other person to disclose without making your partner feel uncomfortable.

Second, in what ways are you and the other person's lives interdependent? As you and this person share and learn to depend on each other for support, understanding, and maybe security, you become mutually dependent for the satisfaction of your needs, wants, and desires. Intimacy and interdependence, however, are not related in a simple way. The most intimate relationships are characterized by an interdependence that allows each person's maximum satisfaction but also has limits and flexibility so that one person doesn't feel overwhelmed or smothered by the other. A relationship in which one person is dependent on another to meet all of his/her needs can be unhealthy. Few of us like to be controlled by another person. If the other person restricts us due to his or her jealousy, needs physical or emotional domination of the other, or places the other person on a financial or emotional tightrope, conflict can erupt. The conflict can be emotional or physical. Emotional conflict can result in the controlled person feeling depressed, manipulated, or powerless. Physical control can manifest itself as the need to escape through suicide, fleeing the scene, depression, or killing the other person.

Third, how much do I trust my partner to accept me just the way I am? Will s/he avoid purposely hurting me, keep my best interests and the best interests of our relationship in mind, to share with me, and to continue the relationship? Your answers determine the degree to which you allow yourself to be vulnerable to your partner. Without trust, relationships tend to be communicatively closed. You might fear being exploited, so you keep information to yourself, hide your real thoughts and feelings and have little faith in what the other person has to say.

LEARNING EXPERIENCE: Interested in finding out what your perceived level of intimacy is in a relationship? If so, do Activity 6.6.

Research shows that Euro-American men and women establish intimacy differently and often have a different definition of what intimacy means.[21] Men generally tend to develop their intimacy by doing things together. A friend is someone you do

ACTIVITY 6.6
Intimacy Probe

Think of a relationship you have with a good friend or intimate partner—whether you are dating, exclusively involved, or married—and with that relationship in mind, mark each statement according to how strongly you agree or disagree with it using this scale:

Mark 1 if you strongly disagree with the statement.
Mark 2 if you disagree with the statement.
Mark 3 if you neither disagree nor agree with the statement.
Mark 4 if you agree with the statement.
Mark 5 if you strongly agree with the statement.

_____1. The other person and I have a great deal of information about each other.
_____2. The other person and I are highly interdependent.
_____3. The other person and I perform a great many services for each other.
_____4. The other person and I support each other.
_____5. The other person and I understand each other.
_____6. The other person and I satisfy each other's needs, wants, and desires.
_____7. The other person and I accept each other as we are.
_____8. The other person and I avoid hurting each other.
_____   Total your eight responses. This is your intimacy score.

KEY:
A total score of 32 and above indicates a high degree of intimacy, while scores of 20 and below indicate a low degree of intimacy. High scores tend to indicate a relationship that is more fulfilling. Examine each of the eight scores for each relationship. The higher a particular score, the higher is that aspect of intimacy in the relationship and, therefore, the greater the possibility that the individual item may be an integral part of the relationship.

What did you learn about your relationship from doing this activity?

things for, such as favors, and with whom you participate in sports or fixing a car. For men, mutual liking and closeness, feelings of interdependence, and mutual appreciation are an outgrowth of shared activities that do not depend on disclosure. A team rather than a person is often the basis for male relationships. Even if a man has a best "buddy" it is unlikely that they will share intimate personal data.

Women, on the other hand, tend to establish intimacy through personal talk, disclosure, mutual projects. Women tend to have "best friends"; men tend to have group friendship relations.

As you can imagine, differences in female and male means of establishing relationships and intimacy can be a source of problems. The "inexpressive" male shows his caring and desire for intimacy by fixing his wife's car or talking about work in a nonpersonal way. The "disclosive" female interprets his lack of expressiveness as avoiding closeness. This problem escalates when considering the meaning and timing of sex in a relationship. Whereas many women think of sex as a way to *express* intimacy that is already developed, for many men sex is a means to create intimacy.[22] A female, for example, may give in to having sex with a man if she perceives it as a means to get relational commitment. She may perceive that being intimate means emotional commitment. This is not necessarily what it means to many males.

Relational Resources

Relationships, whether intimate or not, serve as sources for tangible benefits, such as money and gifts; intangible benefits, such as affection and emotional support; and service benefits, such as help with your gardening or getting you a book from the library. Important resources in a relationship include affection (expressing and receiving warmth, tenderness, and caring), esteem (obtaining confirmation of who you are in relation to others), services (having things done for you), and information (receiving needed information about yourself and the environment).

Affection and esteem are more important resources in love and friendship relationships than they are in work relationships. By contrast, service and information resources are more important in work relationships than they are in love and friendship relationships. Although some resources may be more important than others in a particular relationship, most relationships have many resources.

What are the resources available to you in your important relationships? Do the resources tend to be the same from relationship to relationship, or do they differ? What do the resources you consider important in a relationship tell you about who you are and what kinds of relationships you desire?

People often make judgments about interpersonal contacts by comparing relational rewards and costs—**The Economic Model of Relationships**.[23] When there are more rewards than costs, or a big reward that outweighs the cost, then we will value the relationship. When the relationship costs more than it is worth, most people end the relationship or let it fade away. For example, if one person believes that the investment (relational costs) of such factors as money, time, and/or emotion is met with such factors as security and affection (relational rewards), then that person will want to continue the relationship. If he or she is doing all the giving and the partner is only taking, however, then the relationship will probably end.

With this in mind, examine a friendship. Why have you continued to associate with this person? You probably do so because you receive at least as much as you are giving from being with the person. In contrast, if you have taken the initiative to end an association with someone, your action was probably caused by your belief that you were giving too much and not receiving enough, that the relationship was tilted against you or one-sided.

A way of examining a relationship is to take a sheet of paper, divide it vertically with a line down the middle, write the word "costs" on the top of the left column and "rewards" on the top of the right column. List all your costs and rewards in the appropriate column. Put the paper aside and come back to it several hours or days later. Add any new data to either side of the paper. When you think you have all your documentation listed, read and reread your list. Using this information, on an additional page write one paragraph on the topic: "I should remain in this relationship because . . ." and another paragraph with the topic of "I should leave this relationship because . . ." This information should allow you to examine the relationship. What did you learn about your investments and paybacks? Are you getting what you need from the relationship? Is the relationship costing you more than it's worth? If so, is that extra cost worth what you are getting? Again, this may seem like a very theoretical way of dealing with relationships, but the attempt here is to get you *thinking* rather than acting *emotionally*. Observing only emotions often makes us blind to the realities.

Relationships, no matter the type, are dynamic—continually adapting and developing—as they pass through time. A relationship is not a thing, but a process—an ever-changing process that often needs evaluation to keep it productive for both parties.

Key Terms

relationship
relational fusion
dialectical tension
relational structure
complementary relationship
symmetrical relationship
parallel relationship
relational rules
commitment phobia
system of relational operation
functional relational system

dysfunctional relational system
recalibration
Theory of Love/Like
love
like
commitment
intimacy
revealing culture
nonrevealing culture
The Economic Model of Relationships

Competencies Check-Up

Interested in finding out what you learned in this chapter and how you use the information? If so, take this competencies check-up.

Directions: Indicate the extent that each statement applies to you:

1—Never   *2—Seldom*   *3—Sometimes*   *4—Often*   *5—Usually*

____1. I am aware that relationships are at the center of my social and psychological existence.

____2. I acknowledge that relationships are based on connection, association, and/or involvement with other persons.

_____ 3. I know that relationships are in a constant state of flux.

_____ 4. As for relationships, I recognize that people come into our lives for a reason, a season, or sometimes forever.

_____ 5. I can identify the similarities and differences between role relationships, acquaintances, friends, good friends, and intimate relationships.

_____ 6. I accept that communication plays a key role in all types of relationships.

_____ 7. I am aware that culture plays a major role in relationships.

_____ 8. I am aware that good relationships allow freedom of expression and reflect acceptance that the feelings of both people are important.

_____ 9. I understand that love is the ability and willingness to allow those that I care for to be what they choose for themselves without any insistence that they satisfy me.

_____10. I accept that each person is totally responsible for his or her own happiness.

_____11. I am aware of the difference between "I" and "you" messages.

_____12. I know that successful relationships require time.

_____13. I accept the concept that we teach others how to treat us, and a healthy relationship requires awareness of my role to moderate any relationship in which I am involved.

_____14. I know that relational fusion takes place when one partner defines, or attempts to define, reality for the other.

_____15. I understand that dialectical tension centers on my intrapersonal and interpersonal conflicts over my wants and needs.

_____16. I am aware that intimate relationships are complex and involved.

_____17. I accept that all relationships are both goal- and rule-centered.

_____18. I can explain the similarities of and differences between complementary, symmetrical, and parallel relationships.

_____19. I understand the differences between a functional and dysfunctional relational system.

_____20. I am aware of the process of recalibrating a relationship that has become dysfunctional.

_____21. I can define and explain the concepts of love and like.

_____22. I acknowledge the role of commitment in a relationship.

_____23. I recognize that intimacy is both emotional closeness and intellectual sharing.

_____24. I know the differences between revealing and nonrevealing cultures.

_____25. I understand and can apply the Economic Model of Relationships.

Scoring: A total of 75 suggests that you have minimum competencies in the principles of relational communication. Given the important role of relationships in our lives, a high skill level is needed. Examine any item on which you scored less than 3 and figure out how you will improve your skills.

I-Can Plan!

As you think about the chapter content and your test responses, create a concrete method for improving one of your relationships. Plan your action, and then act on your plan.

Activities

1. Find two personal advertisements in a newspaper or online. One should be an ad that you find appealing, the other, an ad that you find unappealing. Bring the ads to class. The class will be divided into small groups. Each person is to read each of the ads and indicate why they found them positive or negative. The group should then discuss, based on the concepts introduced in this chapter, what you each learned from doing this exercise.
2. A. Make a list of what it costs to be in a relationship.
   B. Make a list of what you get out of a relationship.
   C. Share your list with others in the class and discuss what are the most important "payoffs" and what are the real "deal breakers" in relationships.

CHAPTER 7

Beginning, Maintaining, and Ending Relationships

Learning Outcomes

After reading this chapter, you should be able to:

- Explain that relationship beginnings, maintenance, and endings vary greatly.
- Define and illustrate the roles of task-orientation, friendship-orientation, and intimate-orientation in relationships.
- Recognize the high levels of uncertainty when people meet for the first time.
- Define love as it relates to intimate relationships.
- Explain that culture influences nearly every aspect of relational development.
- List and explain each of the sequential patterns of relationship beginnings, maintenance, and endings.
- Explain and illustrate why people are attracted to each other.
- Describe the process of meeting potential relational partners.
- Define and illustrate cyber-meeting/cyberdating, including fee-based relational introduction services, speed dating, matchmaking, and relational coaching.
- Explain how to initiate relational communication.
- Clarify how to maintain a relationship.
- Explain the concept of right-brain/left-brain thinking in relationships.
- Analyze the stages and reasons for ending a relationship.

A couple from Minneapolis decided to go to Florida to thaw out during one particularly icy winter. They planned to stay at the very same hotel where they had spent their honeymoon twenty years earlier. Because of hectic schedules, it was difficult to coordinate their travel. So, the husband left Minnesota and flew to Florida on Thursday, with his wife scheduled to fly down the following day.

The husband checked into the hotel. There was a computer in his room, so he decided to send an e-mail to his wife. However, he accidentally left out one letter in her e-mail address, and without realizing his error, he sent the message.

Meanwhile . . . in Houston, Texas, a widow had just returned home from making arrangements for her husband's funeral. He had died suddenly of a heart attack. The widow decided to check her e-mail, expecting messages from relatives and friends. After reading the first message, she fainted. The widow's son heard the crash and rushed into the room, found his mother on the floor, and saw the computer screen which read:

To: My Loving Wife

Subject: I've Arrived

I know you're surprised to hear from me. They have computers here now and you are allowed to send e-mails to your loved ones. I've just arrived and have been checked in. I see that everything has been prepared for your arrival tomorrow. Looking forward to seeing you then! Hope your journey is as uneventful as mine was. P.S. Sure is hot down here!

Yes, relationships can take many unexpected turns from their beginning, through their maintenance, to their endings.

A **relationship** is a bond, connection, interaction, or engagement between two people who have an emotional link. Because of the variety of possible relationships, few rules exist that can cover all cases. One way to look at relationships is according to their function or goal. We have relationships that are friendship-based, task-based, and intimacy-based.[1]

The Role of Culture in Relationships

Relational development is greatly influenced by the participants' cultures. Culture influences nearly every aspect of relational development. How people meet, what rules the relationship will follow, what role each participant plays, all are the result of the culture in which the participants have been raised or in which they live.

Ethnic traditions can set the procedure for meeting. In many Western cultures, people somehow meet, date, fall in love, and get married or live together or live together and then get married. In other cultures, dating and even love are not even part of the equation. For example, in some Arab, Indian, Chinese, Japanese, and African cultures, many people have their partners selected through arranged marriages. The parents or a professional matchmaker decides who will be matched. In some cultures, such as in some sects in India, the first son must get married before the younger brothers can get betrothed. In some cultures same-sex marital relationships are sanctioned, as in Belgium, Canada, South Africa, Sweden, Norway, Spain, and the Netherlands, and some of the U.S. states, while in other cultures it is not. Even the ending of a relationship may be prescribed. Some religions forbid divorce, such as traditional Catholicism. Others, such as Orthodox Judaism, give the right of dissolving the relationship only to the male.

Though this book takes a culture-centered approach, most of the discussion about personal relationships that will be presented reflects a very traditional U.S. Euro-American point of view. Please keep this point of view in mind as you read the chapter. In addition, you will want to remember that any generalizations—including those based on scientific research and expert observation—cannot be applied in every case. Even a single culture contains great variation. What holds true for one family member may not hold true for an-

other family member. We seek research-based generalizations as a way of helping us adapt, predict, and show sensitivity in individual communication contexts.

Relational Development: Beginning, Maintaining, and Ending

Relationships have a sequential pattern: an *entry phase* (beginning), a *personal phase* (maintenance), and an *exit phase* (end). Although you may think it pessimistic to say that every relationship will end, the prospect of death does suggest that phase is universal. Be aware that not every relationship necessarily moves through the stages at the same rate. The personalities and needs of the participants and the basis for the relationship determine the rapidity of movement through the stages.

Usually, in the *entry relational development phase*, biographical information and general attitudes are exchanged. In the *personal relational phase*, information about central attitudes and values is exchanged. In the *exit relational stage*, questions concerning the future of the relationship are raised and resolved. This stage may include an agreement to reestablish and continue the affiliation (continuing the personal phase) or to terminate the relationship in its present or a modified form.

BEGINNING A RELATIONSHIP

Establishing a new relationship—one that goes beyond a few minutes of superficial chatter—is difficult. Meeting strangers often brings out our insecurities and our self-perceived flaws.

Although the romantic view of relationships is that they "just happen"—from the magical moment when two lovers swoon at first sight—relationships do not drop from the sky fully formed, are not a gift from some relationship fairy.

When two persons meet for the first time, their levels of uncertainty about each other and themselves are fairly high. Powerful barriers to establishing connections exist: *fear of saying the wrong thing* (the decision not to tell certain things as they may be perceived as weaknesses or make you an undesirable partner); *fear of abandonment* (if the relationship begins, what happens if the other person decides to leave it?); *fear of reprisal/attack* (what if something goes wrong and the other person physically or verbally assaults me?); *fear of loss of control* (not being able to make decisions for and about oneself); *fear of loss of individuality* (the potential loss of *me* as *I* and *you* become a *we*); and *fear of creating a power imbalance* (the potential for giving power to the partner, thus losing my own power).

A relationship begins when you are attracted to someone and initiate an interaction, or are assigned or selected to enter into a working relationship with another person. On a personal level, being attracted to someone does not automatically mean that you will initiate interaction. Interaction is usually initiated when you are motivated to take some action, such as starting a conversation, e-mailing or sending a letter to the person, responding to a personal ad, or allowing someone to arrange for you to meet someone.

When two persons meet for the first time, their levels of uncertainty about each other and themselves are fairly high.

The bottom line to remember in attempting to begin a relationship is that you have little to lose if the relationship attempt is unsuccessful. Individuals will often say, "I'm afraid to make the first move." "What if she/he says, 'No?'" Think of it this way . . . you don't have a relationship now, and if the person says "no" then you still don't have a relationship. Nothing lost here. On the other hand, if you don't even attempt to begin the relationship, there is absolutely no chance of its developing. If you attempt to break the ice and the other person says "yes," then you are ahead of where you were before you attempted your task. Are you afraid your ego will be bruised by a rejection? Get over it. We all experience rejections. It's how you react to the rejection that counts. Thinking, "I'm (fill in a self-deprecating word such as 'ugly') and no one is ever going to be interested in me," is self-defeating. You'll never succeed with that attitude. On the other hand, accepting that the person is being honest with you, for whatever reason, and she/he doesn't know what they are missing by rejecting you, is a positive defense mechanism and allows you to continue on with your search.

On any given day, you encounter many people with whom you can choose to form a relationship. Not everyone, of course, has an equal probability of being chosen. You are drawn to some people and not to others, just as some are drawn to you and some are not. Whether you are aware of it or not, you carry a mental list of desirable characteristics that make others attractive to you. Any person's list is the yardstick for measurement of who they might be interested in and reflects his/her culture. Your list might include such factors as physical beauty—height, weight, hair color, skin color; financial status; educational level; health habits—not smoking or drinking or engaging in recreational drug use; religion; age; race; nationality; societal standing. Your list is neither right nor wrong. It is what it is at this particular moment in time and may change later on.

LEARNING EXPERIENCE: Interested in finding out what your desired characteristics are for an intimate long-term relationship? If so, do Activity 7.1.

Think of people to whom you are attracted and the traits they share. Do they seem to have similar physical characteristics? Do they live nearby? Do they do things for you

---

ACTIVITY 7.1
My Desired Characteristics
for a Long-Term Relationship

Rank the following characteristics in the order of their importance to you in describing a person with whom you would form a long-term relationship. Rank the most important characteristic 1 and the least important 15.

_____able to get a good job
_____adaptable
_____attractive physically
_____creative
_____cultural background
_____engaging personality
_____good genes
_____college graduate
_____healthy
_____kind and patient
_____much in common
_____neat and clean
_____same religion
_____smart
_____wants to have children

What did you learn about your relational desires from doing this activity?

without asking for too much in return? Do they have qualities you lack but that seem to fit well with your own? Are they similar to you? Do you have some personal motives for forming a relationship that are more important to you than who or what the other person is? Does being with them help you feel good about yourself? Do they remind you of members of your family? If you are typical, you answered "yes" to many of these questions, as these are the so-called seven bases of attraction: attractiveness, proximity, familiarity, personal rewards, complementarity, similarity, personal motives, self-esteem enhancement, and attempting to overcome family-of-origin problems.

Attractiveness

Attractiveness is your impression of someone as appealing. How important is attractiveness in seeking someone for you to be involved with in an intimate relationship? Although it seems undemocratic to judge people by the way they look, the reality is that we do.[2] A survey reveals that men rank the item third and women rank it sixth, which indicates that both groups give importance to physical beauty.[3] The more someone is considered physically attractive, the more she or he may be seen as desirable, especially in the early stages of personal relational development.

Proximity

Marrying the person next door doesn't just happen in Hollywood musicals, such as *Meet Me in St. Louis* with its love song, "The Boy Next Door." To be attracted to someone takes some interaction, and you are most likely to interact with people whom you encounter frequently. Whether meeting daily when you both get the mail or sitting next to each other in a class, the effect is the same: you get the opportunity to communicate.

Proximity, how near you are geographically to someone, may be an important determinant of relationship. The bottom line is, if you aren't near a person, or don't ever meet that person, you will never form a relationship with the person. Computer communication has broken down some of the nearness barrier walls, but eventually, in order to form a physical bond, the partners must meet face-to-face. If you believe that there is a perfect match for you somewhere out there, you had better hope that he or she is physically close by or makes himself/herself available on the same online service.

Familiarity

Familiarity, a knowledge and understanding of someone, although it may breed contempt, more often breeds liking. As the other person becomes more predictable, and you develop positive thoughts and feelings about his/her, interaction likely increases. Increased interaction, in turn, leads to other bases of attraction. You may go on to discover interests, physical attributes, and personality traits that enhance attraction or find that the initial attraction fades as you get to know the other person better. In fact, the main purpose of dating in the U.S. American culture is based on the concept that as people spend time together in various settings, they get to know each other better and can determine whether they want to maintain their relationship, end it, or move it on to a higher level.

A lack of familiarity is one reason people often fail to develop relationships with those from other cultures. The movement following the civil rights and equal rights era in the United States, with the integration of schools, the workforce, and neighborhoods, started to break down the barriers prohibiting racial and religious contact and led to familiarity between individuals who might never have had the opportunity during the many years of segregation.

Self-Esteem Enhancement

How important is it to you that your potential partner or friend enhances your self-esteem? Have you ever thought about what it would do to your self-esteem to be seen with this other person? You may feel that being seen with the school's smartest, or strongest, or most attractive person, reflects positively on you. Your perception is that being with this person increases your self-esteem, and therefore the appeal for this person may be heightened. On the other hand, if you feel that being seen with someone who acts foolish or inappropriately, or is known to be a "bad" person reflects negatively on you, you may experience a decrease in self-esteem. In reality, of course, these people are not you, and other people's view of you should not be affected by your presence with the person. Unfortunately, many people do perceive themselves based on how others view them because of their relationships. In the Euro-American culture there are catchphrases that enforce this myth. Have you been told "you are judged by the friends you keep?" Have you ever evaluated someone either positively or negatively because of their parent, sibling, or other relative? If so, you have fallen into the "judged by the friends you keep" myth. Is that a reason to choose relational partners? For some *yes*, for others *no*.

Meeting Potential Relational Partners

The two questions confronting individuals looking to date, broaden the number of friendships they have, or meet someone to become involved with in an intimate relationship are: first, "Where do I meet him or her?" and second, "What do I do after I meet him or her?"

Historically, in the United States people have met at school, in their work setting, while participating in religious events, through mutual friends or family members, at social events, while attending singles' clubs, or in bars or similar hangouts. But, as the saying goes, "The world is a changin'." Off-line dating services, online dating services, and matchmakers have joined the scene as a means to take the first step toward starting a relationship. Matchmakers and speed dating are other techniques.

Relational meeting and matching has become big business. In one form or another, it is estimated to be a $917 million enterprise.[4]

Cyberdating   **Cyberdating** and *cyber-meeting* (developing relationships online), have proven to be popular among all age groups. The reason? Finding a date can be quick, fun, and fairly inexpensive.

The Internet has become the world's biggest singles bar. The major differences between cyberdating and face-to-face searches for potential relational partners before interacting with them is that you lose the pressure of making instant decisions and you can surf until you hopefully find what you are looking for. You aren't restricted by settings and time.

Keep in mind that it is not the duty of the Internet to help you find the person of your dreams. It's the Internet's job to allow you to put yourself out there and for the electronics to be a conduit for making others available. The Internet is especially helpful for people who tend to be shy when initially meeting others face-to-face. Developing and maintaining a relationship, however, is the responsibility of the people involved.

As an Internet advertiser for yourself, the major selling tool is your profile. Another piece of information others use to evaluate you is a picture that can be attached to your profile. The profile and the picture are both communication tools that take special strategies. For example, if the whole purpose is to meet people, you don't want to turn them off. A negative profile that lists things you don't like, that shows no sense of humor, and is sexually inappropriate could spell instant doom. Lying seems to be common on the Internet, but it usually comes back to haunt you. Putting a picture online that isn't you, or is you touched up, or you from another era, will be uncovered if you ever meet the person. The dishonesty will surely turn them off.

You will want to avoid using generalized vocabulary and statements. For example, "I am nice and smart and kind and warm." What does that mean? Illustrate what you mean. Tell them that you are the kind of person who brings flowers to someone for no other reason than to say, "It's nice to know you." Or, you're the kind of person who would cook a candlelight dinner on your one-year anniversary. Looking for someone online might be the time to experiment, to try and find someone who is different from a person you've dated in the past, to look for someone who is your opposite. If you are right-brained look for someone who is left-brained. The balance may open a whole new horizon for you.

Other suggestions for online relational searching are:[5]

Be realistic—you probably won't get responses from twenty-two-year-old brain surgeons who are multimillionaires and perform as models and world-class athletes in their spare time.

Eliminate traits you can't live with. Allergic to smoke? Must find someone of a particular religion? Don't like people with certain physical traits? Include that in your list of desirable or undesirable traits. It will eliminate later potential conflicts. Besides, you don't want people with those traits to answer anyway.

Take your time. When you feel reasonably confident, then you can schedule a meeting.

Ask yourself if there are any warning signs of potential abusive or psychotic tendencies. If things seem too good to be true, move too fast, or there are signals of inappropriate anger, obsession, control, or pressure, be careful.

Be safe. Don't reveal your phone number or address in your profile. Schedule your first interpersonal meeting in public, such as a coffee shop or restaurant, never at an isolated location, such as an isolated park, and let friends and relatives know where you are and when you will be back. Carry a cell phone with you that is on.

If you make a contact online, talk via telephone so you can listen to the person's voice and get a sense of how the individual communicates before making any plans to meet. For security purposes, talk on a cell phone, rather than a land line phone, because the cell usually does not reveal the same information to the answerer who has call waiting.

Be smart. Unscrupulous people do use these services. Don't be naive about what people say. They may be lying. Be cautious on the side of safety.

Have fun. The experience can be exciting and relationship-expanding. The worst that can happen, as long as you are smart and safe, is that you won't meet someone significant. On the other hand, you could find that special person or make one or more friends and social acquaintances.

LEARNING EXPERIENCE: Interested in finding out which online or off-line advertisements appeal to you? If so, do Activity 7.2.

Personal Ads   Much research has been done about how to write a personal ad that communicates effectively.[6] Specifically:

Gain attention with a catchy headline.

Tell about yourself with necessary information. Include aspects you think are important. For example, if you are gay, and want to limit your possible choices to other gay men, say so. The same is true if you have specific ethnic or race preferences.

Get to the point. You are just trying to open the door, not tell your life story in the first contact.

Give an idea of what you're looking for. If there are certain characteristics you seek, you can mention them.

Talk about your interests and activities. Explain how you are unique.

Offer a suggestion about how you could spend time together. If you make a suggestion about your interests, the individual will be able to see if they are shared.

ACTIVITY 7.2
Probing the Online Advertisements

Locate two personal advertisements. They can be from an online or off-line source. One announcement should be one that you would be interested in answering, the other you definitely would not answer. Write a statement regarding each ad about what specific information in the ad led you to your conclusion. What did you learn about yourself and your likes and dislikes from doing this activity?

Convey a sense of your personality. Figure out a way to sell yourself and who you are. You want to attract someone who will like you as you are.

Be honest! You've seen or heard of many instances of lying on the Internet. Lying is not a good foundation for a relationship and eventually the lie will come out. Don't fudge on your height or weight. You are who and what you are. Be proud of it.

Select the right picture. The picture is crucial, but think about whether you want to put your face out to the public. Individuals have been stalked once a face becomes known. Also, be aware that once you release a visual image, it can be passed from person to person and, if the recipient wants to do so, manipulate the image with one of the Photoshop-like programs, putting your face on another body or manipulating the visual. Consider whether you want to participate in *sexting*, sending a nude or sexual image. Once it's out, its out there for all to see.[7]

LEARNING EXPERIENCE: Interested in finding out if you can write an interesting and inviting personal online or off-line ad? If so, do Activity 7.3.

Fee-based introduction services   There are numerous sources for being introduced to others. You can do it on your own by entering chat rooms with people who have similar interests. You can find some free listing services such as those offered through *Craigslist*, *Yahoo*, and *AOL*. Or, you can subscribe to a service. The most popular fee-based dating services are *eHarmony.com*, which stresses that its participants take a "Personality Profile and get instant objective feedback on yourself and how you relate to others,"[8] and *Matchmaker.com*, which claims, "Our in-depth profiles make it easy. 100% satisfaction guaranteed—or your money back."[9] One of the best known nonelectronic fee services is *Great Expectations*, which boasts that "members are pre-screened and qualified, so you can enjoy a safe and enjoyable dating experience.[10] Niche services such as out.com, outpersonals.com, and planetout.com are available for gay and lesbian lookers. Christian singles can search at singles.com and christiansingledating.com, African Americans can browse blacksingles.com, while Jdate.com is for Jewish partner seekers.

Speed dating   **Speed dating** is a face-to-face meeting between a prescribed group of people who are brought together to interact with others for potential relational development. The groups can be formed by a nonprofit organization such as a church or synagogue, a recreational organization such as a YMCA or YWCA, or a group of friends getting together and wanting to expand their relational base. The interaction

---

ACTIVITY 7.3
Writing a Personal Ad

Write an ad for yourself to be submitted to an online dating service that is one hundred words or less. Give the ad to a classmate you don't know very well who is the same sex as the person you hope to attract. Ask that person to honestly critique your ad based on the principles discussed in this chapter.

may be sponsored by a for-profit group that runs the activities for an entrance and/or membership fee.

The rules of speed dating are simple. A group of approximately thirty people gathers at a predetermined venue, such as a cafe or a club. The participants are paired and given a specific amount of time, usually three to ten minutes, to get to know another person. Each pair is usually free to ask their partner anything except their address and phone number. Normally, only first names are exchanged. When the time is up, the participants are requested to fill out a score card indicating whether they would like to meet this person again. Each person then moves on to the next station and the process is repeated again. In about a day after the event, any two people who have indicated mutual interest are notified of each other's e-mail address and/or phone number so they can further pursue the relationship. Estimates are that about 50 percent of the participants walk away with a potential match.[11]

Compared to customary blind dates, this form offers a wider and much easier way to find someone to date or mate with. On the other hand, it is difficult to really get to know a person in just three to ten minutes. If you are a slow starter, not an easy conversationalist, or a slow thinker, you might never get the other person to know the real you. And after a while people start to blend together. To prepare yourself, try a roleplay with a friend of the gender of the person you are interested in finding. Have him or her critique your presentation. If it will make you feel more comfortable, write out a series of questions you could use in a speed dating situation. Don't whip out the cards at the event, but at least you will be prepared and won't have to ad lib questions.

As with any other process, practice helps develop the skills and approaches that work in this environment. If you don't find a relationship the first time out, put yourself out there again, as each time you participate, you'll hopefully learn from the experience.

Matchmaking   According to one dating researcher, "I am convinced that matchmakers do a better job for a higher percentage of their members."[12]

Matchmaking centers on introducing individuals by a matchmaker, a person supposedly skilled in finding people of common interests and desires. In contrast to electronic matching, the matchmaker personally gets to know his or her clients, gains an appreciation for each person's uniqueness, and matches a person only with people with whom they may be compatible.

As one matchmaker states, we "strive to align the important factors of intelligence level, education, religious orientation, level of professionalism, character compatibility, common life goals and interests. We strive to assess the total person, rather than merely getting an insight into the various, fragmented components of the person."[13] The matchmakers remove from the relational search process the sorting through of many files and biographies which has to be undertaken by interested participants in electronic matching services. Matchmaking, if well done, gets people directly together to find out whether they are a match. There are matchmaking services for niche groups such as religious and racial groups. Doing a Google or Yahoo search for "matchmakers" will give you a list of options.

Relational coaching   Some individuals find that they just don't have the skills to enter into the dating/mating/relationship pursuit process. Interpersonal classes can

In contrast to electronic matching, the matchmaker personally gets to know his or her clients.

help teach some of the skills shy and socially awkward people need. In some cases psychological services may be needed to help an individual overcome negative self-perceptions. Relationship coaching, a rather new service, may be the solution for some before they open themselves to a relational search. A **relational coach** teaches clients people skills such as how to be a competent communicator, effective conversational techniques, and confidence. They help people deal with issues related to dating, defining problems, setting goals and appropriate methods for obtaining what a person wants. This is usually done one-on-one, but may be taught in a group or classroom setting. Relational coaches often advertise in local alternative weekly newspapers and in the yellow pages of telephone books.

Initiating relational communication   Once you identify someone with whom you hope to form a relationship, you may want to initiate contact and ascertain whether you want to get to know the person.

Here are several steps that you might consider in initiating relational communication:

Step One: Look for Approachability Cues. A possible first step in meeting new people is to look for **approachability cues**, indications that the other person is available for conversation. A person may be approachable when she or he smiles at you; is alone, relaxed, not busy; in a place where talking with strangers is okay (such as the student union or a coffee shop); maintains eye contact with you for a period beyond what is usual (which is more than three to ten seconds); has an open body position (faces you directly); displays a positive mood (pleasant facial expression); says or waves hello. (If you're looking for a prospective mate, check for "an empty ring finger," probably meaning not married.)

There are, of course, cultural differences in the use of such factors as eye contact, facial expression, gestures, use of space, and vocal variety (e.g., volume and pitch variations). People from Asian cultures, for example, don't smile as frequently or have as much eye contact with strangers. Hispanic females have often been taught not to look males directly in the eye. People who are autistic, often don't establish direct eye contact.

Step Two: Initiate a Conversation. Once you decide to approach someone, the next step is to initiate a conversation. The "opening line" when initiating contact poses a special problem for most people. "What should I say first?" is a common question. Asking a question is usually a good icebreaker. Try and be creative. Such overused lines as "Nice weather, isn't it?" "Do you come here often?" "What's your sign?" and "Seen any good movies lately?" might work, but they have reached the level of being trite. Phrases such as, "I haven't decided on a major yet. How did you decide what you wanted to do after you graduate?" or a simple statement such as, "Hi, I'm Noah, and your name is?" will usually elicit a response. Many people, at least in the U.S. American culture, tend to like to talk about themselves. Asking about their career, hometown, and likes may open the door to conversation. Listen and then ask a follow-up question. Another device is to be totally honest. If you are uncomfortable in social situations, you could say, "I always find it so uncomfortable to start conversations with people I don't know." Just that honesty may open up the verbal door to an honest exchange of beliefs and attitudes. You may ask for information ("I'm new on campus. Can you tell me where the Student Union Building is located?"); introduce yourself ("I'm Bill. I wanted to meet you since we'll be sitting next to each other in this class."); talk about something you have in common ("Did you understand one word of the professor's lecture?"); or offer a sincere compliment ("You have great taste in music, as evidenced by that Adam Lambert T-shirt you're wearing.").

When initiating a conversation with someone from a different culture, you should keep in mind that in many cultures the members feel uncomfortable talking to strangers. A person from China, Japan, or Vietnam, therefore, might not respond as favorably or respond at all. While you may have the best of intentions, he or she may perceive your actions as aggressive and a sign of poor manners.

Step Three: Find Topics to Talk About. The third step, finding topics to talk about, quickly follows initiating the conversation. Perceived similarities often provide topics of conversation. For example, you may attend the same school or classes, enjoy the same types of food, sports, or movies, or come from the same town. Although perceived differences also may suggest topics of conversation, such talk tends to separate you from the other person rather than bring you closer together.

Recognize that not all cultures are interested in the same topics. What seems like normal conversation in your culture might not be of the least interest in another culture. In the Buddhist tradition, for example, people refrain from gossip. In North America and England, gossip is often a favorite pastime as illustrated by the number of exploitation TV shows and tabloid newspapers. If you were to employ this conversational technique with a Buddhist, he or she would most likely only respond out of politeness, not interest.

Step Four: Talk about a Variety of Topics. The fourth step builds on the third. To gather enough information to decide whether to pursue a relationship, you need information on a variety of topics.

You can make transitions to new topics by noting what the other person says and using the information to guide you. Rarely are casual conversations so structured that everything communicated is immediately pertinent. More often, *free information*—elaboration—is provided. Use this free information to find new topics of conversation. For example, if you ask someone whether he likes Mexican food and he responds, "Yes. I also like Italian food, French food, and hamburgers and fries. In fact, I like just about every kind of food." You can then use this free information to extend the conversation to talk about food in general, diets, and even travel to foreign places.

You can increase the probability of getting free information by asking questions that require detailed answers instead of ones that can be answered "yes" or "no." Asking "Have you traveled outside of the United States?" will normally give a "yes" or "no" answer. If the answer is "yes," asking, "To which countries outside of the U.S. have you traveled?" will get you information on which to build the conversation. The answer "no" can be used as a pathway to ask, "If you could travel outside the U.S., where would you like to go?"

Other techniques for obtaining free information include giving compliments—direct ones, such as "That's a nice dog." Indirect compliments, such as "How would you conclude this report?" implies the other has knowledge you don't. Telling something about yourself implies that you trust the other person, which encourages the other person to speak about herself or himself. Use a comment such as, "I tend to be rather shy when I meet people. I'm amazed at people like you who seem comfortable talking to others as soon as they meet them."

Step Five: Share Plans for Future Interaction. The fifth step is sharing your plans for future interaction. If at the end of your first conversation you have enough information to conclude that another meeting is a good idea, communicate this to your partner. You may be indirect ("Are you planning to see the movie the professor recommended this weekend?") or direct ("Would you like to come with me Saturday night to see the movie the professor recommended?"). Indirect statements or questions may be safer, but they are also less useful. Being direct is more threatening than being indirect—for both of you; but, it is also more honest and likely to yield the information you want. Direct communication reveals what people are really thinking, feeling, and wanting, and eliminates guessing about the other's intentions.

A relationship is made up of more than one person. Not only must you decide if you are interested in the other person, but he/she must determine interest in you.

Therefore, in meeting new people you are probably going to try and create a favorable impression upon first meeting.

Creating a favorable impression can enhance the other person's attraction toward you. Therefore, you should convey certain characteristics if you want to continue to interact. Cooperativeness, caring, and being memorable are the characteristics that can be important in creating a positive first impression.

To be perceived as caring, you should listen attentively. Such attention tells the other person, "I care about what you have to say," which creates a favorable impression.

As with many interpersonal situations, an awareness of cultural differences is important to keep in mind when attempting to be friendly. Many people from English, German, Asian, and Scandinavian cultures feel uncomfortable when others become too friendly and ask what are perceived to be personal questions. People from these cultures tend to be rather private and believe that only close acquaintances should know about very personal matters. Sticking to surface level topics is advisable at the start.

To be perceived as memorable, you should communicate your most dynamic and interesting self. You may communicate information that shows you are adventurous (you participate in a dangerous sport); that you are creative (you write poetry); that you are industrious (you hold down several jobs while attending school full-time); or that you have had unique experiences (you were an exchange student your senior year of high school).

You need to remember that many cultures do not value individualism as much as they do collectivism. Being memorable to people from a Chinese culture, for example, is not based on what you have done as an individual, but what you have done as a group member. In their thinking, helping your family or your company is far more important than helping yourself.

LEARNING EXPERIENCE: Interested in learning how to create a more favorable impression? If so, do Activity 7.4.

MAINTAINING A RELATIONSHIP

When you think you have enough information to decide whether to continue a relationship, the initial phase of relationship development is complete. Deciding to pursue a relationship requires that you examine your goals and quickly assess the probability of attaining them. Will this person be helpful on the term project? Will this person be a good friend? Will this person be the type to be a long-term partner? Whatever your needs, if the response is a "yes," you move into the second phase of relationship development: maintaining the relationship. Of course, moving to that level assumes that the other person is also willing to move to that level.

Relationships are two-sided. You have control over only one of those sides . . . yours. If you want to develop and/or work on and maintain a relationship be aware that:

Relationships have goals. Understanding your goals, the other person's goals, and your mutual goals should provide a firm foundation for reaching those goals. At the least, understanding the goals should help you assess the relationship's possibilities.

ACTIVITY 7.4
Creating a Good Impression

To ensure that your relationship partner perceives you as cooperative, caring, and memorable, prepare several alternative means for communicating each impression.

COOPERATIVE
List two conversational rules you can follow to communicate that you are co-operative. For example, you can provide the other person with opportunities to speak and you can maintain sustained eye contact with her or him.

a.

b.

CARING
List two ways you can communicate "I care" to the other person. For example, you can lean forward while listening and ask meaningful questions.

a.

b.

MEMORABLE
List two facts about yourself that are memorable. For example, maybe you have a twin sister or brother, or perhaps you are finally able to return to school and finish the degree you started several years ago.

a.

b.

Relationships have structure and that structure can be changed to meet changing needs. Changing patterns of behavior is difficult, but recognizing the patterns that exist and determining which patterns might be better can help the relationship grow in responsible and beneficial ways. If the participants in a relationship cannot make the changes themselves, turning to a marriage counselor, mediator, or personnel expert may be appropriate.

Relationships have rules. Relational rules coordinate interaction and make the relationship more predictable. You have to know the rules to follow them, so talking about rules and reaching mutual understanding can benefit you and your partner.

And if you want to change a rule, recognize that doing so is a slow process, one that requires understanding the reasons for the rule in the first place and searching for and evaluating the options.

Relationships are always in process. Like everything else, relationships change with time. Attempting to freeze a relationship at one moment in time is bound to fail. Relationships change as you and the other person change, and as the context for the relationship changes. Although this progression may seem obvious, few people behave as if change is inevitable. The comfort of old habits, old patterns, and old viewpoints can be powerful. A moment may come when the relationship *as it is* no longer matches what either of the partners *thinks* it is, resulting in conflict. If the relationship does grow stagnant, it may die from a lack of nourishment. If it gets to be boring, the boredom can lead to relational disintegration.

Relationships require attention. Creating a supportive and confirming communication climate, appropriately self-disclosing, and using suitable affinity-seeking and compliance-gaining strategies, are important ways of attending to a relationship. They ensure the exchange of information necessary for meeting your needs and your partner's as well as the needs of the relationship. Talk about your relationship with your partner and deal directly with relational issues.

Does this discussion sound theoretical, not practical? According to relational experts, if attention is not paid to the goals, structure, rules, process, and communication, then relational destruction may take place.[14] This destruction does not have to take place. As one expert states, "Your relationship doesn't have to be in trouble. You do not have to become one more fatality in the runaway epidemic to broken hearts. You can reach out and reconnect with your partner and build a life together. But the deck is stacked against you unless you start dealing with the truth about you and the life you and your partner have created together."[15]

For many people the necessity to analyze and work on a relationship is an abstract process. They don't make lists, think through the answers or even realize they are probing for answers. They react on emotions and instincts. They may not even be aware that they need to carefully examine their motives or goals. Individuals who quickly fall in and out of love often follow an emotions-only path. Perhaps they like the excitement of falling in love, but lack the skills or motivation to do the work to stay in love. Also in this group are those who seek short-term rather than long-term satisfaction. Those who are young (think back to junior high school crushes and going-steady patterns), are inexperienced in the dating-mating experience, or aren't concerned about tomorrow but only today, and often fall prey to problematic relationships. Their spontaneous actions may be exciting or even perceived as being fun, but the long-term consequences can be drastic. The high divorce rate, unwanted pregnancies, and abuse attest to unwise relational decision-making.

Achieving Your Objectives

Information is the basis for effective relational decision-making. You need information, and you will continue to need information throughout the life of the relationship. Setting the stage for information sharing—making it appropriate to share, as well as encouraging sharing—requires that you use your communication skills to create a confirming, supportive communication climate.

Self-Disclosure   **Self-disclosure** is the process of revealing a depth and breadth of your self so that you can begin, maintain, and develop a relationship. It creates a pool of shared knowledge and, therefore, makes it possible to develop joint views, joint goals, and joint decisions. It also helps the partners in a relationship to help each other, keep up with each others' lives, and learn what the other person is thinking, doing, and feeling.

Self-disclosure varies by type of relationship and the cultural background of the participants. In a healthy intimate relationship there is much self-disclosure because the relational partners usually reveal a great many personal thoughts and feelings on a large number of topics. Dysfunctional intimate relationships are highlighted by cover-ups, lying, and manipulation of information. This results in a lack of trust, jealousy, and misunderstandings.

In contrast to intimate relationships, nonintimate relationships (work friends, classmates, neighbors), self-disclosure has little breadth and depth and accounts for only a small percentage of total communication. Business partners, for example, may discuss their thoughts and feelings about their work setting in great and personal detail, but tend to avoid discussions of non-work-related and personal matters. Think about it. Compare the revealing you do with your best friend or intimate partner with the revealing you do with a classmate or person at work.[16]

Some people don't understand or take into consideration the culturally accepted rules of disclosure. They shoot their mouths off without thinking, fail to choose appropriate words, or just don't think about what is right for the context. They "keep putting their feet in their mouths." They lack impulse control. They are perceived to be socially inept, but don't know why. They lack rhetorical sensitivity. Much of their problem centers on not knowing the "rules of disclosure." Before you disclose personal information, ask yourself:

Is the disclosure relevant to the relationship? Disclosure about your family to your employer, for example, may not be pertinent or appropriate.

How likely is the other person to treat the disclosure with respect? Is the person a gossip? Will he or she realize that not keeping the information confidential may bring undue stress or embarrassment to you?

How constructive is the disclosure likely to be for the relationship? What is the purpose of telling the person that information? Will your revealing help or hinder the relationship? Does the other person deserve to know what you are sharing?

Can you communicate your disclosure clearly and understandably? Some people have difficulty in sharing certain types of information. Can you say what you want to say in a manner that will clearly state what you intend for the person to know?

LEARNING EXPERIENCE: Interested in increasing your self-disclosure and receptiveness to feedback? If so, do Activity 7.5.

Self-disclosure isn't an all-or-nothing proposition; it normally begins slowly with revealing positive aspects of yourself and progresses—if at all—to greater breadth, depth, and amount. And, in general, openness will wax and wane throughout a con-

---

ACTIVITY 7.5
Receptiveness to Feedback

In order to increase your self-disclosure and receptiveness to feedback:

1. Make a list of some of the information you would keep to yourself—your secrets—in your relationship with an acquaintance and in your relationship with a good friend.

2. Select your *least* threatening secret for each relationship and ask yourself what the most horrible consequences would be if you were to reveal it. What would be the consequences for your acquaintance relationship? What would be the consequences for your good friend relationship?

3. Optional step: With your *least* threatening secret and its presumed consequences in mind, select either your acquaintance *or* good friend to tell your secret (select the person with whom you would feel more comfortable).

4. Optional step: Tell your secret. Note: *Remember in making your decision to reveal the secret it is no longer a secret.*

5. If you did step 4: What did you learn from revealing your secret? Would you be willing to take that action again? If so, why? If not, why not?

You will probably learn that your secret is more threatening to you than it is to others, and that the horrible consequences you imagine rarely come to pass.

---

versation as well as an entire relationship. Early disclosures test the situation: Is this person trustworthy? Does this person care about what I say? Each perceptual "yes" answer bolsters your willingness to self-disclose.

Despite its benefits, self-disclosure is risky. Telling a boss your negative feelings about the new organizational chart may lead to rebuke, just as telling a friend how you *really* feel about his new significant other may result in hurt feelings. How will the other person feel after the disclosure? What will happen to your relationship if you disclose your real feelings? You may have to question the extent to which you should be honest. Total honesty may not always be the "best policy."

The primary fear associated with self-disclosing is fear of rejection. Many men also fear that disclosing will make them look bad and cause them to lose control over other people: "If you know my weaknesses, I will no longer be powerful." Many women, on the other hand, fear the consequences of disclosure for the relationship: "If I disclose, you can use the information against me" or "Disclosing could hurt our relationship." For the majority of men, control is the primary objective; for the majority of women, the relationship itself is the primary objective. These objectives affect how each gender discloses and the reasons each chooses to avoid disclosure.

Compliance gaining   Relationships are satisfactory to the extent that they meet your needs and help you accomplish your goals, whether the need is for intimacy or the goal is to finish a group project successfully. **Compliance gaining** is an active process to direct and influence your communication partner's behavior.[17] Mutual influence is a defining characteristic of relationships. It must be remembered, however, that you cannot change anyone's behavior or beliefs unless the person wants to change, or is forced to change. Yes, threats to fire an employee or verbally attacking an individual may bring about the desired reactions, but that doesn't mean the person has changed. In fact, coercive actions often result in a person attempting to get back at the perpetrator through counterattacks, running away, divorce, or quitting, depending on the nature of the relationship.

Communication in a relationship is more satisfying if compliance-gaining strategies are positive, like being supportive and social as a way to induce cooperation, rather than negative, such as using threats of punishment or denials of your partner's future requests. Greater satisfaction with communication relates directly to greater willingness to comply.

Findings from a study comparing compliance-gaining strategies in the United States and Colombia reveal the importance of taking cultural differences into account when describing communication behaviors. For example, whereas giving explanations or reasons is an often-used strategy in the United States—implying that anyone given relevant and sufficient information will choose to comply, and that whether or not to comply is an individual choice—invoking shared obligations is more powerful in Colombia, where relational connectedness and duties are paramount. In Colombia, the obligations of relationships often outweigh the desires of individuals.[18]

LEARNING EXPERIENCE: Interested in finding out your degree of fulfilling expectations of an interpersonal relationship, your degree of intimacy? If so, do Activity 7.6.

Right-Brain/Left-Brain Thinking in Relationships

When people are "in sync" communication is effortless. When partners have difficulty relating to each other, too often they give up out of frustration rather than commit themselves to bridging the gap.

One factor that makes for ease or difficulty in relational communication is **brain dominance.** It is known that "People possess, to varying degrees, dominant characteristics associated with either right or left brain activity, and these form certain patterns

ACTIVITY 7.6
Measuring Effectiveness
and Intimacy in a Relationship

Select two persons with whom you are in relationships. The persons can be perceived as anything from friends to being your partner in an intimate relationship. Go through all of the questions for Relationship 1, then do the same for Relationship 2. After completing both lists follow the directions at the end of this activity.

Mark 1 if the statement is definitely false about your actions in the relationship.
Mark 2 if the statement is mostly false about your actions in the relationship.
Mark 3 if the statement is neither true nor false about your actions in the relationship.
Mark 4 if the statement is mostly true about your actions in the relationship.
Mark 5 if the statement is definitely true about your actions in the relationship.

_____ _____ 1. I respect the other's privacy.
_____ _____ 2. I never discuss what the two of us say in confidence with anyone else.
_____ _____ 3. I look the other person in the eye during our conversations.
_____ _____ 4. I never criticize the other person in front of anyone else.
_____ _____ 5. I never force sexual activity on the other person or expect the other to do something sexual with which they find discomfort.
_____ _____ 6. I seek to repay debts, favors, and compliments no matter how small.
_____ _____ 7. I stand up for the other person in her or his absence.
_____ _____ 8. I share news of success with the other person.
_____ _____ 9. I offer to help the other person, including helping with mundane, material, and emotional needs.
_____ _____ 10. I trust and confide in my relational partner.
_____ _____ 11. I show emotional support and bolster the other's self-esteem.
_____ _____ 12. I strive to make the other person happy.
_____ _____ 13. I am not jealous or critical of the other's relationships.
_____ _____ 14. I ask for personal advice.
_____ _____ 15. I avoid nagging.
_____ _____ 16. I joke or tease in a friendly, not attacking way.
_____ _____ 17. I disclose personal feelings or problems.
_____ _____ 18. I feel attraction and physical or emotional arousal.
_____ _____ Total

(continued)

ACTIVITY 7.6 *(continued)*

Add your scores. The higher your score, the more effectively you follow the basic expectations of interpersonal relationships. The person for which you had the higher score should be your more intimate relationship. Positive answers to questions 9 through 18 suggest deeper levels of intimacy. For each item you marked less than 5, create a technique for effective communication in your I-Can Plan.

Source: Adapted from concepts developed by Michael Argyl and Monika Henderson as reported in Argyle, M. (1985). *The anatomy of relationships and the rules and skills needed to manage them successfully*. London, England: Heinemann.

in their way of relating to self and others, communicating, problem solving, and even making love."[19]

Most people can use both halves of their brain. Therefore, classifying people as right-brain or left-brain dominant is an oversimplification. Human beings are far too complex to be captured so easily.[20] However, in reality, when a **right-brained dominant person** and a **left-brained dominant person** form a couple, it is a joining of "opposites."[21] And, because of the differences in the way the partners think and communicate, problems can result. The question arises, "What are those differences?" Left-brainers (LBs) use a language of facts. They tend to speak with precision, are rational, use impersonal language, and present facts. Their counterparts, the right-brainers (RBs), tend to use a language of feelings. They tend to be more ambiguous as they speak, use emotional rather than logical words to describe thoughts, explain with examples, emphasize attachment, regard communication as a connecting process, and use questions as tools to determine how experience has led to perspective.[22]

Often when people in a relationship, whether in an intimate, personal, or work relationship, are unaware of the concept of brain differences, they don't understand why they are in communication conflict. "Opposites who do not truly understand that they are wired differently complain, 'If I can do it, why can't she?' or 'If he really wanted to he would.'"[23] Bosses mistakenly say this to employees, husbands to wives, teachers to students.

Unless effort is placed into making change, conflicts will continue. People tend to stay in their dominant hemisphere and, unless they understand the consequences of how their style is causing problems, they don't change their attitudes and modes of operation.[24]

One of the first steps in working toward change is first to recognize if your relational partner uses a similar or different side of the brain to think, listen and communicate.

LEARNING EXPERIENCE: Interested in knowing whether you and your relational partner think, listen, and communicate in the same way or differently? If so, do Activity 7.7.

ACTIVITY 7.7
Identifying Left-Brain or
Right-Brain Relational Partner

A. Place a check mark in the space to the left of the alphabetical numbers next to the general traits/actions of your relational partner. B. Place an "x" on the space provided to the right of each sentence for those factors that represent you.

Relational partner   You
_____a.   Focuses on one thing at a time; resists getting sidetracked.   _____
_____b.   Approaches problems sequentially, thoroughly.   _____
_____c.   Often does many things at once.   _____
_____d.   Deals in hunches, uses intuition.   _____
_____e.   Very logical, rational, and analytical in their approach
          to problem solving.   _____
_____f.   Are predictable in their actions.   _____
_____g.   Focus on feelings.   _____
_____h.   Do not have to have things make sense to register as "true."   _____
_____i.   Is comfortable with routine.   _____
_____j.   Expects others to operate with the same rules of logic as
          he/she does.   _____
_____k.   Deals in facts, rejects intuition as source.   _____
_____l.   Has difficulty remembering names.   _____
_____m.   Avoids routine if possible, doesn't like to do things over
          and over.   _____
_____n.   Stimulates others into action.   _____
_____o.   Expects other person to be as interested in a relationship
          as they are.   _____
_____p.   Seems to be emotionally unavailable.   _____
_____q.   Is inhibited, can't let go and play, let loose.   _____
_____r.   Gets emotional when talking about problems.   _____
_____s.   Personalizes things; too sensitive.   _____
_____t.   Won't talk about feelings.   _____

A. Total the other person's scores:
    Left Brain: Count the check marks for answers to:
        a, b, e, f, i, j, k, p, q, t = _____
    Right Brain: Count the check marks for answers to:
        c, d, g, h, l, m, n, o, r, s = _____

If a person has a score of 7 or above as an LB total, you perceive your partner as being left-brained. A score of 7 or above as a total on the RB line means you perceive your partner as being right-brained.

(*continued*)

ACTIVITY 7.7 (continued)

B. Total your perceived scores of yourself:
   LB: Count the X's for answers to: a, b, e, f, i, j, k, p, q, t = _____
   RB: Count the X's for answers to: c, d, g, h, l, m, n, o, r, s = _____

If you indicated that you had a score of 7 or above as an LB total, you perceive yourself as being left-brained. A score of 7 or above as a total on the RB line means you perceive yourself as being right-brained.

If neither of you had scores of 7 or above, you perceive that neither of you is dominantly right-brained or left-brained.

What are the implications of the similarities or differences between you and your relational partner? How might you adapt for more effective communication?

Source: Based on lists presented in Cutter, R. (1994). *Right brain/left brain relationships and how to make them work.* New York: Penguin Books, pp. 24–26.

Associates need to learn to accept and respect that their partner's way of thinking is not wrong, it is just different. Differences can be expected and appreciated. Rather than trying to change the partner, accept who he/she is. This, of course, is easier to understand than to put into action, but it is worth the effort, as it causes major changes in relational conflict and encourages relational understanding.

Relational opposites need to work out methods to reach conclusions in a constructive manner. For example, the right-brained partner will often make decisions quickly, the left-brainer will want to think things over. Let the "quick" thinker come up with alternative decisions that are acceptable to him/her, share the list of decisions with the more tentative partner, and give the thinker a period of time to ponder the options and reach a conclusion.

Different thinkers need to realize that there doesn't have to be a winner in decision-making. The relationship is more important than the decision. Neither partner has to be a winner. Think of it this way: if one person wins, the other has to lose. A goal of defeating your partner does not make for a healthy relationship.

Those in healthy relationships learn to share not only facts, but emotions. This technique allows for both partners in opposite brain relationships to feel heard. Questions should include both, "What are you thinking?" and "What are you feeling?" Again, neither of their thoughts or feelings are always right, but being able to consider both may lead to a constructive solution and open the possibility of neither partner's feeling used or abused.

"Differences need not stand in the way of good communication. They actually provide an opportunity for an altered sense of what is possible, opening the partners up to avenues they have never considered."[25] Of course, knowledge and skills must be acquired. Although change is usually slow, opposites are capable of making significant alterations in the way they interact. Research indicates that RBs tend to change first and rather quickly. Since LBs often don't understand the need for connectedness, they often assume they can deal logically with all relational issues. Unfortunately, opposites who are heavily invested in their own ways and fail to consider alternative possibilities and explanations, may not understand that their inflexibility might be perceived as intentionally thoughtless by the other person.[26] Truth is a major issue in the conflict between different brain styles. Since left-brainers tend to ignore feelings because in order to analyze a situation, one needs to make it as impersonal as possible, they often find it impossible to divorce themselves from any beliefs or emotions and rely on pragmatism as a guide.[27] On the other hand, those with right-brain tendencies may resort to intuition and feelings to reach conclusions. Letting each partner develop a conclusion, and then explain that conclusion to their relational partner often allows each to understand the other. To do this, respectful listening becomes paramount.

The bottom lines regarding differences in partners are: "Unless opposites reach an understanding of how their differing styles contribute to their issues and learn specific skills for managing their polarized ways of being, they will enter a crisis state."[28] And, "Although couples may spend time talking to each other, many lack the skills to get their messages across effectively, express their feelings, or resolve conflicts without hurting each other or provoking anger."

ENDING A RELATIONSHIP

Whether we are dealing with dating, friendship, or marriage, we must realize that these relationships will not go on forever. Rather, we must accept that the ending of relationships is part of the life cycle. We grow up, relocate, change jobs, have different needs, grow in different directions, and ultimately die. We must realize that just as change is inevitable, so are endings, unless you believe in life-everlasting, life-after-death, or reincarnation.

Ending a relationship can feel devastating. If you have invested considerable time, emotion, and energy in developing and maintaining the relationship, you may feel shocked and betrayed when it ends, even if you are the person who initiated the break-up.

If you felt sure "this is the one," you may question yourself and your judgment when it ends. If the person turns out to be someone totally different from the person you first met, you may wonder how you made such a mistake.

How do break-ups happen? Sometimes both people decide to end the relationship. Or, one person may desire to terminate the relationship while the other wants to continue. Some people allow the other to "discover" the relationship is over by finding out about infidelity. In other cases, the relationship just fades away as the two people do other things and see less and less of each other.

A more positive ending is most likely when the two people meet and talk about what has happened and how they will move forward without each other.

For some people, the end of a relationship is filled with feelings of hostility, blame, rejection, loss, and failure. The same can happen when employees are fired. You've probably read or heard of instances of employees returning to their former place of employment and killing their supervisors in situations where the employee was mentally ill.

Relationships are fragile, and the possible threats to their well-being are numerous and powerful. Relationships end for a variety of reasons:

Goals may be fulfilled and no new goals established. The team was put together to perform a task, the task has been accomplished. The purpose for the relationship is gone.

Goals may not be accomplished and there may be little chance of achieving them. A jury is formed, they are deadlocked and cannot reach a conclusion. The jury is dissolved and the relationships for the purpose of jury duty are over.

The partners may continue to feel lonely despite their relationship. The two may have come together out of a need for having someone in their life. Unfortunately, the person chosen doesn't fill that need as expected.

The patterns of interaction may be too fixed, too inflexible, or too boring. The relationship is too restrictive, it emotionally costs too much to be in the relationship. A Euro-American female who marries a man from a Muslim culture in which the male makes all the decisions may find herself frustrated. Or, a male may find that the passive, nice girl he married is just not adding any variety or excitement to his life.

The initial attractiveness may fade and nothing new may replace it. Remember the high school cheerleader who married the captain of the school's football team? They were the "hot" couple in high school, envied by all. Five years later that was no longer the case. They are different people, their former popularity and positions are gone, they are surrounded by different people, and they may have developed different relational expectations.

New relationships may appear more attractive. New people are constantly entering our lives. One of those "newbies" may be of more interest, be more exciting, or better fulfill the "relational wish list" of one of the partners.

The list goes on and on. Sexual dysfunction, conflicts with work, and financial difficulties may doom relationships.

Reactions to relationship termination may vary from relief to self-recrimination, from happiness to deep depression. Similar to the death of a loved one, the death of a relationship evokes strong responses, which are often accompanied by denial that the relationship is over, creating logical but untrue explanations for "what went wrong," anger that's generalized to everyone and everything, and the presumption that how you feel is how everyone should or must feel.

Terminating a relationship often involves changes in other relationships. New groups of friends may need to be formed and explanations to friends, relatives, and parents may be necessary. Sides may be taken. Ill will may be created.

Critical dimensions describe the variations in relationship disengagement. Three of these are:

- Whether the onset of relational problems is gradual or sudden. Most problems emerge gradually, making it difficult to determine their specific causes and the most clearly related consequences.
- Whether one or both partners wish to end the relationship. Does only one partner want to end the relationship (*unilateral desire*) or do both agree (*bilateral desire*).
- Whether a direct or an indirect strategy is used to end the relationship.

If you want to end a relationship and the other person wants to continue the relationship, you may confront the other person with your desire—*a direct relational dissolution strategy*. You may also arrange to see the other person less—*indirect relational dissolution strategy*. If both you and the other person wish to end your relationship, a direct strategy would be to talk it out and an indirect strategy would be to decrease the amount of time you spend together.

Strategies vary not only according to whether they're direct or indirect, but also according to whether they're self-oriented or other-oriented. Strategies that seem to have a self-orientation are *fait accompli* ("I've decided this is over!"), *withdrawal* ("I'm going to be busy all next week"), *cost escalation* ("If you want me to go with you, you'll have to give up going out on Fridays with your friends"), and *attributional conflict* ("It's your fault, jerk!"). Fait accompli takes control away from the other person, inflicting a blow to the other's self-esteem. Withdrawal also limits the other's control. Cost escalation raises the relationship's costs for the other person, and attributional conflict results in hostile communication and disparaging remarks.

In contrast, *state-of-the-relationship talk* ("Where is this relationship going?"), *pseudo-de-escalation* ("I think we should see less of each other for a while"—when *no* contact really is desired), *negotiated farewell* ("Let's rationally discuss how to end this without fighting"), and *fading away* (seeing the other person less and disclosing less) are more other-oriented. They allow some face-saving for both relationship partners.

The other dimensions on which disengagement processes may be distinguished are:

• Whether it takes a long time or a short time to break away. Using an indirect strategy is likely to result in a drawn-out disengagement with several rounds of negotiations. Overreliance on indirectness also is likely to lead both partners to regret that they didn't use a more direct strategy to make the break quicker and less complex.
• Whether there are any attempts to repair the relationship. If they use an indirect disengagement strategy, relational repair is more likely.
• Whether the final outcome is termination or a restructured relationship. Restructuring may result in a relationship that is successfully repaired and restored to approximately the same state it was in before problems arose, or it may lead to a different relationship with new goals, structure, or rules, or modified commitment, intimacy, or resources. The infrequency with which relationships are successfully restructured demonstrates the difficulty of accomplishing this task to both partners' satisfaction.

The most frequently used disengagement process involves a unilateral desire to exit (one person wants out), coupled with an indirect strategy (the person decreases contact, claims a desire to reduce contact when no contact is really the goal, or makes contact very costly for the other person), with no attempts at repair, which leads to termination without trying to structure a new relationship (the pair say good-bye with no expectation for future contact). For example, Dale wants to break off with Lupe. Dale stops calling Lupe. Lupe calls Dale and asks, "What's wrong?" Dale tells Lupe, "Nothing. I don't want to talk about it. Good-bye." Dale hangs up.

The discussion so far about ending relationships makes it seem as though this final stage to relational development is clear-cut, that when a relationship ends, it *ends*. This interpretation, however, is misleading because relationships, in a very real sense, *never end*. Even though people are no longer in your life, the experiences you had together, the ideas you exchanged, the lessons that were taught, the modeling of value and ethics, among other things, remain.

The ongoing influence of your relationships with people with whom you no longer interact attests to the fact that relationships—certainly the important ones—have lasting effects.

Alternate Ways of Examining Relational Stages

An alternate way of examining relationships is the **Knapp Relationship Escalation Model**,[29] which is a communication-based explanation of how relationships develop and disintegrate.

Knapp describes the developmental stages as initiation, experimenting, intensifying, integrating, and bonding.

The *initiation stage* tends to be short. Think about a time when you met someone who later became your friend. At the start, basic information is exchanged such as each other's names and observing each other's appearance or mannerisms takes place. Though superficial, this stage is critical in determining whether there is interest on the part of either person to progress to the relational escalation level. Much of the information at this level is at the superficial level.

The *experimenting stage* centers on asking questions of each other in order to gain more information that will determine whether there is interest in furthering the relationship. More in-depth demographic information may be investigated (e.g., Where do you go to school? Where are you from?). Light probing about belief systems and attitudes may take place.

In the *intensifying stage*, self-disclosure starts. The relationship often becomes less formal, the participants start perceiving each other as individuals and "nicknames" and more depth of personal information becomes known. Knowledge about attitudes, beliefs, family, and other friendships are exchanged. There is often common "language" about actions that have been coexperienced.

The *integrating stage* normally includes such duo-based terms as "best friends," "couple," "boyfriend-girlfriend/boyfriend-boyfriend/girl friend-girl friend," "engaged." Others perceive the dyad as a pair as they have developed a shared relational identity.

During the *bonding stage*, a formal, sometimes legal, announcement of the relationship takes place. Terms that identify the transition into this phase include getting engaged, or going through a marriage or civil union, or forming a business partnership. Other actions which may indicate that the couple is bonded may include living together, buying property together, or having or adopting a child. Very few relationships reach this level.

Knapp's Relationship Termination Model describes how, at any stage of the model, participants may work toward ending the relationship. The ending stages include differentiating, circumscribing, stagnating, avoiding, and terminating.

The *differentiating stage* is highlighted by one or both of the partners" being aware that he or she needs to be independent. "We" is no longer as important as "me." In terms of the **Economic Theory of Costs and Rewards**, it is perceived by one or both that the cost(s) of being in the relationship are exceeding the reward(s) being received. This could be a warning sign that the relationship needs to be recalibrated or that it is beyond help and heading for termination.

The *circumscribing stage* is illustrated by the diminishment and quality of the intercouple communication. Again, this awareness can be used as a sign that the relationship needs to be discussed and, if possible, recalibrated.

During the *stagnating stage*, the individuals may start to avoid discussing the relationship because one or the other is afraid of the consequences of sharing thoughts and/or feelings. The relationship may take on the air of suspended animation, with little or no mutual feelings taking place. If there has been a sexual component to the relationship, the intimacy may cease or become automatic rather than meaningful. Often words of endearment start to disappear.

The *avoiding stage* is keyed by the partners' physically separating. Little or no discussion takes place, as it is often thought that the relationship is on a strong downhill slope and is basically over.

The *terminating stage*, the final stage, may come naturally, such as at the end of the semester when roommates move out, or arbitrarily, through divorce or legal separation.

Communication and Relational Stages

Communication is an extremely powerful process. Accepting the responsibility of entering into a relationship means (whether you care to or not) accepting the responsibility for influencing and being influenced by another person. Every relationship opens the possibility for change, change that may last a lifetime. In one form or another, you will always be with your relational partners. These concepts are well developed in the closing speech of a play:[30]

In the beginning of our relationship, we learned each other's language
Like over-eager babies
Mouthing unintelligible gaggles and sounds
Unable to articulate
Clumsily tripping on words
Falling into abject frustration
But once we found the common language
Each action and deed, every word and sentence was a joy and an excitement
A tingling of senses
A radiant discovery

Then, as if through osmosis, we used each other's words and expressions
Borrowing shamelessly and
Indeliberately incorporating them into our language
Speaking as one
Thinking as one
Feeling as one
And in the course, we invented new words
Gave existing words new meaning

Redefined and polished our language
Making it a special one of our own
One that we selfishly shared
One that no one could decipher or understand
One that we used in the comfort of each other's arms in quiet evenings

Then we tired of it
Lost interest
Got lazy
Became indifferent
Words gradually lost their meaning and significance
Like drunken dancers, we emphasized wrong accents in words
Sentences led to misinterpretations
Misinterpretations led to misunderstandings
Misunderstandings led to inevitable silence

In the end, we spoke different languages
Even though we wanted the same thing

Key Terms

relationship	compliance gaining
cyberdating	brain dominance
speed dating	right-brained dominant person
matchmaking	left-brained dominant person
relational coach	Knapp Relationship Escalation Model
approachability cues	Knapp's Relationship Termination Model
self-disclosure	Economic Theory of Costs and Rewards

Competencies Check-Up

Interested in finding out what you learned in this chapter and how you use the information? If so, take this competencies check-up.

Directions: Indicate the extent that each statement applies to you:

1—Never   2—Seldom   3—Sometimes   4—Often   5—Usually

____1. I recognize that the sequential pattern of relationships includes the entry phase, a personal phase, and an exit phase.

____2. I am aware that in establishing a relationship there are levels of uncertainty.

____3. I know that each person has a different list of characteristics that they find desirable in others.

____4. I can list the characteristics I look for or looked for in a person to be acceptable to me as a potential partner in an intimate long-term relationship.

_____ 5. I am aware that the so-called seven bases of attraction are attractiveness, proximity, familiarity, personal rewards, complementarity, similarity, personal motives, self-esteem enhancement, and attempting to overcome family-of-origin problems.

_____ 6. I am aware of advantages and disadvantages of cyberdating.

_____ 7. I am aware of the various types of activities that are available for meeting individuals for relationships, including such systems as fee-based introducing services, speed dating, cyberdating, and matchmaking.

_____ 8. I know of the role of relational coaching as it relates to learning needed social skills to be an effective communicator.

_____ 9. I am aware of the role of approachability cues as a factor in relational development.

_____10. I know and can apply the steps to initiating relational communication.

_____11. I recognize the factors that allow for favorable impressions in relational communication.

_____12. I know that relationships are two-sided and can explain why this is an important concept in relational maintenance.

_____13. I understand the roles of self-disclosure and receptiveness to feedback in relational development and maintenance.

_____14. I can define compliance gaining and explain its role in relational maintenance.

_____15. I can explain and apply the concepts of right brain/left brain thinking in relationships.

_____16. I realize that the ending of relationships is part of the life cycle.

_____17. I am aware that the ending of a relationship can be a positive or negative experience.

_____18. I am aware of the procedures that are likely to lead to a positive ending to a relationship.

_____19. I can explain the Knapp Relationship Escalation Model.

_____20. I can apply the Knapp Relationship Termination Model.

Scoring: A total of 60 suggests that you have minimum competencies in the principles of relational communication. Given the important role of relationships in our lives, a high skill level is needed. Examine any item on which you scored less than 3 and figure out how you will improve your skills.

I-Can Plan!

Think over the content of this chapter. Consider a relationship in which you are involved (intimate, friend, etc.). What stage is it in? What can you do to enhance that relationship. Or, select a relationship which you are in. Both you and the other participant should take the right-brain, left-brain questionnaire presented in this chapter. Afterward, discuss your relationship from the perspective of the test results and try and develop a plan to adjust problems within the relationship based on this information.

Activities

1. Class activity: This activity is intended to allow class members to generate, try out, and evaluate ways to probe for information and start conversations.
   a. As homework you are to write a question someone could ask you about something you know. (*Example*: "What do you like to do on vacations?").
   b. List two follow-up questions the other person could ask you based on your answer. (*Example*: If you like to travel, follow-up questions could be, "Where have you been lately?" and "What's the nicest place you've ever visited?")
   c. What two questions could you ask someone who tells you, "I'm planning on going into sales when I finish my education."
   d. During a class period the students are divided into groups of four. If possible, each group should be equally composed of males and females. One person in the group reads her/his answer to question a. People in the group evaluate the question. Then the second person reads his/her question. After all the answers to a question have been presented, the answers to question b are read and evaluated. Continue the process until all of the questions have been presented.
   e. Two people are selected to be the first "couple." Using the questions generated during the evaluation segment of this activity, the couple carries on a conversation of about five minutes. The rest of the group observes the interchange of the couple. Following the interaction, a discussion is held about how successful the questions and the follow-ups were. The next duo carries out the same task.
2. Class activity: Learn how to communicate with someone from an opposite brain perspective.
   a. The class will be divided into dyads. If possible, a right-brained person will be matched with a left-brained person.
   b. Students are to select one of these issues to discuss and reach a conclusion. If they finish one topic they are to go on to the next. (If all of the dyads are of the same brain type, one of them should play the role of a person who is strongly right- or left-brained based on the concepts taught in the discussions of how individuals of that brain tendency act.)
      (1) Decisions in a relationship should be made by the person who is most logical.
      (2) Emotions should have no place in decision making in intimate or work relationships.
      (3) In a relationship, such factors as caring, mutual dependency, and emotions have no role in how problems should be solved.
   After the discussions, each dyad should come to some conclusions about what they learned from the transactions and report those findings back to the class.
3. Using Google and/or Yahoo, do an online search for matchmakers. Ascertain what niche groups may avail themselves of their services.
4. Go online to a dating service or speed dating service and investigate how it operates.

CHAPTER 8

Conflict Resolution

Learning Outcomes

After reading this chapter, you should be able to:

- Define and explain the concept of conflict.
- Compare and contrast conflict-active societies and conflict-avoidance societies.
- Explain the differences between thinking and feeling.
- Explain the levels of conflict.
- Analyze the influence of personal anger in a conflict situation.
- Identify and explain the sources for conflict.
- Explain the role of the family, media, educational institutions, and the government in developing conflict resolution perceptions.
- Understand the technique of fair fighting.
- Identify the advantages and disadvantages of using the various methods of managing conflict.
- Respond assertively in conflict situations.
- Describe the advantages and disadvantages of win-lose, lose-lose, and win-win approaches to conflict.
- Define and explain negotiation.
- Appreciate cultural differences in interpersonal conflict.

Dan and Ming, who are in their early twenties, have been married for nine months. Ming's parents were against the marriage as they felt Dan was immature. Dan is aware of their feelings.

Dan	*Let's go out Friday night.*
Ming	*Where do you want to go?*
Dan	*How about going to a movie?*
Ming	*OK, but I don't want to see one of your usual choices—a movie with lots of killing.*

Dan	What's the matter with action flicks?
Ming	You're just trying to act macho by going to that kind of film.
Dan	You think I have to act at being macho?
Ming	I didn't say that.
Dan	I'm not man enough for you? You never complained before. I'm more of a man than your wimpy father.
Ming	Of all the . . . why are you making nasty cracks about my dad?
Dan	And your mother is no better, she's always nagging. I guess that's where you get it from!
Ming	You can just go out by yourself Friday night, and maybe forever, you jerk!

When you think of the word "conflict," what metaphors do you think of? Many people probably conjure up: "conflict is war," "conflict is explosive." Whatever your metaphor, the words that are used to describe conflict tend to be negative.

Interpersonal problems are inevitable whenever two individuals participate in an ongoing relationship. The inevitability of conflict, however, shouldn't disturb you. In fact, it might surprise you to know that conflict can play a positive role in healthy and growing relationships. And though conflict may be impossible to eliminate, it can be managed successfully with appropriate communication skills.

As shown in the Chinese pictograph in Figure 8.1, conflict contains the concepts of both *danger* and *opportunity*. Although you probably understand the danger of conflict, you may not recognize the opportunity for promoting interpersonal relationship growth and communication. By confronting conflict you can become aware of what changes you or the other person or people need to make in order to create harmony. Without confronting the basis of the conflict, this never would normally happen.

Figure 8.1. Opportunity: In Chinese, the symbol for the word *crisis* is a combination of the symbols for the words *danger* and *opportunity*.

What is your response to conflict? Do you scream, cry, call names, throw things, slam doors, or hit people? Do you stop talking, withdraw, glare at the other person, mutter hostile remarks under your breath? Do you try to reason things out, discuss the problem, seek answers that help both you and the other person? Do you behave differently in different conflicts?

The Concepts of Conflict

"A **conflict** is any situation in which you perceive that another person, with whom you're interdependent, is frustrating or might frustrate the satisfaction of some concern, need, want, or desire of yours."[1] The origins of the conflict may be simple, complicated, or something in between. You may be involved in conflict, for example, over competition about limited resources (such as a job or money), or gender influences that result in a different perception of the relationship. Whatever the cause, conflict is a natural part of life and interpersonal communication.

Conflict occurs when one person feels upset or frustrated because of a perception that another person has interfered with the first person's goals. A specific conflict can be identified by filling in the blanks of this sentence: "*I want* (a personal need, concern, or want), *but* (insert the name of the person or thing which is perceived to be stopping you from accomplishing your goal) *wants* (insert his or her need, concern, or want). For example:

I want to switch jobs with a coworker,
but the supervisor
wants people to stay in the jobs they were hired to do.

I want to go to a comedy club Friday night,
but Jose
wants to go to a concert.

I want to borrow money,
but Caletta doesn't
want to lend it to me.

From these statements comes a conflict or crisis situation in which mismatched goals and behaviors are revealed. The opposing or clashing behavior of the two people hinder or interfere with each other.

Many times conflicts are based on *feelings* (e.g., "I feel that . . ."), other times on *thoughts* (e.g., "I think that. . . ." Be aware that there is a difference between thinking and feeling. Thinking, a left-brained activity, is based on awareness, facts, examples. Feeling, a right-brained activity, is based on instinct, awareness, and examples. Sometimes conflict is a combination of both feelings and thoughts. It is important for you, as a participant in a conflict, to attempt to determine whether your reactions are emotional or logical, a "gut level feeling," or reality. As will be discussed later in this chapter, how you deal with the conflict is often based on this awareness.

LEARNING EXPERIENCE: Interested in practicing how to analyze relational discord? If so, do Activity 8.1.

ACTIVITY 8.1
Analysis of Relationship Discord

A. Reread the Ming and Dan scenario presented at the beginning of this chapter. Assuming you are Dan, complete the following using the information presented in that interchange.

I (Dan) **want** (Dan's concern, need, want)_____
but (the other person) Ming **wants** (Ming's concern, need, want) _____

_____.

B. Think of a recent relational conflict you have had. Complete the "I want . . . but . . . wants" for that conflict.

I **want** _____,
but _____ **wants** _____.

Do you seek to avoid conflict? One researcher found that "students try to avoid about 56 percent of their conflicts. They become skilled at turning away from conflict."[2] Avoidance of conflict can cause problems. When people fail to say what is bothering them, their response often becomes an intrapersonal conflict in which the person internalizes the feelings and ideas.[3]

When people use disagreements as a springboard for talking about and resolving differences, conflict can lead to improved interpersonal communication and increased relationship satisfaction. In these cases, conflict has positive effects. We are often taught constructive ways of handling anger in our families, schools, and the media.

LEARNING EXPERIENCE: Interested in identifying how you learned your conflict resolution style? If so, do Activity 8.2.

Just as conflict can serve a useful function, so too can it cause problems. Conflict is detrimental when it stops you from doing your work; threatens the integrity of a relationship; endangers the continuation of a relationship or your ability to function within it; causes physical, mental, or sexual abuse; or leads a person to give up and become inactive in a relationship or life in general.

Different cultures use different approaches to conflict. In many Mediterranean and Middle Eastern cultures, conflict is accepted as a normal part of life. In these **conflict-active societies**, people—particularly men—enjoy arguing, negotiating, and haggling. Haggling is commonly used as a way of negotiating the price of goods and services in many Arabic and Central and South American countries. Israelis jokingly call conflict their national sport. "African Americans tend to be more emotionally engaged in their

ACTIVITY 8.2
The Role of Family, School, Media
in Developing Conflict Strategies

List several positive messages or "healthy" techniques that were given to you by each of these sources regarding conflict and conflict solution.

Family (e.g., "In this house we talk out our problems, we don't hit.")

School

Media

Other (identify the source: e.g., religious institution)

conflict approach [than Euro-Americans]."[4] "The Black mode of conflict is high-keyed (e.g., energetic, nonverbally animated and emotionally expressive)."[5]

Remember that in this text, generalizations are made based on research findings about gender and cultural groups. Although scientific findings and expert observations do not always apply to every individual, they can provide communication guidelines, which help individuals respond with flexibility to others.

People from **conflict-avoidance societies** believe that people should stay clear of disagreements.[6] People from certain Asian and Native American cultures find haggling to be offensive.[7] This does not mean that they will not engage in mild forms of it. You may find yourself bartering for prices in the People's Republic of China, but it will not be the loud haggling in a Turkish or Moroccan bazaar. Individuals from many Asian cultures consider argument to be repulsive.[8] A Chinese proverb states, "The first person to raise his voice loses the argument." In Japan, so strong is the notion of self-restraint in dealing with conflict that the Japanese have a word in their language ("wa") that reminds their members that interpersonal harmony is essential. The Japanese believe that each of us comes to an encounter with this feeling of "wa" already inside of us, and that communication between people should foster this harmony, *not* disrupt it. This concept pervades nearly every aspect of Japanese life. People often wear surgical masks in public to keep from giving their colds to others. The words, "I am very sorry" ("soo-mee-mah-sehn") are heard with great regularity. In the Native American and Mexican cultures people seldom compete with the same aggressive attitude as do members of the predominantly Euro-American culture of the United States. People from these cultures are apt to withdraw rather than stand toe-to-toe and "slug it out." In fact, "assertive speech and behavior are a sign of discourtesy, restlessness, being self-centered, and a lack of discipline."[9] Historically, this is one of the factors that caused Native Americans, unlike their image as portrayed in old Hollywood movies, to be taken advantage of. The same is true of Indian tribes in Mexico, especially the kind and trusting Mayans, as they met and dealt with their European invaders. This does not mean to imply that these cultures avoid conflict, but rather it underscores the notion that conflict and competition are defined differently.

Since most of the readers of this book will be dealing with conflict in the predominantly Euro-American society, an investigation of that society's conflict patterns will be undertaken. However, even if you are Euro-American, please remember that because the United States and Canada are nations of immigrants, a great number of the people with whom you come in contact have strong other-cultural ties and may follow the patterns of their native culture. Your pattern or their pattern are not right or wrong, they are just different.

Types of Conflict

If you think that another person is infringing on your rights, taking advantage of or threatening you, and you communicate your concern to the other person, you have an **interpersonal conflict**, a conflict between people. In the examples presented at the start of this chapter, *you request* the job swap *from* your supervisor, you tell your date *you want* to go to the comedy club, *you want* to borrow money from your roommate. The conflict is between you and another.

If you decide to resolve the conflict on your own, you have an intrapersonal conflict. You may decide that the supervisor is too inflexible and that it wouldn't pay to ask about switching jobs. You may decide to keep your frustration about not being able to go where you want to go on the date because you fear you'll harm your current relationship if you say something. Without talking to your roommate, you may decide that your roommate wouldn't lend you the money even if you asked for it. However, you may communicate your frustration by being curt with your supervisor, withdrawing from your date, or being sarcastic with your roommate. Recognizing interdependence, and resolving conflicts interpersonally may well be less taxing in the long run.

Levels of Conflict

Conflict usually develops sequentially and can be analyzed according to its stages. It can take many forms, such as minor bickering, a dysfunctional relationship, uncertainty, or the need to assert yourself.

The levels of conflict are:

Level 1: No conflict. At this stage, the individuals face no key dispute and have compatible goals.

Level 2: *Hidden conflict*. No one is talking about a conflict, although an individual may believe there is an undercurrent of tension. Although no overt signs of conflict exist, something seems to be brewing.

Level 3: *Problems to solve*. The conflict is in a positive stage, as people recognize a problem exists, talk to each other about the problem, and work to solve the problem. The individuals take the risk to discuss their needs, concerns, or wants in a context of concern.

Level 4: *Argument*. In this stage, the conflict escalates to a disagreement using personal attacks and destructive comments or actions. The clash has negative effects on the communication, problem-solving process, and relationship.

Level 5: *Help*. At this stage, the conflict has grown out of control, so that one or more parties seek help to manage the differences. An individual may ask a friend, supervisor, religious leader, counselor, professional mediator, arbitrator, or adjudicator.

When turning for help, a good choice is a third party who is a neutral person who has no investment in the outcome of the disagreement. The help may be direct (telling the person what to do) or nondirect (drawing a solution out of the parties involved). Compliance with such a solution should be by choice, otherwise, it can carry resentments, and the individual may sabotage any hope for success.

Level 6: *Fight or flight*. At this stage, one or both individuals may run from the situation or remain and escalate the clash. The difference of opinion has usually turned into an interpersonal war. Often the purpose of one or both is to prove how right he or she is and then how wrong the other person is. This is the time when the stress may be so bad that one or the other leaves. For example, in a conflict between a teen and his parents, the teenager may run away. It is at the fight stage that physical and verbal aggression, battering, or murder may take place.

Level 7: *Intractability*. At this stage, one or both people have passed the point of no return. The participants may be more concerned about maintaining the conflict than resolving it. Often it becomes a point of no forgiveness and justification for how "good" one person is and how "bad" the other person is. The relationship can be devalued and/or destroyed, and the people involved may suffer irreparable harm, psychological or physical. If the conflict ends, it is only because one of more of the participants lacks the energy to continue to fight.

The Role of Personal Anger in Conflict

Explaining their reactions to conflict, people may say, "He made me mad" or "I was so angry I couldn't control myself." This is the verbalization of the *emotion of anger*.

Anger is a feeling of irritation, frustration, resentment, or antagonism toward oneself or another person, "Anger is a signal, and one worth listening to. Your anger may be a message that you are being hurt, that your rights are being violated, that your needs or wants are not being adequately met, or simply that something is not right."[10]

Anger is a way of communicating, above or beneath your conscious level. In other words, you may not actually be aware that you are angry. The meaning of anger comes when you communicate your thoughts and feelings to others. It also can be analyzed

Figure 8.2.   Forms of Expression for Anger

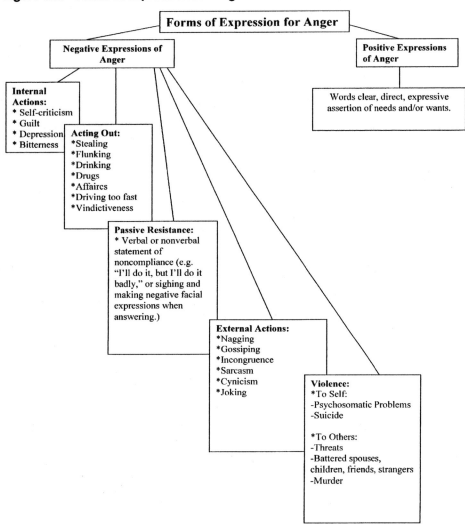

by what you do. The words and your nonverbal reactions can help in analyzing and expressing what is wrong.

The emotion of anger is never a problem, but the way anger is *expressed* can be a problem for the individual or others.

Implosive anger is directed toward the self. A person who uses negative self-talk, is exhibiting implosive anger. If an individual responds by overeating, getting drunk, taking drugs, or self-mutilation, the anger can have severe personal effects. Sometimes individuals say or do things that destroy relationships as part of the feeling of being unworthy of conflict resolution. Implosive anger may result in suicide.

Explosive anger is directed outward. Yelling at someone; attacking another person; storming out of a meeting; walking out of a relationship; disowning people; ending friendships; cutting off another's emotional, physical, or financial support; self-mutilation; and developing an eating disorder are all explosive anger strategies. Anger can result in legal and psychological effects if you attack someone verbally or physically. It can result in physical harm when you attack yourself. Common forms of explosive anger are physical or mental abuse or rape. But, it can also take more subtle forms such as a parent who stops talking to a child, a spouse withholding physical love, a lover verbally abusing a partner. The verbalization of explosive anger may include an arsenal of terms called a *verbal shooting gallery.*

During the reform of health-care debates during the late summer and early fall of 2009 there was a display of much explosive anger. Part of it was instigated by right-wing radio talk show hosts (e.g., Rush Limbaugh),[11] part by Republican conservative politicians (e.g., Sarah Palin).[12] Some was a reaction of frustration. As one anger management expert stated, "You have months and months of built up anger, whether it's over unemployment or losing your home."[13] He went on to say it may not be a bad thing. "If people are getting that [anger] out in a verbal way without violence, then it can have a certain amount of mental catharsis."[14] However, "the relief that screaming matches offer is only temporary."[15] "It's like taking speed or amphetamines or a big Starbucks. It gives you energy and temporary confidence. Primates, especially men, were designed to roar at the sign of danger. But it's meant to warn, threaten and intimidate a saber toothed tiger, not express opinions about health care reform."[16] The bottom line, when it comes to anger being an effective tool for getting results is, "It is socially unacceptable to make people uncomfortable, and it really doesn't accomplish anything."[17] As a U.S. Senator said during a town meeting when she was being screamed at by a constituent, "I don't understand this rudeness—what is it? Do you think you're persuading people when you shout out like that?"[18] Realizing that they were doing their cause more harm than good, a state director of a conservative activist group sent e-mails to their members encouraging all members to ask touchy questions, "but to do it in a polite tone." He went on to say, "It's got to be a civil discussion. Otherwise, the point we're trying to make won't be the story. Shouting and yelling will be the story."[19]

LEARNING EXPERIENCE: Interested in identifying if you use a verbal shooting gallery of attack phrases, and what those phrases are? If so, do Activity 8.3.

Most people see anger as a negative. Perhaps you direct anger toward yourself, chastising yourself for your behavior, blaming yourself for the problem. Your reaction may be depression, withdrawal from people involved, or acting defensively. All of these responses are intrapersonal anger, where you direct your anger internally.

By using effective interpersonal communication strategies, you can respond in a positive instead of negative direction.[20]

Wait before you react in anger. You may have heard of the "count-to-ten" and "sleep on it" techniques. They are suggestions that encourage you to stop, think, and calm down before you do or say anything. The intention is to stop you from making

ACTIVITY 8.3
Inventory of Your Verbal Shooting Gallery

Think about conflicts you have had with your parents/caretakers, siblings, coworkers, and friends. Which of these phrases (or similar ones) did you use? Circle all the attacking phrases that are part of or similar to your verbal shooting gallery or add some of your own.

"You're stupid!"
"I hate you!"
"You're just like your father/mother/sister/brother!"
"I wish you were dead!"
"If you loved me you wouldn't . . ."
"You think that's a problem? That's nothing!"
"If you'd do it my way . . ."
"I told you so!"
"Your problem is easy to trace: poor toilet training!"
"Why do you always . . .?"
"Can't you ever do anything right?"
"For an idiot, that's a good answer!"
"That's ridiculous!"
"You're ridiculous!"
Others:

A. How many did you circle? _____ If you didn't circle any, or didn't add any to the list, you probably have learned not to verbally attack others as part of your conflict resolution pattern.

B. How do you feel or what do you think when someone says any of the circled phrases to you?

a decision while angry. For example, if you are under stress and feeling angry, you should never tell a partner you want to break up, ask for a divorce, quit a job, send an e-mail, or fire an employee. Wait until you have time to think and analyze, so you avoid making a hasty decision.

Use the extra energy generated by anger constructively. You receive the adrenaline rush, clean the house, go jogging, write down your thoughts (but don't mail them), or play a game of basketball. Often when you are angry, you are actually afraid of something. Figure out what you are afraid of, and think about appropriate behaviors. These kinds of actions will help you use your physical energy without saying or doing anything that can result in the destruction of a relationship.

Apologize if necessary. If you really behaved badly, an **apology**, a statement of remorse to the wronged person, is in order. You can express regret by saying, "I apologize for _____. I was upset because _____. It won't happen again because in the future I will _____." This act may be difficult because your ego is involved, but it may save the relationship.

Sources of Conflict

There are various sources for conflict. The most common are dependence/interdependence, frustration, limited resources, individual differences, differences in defining relationships, and competition.

DEPENDENCE/INTERDEPENDENCE

You and the other person in your "I want . . . but . . . wants . . ." formula are interdependent; that is, you depend on each other and need each other in some way. Parents and children, workers and supervisors, and partners in a relationship all depend on each other for something, whether it's care, affection, goods, or services. Without interdependence, there is no interpersonal conflict.

You and your supervisor need each other to solve the problem of how you can swap jobs with a coworker. If you both saw the job change in the same way, there would be no conflict.

You and your friend need each other to solve the problem of how to satisfy your desire to have some influence over where you go. If you both defined your relationship the same way—as casual and nonexclusive or as serious and exclusive—there would be no conflict.

As a teenager who needed the family car, you and your parents together owned the problem of who got the car Saturday night. If you each had a car, or both had cars, or none of you had a car, you would not have been interdependent. If you were not interdependent there would have been no conflict.

FRUSTRATION

The frustration that triggers your conflict has a source. Common sources of frustration are limited resources, individual differences, differences in defining your relationship, and competition.

Limited Resources

Limited resources are a widespread source of conflict. You may feel that any problem could be solved if there was more money, more time, more space, more tools, or more

Parents and children, workers and supervisors, and partners in a relationship all depend on each other for something, whether it's care, affection, goods, or services.

people to help. If you and your family or caretaker have only one car to share, or no car, the limited resource—the car—becomes a source of conflict.

Individual Differences

Individual differences are probably the most common and least-often acknowledged source of conflict. Each person's perceptions of the world are uniquely her or his own, based on her or his past experiences, background and history, and interpretations and responses to events. No two people view the same object or event in exactly the same way. These perceptual differences may trigger conflicts.

Among the typical sources of frustration are individual differences in gender, attitudes, beliefs, values, experiences, upbringing, and education. For example, your supervisor may believe that not causing problems is an important goal. You might enjoy trying different approaches to finding solutions to problems. The differences may not matter under most circumstances, but when you propose to swap positions with a coworker, as illustrated in the example earlier in this chapter, the stage is set for conflict.

Differences in Defining a Relationship

Another source of conflict stems from your view of your relationship. People tend to define a relationship in their own way. For example, you may want to socialize with other people because you see your current relationship as unable to fulfill some of your social needs; or, you view yourselves as present-tense but not long-term partners. The other person, however, may define the relationship as serious, and define your roles as intimate friends, mutually exclusive, and prospective spouses or permanent partners. Under these circumstances, your desire to date other people triggers a conflict, one born of different definitions of your relationship.

Competition

Competition is an inescapable fact of life. From the nursery to the nursing home, people compete with each other. They may compete for affection, success, advancement, friendships, social status, power, and money. So pervasive is the competitive urge that it frequently governs your behavior even when you are unaware of its influence. From the time you were very small, competition was a fundamental aspect of the process by which you developed your self-esteem, your social assurance, your very identity.

Sources for Perceptions of Conflict

The family, educational institutions, and the media are among the social agents that teach us how to deal with conflict. Of course, there are other sources such as the legal system, religious organizations, and the government, that teach us about dealing with conflict.

FAMILY

Perceptions of conflict are often based on your experiences with your family or those who raised you. How was conflict treated by your parents or caretakers? Was it something dealt with openly, in front of you and your siblings, or was it something to be hidden behind closed doors? Was it handled in productive ways so that the outcomes were positive, or were most conflicts screaming bouts followed by periods of cool silence, or physical battles?

As conflicts raged around you, you may have been taught such coping techniques as "Don't fight with your sister!" or "If your brother hits you, hit him back!"

EDUCATIONAL INSTITUTIONS

Few schools teach courses or have programs related to conflict resolution, programs that teach how to define problems and communicate feelings and needs to each other to find a mutually satisfactory resolution. Instead of teaching youngsters how to deal constructively with conflicts, schools typically punish children. This may stop the conflict, but doesn't teach how to handle future conflicts. Fortunately, there are some schools that teach their students how to be conflict mediators and allow students to mediate conflicts.

MEDIA

The average person often spends more hours watching television than in school or at work. In half-hour programs, you see complex problems being solved in twenty-four minutes, plus commercials. In one-hour programs, you see even more complex problems being resolved in about fifty minutes, plus commercials. But real life is *not* made up of half-hour or one-hour segments. Many television programs illustrate that guns, knives, poison, and fights are the way to deal with conflict. It makes the shows exciting and teaches bad styles of conflict resolution.

Your own life is not realistically portrayed on television, not even on "reality" television. Television may embody the modern fairy tale where, in the end, everybody but the villain lives happily ever after, but is that reality? Add to this the influence of computer and electronic games, sensational journals, rap music, DVDs, video tapes, movies, concerts, plays, and books, and we have a whole fantasy system on how to deal with conflict.

Dealing with Another Person's Anger

SELF-RESPONSIBILITY

To deal with someone's anger, one expert advises, "Don't let them dump on you; it only encourages their craziness."[21] Figure out what you need to do for yourself, and do it. You don't have to accept communication that is emotional blackmail (e.g., threats that she or he will leave you or stop being your friend), personal attacks, yelling, or other abusive behavior from other people.[22] If you accept the other person's craziness, you set yourself up for a pattern in which this kind of behavior will occur again.

Often, when people are angry, they attack someone who is handy, not necessarily the person who is at fault or who can change the situation. You may simply encounter someone who is distracted by anger from another context, and the person unloads on you. You can allow the person to vent, then redirect them into taking responsibility for the conflict situation. At the same time, you can remember that people under stress often have difficulty handling conflict. If the person continues to be inappropriate, you could respond: "Yesterday you yelled at me when Mary didn't get her report in on time, and again when John didn't reach his sales quota. I wasn't responsible for either of those things. I know you were angry, but I'd appreciate it in the future if you discussed other people's problems with them, and not take it out on me."

If you use "fighting fair," you can translate negative conflicts into constructive interpersonal communication.[23]

FAIR FIGHTING

Fair fighting is a respectful way of confronting others on issues that are causing conflict. It provides a way to support a person's point of view while recognizing the other person's needs. The basic idea is to provide an alternative to *dirty fighting* which uses blaming, yelling, accusing, and humiliating.

Fair fighting strategies include:

Find out information and adapt to the problem using that information. By focusing on facts and information, you can take some of the emotional distractions out of the conflict.

Keep arguments in the present tense. Focus on the now. A conflict is no time to go through a graveyard of past problems. "You always . . ." or "This is just like the time you . . ." Leave the past out of it. You cannot change the past, so when you are in a conflict situation, focus on what is happening now. State the facts and use specific examples to clarify your views.

Change yourself and what you can control. In a conflict situation, many people try to persuade the other person to change. You can present information and ideas. You can express your needs and wants. Ultimately, however, no one can make other people change. So, you will probably become even more frustrated if you try to suggest changes in things over which you have no control.

Use appropriate timing. If you start an argument with someone just before bed, or when the person is leaving to go to work or school, or when the other person is stressed about final exams, you could have disastrous results. Raise your concerns at a time when you and the other person can reasonably discuss the problem without outside interference or distracting stressors.

Select an appropriate setting. Avoid talking in front of other people or arguing in a public setting. If you want to solve the problem rather than lining up allies or witnesses, you should have your disagreement privately. Select a setting that is comfortable for everyone involved.

If you're in a destructive conflict, stop. Two people are needed for an argument, so if the situation begins to deteriorate, stop participating. The length of a *constructive* argument is normally about twenty minutes or until the same argument gets repeated. Once people run out of things to say, they are likely to make personal attacks.[24] Your energy has waned so you will have trouble employing good communication skills. At the point of the change from positive to negative interaction, you can say, "I think you've heard my point of view," or "I need to think about this. Let's talk more later," or "I'm all talked out. Let see how we feel about everything tomorrow." If the conflict is getting out of control or has gone on too long, then one party can simply stop participating.

Identify realistically what you need to get out of the transaction. Unless you know what you want or need, why are you engaging in an argument? Repetitive arguments are often about power and control, not solving problems. So, figure out the problem that needs to be solved and have ideas about solutions before you engage the other person. Then be open to the needs and suggestions of the other person, which can be adapted to meet your needs. Too often people fight without having a goal or even knowing what they are fighting about.[25]

Approaches to Dealing with Conflict

Different people have different responses to conflict. Sometimes their responses are based on their personality, sometimes in repeating the formats they've been taught, and sometimes their reactions are what they consider appropriate for the context. Most people have a preferred or habitual conflict style. By understanding your preferred style and how it affects you and others, you will be able to make better choices for adapting to various conflict situations and the response style of others. The styles include: avoidance, accommodation/smoothing over, compromise, aggression, and assertiveness.

LEARNING EXPERIENCE: Interested in identifying your habitual pattern for conflict resolution? If so, do Activity 8.4.

CONFLICT AVOIDANCE

Some people respond to conflict through **conflict avoidance**. Instead of engaging and communicating with the other person, they ignore, stay away from, or procrastinate about the problem. In this case, no matter what, the person allows things to continue as is (the status quo). If the problem is minor or may resolve itself with a little time, conflict avoidance can work well. In other cases, conflict avoidance may result in a festering problem, a loss of self-respect, or feelings of being oppressed. Problems that are persistent or are of serious concern need to be dealt with because they won't go away on their own. An example of a conflict avoider is the person who doesn't like certain things that her roommate does, but never expresses the concern. All of a sudden, one day the person says to the roommate, "I'm moving." The roommate has no idea why because she didn't know anything was wrong.

Avoiders may have been brought up in an environment where they were taught to keep their opinions to themselves. Perhaps they were told to be nice and problems would disappear. Or, avoiders may have been raised in an abusive environment, and learned that if they avoided any chance of inciting conflict there might be no abuse. Or, they may be members of pacifist religious groups such as the Quakers, Brethren,

ACTIVITY 8.4
Patterns of Dealing with Conflict

We each have a general pattern by which we deal with conflict. To learn your approach to dealing with conflict, circle T (true) or F (false) to indicate how you would respond in each of the situations. Although you may not agree with either choice, you must select either T or F. Read quickly, and react quickly.

Directions: Circle T (true) or F (false) to indicate which of the following statements best describes how you would respond in each of these situations. Although you may not agree with either choice, you must select either true (T) or false (F). Your first instinct will be your best response.

	1	2	3	4	5
1. When there is a difference of opinion, wants, or needs, I would rather explore our differences than try to convince the other person that I am right and he or she is wrong.	F				T
2. When there is a difference of opinion, wants, or needs, I would rather disagree openly and explore our differences than agree with the other point of view simply to have someone agree with my point of view.				F	T
3. When asked to perform an unpleasant task, I would rather postpone the task indefinitely than follow orders without discussion.		F	T		
4. When there is a difference of opinion, wants, or needs, I would rather try to win the other person over than withdraw from the conversation.	T		F		
5. Sometimes it's easier to agree and appear to go along with something without discussion than to avoid making any comment on a controversial subject.		T	F		
6. During a disagreement, I would rather admit that I may be half wrong than try to convince the other person that I am 100 percent right.	F		T		
7. When there is a difference of opinion, wants, or needs, I would rather give in totally than try to change the other person's mind or opinion.	F		T		
8. I would rather postpone a potential disagreement than explore our different points of view.			T		F
9. During a disagreement, I would rather meet the person halfway than give in totally.		F		T	
10. Sometimes it's easier to agree without discussion than to try to convince the other person I'm right.	F	T			
11. During a disagreement, I would rather admit that I am half wrong than not say anything and withdraw from the conversation.			F	T	
12. When asked to perform a task I don't want to do, I would rather postpone it indefinitely than make someone else do the task.	F		T		
13. During a disagreement, I would rather try to win the other person over than to split our differences.	T			F	
14. When there is a difference of opinion, wants, or needs, I would rather explore our differences and reach a mutually satisfactory solution than withdraw from the conversation or conflict.	F		T		
15. When asked to perform a task I don't want to do, I would rather postpone the task indefinitely than discuss my feelings and attempt to find a solution we can both agree on.			T		F
16. During a difference of opinion, wants, or needs, I would rather try to convince the other person that I am right than explore our differences.	T				F
17. During a disagreement, I would rather admit that I am half wrong than explore our differences.				T	F

(continued)

ACTIVITY 8.4 (*continued*)

		1	2	3	4	5
18.	Sometimes it is easier just to agree without discussion than to give up half of what I believe to reach an agreement.		T	F		
19.	When there is a difference of opinion, wants, or needs, I would rather explore our differences than give in without a discussion.			F		T
20.	During a difference of opinion, wants, or needs, I would rather try to win the discussion than sacrifice my point of view by not discussing it.	T	F			
21.	During a disagreement, I would rather try to find a solution that satisfies both of us than to let the other person find a solution without my input.			F		T
22.	During a disagreement, I would rather try to win the other person over than give in totally.	T	F			
23.	When asked to perform a task I don't want to do, I would rather agree to perform just half the task than to find a solution that is mutually satisfactory.				T	F

Scoring Instructions:

1. Count the number of items circled in each of the five columns. Record your totals in the boxes below. Multiply each score by 10.

	1	2	3	4	5
× 10 =					

2. Chart your score on the graph below. Place an X next to your score for each of the five strategies. Draw a straight line connecting the Xs from one column to the next. This will give you your conflict management strategy pattern.

	1 Competition/ Aggression	2 Accommodation/ Smoothing Over	3 Avoidance	4 Compromise	5 Integration
120					
110					
100					
90					
80					
70					
60					
50					
40					
30					
20					
10					
0					

Mennonites, Hutterites, or Jehovah's Witnesses, or philosophies such as the Bahá'i Faith, Jainism, or Buddhism.

A person who attempts to respond to conflict through conflict accommodation puts the other person's needs ahead of his or her own, thereby giving in. As an accommodator you meet the other person's needs, but don't express your own needs.[26] The accommodator often feels like the "good person" for having given the other person his or her own way. Accommodation is quite acceptable, provided the other person's needs are more important or if you believe that conflict is not an acceptable means of dealing with problems. Unfortunately, many accommodators fail to express their needs and are often taken advantage of.

Smoothing over is a style that preserves the image that everything is okay above all else. The individual is more concerned about appearances than solving problems. It can work. Sometimes keeping a positive approach will calm others so the problem dissipates. More likely, the problem continues to fester under the surface and one individual continues to feel frustrated.

Each conflict style can be useful in certain situations. Avoidance, accommodation, and smoothing over can work. All of these approaches count on the problem to go away with time, which could happen or may not happen. Ignoring the problem may mean it will grow and explode in the future.

Conflict avoiders sometimes come from backgrounds where they were exposed to a martyr who gave and gave and got little in return, but who put on a happy face. Avoiders may have low self-esteem, so they seek strokes from others by being nice and putting up with everything from everyone. They may come from backgrounds in which they were taught that the way to be liked is by being nice, even if they suffered as a result.

CONFLICT COMPROMISE

Conflict compromise is about "trading some of what *you* want for some of what *I* want. It's meeting each other part way."[27] People typically see compromise as a positive approach, and it can be, but this style can mean that neither person is going to be satisfied or feel like a winner because both people have to *give up* something they want in order to *get* something they want. Often, no one is totally happy with the solution. For example, in wage negotiations, assume the union wants a 5 percent increase in pay, and management wants to give no raise. Finally, a 2 percent raise is agreed on. They have compromised, but neither side may be happy as one gave more than it wanted, the other got less than it wanted. On the other hand, from the workers' standpoint, 2 percent is better than nothing, and from the managements' view, giving up 2 percent is better than giving up 5 percent.

People who work in negotiation may use conflict compromise in a positive way. Negotiators are skilled at figuring out what means the most to the individuals involved. When people give up something they don't care about, they can feel quite positive about gaining what they want most. The problem can come when individuals have to give up what is important to them, when they feel like they have given up more than they received, or when they feel that the compromise was not worth doing.

CONFLICT AGGRESSION

Conflict aggression is driven by the need for power. "Its purpose is to get another person to comply with or accept your point of view, or to do something they may not want to do."[28] In this case, one person wins and the other person loses. The Euro-American approach based on competition often endorses conflict aggression in business, athletics, and even interpersonal relationships. Unfortunately, some people are not satisfied unless they win and the other person loses. The road rage displayed by drivers is an act of aggression. The child who has to control others by being the school bully and verbally or physically attacking others, is showing aggressive actions. The sports coach who tells his team, "just win, I don't care how," is encouraging aggression.

There seems to be little value in this approach for resolving interpersonal conflicts because of the potential resentment of the loser, sabotage that may happen in retaliation, and hardened stances for future interactions. An aggressive conflict style can result in the hatred of a child for a parent caused by continuous losing. An aggressive supervisor can cause a hostile work environment. The negatives can be far more destructive than compromise or the occasional loss of a battle. Many sales, friendships, and relationships have been irreparably damaged or totally lost based on the win-at-all-costs philosophy. On the other hand, if you only care about winning, being the best, controlling others, then conflict aggression is probably your style of choice.

A form of aggression that may sneak under the observation net is **passive aggression**, communication tactics that attack in subtle, often unobtrusive ways.

Passive aggressive acts include:

- *Attacking the person indirectly* (For example, you've received a grade of *D* on a paper and you go into the professor's office and say, "Most professors seem to curve the grades so that most of their students pass their classes.")
- *Lying about your real feelings* ("I've thought about the *D* you gave me, and I really think I deserved it.")
- *Manipulating the situation* ("I know you don't believe in extra-credit assignments, but if I do another paper on the same topic, will you read it and give me your comments?")
- *Embarrassing the person* (A student says to his English teacher, "My lack of ability to write reflects your lack of ability to teach!")
- *Hinting about a problem* ("It seems like a lot of students in this class are failing.")
- *Keeping something from the other person* ("I forgot to pick up the papers that you wanted to give out in class today.")
- *Inviting the person to feel guilty* ("No, no, it's okay if you give me a *D* and I lose my scholarship.")
- *Using sarcasm* ("You want me to write better papers? Great advice coming from a teacher with six typos on a five-page exam!")

Passive aggression is risky for several reasons. First, because the person communicates concerns indirectly, the other person may miss the point. Second, even if the other person understands the message, she or he may decide to ignore it because the indirectness offers a ready excuse: "I didn't know what you wanted!" Third, indirect aggression is risky because people who feel manipulated often respond angrily. The relationship may be damaged, and future conflicts may be more difficult to resolve.

ASSERTION

Assertion is an approach to conflict that uses the best of communication skills. In this approach, the individual expresses needs while respecting the needs of others. All parties feel free to openly engage with each other in a collaborative way. The goal is for everyone to come away feeling a winner, thus assertion is considered a win-win strategy. The most important aspect of assertion is the realization that the relationship, the value of self-worth, as well as the issue, are all important. A time-consuming approach, integrative solutions involve considerable effort and energy.

If you are competitive by nature, communicatively apprehensive, or nonassertive, you may have trouble employing assertive techniques. Competitive people think that they must win. Individuals who are communicatively apprehensive think they cannot stand up for their rights. Assertive people, however, believe they have worth, value the nature of relationships, and don't want to be victimized, so they usually attempt to work toward assertiveness.

LEARNING EXPERIENCE: Interested in identifying your conflict behavior regarding assertion, aggression, nonassertion? If so, do Activity 8.5.

Assertive Communication

Have you ever found yourself saying something like, "I didn't want to come here, but *he* insisted," or "I ordered this steak well done and it's rare. Oh well, I guess I'll eat it anyway"? In these cases, you may have needed to use an assertive communication technique to get the issue resolved and your needs met (e.g., not going when you didn't want to go, and getting the steak the way you ordered it.)

ASSERTIVE BEHAVIOR—DEFINED

Assertive behavior occurs when an individual communicates his or her needs in a way that shows self-respect and respect for others.

The assertive person believes in the right to control one's own life and, therefore, acts in a way to accomplish the goal of attempting to get his/her needs met. Instead of thinking about what they *could or should* have said, assertive people say what they need to say to appropriately engage other people.

What are often called "communication misunderstandings" have a lack of assertion at their roots. For example, if a coworker takes advantage of you, but you are afraid to say anything because you think you'll get in trouble, lose the coworker's cooperation, or be seen as not being a team player, you might not say anything. Your lack of response may become part of a pattern where your coworker takes advantage of you again, you fail to say anything, your coworker takes advantage again, you become more

ACTIVITY 8.5
Conflict Behavior Scale

Directions: Indicate, on a scale of 1 to 7, the degree to which each of the statements describes your conflict behavior. Use the following scale: 1 = never, 2 = very seldom, 3 = seldom, 4 = sometimes, 5 = often, 6 = very often, and 7 = always.

_____ 1. I blend ideas with others to create new solutions to conflict.
_____ 2. I shy away from topics that are sources of disputes.
_____ 3. I steadfastly insist on my position being accepted during a conflict.
_____ 4. I try to find solutions that combine a variety of viewpoints.
_____ 5. I steer clear of disagreeable situations.
_____ 6. I do not give in to other people's ideas.
_____ 7. I look for middle-of-the road solutions that satisfy both my needs and the needs of the other person.
_____ 8. I avoid a person I suspect of wanting to discuss a disagreement.
_____ 9. I minimize the significance of a conflict.
_____10. I build an integrated solution from the issues raised in a dispute.
_____11. I stress a point I am making by hitting my fist on the table when I insist the other person is wrong.
_____12. I threaten people to reach a settlement that helps me satisfy my needs.
_____13. I shout when trying to get others to accept my position.
_____14. I look for mutually satisfying creative solutions to conflicts.
_____15. I keep quiet about my views in order to avoid disagreements.

Scoring:
Add your scores for questionnaire items 2, 5, 8, 9, 15 = _____, then divide by 5 = _____. This is your score for _nonassertiveness_. A high numerical score (29 or above) means you perceive yourself to have a tendency to use this style often. A low numerical score (11 or below) means you perceive that you use this style rarely.
Add your scores for items 1, 4, 7, 10, 14 = _____, then divide by 5 = _____. This is your _assertion_ score. A high numerical score (29 or above) means you perceive yourself to have a tendency to use this style often. A low numerical score (11 or below) means you perceive that you use this style rarely.
Add your scores for items 3, 6, 11, 12, 13 = _____, then divide by 5 = _____. This is your _aggression_ score. A high numerical score (29 or above) means you perceive yourself to have a tendency to use this style often. A low numerical score (11 or below) means you perceive that you use this style rarely.

Compare the scores on the three dimensions to see which style you perceive yourself using most.

Source: Based on Hocker, J. L., & Wilmot, W. W. (1986, February). _Teaching a college course on conflict and communication._ A paper presented at the annual meeting of the Western Communication Association, Tucson, AZ.

resentful, and so on. If you look at the long term, it may actually be more productive to assert yourself and change to a different pattern.

As illustrated in Figure 8.3, the purpose of assertive behavior, in contrast to non-assertive or aggressive communication, is to honestly and directly express your needs. Assertion is the act of taking control of yourself and your world while respecting the needs and worth of others.

Figure 8.3.   A Comparison of Nonassertive, Assertive, and Aggressive Behavior

	Nonassertive	Assertive	Aggressive
Characteristics of the behavior	Does not express wants, ideas, and feelings, or expresses them in self-deprecating way Intent: to please	Expresses wants, ideas, and feelings in direct and appropriate ways Intent: to communicate	Expresses wants, ideas, and feelings at the expense of others Intent: to dominate or humiliate
Your feelings when you act this way	Anxious: Disappointed with yourself. Often angry and resentful later	Confident: You feel good about yourself at the time and later	Self-righteous: Superior, sometimes embarrassed later
Other people's feelings about themselves when you act this way	Guilty or superior	Respected, valued	Humiliated, hurt
Other people's feelings about you when you act this way	Irritation, pity, disgust	Usually respect	Anger, vengefulness
Outcome	Don't get what you want; anger builds up	Often get what you want	Often get what you want at the expense of others. Others feel justified in "getting even"
Payoff	Avoids unpleasant situation, conflict, tension, and confrontation	Feels good; respected by others. Improved self-confidence. Relationships are improved	Vents anger; feels superior

Source: Created by Phyllis DeMark. Used with permission.

To learn to use assertive communication, consider these concepts:

No one can read your mind. The only way another person will know what you think or want is if you tell them.

Habit is never justification. Having always done something one way doesn't mean you can't do something differently. Tradition, patterns, and habits do not justify continuing behaviors that need to be changed.

People can only make themselves happy. You are not responsible for anyone's happiness, nor can you make others feel happy. Often people feel guilty because parents, friends, and culture influencers (e.g., religious leaders) teach you to think that you have to act a certain way to make others happy. Remember, each person is responsible for his or her own happiness.

What you think of yourself is what matters most. Your partner, parents, friends, supervisor, children, and others will not like everything you do, but that should have no effect on who or what you are. The very act of interacting with others means that someone sometime will probably disapprove. Instead of being upset by their disapproval, you can accept the principle that in spite of the criticism, only you can determine what is best for you. Consider their comments, but select the course of action that pleases you, not them. Don't let others guilt you into being their puppet.

Whenever you find yourself avoiding taking some action, ask yourself, "What's the worst thing that could happen to me?" Instead of being controlled by fear of consequences that may never happen, analyze the potential consequences. If the negative potential consequences of assertion outweigh the positive potential consequences, then take the action. Often, the negatives aren't that bad, so if the positives are more important, then you also know what to do. Ask yourself, "What really will or won't happen if I take this action?" Don't let the fear of the unknown paralyze you.

Insist on proper treatment. Don't allow another person to offend, persecute, or mistreat you. You should not be a victim, and you can often stop a victimizer. A *victimizer* is a person or establishment that interferes with another person's right to decide how to live his or her own life, and a *victim* is a person who is denied that right or permits victimization. For example, both men and women have been wronged because of failure to stand up to a victimizer who sexually harassed them. Cultural traditions, religious institutions and their leaders, school policies, and family customs may be victimizing sources.

Sometimes a person is actually a *self-victimizer.* Self-victimizers think of themselves as losers who are unworthy of having their needs met and allow the victimization to continue.

Assertive communicators use the resources around them and remove themselves from victimizing situations rather than submitting to the abuse. By reporting the victimizer or removing yourself, you take control (e.g., resign from the church, transfer schools, drop the class, divorce yourself from the family or the significant other). Assertive people believe they are worthy of proper treatment and simply will not accept anything else.

Action, not worrying, is needed. Worrying about a problem doesn't help, but action can. Even if the overall action seems overwhelming, you can take small steps in the right direction. Most people are reasonable human beings and will behave accordingly if they have the needed information and skills to do so.

Adopt the attitude that you will do the best you can, and if someone else does not like it, that is her or his problem, not yours. As an effective interpersonal communicator, and a person of self-worth, you can be an evolving person, you can strive to do your best, improve yourself, and be responsible for yourself. For the people around you who don't think your best is good enough, that is their problem. Often people with a poor self-concept are the ones who try to make themselves feel better by denigrating others. Don't fall into their trap. Their criticisms are about themselves, not you. You can listen, consider if there is merit, and say "I hear what you're saying." Then you continue to set your priorities according to your ethical value system, and continue to do your best, according to your definition, not theirs.

Be aware that assertiveness has consequences. Shallow people who only liked you because you were always nice may end the "friendship." Control freaks who can't control you will end the "friendship." If you threaten to quit your job if your coworker keeps taking advantage of you, then start looking for another job.

ASSERTIVENESS TECHNIQUES

Assertion might help you have your needs met so you can take control of yourself. Assertive communication is a skill anyone can learn.

Simple, Empathic, and Follow-Up Assertions

When you desire to be assertive, start with a **simple assertion** in which you *state the facts* relating to the existence of a problem. This in itself may be enough to solve the problem because people are often unaware that something is bothering you or that they have done something you consider wrong. A simple assertion alerts the other person to the problem. If they act, the solution is at hand.

Sometimes, however, you need to recognize the other person's position but state your needs. This is an **empathic assertion**. It may follow a simple assertion or be the first step in the assertive process. By recognizing the other person's problems or rights, you may find that she or he understands that you are not on the attack. The person may then become quite cooperative.

In neither the simple nor empathic assertion do you tell the person *how* to do what you think needs to be done. This forestalls a defensive response. Defensiveness is common when you command someone to do something, when you overstate your case, when you don't clearly state what's wrong, or when you implicitly communicate that you know what another person should do or think.

Sometimes what you were expecting fails to happen, so you need a **follow-up assertion**. In this case, you simply restate the simple or empathic assertion, give your position, and tell the person what you need. For example, you receive a bill from your college charging you for a class you did not sign up to take. You call the college's business office and say:

"Hello, this is . . . . My student number is _____. I received my tuition bill today and I'm being charged for Psychology 101, Section 9, a class which I'm not taking." (*simple assertion*)

-or-

"Hello, this is . . . . My student number is _____. I know you're probably not the person who's responsible, but I received my tuition bill today and I'm being charged for Psychology 101, Section 9, a class I'm not taking." (*empathic assertion*)

—you do not achieve your goal with either or both of the previous assertions—

"Hello, this is . . . . My student number is _____. I received my tuition bill yesterday. I called the day before yesterday to report that I'm being charged for Psychology 101, Section 9, a class I'm not taking. I have not received the call back that I was promised. I would like the overcharge removed. I'll come to your office at noon and pick up the adjusted bill." (*follow-up assertion*)

Remember, assertive communication doesn't mean you always get what you want. There is a better chance you will receive what you want than if you do nothing. Taking no action or using aggression will probably ensure that your goals will *not* be met, but assertion can increase the likelihood that a workable solution may be obtained.

LEARNING EXPERIENCE: Interested in knowing your ability to use assertive communication strategies? If so, do Activity 8.6.

Assertive Techniques for Complex Situations

A conflict situation becomes complex if it is a long-term dispute, or it involves people to whom you're emotionally close, or there is a strong possibility of physical or verbal violence, or if there are differences in power. Such cases require more detailed assertive responses. .

A complex assertive message can be expressed by using the **A*S*S*E*R*T formula**:

A: Describe the *action* that prompted the need for the assertive message. Your description should be behavioral; that is, it should focus on *who* is involved, the *circumstances* that are relevant, and the *specific behaviors* that are the source of your frustration and that trigger the assertive message. The expression of a descriptive message is clear and objective. For example, you say to your roommate, whom you consider your best friend, "Yesterday when I told you that I was really upset because Dale was mad at me, you just laughed and said, 'Get over it, you blow everything out of proportion. Stop being a drama queen.'"

S: Express your *subjective interpretation* of the action. Using *"I" language*, offer your interpretation of the behavior you describe. Separate this subjective interpretation from the objective description. For example, "When you joke around, I think you want to avoid talking about a serious issue under discussion or don't take my feelings or concerns seriously."

S: Express your *subjective interpretation* of the action. Say how you *feel* about the behavior as precisely as possible. Include the intensity of your feelings. Does the

ACTIVITY 8.6
Using Assertive Communication Strategies

You and Leslie are from the same hometown. Leslie has a car, and the agreement you made at the beginning of the semester was that if you did his laundry, Leslie would drive you home for Thanksgiving vacation. It's the Monday before vacation and Leslie tells you that his Wednesday class has been canceled and the new plan is to go home Tuesday. You have an exam on Wednesday. Your instructor has stated that there will be no makeup exam, no matter the excuse.

A. Write a simple or an empathic assertion that you might state to Leslie:

B. When you present your simple or empathic assertion, Leslie does not respond as you would like. Write a follow-up assertion:

Answers: (Presented are assertions that would fulfill the definitions)
A. Simple assertion: "We agreed at the beginning of the semester that if I did your laundry you would drive me home for Thanksgiving. As agreed, I did the laundry every week. Now that your class has been canceled, you want to leave on Tuesday and I have an exam on Wednesday which makes it impossible for me to leave on Tuesday."

Empathic assertion: "I realize that it might be inconvenient for you, but we agreed at the beginning of the semester that if I did your laundry you would drive me home for Thanksgiving. As agreed, I did your laundry every week. Now that your class has been canceled, you want to leave on Tuesday and I have an exam on Wednesday, which makes it impossible for me to leave on Tuesday."

B. Follow-up assertion: "I know it is inconvenient for you, but we did make an agreement and I think that you should either wait to leave until Wednesday when my exam is over, find me another ride, or pay me for the laundry I did for you so that I can buy a bus ticket home."

joking make you thoughtful, sad, or upset? Are you distracted, surprised, or amazed? Are you apprehensive, fearful, or filled with terror? Are you annoyed, angry, or enraged? For example, "I feel angry when you kid around and make it sound like my problems are trivial. I'm frustrated because I don't know what to do to get you to take me seriously."

E: Indicate the *effects* of the action. Effects can focus on *you* ("I want to avoid discussing serious matters with you because you joke around"), on the *other person* ("I listen when something is bothering you. How would you feel it if I laughed your problems off?"), or on *others* ("I think people think I'm a jerk when they see you laughing at what I think is important.").

R: Make your *request*. Indicate what specific behaviors you want. For example, "When I try to discuss a serious matter, I want you to stop mocking and kidding around." (Note that the request ends with a period, not an exclamation point—it is a statement, not a command.)

T: *Tell* your intentions: "If you mock me again when I try to tell you something that is of concern to me, I'm going to change room mates. I don't think friends should treat each other like that."

This may seem to be very theoretical and a paint-by-numbers concept, but if your present mode of operation is not working, then maybe you need an alternative system. We use formulas to solve problems in mathematics and science, why not in communication?

LEARNING EXPERIENCE: Interested in testing your ability to A*S*S*E*R*T? If so, do Activity 8.7.

Negotiation

Negotiation is a "discussion between two or more disputants who are trying to work out a solution to their problem."[29] When negotiating, for a win-win solution, everyone should express their needs and why those needs exist. In other words, both parties must make clear what the consequences will be. They must also make sure that the consequences are relevant to the other person or organization and can be carried out.

WIN-WIN/WIN-LOSE/LOSE-LOSE NEGOTIATION OUTCOMES

In a **win-win negotiation**, the goal is to find a solution that works for everyone. Success for one side can include success for the other side, so that everyone feels satisfaction about the results (see Figure 8.4).

Win-lose negotiation centers on one person, whose needs are met when the other person receives nothing or worse than nothing.

In a **lose-lose negotiation**, no one receives what they want or need. If conflict goes on too long, everyone could be a loser.

ACTIVITY 8.7
A*S*S*E*R*T Yourself

Early in the semester a friend asked you if she could copy your accounting homework. Throughout the semester she has continued to ask, each time apologizing
and saying she won't ask again. She has all sorts of excuses why she can't do the
homework, including "no time," "don't understand," "forgot to write down the
assignment." Last night you told her you won't give her your homework again.
Today she again asks for it, pleading this is the last time, and, "anyway, that's
what friends are for." You've had it! Use the A*S*S*E*R*T formula to present
your view of the situation to your friend.

A:

S:

S:

E:

R:

T:

Figure 8.4. Options for Negotiation Resolution

Negotiation Options	You Win	You Lose
Other Wins	All parties try to find a solution that is satisfying to everyone	Other gets what s/he wants You come up short
Other Loses	You gets what you want Other comes up short	Neither person is satisfied with the outcome

In lose-lose negotiation, no one receives what they want or need.

LEARNING EXPERIENCE: Interested in testing your ability to identify win-win, win-lose, lose-lose negotiating styles? If so, do Activity 8.8.

The steps used to help create a win-win situation are described here:

Step 1. Define the conflict for yourself before approaching the other person. This requires some self-analysis: What is your concern? Who or what is frustrating you? What is the source of conflict?

Once you understand the conflict from your perspective, approach the other person and agree on a time to talk. Don't spring the conflict on the other person without warning or bring it up when there isn't enough time to deal with it. If the other person feels attacked, he or she may become defensive, which will make it difficult for you to establish a supportive climate. Agree on an appropriate place for your discussion. Certain locations, such as where others can observe or interrupt the negotiations, may inhibit open and honest interaction. Attempting to deal with conflict in a public place, such as a restaurant, virtually assures failure.

Step 2. Communicate your understanding of the problem assertively to the other person. This includes describing the other person's behaviors, as they affect you, in a direct, clear, nonjudgmental way.

ACTIVITY 8.8
Identify the Negotiating Outcomes

Identify the negotiating outcome that is anticipated in each of the following situations based on each situation of my wanting to go to a concert, when you need to stay home and study.

Choices: win-win, lose-lose, lose-win

A. We discuss it and both agree that we will study until a half-hour before the concert starts, go to the concert, and then come right back to finish studying. Style_____
B. I tell you that for the past three weeks I've done what you wanted to do. You give in, we go to the concert, but are upset the rest of the evening. Style_____
C. I refuse to study and you refuse to go to the concert. We get so angry that I don't go to the concert, you don't study, and we both spend the evening pouting, slamming doors, and being obnoxious to each other. Style_____
D. I go to the concert and you study. Style_____

Answers:
A—Win-Win; B—Win-Lose; C—Lose-Lose; D—Win-Win

Once your own concerns are clear, invite the other person to express her or his concerns. Listen carefully to the content of the message and try to perceive the feelings that accompany it.

Share your perceptions of the other person's point of view without labels ("That's stupid!") or insults ("You're crazy!"). Then reverse the process and encourage your partner to reiterate your point of view to your satisfaction.

When you complete this step, both you and your partner will have defined the problem specifically, described your feelings, and recounted the actions that led to the conflict and perpetuated it.

Step 3. Based on your understanding of your own and the other's perspective, try to arrive at a mutual, shared definition of the problem and a mutual, shared goal. Consider your areas of agreement and disagreement; figure out how you're dependent on one another. Discuss the consequences of the conflict for each of you.

Step 4. Communicate your cooperative intentions. Let your partner know that your aim is to satisfy the needs of both of you and to achieve your shared goals, and that you do not want to win by being competitive or combative. If you can (and it may be difficult under stressful conditions), communicate your intention in a calm, firm voice and invite your partner to join you in being cooperative.

Successful conflict resolution is impossible unless both you and your partner are motivated to behave cooperatively. If your partner is reluctant to cooperate, you may want to discuss what each of you gets out of continuing the conflict. Perhaps the conflict gives you something to complain about or an excuse to end the relationship. Or perhaps you feel threatened because a solution to your shared problem will require changes in your behavior. Whatever the reasons, they must be recognized and overcome before you can proceed.

Step 5. Generate solutions to your shared problem. Avoid discussing or evaluating each solution as it is generated. Instead, generate as many ideas as you can. If you and your partner agree to defer evaluation, the number of possible solutions should be high. Be spontaneous and creative and build on each other's suggestions. Remember that even a foolish-sounding solution may contain a shred of useful information.

Step 6. After you've suggested all the solutions you can think of, evaluate them and select the best one. How might each solution satisfy the shared goal? How easy or difficult would each be to implement?

Step 7. Implement the solution. First, be sure that you and your partner truly agree on which solution to implement. Make sure that you both agree fully and that you're not agreeing because you're tired, because you want to please your partner, or for some other reason that will later undermine the solution. Second, agree on who does what, when, and how. If you don't specify the particulars, the groundwork may well be laid for the next conflict. Third, do what needs to be done.

Step 8. Plan to check on how the solution is working. You may have to adjust your plan or scrap the solution and generate a new one. The need for modification is a predictable consequence of changes brought on by time and an inability to foresee all possible outcomes during the initial problem-solving stage.

Another approach to a win-win solution is to prescribe particular behaviors to enact when particular circumstances arise. The prescription takes one of two forms:

If _____ happens, then _____ *must/should* be done.

or

If _____ happens, then _____ *must not/should not* be done.

Examples of ways to change the conflict situation are described here:

Situation 1: Danny is the one-year-old child of Mary and Tom. He has gotten into the habit of screaming and crying when he doesn't get his way. Tom and Mary have been arguing over this matter for weeks. A child psychologist who was consulted has indicated that it is her opinion that as long as Mary continues to pick up the child as soon as he cries, the child will become more and more manipulative.

Prescribed behavior: *When* Danny throws a tantrum, then Mary *must not* pick him up.

Situation 2: Dennis has a pattern of withdrawing and pouting when he perceives someone is "picking on him." This is a source of major conflict between Dennis and his friend Chris.

Prescribed behavior: *When* Dennis withdraws because his feelings are hurt, Chris *must* let Dennis know how this is making Chris feel and let Dennis know that Chris will leave the apartment for a cooling-off period.

The prescribed behavior approach is an excellent method to use when the problem can be isolated and the participants are willing to work toward changing past patterns.

LEARNING EXPERIENCE: Interested in practicing the prescribed behavior approach? If so, do Activity 8.9.

Sound too theoretical and impractical? What are your relationships worth? What is family peace worth?

NEGOTIATION CONSIDERATIONS

A number of considerations must be kept in mind during negotiating:

Look closely at the other person's point of view to understand where you differ. Conflict is often cleared up as soon as one party realizes that they did not understand the other person's viewpoint, or their own point of view.

Identify your needs. What do you really want? What does the other person want? Are your needs similar, or different?

Decide on a negotiating style. You need rhetorical sensitivity, which means you adapt to the particular situation in the most appropriate way. Because of this, one of

---

ACTIVITY 8.9
Putting the Prescribed
Behaviors Approach into Action

Situation: Jill, Diane, and Marci have been friends since junior high school. Recently, Marci feels overwhelmed because Jill and Diane make plans to do things without asking her and then expect her to go along with them. If Marci refuses they get angry and accuse her of trying to break up the friendship by being selfish. The three of them agree that they don't want to break up the long-standing friendship, but need some guidelines by which to operate.

Write two prescribed behavior resolutions, one positive, the other restrictive.

When _____

must _____.

When _____

must not _____.

your basic considerations should be whether you want a win-lose, lose-lose, or win-win resolution.

Select a positive communication setting. The environment or context of the communication needs to be conducive to negotiation. If the communication climate is supportive, you may be able to collaborate in ways that achieve a win-win result. If the communication climate is hostile, you may find yourself with a win-lose or lose-lose result. You will want to make sure there is adequate time, appropriate resources, and whatever else is needed to succeed. The communication environment or climate affects the way people communicate.

Keep the discussion focused. Focus on information sharing, generating ideas, and being open minded. There's no place for personal attacks in negotiation.

Everyone can win in a negotiation. There is no need for someone to lose, when everyone can leave the conflict feeling satisfied with the solution. You can focus on the goal of everyone having what they need most.

Key Terms

conflict	conflict aggression
conflict-active societies	passive aggression
conflict-avoidance societies	assertion
interpersonal conflict	assertive behavior
anger	simple assertion
implosive anger	empathic assertion
explosive anger	follow-up assertion
apology	A*S*S*E*R*T formula
fair fighting	negotiation
conflict avoidance	win-win negotiation
smoothing over	win-lose negotiation
conflict compromise	lose-lose negotiation

Competencies Check-Up

Interested in finding out what you learned in this chapter and how you use the information? If so, take this competencies check-up.

Directions: Indicate the extent that each statement applies to you:

1—Never   2—Seldom   3—Sometimes   4—Often   5—Usually

____1. I express conflicts so that I avoid internalizing negative feelings and ideas.

____2. If conflict stops me from doing my work; threatens the integrity of a relationship; endangers the continuation of a relationship or my ability to function within a relationship; causes physical, mental, or sexual abuse; or leads me to

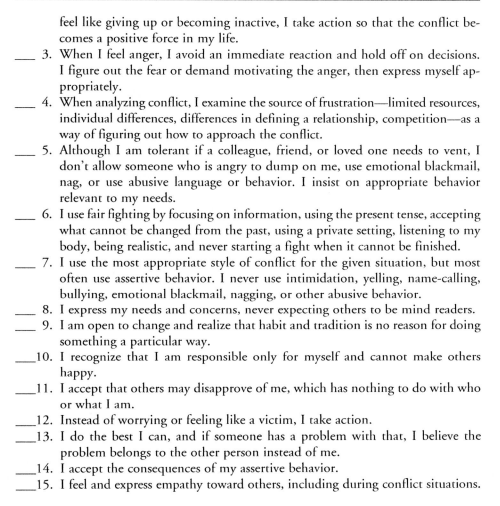

feel like giving up or becoming inactive, I take action so that the conflict becomes a positive force in my life.

___ 3. When I feel anger, I avoid an immediate reaction and hold off on decisions. I figure out the fear or demand motivating the anger, then express myself appropriately.

___ 4. When analyzing conflict, I examine the source of frustration—limited resources, individual differences, differences in defining a relationship, competition—as a way of figuring out how to approach the conflict.

___ 5. Although I am tolerant if a colleague, friend, or loved one needs to vent, I don't allow someone who is angry to dump on me, use emotional blackmail, nag, or use abusive language or behavior. I insist on appropriate behavior relevant to my needs.

___ 6. I use fair fighting by focusing on information, using the present tense, accepting what cannot be changed from the past, using a private setting, listening to my body, being realistic, and never starting a fight when it cannot be finished.

___ 7. I use the most appropriate style of conflict for the given situation, but most often use assertive behavior. I never use intimidation, yelling, name-calling, bullying, emotional blackmail, nagging, or other abusive behavior.

___ 8. I express my needs and concerns, never expecting others to be mind readers.

___ 9. I am open to change and realize that habit and tradition is no reason for doing something a particular way.

___10. I recognize that I am responsible only for myself and cannot make others happy.

___11. I accept that others may disapprove of me, which has nothing to do with who or what I am.

___12. Instead of worrying or feeling like a victim, I take action.

___13. I do the best I can, and if someone has a problem with that, I believe the problem belongs to the other person instead of me.

___14. I accept the consequences of my assertive behavior.

___15. I feel and express empathy toward others, including during conflict situations.

Scoring: A total of 45 suggests that you have minimum competencies in conflict resolution. Given the crucial and complex nature of interpersonal conflict, however, even a high skill level may not be enough for success in this area. How close are you to a score of 75? For a skilled approach, you will want to use these conflict resolution strategies most of the time. Examine any item on which you scored less than 3 and figure out how you will improve your skills.

I-Can Plan!

While the chapter information is fresh on your mind, create a list of strategies that you will use to help you on your journey toward a high level of interpersonal communication competence in conflict situations.

Activities

1. Schools are developing conflict resolution programs.
   A. If you attended a middle school or high school that had such a program be prepared to discuss it in class.
   B. If you did not attend a school that had a conflict resolution program, go online and find out about such programs. One source is: www.charityadvantage.com/communityboards/SchoolsProgramming.asp. Prepare to explain the program to your classmates.
2. Prepare to debate one of these topics: (Be sure you have research to back up your view.)
   A. Being the winner is the most important aspect of any conflict.
   B. To be less than a winner is to be a loser!
   C. Television programs and video games teach children to be aggressive.
   D. Solving issues by win-win is a nice theory, but an impossible reality.
   E. Organized sports for children and teens, such as Little League, teaches children to do whatever it takes to be a winner.
   F. Males and females generally view winning in different ways.
3. Identify a conflict situation in which you've been involved in the last several weeks. Write out the details of the conflict (e.g., the participants, the exact cause of the conflict, where it took place). During a specified class session, each student's conflict description will be collected. The class members will be divided into dyads and given two randomly distributed situations. Each student will read his or her selected situation aloud. The partner will then word a simple or empathic assertion. The reader will comment on the quality of the assertion. Then, the partner will read his or her assertion and the other person will make a simple or empathic assertion. No matter the quality of assertion, the assumption is to be made that it was not successful in getting the desired results. The speaker will then word a follow-up assertion. A short, classwide discussion about simple, empathic, and follow-up assertions will then be held.

CHAPTER 9

Interpersonal Relationships in the Family

Learning Outcomes

After reading this chapter, you should be able to:

- Explain what a family is and how a family is positively and negatively affected by their communication.
- Identify and define various family configurations.
- Explain the relationship between family and culture.
- Identify family images, themes, boundaries, and biosocial beliefs.
- Explain the family as a system.
- Differentiate between less healthy and more healthy families.
- Describe family conflict and parental authority.
- Identify and explain aggression in family settings.
- Identify and put into operation some techniques to improve family communication.

"When I was growing up my grandmother lived with us. She was a simple woman, limited in her formal education, but wise in common sense. Her philosophical concepts formed much of my present-day thinking and saved me much frustration and internal conflicts. If I came home from school after taking a test and proclaimed, 'If I didn't get an A on that test, I'm never going back to school again,' she would look at me and make her 'pronouncement,' as my cousins and I came to name it. The same would happen when I would state, 'I tried out for a play today and if I don't get the part I'm never going to try out again!' Again, the 'pronouncement' would be made. When my oldest cousin was applying to optometry schools and was bemoaning that he wouldn't get in, she again gave the 'pronouncement.'

What was the pronouncement? In her heavily accented English it sounded like, "Iv posed ta be, vood. Ifen nut, voodn't." The translation: "If it is supposed to happen, it will, and if not, it won't." Fatalistic? Maybe. Practical? Absolutely!"[1]

Definition of a Family

"We are born into a family. We are socialized by a family. We mature from a family. We often create a family, and, if so, use the information and behaviors we learned from a family. And, when we die, we diminish a family. Families affect us greatly . . . they surround us, shape us, and often determine our destiny."[2]

In order to understand **family communication**, how members of a family unit communicate within the family, we must understand what a family is. A **family** traditionally has been defined as a group of interconnected people typically with blood or legal ties.[3] Other definitions include: A family is "any group of two or more people who make their lives together and consider themselves a family";[4] and "a variety of household arrangements, from husbands and wives who work outside the home to heterosexual couples without children at home, to gay couples to widowers living in a nursing home community."[5]

Besides the definitional approach, a family may be classified by its configuration (see Figure 9.1). The configuration of your family can have an effect on your communication. Being part of a blended family means dealing with step-parents and often step-siblings. Being a member of a gay or lesbian family introduces the awareness of

Figure 9.1. Family Configurations

Nuclear family
   Wife, husband, and their biological child(ren) or adopted child(ren).

Gay or lesbian family
   Two same-gendered people (male-male or female-female in an intimate relationship, with or without their own biological or adopted child(ren).
   The same-gendered persons may have made a formal commitment or be married, in a civil union, part of a registry, or in a paperless marriage.

Extended family (biological)
   Relatives, such as grandparents, aunts, uncles, and cousins, as well as parent(s) and child(ren) who may or may not be living in the same residence.

Extended family (communal)
   A designated family of acquaintances who have declared themselves to be a family, such as members of a cult or religious community.

Stepfamily
   Two adults and child(ren) who are not the biological offspring of both adults who have combined into a family unit. Usually, the adults are married, but could be in a paperless marriage.

Single-parent family
   One adult with child(ren).

Couple
   Two adults living together in a relationship, commonly a paperless marriage, with no child(ren).

Source: Based on Turner, L., & West, R. (2006). *Perspectives on family communication* (3rd ed.). Boston, MA: McGraw Hill, p. 40.

societal attitudes toward that family configuration. A child of a single parent may find communication difficult with members of the gender absent in the family of origin (e.g., males of a single mother family may encounter a problem in male-male interaction). Being in a *paperless marriage*, living together without being legally married, eliminates lawful protections and obligations.

You can be a product of more than one configuration. For example, you can be a member of a nuclear family composed of a wife, a husband, and their biological children, while also being a member of your original family of origin. Traditionally, a *family of origin* takes us from the womb and begins to teach us self-reliance, how to please and displease others, responsibility, obedience, dominance, social skills, aggression, loyalty, gender roles, age roles, values, ethics, morals, family traditions, theological beliefs, and aesthetic values.

Single-parent families consist of one adult and at least one child. A woman generally heads the single-parent family, though men do guide a very small number of single-parent households.[6]

Cohabiting families (paperless marriage) are two adults living together who have not participated in a formal legal or religious ceremony. Children may or may not be present in the cohabiting household.[7]

"*Gay and lesbian families* include two people of the same sex who maintain an intimate relationship, with or without the benefit of marriage or civil union, and who may or may not serve as parents of at least one child. This family type may also include a lesbian mom or gay dad who is not in a relationship but has full custody of a child."[8] The 2000 census listed "601,209 same-sex unmarried partner households in the United States, but the total number still represents an undercount of the actual number of gay or lesbian coupled households in the country.[9] Possible explanations for this include continued prejudice and discrimination against homosexuals which may keep gay couples from reporting their living arrangements.

A *blended family* or step-family is a reconstituted family. Exemplified by "The Brady Bunch" television show household, it includes a couple, at least one of whom enters the relationship with children, who combine their families to form a new living unit.

Why is it necessary to have a definition for "family," "marriage," and those who are members of the family? A communication concept indicates that if we don't have a name for something, it is hard to fathom exactly what is being discussed. For example, should there be a name assigned to gay unions to distinguish their family unit from "traditional" marriages? Does using the term "civil union" make the relationship of gays and lesbians less than that of "straight" couples? Because the relationship has no precise name, there is a problem of common understanding in our culture of what these relationships mean.[10]

Even if we understand the nature of the union, what do we call same-sex couples who are committed to each other without a legal union? "Our language contains no term except maybe 'partner,' which is imprecise because it can refer to a business relationship or a gay union that is not marriage."[11] As a representative of the American Dialect Society stated, "Because the situation is unsettled, the terminology is unsettled—and when it gets settled, the terminology will, too."[12]

The Family and Culture

While most of the discussion in this chapter focuses on the family unit in the United States, remember that families from other cultures offer their children different messages, and hence produce people with specific cultural and societal perceptions and with specialized communication styles.

Please be aware that throughout this chapter generalizations are presented regarding families in general and families in various cultures. These are based, whenever possible, on research findings and expert observations. They are in no way intended to lead to the conclusion that all families and the members of any family configuration conform to the generalized patterns.

Children born into a family in India often notice women eating after the men have finished, and for these children this pattern is appropriate behavior. In the People's Republic of China it is common for meals to be served from a common bowl, whereas in the United States people usually have their separate plates brought to the table. This focus on communal responsibility, family discussions, and group interactions is the norm in China, while a focus on the individual and self is the norm in much of the United States (e.g., own plate, own room). Each culture teaches its version of sharing and the concept of collectivism versus individuality. In Mexico, grandparents typically live with the family. In the United States grandparents generally live in their own home or in a retirement community. In Arabic countries the mother of the groom often lives with her oldest son's family. A child observing these patterns learns about the gender, age, and self or other operational patterns expected and accepted in each culture.

The examples are endless. But they all should convey the same message: as cultures differ, so do families—and as families differ, so do individual patterns of communication.

The Family and Communication

Communication is at the very heart of a family. Families create and maintain themselves through their own interactions and their interactions with others outside of the family unit. Families use communication to deal with issues of closeness and distance, to maintain traditions, make decisions, and deal with problems. Communication shapes family life, reflects family relations, and is instrumental in family functioning.

Family conversations serve several purposes for the family. They "(1) inform others about the kinds of relationships you have with members of your family, (2) explain to others how your family fits within the larger culture, (3) define family relationships with individual family members."[13]

Families don't just communicate, they have **communication rules** (common interaction procedures) by which they operate. These rules can include such topics as "(1) what family members can talk about, (2) how family members can talk about these topics, and (3) to whom family members can talk about these topics.[14] For example:

Families create and maintain themselves through their interactions.

"We don't speak about sex in this family." "We don't swear in this house!" "Don't talk to your sister like that." "I am the adult and you are the child, speak when you are spoken to." "This is between your father and me." In some houses where languages besides English are spoken, conversations between adults are conducted in that language so that others, who do not speak the language, can be cut off from restricted information.

"Families not only make rules about communicating around certain topics and with certain people, they also create rules about whether or not to overtly acknowledge that they have these rules."[15] In some households, there are "hidden" rules. Certain topics are "off limits," such as not discussing grandpa's being an alcoholic or your uncle having been in jail. You may have learned not to ask a parent for something when he/she was in a bad mood or that "your room" wasn't really yours because your parents could enter at will and invade "your" territory.

One of the most common topics that families struggle with is sex and sexuality. "A large percentage of both children and parents report dissatisfaction with the quantity and quality of family sex communication."[16] Some families avoid talking about sex entirely, some set up a series of agreements about who talks to whom (e.g., dad talks to boys, mom to girls), some are completely open and encourage family members to ask questions and confront sexual topics directly.

The Family Matrix

Each family, knowingly or unknowingly, has a matrix, a set of images, themes, boundaries, biosocial attitudes, and stories that describe the unit and affect their interpersonal communication. In some families these traits stay the same for generations, whereas in other families they are in constant flux, paralleling the changes in society. Knowing your family's traits—its images, themes, boundaries, and biosocial attitudes—aids in understanding its communication.

FAMILY IMAGES

Family images are the mental pictures and illusions the family holds of itself and its members. They are the definitions of people that predict how they behave, including how they communicate. Think of members of your family. What is your image of each of them—helper, helpless, dynamic, stable?

LEARNING EXPERIENCE: Interested in finding out your family's images? If so, do Activity 9.1.

FAMILY THEMES

Family themes are the patterns of feelings, motives, roles, fantasies, understandings, and rules that family members hold about the family and their relationships with the outside world. Themes are revealed in special nicknames, roles (who does what), and made-up words families use and which only the family or groups within the family understand. Themes affect communication because they contain the rules that guide who talks to whom and who does what and when. For example, if a family rule is, "Children should only speak to their parents when they are spoken to," the theme revealed is that "children should respect their elders and know their place, and the parents are in control."

  Through its themes, a family describes its reality and how it deals with that reality. Some family themes are, "Family business is kept inside the house—we don't show our dirty linen in public," "It is our responsibility to help others less fortunate than ourselves," and "If you're going to do something, do it right."

LEARNING EXPERIENCE: Interested in finding out your family's themes? If so, do Activity 9.2.

FAMILY BOUNDARIES

Families create boundaries to regulate their communication. **Family boundaries** are the limits a family sets on its members' actions. These boundaries typically include

ACTIVITY 9.1
Identifying Your Family's Images

Who, if anyone, plays these roles in your current family or family of origin. (Not all of the roles may be represented in every family.)

1. The martyr—does most of the cooking, serving, and cleaning up.

2. The pet—the spoiled one who always gets the last spoonful of stuffing and the biggest slice of cake.

3. The victim—two hours late, but it's not her or his fault. It never is!

4. The rebel—if everyone's dressed up, he or she wears old jeans, and then sits back and waits for the fireworks.

5. The peacemaker—he or she will make sure that everyone stays civil and then be the one to suffer with heartburn.

6. The smart one—she or he hasn't seen the movie, but knows it's rotten. You don't even argue. Why invite the fight you know you'll lose?

Was it easy to identify the images you hold of your family members? What images are shared by all the members? How do you feel thinking of yourself in one or more of these roles? Do you think each member of your family would complete this check-up similarly?

regulations for dealing with specific ideas, people, and values. Boundaries may encourage or restrict contact with people outside the family's religious or ethnic group. A family may allow or forbid intermingling with certain races or social classes. A family may encourage or discourage certain liberal or conservative attitudes.

Family rules form a large part of family life, whether they are spoken or implied. These rules determine what *cannot* be talked about (e.g., death, alcohol, the way money is spent, sex, or weight), what *can* be talked about (e.g., academic, athletic, and work achievements), how certain topics can be expressed ("mommy is sick," versus "mommy is drunk"), where certain topics can be talked about (at the kitchen table, only in the house, only in the bedroom), and who can talk about certain things with whom (parents only, one parent to a particular child).

Boundaries also create the framework within which family members speak to each other. In a **position-oriented family**, there are sharp boundaries for family roles based on status and social identities related to sex and age. The child in a position-oriented family, for instance, is expected to communicate in defined ways. Such guidelines as "honor thy mother and father," and "act your age" must be respected. Even as an

---

ACTIVITY 9.2
Identifying Your Family's Themes

What are some common themes in your current family or family of origin?

1. Describe one family custom that is important for all members to follow.

   _____

2. Describe one family story that is repeated over and over at parties, during holidays, and at family get-togethers. _____

3. Describe one wish that all or most family members repeat over and over.

   _____

4. Describe one family belief that restricts or encourages family thinking.

   _____

Was it easy to choose themes to describe?

Do you think each member of your family would complete this checkup similarly?

How do these themes describe your family?

What do they tell you about how your family members interact?

---

adult, if the off-spring is still seen as the "child," then she or he often feels obligated to fulfill the same role as she or he did as a child.

A **person-oriented family** has flexible boundaries and allows a wide range of communication behaviors related to an individual's needs rather than her or his position in the family. A person-oriented family fosters open communication in which roles are continuously accommodated and the different intents of family members are recognized and dealt with. For example, when a "child" in a person-oriented family grows to adulthood, she or he is treated as an adult and not a child.

LEARNING EXPERIENCE: Interested in finding out whether your family is position-oriented or person-oriented? If so, do Activity 9.3.

BIOSOCIAL ATTITUDES

Biosocial attitudes determine the way the family deals with male and female identity, authority and power, and the rights of family members. Each of us was brought

---

ACTIVITY 9.3
Characteristics of Position-Oriented
and Person-Oriented Families

Directions: If the statement is true of your family, place 5 on the line before the statement. If the statement does not represent your family, place a 0 on the line before the statement. If the answer is neither clearly yes nor no, put a 3 on the line.

___1. People in my family were generally assigned specific tasks and chores to do according to their age.

___2. Each person in my family was discouraged from doing "his/her" own thing.

___3. Each person in the family is/was discouraged or restricted from saying whatever he/she wanted to whomever he/she wanted.

___4. Family members were/are assigned clear-cut roles or tasks based on their gender.

___   Total

If the total score was:
between 15 and 20 = you probably come from a *position-oriented* family.
between 6 and 14 = you come from *neither* a position-oriented nor a person-oriented family.
between 0–5 = you probably come from a *person-oriented* family

What is one way this orientation has affected your interpersonal communication?

---

up with notions of what males and females are allowed to do, supposed to do, and capable of doing. These may have included household roles (boys do the cooking and cleaning, and girls do the car repairs), occupational roles (girls are mechanics, boys are elementary school teachers), areas of responsibility (women are the principal wage earners, and men take care of the home), and emotional roles (girls don't cry, and boys don't get angry). *If you were taken aback by some of the example role identifications because you thought they were role-reversals, you have identified some of the biosocial roles you learned in your family.* If you had no awareness of the role-reversal, that also reveals your biosocial expectations.

The task of identifying the self as a male or a female is apparently not very difficult. By age three, for example, most children will identify not only which gender they belong to, but also which jobs are done by men and women, what roles mommies and daddies play, and what kind of behavior is allowed for each sex.[17]

LEARNING EXPERIENCE: Interested in finding your biosocial role attitudes? If so, do Activity 9.4.

ACTIVITY 9.4
Identifying Your Gender Role Attitudes

Directions: Indicate whether primary responsibility for each task should belong to a male (M) or a female (F).

_____a. taking out the garbage
_____b. writing thank-you notes for a family gift
_____c. initiating sexual activity
_____d. changing diapers
_____e. bringing home the major paycheck for household use
_____f. disciplining the children
_____g. cooking
_____h. cleaning the bathroom
_____i. fixing or making arrangements for fixing the car
_____j. taking the children to piano lessons
_____k. taking the son to baseball practice
_____l. fixing the leaky faucet
_____m. changing the bed sheets and pillow cases
_____n. making family investments
_____o. selecting new furniture for the living room

Research indicates Euro-Americans have traditionally perceived items a, c, e, i, l, and n to be "male activities," and b, d, f, g, h, j, k, m, and o as "female" activities. Give yourself one point for each of your answers that conforms to what was found in the research.

My score is _____

A score of 10 or more indicates your biosocial attitudes are parallel to traditional societal thinking from the mid-1980s. There has been much change in Euro-American attitudes due to the women's movement.

How much did your results differ from these?

Are your attitudes similar to those followed by your family?

Source: Based on questions from an activity developed by Gordon, T. (1975). *Parent effectiveness training.* New York: New American Library.

In addition to gender roles, the way authority and power are dealt with also reflects a family's biosocial attitudes. Authority and power can be examined by acknowledging who creates and enforces the rules ("Your father makes those decisions"), and the rights of family members regarding such issues as privacy ("If a door is closed, don't enter without knocking), setting of curfews ("You must be in by midnight."), and appealing a parent's decision ("Your mother and I agree, so don't even think about it!").

LEARNING EXPERIENCE: Interested in finding your family's images? Do Activity 9.5.

FAMILY STORIES

A family's images, themes, boundaries, and biosocial attitudes are passed down through family stories. **Family stories** are narratives, told in the family context, that

---

ACTIVITY 9.5
Family Images, Themes, Boundaries, and Biosocial Attitudes

Using your family or a family with which you are familiar (a family on television or a friend's family) answer these questions:

1. What are some of this family's important images? How do these images affect how the family members communicate?

2. What themes did you have to learn in order to understand the family's interaction?

3. What are some boundaries that guide how members of the family communicate with one another?

4. List several biosocial attitudes found in this family that regulate how the parents and children talk to each other.

5. Based on your analysis, how do the images, themes, boundaries, and biosocial attitudes combine to create the communication pattern unique to the family?

feature a family member or several members, involve a plot line, furnish a sense of family identity, and provide lessons, morals, and a sense of connection to family members who tell and listen to them. "Family stories shape the private world of the family by developing the family's world view."[18] Types of family stories include: courtship stories (love, marriage, and the interplay between cultural expectations and family mores and customs); birth stories (a sense of how each child fits into the family, the roles they are expected to play, and some of their parents' hopes and dreams for them); stories of survival (how to cope in a world that is not always welcoming and charitable).[19]

LEARNING EXPERIENCE: Interested in identifying some of your family's stories? If so, do Activity 9.6.

ACTIVITY 9.6
Family Stories

A. Make a list of at least five specific stories that you have related or heard told about you or members of your family. This can either be a topical list or a series of short story summaries.

B. Using your answers for answer A, identify which of the following is represented by each of your stories: courtship stories, birth stories, the roles family members are expected to play, some of their hopes and dreams for the family or family members, a story of survival.

C. What did you learn about yourself or your family from doing this activity?

D. *Additional learning experience*: Talk to members of your family, especially older members, and ask them to relate family stories. This assignment makes for great "table talk" at family gatherings, such as holiday dinners.

Characteristics of the Family System

Regardless of the countless ways that the infinite number of themes, images, boundaries, biosocial attitudes, and family stories come together to form unique families, several characteristics of **family systems**, the format for how families operate, seem universal.[20]

Any change in one part of the system causes the entire system to change. Family members are interdependent. The unit creates a synergy—that is, the whole is greater than the parts. Much like the pieces of a mobile, if one part moves, all the other parts move. If a family member leaves home to go to college, the system is no longer the same. If a parent loses a job, becomes permanently disabled, or becomes angry with another member, the system is no longer in balance. When that happens, adjustments are needed to bring the system back into balance. When siblings continually argue, that affects the entire system, as does divorce, a step-parent entering the family structure, or the relocation of the family. Healthy families are capable of recreating a balance. If the system needs to be recalibrated, they can do so. The psychologically and communicatively competent family can make these adjustments. In dysfunctional systems, these changes are often very hard to make.

LEARNING EXPERIENCE: Interested in ascertaining your family's ability to deal with changes in their system? If so, do Activity 9.7.

Family systems are complex, adaptive, and information-processing. A family system is complex because it is constantly in flux. Because a family is made up of people, and because people change as they gain new experiences, age, and mature, the system continuously modifies itself. A healthy family system is adaptive because a flexible system develops in response to interaction among its members. The ongoing interaction is bound to lead to strains and tensions, but a well-developed family system accommodates itself to such difficulties. And systems are information-processing because the basis of a family is the exchange of ideas, attitudes, and beliefs. In dysfunctional families a lack of clear rules, inconsistent rule-following, or rigidity in enforcing poorly set rules creates chaos and often resentment.

People act out what is wrong in their family system. Arguments, physical conflicts, pouting, and isolation of a family member are all clues that something is wrong. But things are not always as they appear. Often what is dealt with is the presenting issue, the thing the family members complain about. However, the *presenting issue* is usually only a symptom of the *problem*, the real issue, the thing(s) that needs to be dealt with or worked on. For example, a teen who says, "You never listen to me!" may have identified the situation of the parents seemingly not paying attention to what he says, when the real problem is that the teen is being treated in the same way as when he was a child.

Factors outside the family affect the system. Laws, economic factors, and societal pressures constantly play on family loyalties and prevent even the most effective systems from operating efficiently and happily. No family can protect itself from wars, job layoffs, natural disasters, economic downturns, and random acts of violence. How the family *reacts* to those factors however can be dealt with.

ACTIVITY 9.7
Dealing with Family Adjustments
to Change in Their System

Think back to a situation in which your family had a change in its configuration or experienced some type of major family transformation (e.g., birth of a new child, death of an immediate family member, a major difference in the family's finances such as the loss of the major source of income because of a job loss or due to the inheritance of money, or, someone leaving to go to college or the armed services.

   The situation was:

How did your family adjust to the change?

How did the family cope?

How did the family talk about the change?

If the family operation was *dysfunctional*, operating in chaos, how could there have been *recalibration*, changes made in the patterns that could make the system work effectively?

A family system creates its children's notions of reality when they are young. Families make decisions about who each child is and how the child is to interact with others. In other words, your family laid the foundation for your self-concept and who you are today. All of your current relationships are molded by your past experiences, the rules you followed, and the roles you played, unless you have made the effort to overcome those influences.

There are costs and rewards for belonging to a family system. Costs are the contributions you make for being part of the family—time, money, support, help, expenditure of emotions, loyalty. *Rewards* are the benefits you receive for being in the family—food, shelter, love, attention, emotional support. The payback is not necessarily dollar for dollar, kiss for kiss, and thank you for thank you. Rather, individuals remain satisfied and productive parts of a family as long as their needs are met and they don't feel put upon or taken advantage of. If and when the costs exceed the rewards, *disengagement* may take place and a family member may break ties, either physically or psychologically. Sometimes, when young people disengage, they may try to punish the rest of the family by running away, getting pregnant, isolating themselves, using drugs or alcohol, or committing suicide. Adults who are alienated are likely to break off relationships with all or part of the family, deny access to children or grandchildren, or refuse to attend family functions. These responses are all techniques for communicating personal or family conflict.

To operate successfully within a family system, you must examine and understand the connections between yourself and the other elements of the system. Of particular importance is your understanding of the role you play as a family member. Ask yourself: Who am I in this family? Do I communicate consistently with my role? What are my role identifications? For example, am I the financial provider, the child of a troubled family member who is forcing me to be the parent, the caretaker in a dual parent working family, the oldest child carrying the burden of success for the entire family, the college student who is an occasional home visitor, or the peacemaker among warring factions? Understanding your role leads you to understand whether you are effectively communicating in your family environment and enables you to assess what changes you may want to make in your role as a family member.

LEARNING EXPERIENCE: Interested in checking out your understanding of the family as a system? If so, do Activity 9.8.

More Healthy versus Less Healthy Families

"Every family creates its own balance to achieve some sort of stability. As long as family members interact in certain familiar and predictable ways, this balance, or equilibrium, is not upset."[21]

Communication patterns are the single most important factor in creating a balance that creates a **functional family**, a family system in which the members have learned to make decisions constructively, engage appropriately in conflict with each other, handle pain, and assume risk in constructive ways.

Dysfunctional families are families in which the members find themselves living in fear or chaos or are emotionally and/or physically endangered. The dysfunctionality is usually not the fault of one person, but a lack of communicative teamwork.

The most common problems facing dysfunctional families—and the most common sources of their conflict—often center on their unwillingness or inability to communicate about *power struggles in the family* (e.g., how rules are set up, who enforces them, and how biosocial issues are handled), *differences in intimacy needs* (e.g., showing levels of caring, physical and emotional touching, and sexual activity), and *interactional difficulties* (e.g., how to resolve conflicts, make decisions, and interact with each other).

A less healthy family system is often like a multicar pile-up on a freeway in that it causes damage in one person after another, generation after generation. Dysfunction stems from the accumulated negative feelings, rules, interactions, and beliefs that have been handed down from previous generations and is carried out by the people responsible for creating this new family unit.[22]

For the well-functioning family, there is parental leadership that believes in a caring approach to the development of children and their eventual independence.[23] But parents in a less healthy family have beliefs about children that are selfish and egotistical.

ACTIVITY 9.8
The Family as a Communication System

Which principle of family systems discussed in this section is best displayed by each comment?

1. "My sister doesn't come around much any more. She thinks that all the effort she puts into being a good daughter isn't appreciated."

   _____

2. "As my older brother became a teenager, I noticed his relationship with our younger brother became strained, and we had to spend a lot of time trying to find out what was happening between them."

   _____

3. "With the auto plant closing, my dad is going to be out of work. That's going to put a strain on all of us."

   _____

4. "When my sister left for college we were totally confused about how to act and what to do without her."

   _____

5. "My father has a violent temper, and my sister has been making up all kinds of excuses to stay at her friend's house on weekends."

   _____

Answers:
1. There are costs and rewards for belonging to a family system.
2. Family systems are adaptive.
3. Factors outside the family can affect the system.
4. Any change in one part of the system causes the system to change.
5. People act out what is wrong in their family system.

The parent may think, "Children should respect their parents no matter what," and "There are only two ways to do things, my way and the wrong way." These parents may turn over the philosophy of family practice to religious or cult leadership, many of whom have no expertise in how to develop and maintain healthy family systems. These parents also tend to lack the communication skills and the reasoning perceptions needed to change a dysfunctional system.

"If beliefs are the bones and rules are the flesh of the family system, then 'blind obedience' is the muscle that propels that body. We blindly obey family rules because to disobey is to be a traitor to one's family."[24] In less healthy families there are distorted roles and inappropriate rules, which lead to destructive, self-defeating behaviors. The rule, for example, is that "thou shalt love thy parents." For less healthy families, this seemingly entitles the parents to abuse children who are disrespectful. A child's needs are subservient to pressure to obey. Only when the parents can see the destructiveness of the rules clearly can they exercise free choice. And, only when they have competent communication skills can they create a healthy family system.

Contemporary family theory contends that freedom is an important factor in creating a healthy family system. The family leader or parents need to encourage each person's individual development, responsibility, and independence. Less healthy families fail to encourage individual development and support personal growth. Less healthy families react to problems by acting out their fears and frustration, with little thought about the consequences for family members. On the other hand, this theory is thought to be too liberal for those whose belief system centers on a strong matriarchal or patriarchal family system that enforces blind obedience to a set of principles steeped in narrow religious or ethnic interpretations of what is right and wrong. People with

In less-healthy families there are distorted roles and inappropriate rules, which lead to destructive, self-defeating behaviors.

that family focus would find encouraging freedom of expression to be an invitation to moral and ethical disaster.

Children of parents in less healthy families may mistakenly believe that they are responsible for a parent's abuse. These children develop low self-esteem and guilt because of the parent's behavior toward them. Children who are abused tend to feel unworthy and incapable in many or all aspects of their lives, including how they communicate in their relationships.[25] Children in functional families are most often aware of their role in the family and feel secure in who they are and what they believe in.

Learning about healthy systems and the skills needed to create a healthy system can aid in reinforcing positive patterns and altering negative patterns.

FAMILY CONFLICT

"All families experience some sort of conflict and power issues. Whether within a marriage, sibling relationship, a parent-child interaction, or a cohabiting relationship, conflict is likely to be present in families."[26] "Understanding the relationship among conflict, power and violence is essential to understanding some practices adopted by family members."[27]

Family conflicts are disagreements that center on the exercise of power—the amount of control the family should be allowed to have over individual member's lives. The ideal balance should enable each person within the family to be most effective in gaining access to what he or she wants. You can measure your family's process by examining the degree of freedom or restraint in each of the member's movements and actions. Is there a hierarchy of power? Do one or two people control all or most of the actions of the others? How are decisions made? Can you make some, any, or all decisions about matters that are important to you?

Family members make varying claims on each other for love, affection, recreational companionship, and understanding. Intimacy plays a role in such matters as feeling loved or unloved; inflicting and submitting to sexual, physical, or verbal abuse; getting praise or being ignored; and being included or left out of family activities.

In addition to conflicts concerning power (who's on top and who's on the bottom) and intimacy (how emotionally close or how far family members should be from each other), there are conflicts about how to handle conflicts, including partner conflicts and parent-child conflicts.

LEARNING EXPERIENCE: Interested in your perceptions about parental authority? If so, do Activity 9.9.

The role of parental authority is conflict-loaded. One of the questions you must ask as a parent or prospective parent is, "How do I use or would I use my parental authority?" There is no ideal level of authoritarianism. Some situations, such as when physical danger exists (e.g., the teenager wants to borrow the family car during an ice storm), may call for a very authoritarian approach. On the other hand, responses to conflicts over issues such as room cleaning, curfews, and taking out the garbage depend solely on the extent to which these things are important to the family unit. The more

ACTIVITY 9.9
Use of Parental Authority

Here are some typical things parents do in their relationships with their children. For each statement, mark the column that tells how you as a parent act or would act.

L = likely to act that way
U = unlikely to act that way
? = uncertain how I would act

L	U	?	
—	—	—	1. I would physically remove my child from the piano if he refused to stop banging on it after I had told him it was disturbing me.
—	—	—	2. I would praise my child for consistently being prompt in coming home to dinner.
—	—	—	3. I would scold my six-year-old if she demonstrated poor table manners in front of guests.
—	—	—	4. I would praise my adolescent when I saw him reading literature I approved of.
—	—	—	5. I would punish my child if she used swear words.
—	—	—	6. I would reward my child if he showed me a chart indicating that he had not missed brushing his teeth even once in the past month.
—	—	—	7. I would make my child apologize to another child that she has treated rudely.
—	—	—	8. I would praise my child if she remembered to wait at school for me to pick her up.
—	—	—	9. I would make my child eat almost everything on his plate before being allowed to leave the table.
—	—	—	10. I would require my daughter to take a bath each day and give her a reward for not missing a single day for a month.
—	—	—	11. I would punish my child if I caught him telling a lie.
—	—	—	12. I would offer my teenage son some kind of reward if he would change his style of physical appearance (clothing, piercings, tattoos) to one I approved of.
—	—	—	13. I would punish my child for stealing money from my wallet or purse.
—	—	—	14. I would promise my daughter something she wants badly if she would refrain from using too much makeup.

(continued)

ACTIVITY 9.9 (*continued*)

___ ___ ___   15. I would insist that my child play the piano for relatives or guests.

___ ___ ___   16. I would promise my child something I know he wanted if he would practice his piano lessons for thirty minutes each day.

___ ___ ___   17. I would make my two-year-old remain on the toilet as long as necessary if I knew that he had to go.

___ ___ ___   18. I would set up a system whereby my child could earn a reward if he regularly did his household chores.

___ ___ ___   19. I would punish or threaten to punish my child if she ate between meals after I had told her not to.

___ ___ ___   20. I would promise a reward to encourage my teenager to come home on time after dates.

Tally:

Count the L's checked before the ODD numbers   _____

Count the L's checked before the EVEN numbers   _____

Add the number of L's   _____

The odd-numbered L's indicate the degree to which you do or would use punishment or the threat of punishment to control your child or to enforce your solutions to problems.

The even-numbered L's indicates the degree to which you do or would use rewards or incentives to control your child or to enforce your solutions to problems.

The total number of L's indicates the degree to which you do or would use both sources of your parental power to control your child. Use the following scale to indicate your power-level.

Use of Punishment	Use of Reward	Use of Both Kinds of Power	Rating
0–3	0–3	0–5	Anti-authoritarian
4–5	4–5	6–10	Moderately authoritarian
6–8	6–8	11–15	Considerably authoritarian
9–10	9–14	16–20	Very authoritarian

What is your parenting style? _____

An authoritative parenting approach (unresponsive and demanding) has been shown to be appropriate in very few contexts. More often, an authoritative style, which is responsive and has high expectations, works best. Permissive and neglecting parenting styles are typically the least positive approaches for helping children develop into healthy adults.

Source: Brodericik, P. C., & Blewitt, P. (2006). *The life span: Human development for helping professionals* (2nd ed.). Boston: Pearson, Chapter 4.

important an issue is to you as a parent, the more likely you will behave in an authoritarian manner. The bottom line, however, is to choose your battles carefully. If every incident is a conflict stimulator you can lose the battle while winning little wars.

Family conflicts, whether parent-child, spouse-spouse, or among siblings, often revolve around one erroneous thought: "If only you were more like me, or could see that I'm right and you're wrong, I wouldn't have to be upset." Family members, however, are not identical, and no family member has a corner on the truth, and, therefore, conflict erupts.

Family members participate in conflict because they get something out of it. If not, they wouldn't participate. *Constructive family conflicts* provide new information, excitement and stimulation, and the resolution of mutual problems. *Destructive family conflicts* also have payoffs, such as gaining control over others, placing the blame on someone else in order to get oneself off the hook, and feeling superior to those who are seemingly wrong or inferior. Unfortunately, the "benefits" of destructive conflict sow the seeds for relational dissatisfaction. In spite of the dissatisfaction, many parents and children believe "being right" and "winning the battle" are of paramount importance and continue to battle for control.

VERBAL AGGRESSION IN FAMILIES

A serious problem with conflict in families is that it may turn into verbal or physical aggression. A general acceptance of force and violence exists in many segments of our society. Whether caused by overexposure to violence in the media, the modeling that was done by generations which preceded this generation, or a natural born instinct, violence and aggression exist. Research shows that family violence is not an isolated event, but part of a family's system.[28]

Aggression, which can be a type of abuse, is the taking of actions that advance personal goals without concern for the harm they may cause others. **Verbal aggression** includes the use of words to attack another person, nagging, yelling, insulting, attacking character, crying, accusing, rejecting, refusing to talk, and swearing. Verbal abuse against children and spouses is more common than might be assumed in the United States. Studies indicate that more than two out of three Euro-American children, and more than three out of four spouses, are victims of verbal aggression. Swearing and attacking character are the two most common specific acts of verbal aggression against spouses and children.

Verbal aggression strongly affects people. For example, the more verbal aggression a child suffers, the greater the probability that the child will be physically aggressive, become delinquent, or have interpersonal problems. In addition, the more verbal aggression a spouse endures, the more likely the individual will experience psychosomatic symptoms, poor health, depression, and suicidal thoughts.

Verbal aggression often leads to physical violence. Contrary to the claim that verbal venting releases pent-up anger and thus avoids physical aggression, it has been found that verbal venting contributes to higher levels of physical attack and violence.[29]

PHYSICAL AGGRESSION IN FAMILIES

The nonverbal communication act of physical aggression is also prevalent. **Physical aggression**—hitting, slapping, pushing, beating, or battering another person—is endured by 30 to 50 percent of people in dating relationships.[30] Both males and females experience such physical aggression,[31] including junior and senior high school students, lovers, the engaged, people who are newly married, and people who have been married for some time.[32] "In early marriage, the prevalence of physical aggression increases to a point where over half the men and women are in relationships characterized by physical aggression."[33] Only a small percentage of these acts involve beatings or weapons (such as a knife or gun).[34] "The prevalence of physical aggression is so high in the general population that it is now clear that we need to understand how physical aggression escalates in some relationships, while in others the partner(s) desist from using such aggression."[35] Studies have indicated that there are a series of factors associated with continued aggression (see Figure 9.2).

HEALTHY COMMUNICATION WITHIN A FAMILY CONTEXT

Why is it that at some time in almost every person's life he or she wished to belong to a different family? "In John's family, they discuss everything before a decision is made." "Mary's parents would never make her tell them what happened on a date." The truth is, most families have both healthy and unhealthy communication patterns. The question is one of degree rather than "health": "To what degree is a family's communication system healthy" is a better question than, "Is the family's communication system healthy?"

LEARNING EXPERIENCE: Interested in expressing your beliefs about important aspects of family communication found to be most important for families in the North American culture? If so, do Activity 9.10.

Figure 9.2.   Factors Associated with Continued Aggression

- Acceptance of physical aggression toward a partner
- Alcohol addiction or abuse
- Coming from a family where violence was present
- High levels of psychological aggression
- Jealousy
- Marital conflict
- Multiple instances per year of physical aggression over a two-year time span
- Personality problems such as borderline personality organization or aggressive personality style
- Use of power and control tactics
- High levels of hostility or anger toward a partner

ACTIVITY 9.10
Family Communication Reaction Inventory

In order for you to understand some principles of family communication, it helps to know your beliefs about the process. Tell whether you agree or disagree with each statement.

Agree   Disagree

_____   _____   1. Most family members know how to communicate effectively; they just don't take the time to practice what they know.

_____   _____   2. Family conflict is a symptom of deteriorating family relationships.

_____   _____   3. Family conflict should be avoided at all costs.

_____   _____   4. Most families function more effectively if there is one central leader.

_____   _____   5. Ineffective communication is one of the most important factors leading to family conflict and family tension.

Each of the five items in the knowledge check-up relates to what makes communication in a family effective or ineffective.

Number 1: Communication within the family is often difficult because in many families the members do not know how to communicate effectively.

Number 2: A family may be in trouble and may not realize it unless they are aware of the negative role of continued conflict.

Number 3: The idea that hiding conflict gets rid of it is mistaken. Conflict can be healthy if it is dealt with in a positive way.

Number 4: This point is debatable. If the leader is a constructive leader, the answer could be yes, but if the leader is destructive then the answer would be no.

Number 5: Poor communication, along with financial mismanagement, have been shown to be the most common causes of family tension.

Source: Based on Beebe, S., & Swinton, M. (1987, November). *Teaching the college course: Resources and methods for teaching the family community course.* A paper presented at the annual meeting of the Speech Communication Association, Boston, MA.

Most people do not receive effective communication training in their homes or schools, and typically have poor models to follow. Therefore, even if they want to communicate effectively, most people lack the necessary knowledge and skills. Still, individuals could improve on their own communication if they made the effort. However, no matter how diligent they are, if they don't have the skills, they won't be successful. To be an effective family communicator a person must be aware of how to approach family conflicts, disagreements within the family.

Conflict is natural. Conflict becomes destructive when people, rather than issues, are attacked, when anger is suppressed and allowed to fester, and when problems are solved using authoritarian and divisive means that lead to stress and retaliation. Placing conflict on the back burner, attempting to ignore it, smoothing it over, or denying that it exists creates tensions. The key to resolution lies in how the conflict is dealt with.

It is better to focus on conflicts over small rather than large issues. Small issues can generally be resolved within a reasonable amount of time and with a reasonable amount of effort. Large issues need planning and, sometimes, outside help for resolution.

It is better to recognize the differences in power and ability among participants than to ignore or minimize them. If the family system is based on the dominance of one person, disagreements about his or her use of power may be difficult or impossible to resolve unless that person is willing to give up some of the control role.

It is better to avoid solutions that fail to address important concerns of the participants. A solution, such as, "As long as you live in this house, you will do what I tell you," will not allow all family members to leave the scene with a feeling of satisfaction. Strong feelings that are not resolved in one conflict can resurface later in another conflict.

Many families operate effectively with one leader. However, more often than not, if that leader is dictatorial, even if the system is functioning effectively, a power struggle will eventually arise. Members of families are like citizens of countries. As can be seen again and again throughout history, and as exemplified by the number of revolutions that attempt to overthrow dictatorial or ineffective governments, people can be suppressed only so long. Eventually, they will arise and fight for their freedom by whatever means they have. A family held together by fear and abuse will eventually self-destruct as people run away, divorce from the system, or physically or emotionally destroy the tyrant.

Ineffective communication is one of the most important factors that leads to family conflict and family tension. If ineffective patterns are clung to, family members will inevitably do something to try to change the system. If change cannot be achieved amicably, the next step is to destroy the system.

A family system can change without being destroyed as long as family members understand that their histories are often the problem, and not the individuals, per se. Most problems are generations old and have been passed down from person to person. Eventually, those problems fester into major conflicts.

A family system can develop the flexibility to accommodate bids for individuality. Some family systems make their members slaves to the will and influences of other family members. If people in the system accept this format, there is no problem. If, however, there is conflict concerning the system, then some action must be taken if the system is to survive. One technique is to learn adaptive communication skills. Effective communication in a family allows for a person to be part of a unit while still maintaining an individual identity.

Improving Family Communication

As an individual you have both a right and responsibility to reevaluate the way you are treated, what is expected of you, and what you expect of others. If you are dependent and like your position or role, then the system is working for you. On the other hand, if you want to be more independent, you need to take some action. To be emotionally and communicatively independent (free to have your own beliefs, feelings, and behaviors), you need *not* cut yourself off from your parents or anyone else. It is entirely possible to be part of a family while at the same time being a separate individual who determines what is best for him or her.

LEARNING EXPERIENCE: Interested in assessing the extent to which you have been able to establish an identity separate from your family identity? If so, do Activity 9.11.

Many people fail to stand up for themselves because they confuse self-definition with selfishness. You, like most people, were probably brought up with such rules as, "Don't toot your own horn," "Be humble," and "People don't like braggarts." This advice, if taken to heart, may have led you to believe that you shouldn't be an independent person, that you must always put others' interests before your own, and that you should respect people in authority, whether or not they deserve respect.

Understanding is the beginning of change. Recognizing the existence of a problem leads to the desire to seek new options. This realization, in turn, motivates family members to find ways of altering the present system, the present mode of operation. The change takes place when you examine old patterns, discover what needs to be changed, and learn how to make the appropriate changes.

One useful approach to change-making is the **Workshop Process of Change**.[36] Family members get together, list the family rules of operation, and test them to see if some are unacceptable and if not, are then changeable. Once possible changes are identified, a plan of action is developed. The plan may require you to take some difficult or upsetting risks, but these are necessary to improve the family system. Family members must be honest in dealing with themselves and others so that everyone can start living in and being responsible to the present, rather than retreating into the patterns of the past. This means that all family members must be willing to see and correct their destructive patterns. Consider this example: Rather than continue the battle over the child's not keeping her bedroom neat, the family must accept that old resolutions, such as constant threats, have not worked and that new approaches need to be explored, such as keeping the child's door closed or negotiating a reward-system for cleanliness. The hard part is not slipping back into old and useless patterns while negotiating a change agreement. Sound too theoretical? The system has been used for many years as a constructive counseling tool in dealing with dysfunctional families. Of course, this idea, or any other solution will not work unless *all* of the participants work to eliminate the dysfunctional pattern of operation.

ACTIVITY 9.11
My Parents, My Family, and Me

Directions: Check each statement that is true or mostly true for you:

___ 1. I am very dependent on my parents for emotional support.
___ 2. I have difficulty facing unpleasant truths about my childhood.
___ 3. I fail to see the connections between events of my childhood and adult life.
___ 4. I have difficulty telling my parents my real *feelings* about our relationship.
___ 5. I have difficulty telling my parents my real *thoughts* about our relationship.
___ 6. I have difficulty making my needs a priority when dealing with other family members.
___ 7. I am unwilling to bar family members from my life even if I feel it is in my best interest.
___ 8. I have trouble assessing honestly my relationship with my parents.
___ 9. I don't perceive myself as a particularly powerful and confident adult.
___ 10. I feel incapable of changing my own behavior without seeking advice of parents and family members.

If you checked seven or more of the statements you may feel you are too strongly controlled by parental and family influences. If you think you are too strongly controlled, what can you do about it?

What did you learn from doing this activity?

Source: Forward, S. (1989). *Toxic parents.* New York: Bantam Press, p. 234.

A family system built around protecting an alcoholic, a drug user, an abuser, or a tyrant, is unhealthy. Many families continue to operate with such a pattern even though excusing an alcoholic because he or she "can't help it," or is "a wonderful person when he isn't drinking" is destructive to all concerned. In the process, the family becomes dysfunctional and members become slaves to the person they are trying to protect.

Here's an outline for carrying out a workshop process of change:

Step 1: Each family member lists two family rules that she or he feels enhances family functioning.
Step 2: Each family members lists two family rules that she or he feels causes her or him personal difficulties.
Step 3: Each person reads aloud her or his "enhancing rules."

Step 4: Each person reads aloud her or his "difficulty rules."

Step 5: A discussion is held in which family members acknowledge the "enhancing rules" and talk about the "difficulty rules" with respect to why the rules exist, whether the rules are appropriate, and what changes could be made, if any.

Step 6: Agree on *one* rule that you can realistically institute.

Step 7: Put the rule into effect.

Step 8: Using the information collected, go back to Step 6 and repeat the process.

In some instances, families or some members of a family are unable to make needed changes by themselves and require outside help. One-on-one counseling, family counseling, and support groups are often helpful in solving the problems of dysfunctional families. An alcoholic, for example, may turn to Alcoholics Anonymous for assistance, while the other members of the family attend Alateen or Al-Anon or other support groups for spouses or children of alcoholics. Similarly, an abuser and the abused may seek individual or joint assistance.

Sometimes family members obtain training and support through such organizations as Marriage Encounters, Parents Anonymous, Family Home Evenings (FHE), Family Anonymous for Parents of Drug Addicts, and Family Anonymous for Parents and Friends of Lesbians and Gays (P-Flag). All of these groups stress awareness of verbal and nonverbal communication as it affects other people. All emphasize self-disclosure, openness, sharing, risk-taking, and trust. All use direction and problem-solving techniques to gain insights into interpersonal communication problems and highlight the influence of effective intrapersonal communication and a healthy self-concept as the bases for effective communication with others.[37]

Over one-third of a million parents have turned to PET (Parent Effectiveness Training), a system designed to improve direct interpersonal communication in families. Stress is placed on "I" messages, in which personal feelings and observations are expressed, rather than "you" messages that attack the other person. In addition, a no-lose method of problem solving is taught. In one technique, participants are taught to state how a certain event or activity affects them by expressing their feelings with specific comments, rather than blaming the other person with generalized attacks. For example, an "I" statement such as "I get upset when I walk into the family room and find empty snack boxes and bags littering the floor," is more effective than saying, "You make me so mad. You're a slob. You are always leaving things around."

The Mormon Church, long known for its recognition of the importance of family solidarity, developed the Family Home Evening (FHE) course in which church members set aside Monday evening of each week for a family group meeting or other activities which underscore that the home is the first and most effective place for children to learn the lessons of life. The program centers on intrapersonal and interpersonal communication.[38]

Some programs, such as Family Anonymous for Parents of Drug Addicts, use the techniques of Alcoholics Anonymous to help parents who share a common interest to meet and learn ways to cope with their feelings. Through these programs, parents of drug addicts learn to change negative feelings to positive ones, to replace hostility with understanding, and to live for today without wasting energy on regrets.

Some families have found a simple technique that works well to help build individual self-esteem and encourage communication during family meals. At dinner each evening everyone in the family is encouraged to make one comment regarding something positive that happened to him or her during the day. This puts the emphasis on sharing information and allowing each person to gain positive regard for self and from others. Positive talk about the day also encourages thinking positively rather than negatively. It parallels the philosophy of some child psychologists who urge parents to search out one positive thing their child did each day and praise him or her for accomplishing the task.

We are born into a family. We are socialized by a family. We mature from a family. What a family is and what the individuals in that family are, is dependent on their communication. The more effective the communication, the more healthy will be the family unit.

Key Terms

family communication	family systems
family	dysfunctional
communication rules	functional family
family images	dysfunctional families
family themes	family conflicts
family boundaries	aggression
position-oriented family	verbal aggression
person-oriented family	physical aggression
biosocial attitudes	Workshop Process of Change
family stories	

Competencies Check-Up

Interested in finding out what you learned in this chapter and how you use the information? If so, take this competencies check-up.

Directions: Indicate the extent that each statement applies to you:

1—Never   *2—Seldom*   *3—Sometimes*   *4—Often*   *5—Usually*

___1. I have a family, am part of a family, or have created a family, or had a family with effective communication at the heart of who we are.

___2. My family uses or used open and supportive communication to create intimacy, maintain traditions, make decisions, deal with problems, shape family life, develop effective relationships, and function effectively.

___3. Regardless of my role or image in my family, I use or used leadership skills to enhance the quality of communication in my family.

___ 4. I am part of or was part of a person-oriented family, where we have flexible boundaries and encourage a range of communication behaviors related to individual needs.

___ 5. I communicate or communicated positive family themes, use meaningful family rules, encourage flexible boundaries, and adaptive communication.

___ 6. We use or used family stories to convey our family's images, themes, boundaries, and biosocial attitudes.

___ 7. I recognize or recognized the synergy of my family, and respect how we influence each other.

___ 8. Our family is or was a complex and adaptive group of people, which allows and encourages or allowed and encouraged growth and change.

___ 9. We recognize or recognized that arguments, physical conflict, pouting, stonewalling, and isolation are symptoms of a problem, which we work or worked together to solve.

___10. I am or was an integral part of a functional family, which respects/respected the feelings and needs—including independence needs—of everyone.

___11. We believe or believed that conflict is normal in a family, and we approach or approached differences in a way that enables or enabled each person within the family to be most effective in gaining access to what he or she wants.

___12. We communicate or communicated love in our family by prohibiting any physical, sexual, or verbal abuse, and instead respect our differences and uniqueness, give praise and support to each other, and include each other in family activities and decision-making processes.

___13. Verbal aggression is or was prohibited in our family, so we never use or used words to attack another person, nag, yell, insult, attack character, cry to manipulate, accuse, reject, refuse to talk, and swear at another family member.

___14. Verbal aggression is or was prohibited in our relationships, so no one hits or hit, slaps or slapped, pushes or pushed, beat or beats, or batters another person.

___15. In our family, we communicate or communicated problems when they are small and manageable, we continue or continued to reevaluate our communication patterns, and seek or sought solutions that address or addressed the important concerns of everyone involved.

Scoring: A total of 45 suggests that you have minimum interpersonal communication competencies within your family context. Given the fundamental role of family in your feelings of connectedness, you will want to work toward a score of 75. Carefully examine your answers and needed areas of change.

I-Can Plan!

While the chapter information is fresh on your mind, create a list of strategies that you will use to help you on your journey toward a high level of interpersonal communication competence in family conflict situations. For example, ask each family member to complete the test, then discuss your responses in a family meeting. If the test results underscore a serious problem, use this opportunity to open dialogue and perhaps seek professional family counseling.

Activities

1. Each student in the class is to interview a member of his or her family who is thought to be the most knowledgeable about the person's family rules and customs. The purpose of the interview is not only to identify the rules or customs but from where they were derived.
2. Be prepared to share with your classmates a story that illustrates one of your family's rules or customs regarding an issue such as gender, age, ethnicity, religious background, or birth order.
3. A person in the class will be asked to volunteer to be an artist who will create a sculpture of his or her family. The sculptor will use as many students in class as necessary to "build" the family model. Each classmate will be placed in a body position that shows the verbal and nonverbal personality of each family member and his or her connectedness to other family members. The directions of what pose each person will take are to be whispered to the poser so that the other class members do not know the intent of the pose. After the sculpture is completed, the class members who are not part of the sculpture are to relate what they perceive about each family member and his or her interactions with members of the person's family.

CHAPTER 10

Electronically Mediated Interpersonal Communication

Learning Outcomes

After reading this chapter, you should be able to:

- Define and explain Electronically Mediated Communication (EMC).
- Relate the role of and problems related to cell phones as tools of interpersonal communication.
- Explain why the success of communicating via the Internet is knowing how to be a competent communicator as well as knowing how the technology operates.
- Clarify how individuals can use the Internet to nourish existing relationships.
- List and explain the positive and negative aspects of Internet and texting use.
- Define and explain sexting.
- Define and explain cyber and texting addiction.
- Explain the concepts of flaming.
- Describe how to protect against cyber stalking.
- Relate the positive and negative aspects of social networking tools.
- Explain the relationship of blogging to interpersonal communication.

Sabina smiled as her roommate entered their apartment. "I'm really glad you're here, Trish. Jose just left and I have a problem. He came over with a great idea about our wedding, but I don't know if it's okay." Trish smiled at her and said, "What's the dilemma this time?" Sabina sighed, knowing Trish was right. Ever since she and Jose had set their wedding date, life had become a series of problems about the ceremony, the honeymoon, and trying to make both sets of parents happy. "Since we are both so into computers, Jose thought it would be great to send the wedding invitations and thank-you notes online and set up a web page with links to the places we're listed for gifts. What do you think?" Trish paused for a second. "I'm not sure. You know what a stickler your mom is for doing things absolutely right." Sabina laughed, "You're right. If everything isn't done by the rules, she'll have a fit. I did check my wedding books, but they didn't have anything on using the Internet for announcements and thank-you notes." "Wait, I know where to look," Trish said suddenly.

"Remember in our computer class when we went over unusual sites and someone mentioned that one about manners and we all laughed? Well, for some strange reason I wrote it in my notes. Let me get it. But, just so you know, I don't care what the experts say, I think it's a great idea, and so will most of our friends. You could send out the invitations on Evite. Your parents and friends probably won't like it. I know my parents would have a fit. I guess it's a generational thing."

LEARNING EXPERIENCE: Interested in finding out about the answer to Sabina and Jose's question, or do you have an Internet dos and don'ts question of your own? If so, do Activity 10.1.

ACTIVITY 10.1
Internet Dos and Don'ts

The Internet site Trish was referring to in the dialogue at the beginning of the chapter was www.mywedding.com. Find the answer to Sabrina and Jose's question regarding on-line invitations and wedding gift lists.

Electronically Mediated Communication

Electronically mediated communication (EMC) has become pervasive in personal, academic, and business contexts and continues to grow in importance and types of techniques. EMC includes such technology as blogs, cell phones, computer-conferencing, discussion boards, electronic mail, instant messages, photo-sharing communities, social networks (e.g., texting, Facebook, MySpace, Twitter), videologs, and voice-over IP technology, such as Skyping and YouTube.

Electronic communications are considered interpersonal communication because of the sense of relationship and the connection they create. They may coincide with or substitute for face-to-face and other interpersonal forms of communication.

Although EMC is made possible through an electronic vehicle, in reality it is about intrapersonal and interpersonal communication, not just about computers, cell phones, and other technology. The success of communicating via electronics is not only knowing how the technology operates but knowing how to be a competent communicator. The technology doesn't communicate. You communicate as you use the technology. In fact, a number of technology projects fail because the human dimension is poorly managed.

To those of you under age twenty-five, the statement that EMC is important and continues to grow may seem ridiculous. You might be asking, "What's the big deal? I've always had e-mail and a cell available." Yes, but do you realize that only in the last decade have these become popular and many of those older than you find all of this technology to be mind-boggling as a means of interpersonal communication? With that understanding, let's examine the channels of EMC so you enhance your knowledge of how to use them as meaningful tools for effective interpersonal communication.

Cell Phones

Cell phones, Blackberries, camera phones, and similar devices have changed the way people communicate interpersonally. Whether you want to check on a loved one or conduct work while on vacation, cell phones make interpersonal communication easily accessible. Cell phone connections are often characterized by more frequent, shorter, and perhaps less personal interactions than face-to-face interactions. However, there are minuses. Missing are the visual cues that give communicators emotional content in interpersonal messages. Instead, you have to depend on the words and the sound of a voice to communicate emotion and meaning, which can be a challenge to interpret during a cell phone echo or static laden connection.

The instantaneous nature of e-communications means you can easily and quickly connect to anyone you need. But the bad news is that you can be connected in too many directions at once! Business executives may be on their phones orchestrating deals while they're vacationing on the beach. Parents may be chatting with friends instead of talking with their kids while driving the car. People having dinner at a restaurant can and do talk on their cells to those outside of the restaurant instead of interacting with their dining companions.

Cells can be and are distracting. When the phone rings (or vibrates), the caller often takes precedence over anything else the individual may be doing. You may be in the middle of a personal conversation, a work meeting, or even driving, when your cell phone suddenly interrupts you. Of course, talking and texting while driving can cause accidents because it impairs your concentration.

Listening alone causes the brain activation associated with other tasks to go down by a lot. It seems very clear that driving while being engaged in a phone conversation seems very dangerous.[1] In fact, some states (e.g., Connecticut, New York, and New Jersey) and municipalities (e.g., District of Columbia and Brooklyn, Ohio) have outlawed the use of handheld cells while driving.[2]

Rules of etiquette for the use of cell phones include:[3]

- *If you are engaged in face-to-face communication, keep talking and ignore your phone.* Turn off your phone when the conversation is crucial—such as during a meeting, while in class, while listening to a friend talk about something important, or during a job interview—so you aren't interrupted by the ring or vibrate noise. If you must take a call while engaged with someone else, excuse yourself before answering the phone.
- *Remove yourself from others so you can speak privately.* There is a reason why cell phones are banned from such places as art museums, libraries, and hospitals: cell phone conversations disturb others because they pull bystanders into conversations they don't want to be part of and invade otherwise private and quiet settings.

- *Avoid using the speaker phone* as the noise can be disruptive and outsiders often don't want to know the phone user's business.
- *Tell others in advance if you are waiting for an important call—for example, "my sister is ready to deliver her baby"—so they understand why a phone call may be more important than the communication at hand.*
- *Remember, any time you answer a phone call during a conversation with another person, you are saying "you're not as important to me as the person on the phone."* You risk the other person's attaching negative meanings to your behavior, perceiving you as rude, and losing his/her train of thought. Be certain your phone call is worth jeopardizing your current conversation.
- *Use voice-mail and caller ID so you can bypass unnecessary calls.*
- *Be sure your phone is turned off when you go to a class, library, meeting, conference, speech, interview, worship service, concert, film, recital, stage play, ballet, or court session.* A college freshman was both shocked and mortified when, during his very first college class, his cell phone went off. He answered and said, "Hi mom." His instructor walked back to the student's desk, motioned for the phone, took it and said, "This is Professor XX. Your son is in my Psychology class at this very minute. He was told during orientation that phones were to be turned off during classes. He signed an acknowledgement pledge that if his phone was used, it would be taken and donated to the local abused women's cell phone collection drive. On behalf of an abused woman, I'd like to thank both you and your son for the generous contribution. Bye, mom."
- *Avoid personal calls at the office.*
- *If you must use someone else's cell phone, minimize the amount of time you use their service minutes.*
- *If you have a bad connection, hang up and find a better place to make the call instead of trying to talk over the static.*
- *Avoid discussing personal matters if you are in a public space (e.g., retail store, college cafeteria).*
- *Follow the rules about wireless phone use in hospitals and on airplanes so you won't interfere with sensitive electronic equipment.*

Interpersonal Uses of the Internet

LEARNING EXPERIENCE: Interested in finding out how you use the Internet in relationship to intrapersonal and interpersonal communication? If so, do Activity 10.2.

The Internet offers the user many interpersonal options. A psychologist states, "You can flirt, you can have an affair, you can even consummate the relationship in some way. While on the Internet the person has a sense of belonging, a sense of identity."[4] You know that someone is listening, you are getting attention. You can send and receive information, you can agree and disagree with others. You can take time off from your everyday stress, relax, and gain pleasure by twittering a friend, blogging about your favorite topic, or getting into a chat room concerning an interest or hobby.

ACTIVITY 10.2
My Use of the Internet

Listed are common reasons for and specific ways in which people use the Internet for intrapersonal and interpersonal means. Place a check mark next to each statement or activity which indicates a reason you have used the Internet.

___to gain pleasure
___to relax
___to escape from everyday concerns
___to maintain contact with friends and family
___to make long-distance relationships feel closer
___to meet new people
___to create and sustain new relationships
___to indulge in fantasies
___to cover up for a lack of interpersonal skills
___to find information (e.g., look up a phone number or address, research symptoms of a disease)
___to interact with someone you haven't seen for a while
___to escape for a short time into a fantasy world by becoming someone other than who I really am
___to take academic courses
___to look for employment
___to conduct business
___to contact an instructor
___to participate in a support group
___to participate in a chat room
___to conduct E-commerce
___to investigate product information (e.g., autos, appliances)
___to find out entertainment information (e.g., sports, movies, concerts or theater schedules)
___to flirt
___to find a sexual partner
___to participate in sex talk
___to do homework
___to do academic research
___to make travel arrangements (e.g., plane or hotel reservations)

What did you learn about your Internet usage from doing this activity?

Many individuals use the Internet to nourish existing relationships. They can maintain contact with friends and family, make long-distance relationships feel closer, meet people, keep up with day-to-day activities of loved ones at a distance, create and sustain new relationships, and even indulge in fantasies.

Some people use e-mail to cover up for their lack of interpersonal skills. Those who are introverted may not be able to use the face-to-face method for satisfying their need for social interaction and may, instead, choose a substitute method such as online communication.

On the Internet, people can have power without responsibility They feel they are protected and have nothing to lose. An anonymous hate post, a blog entry that spreads a rumor, an embarrassing photo posted to an Internet site are all examples of how people use interpersonal power without responsibility on the Internet. The shy can become bold. People can be vindictive with little fear of being identified.

The recipient of negative communications can't punish, fire, or divorce the writer. Consequences for inappropriate e-communications seldom carry the same repercussions as ones encountered face-to-face. The risks of online insensitivity are low compared to face-to-face circumstances. The communicator cannot see the hurt expression in the eyes or the anger of a reddening face online as in face-to-face circumstances. If a moderator banishes an individual from an e-mail discussion group, for example, the person can simply join another group or use a new e-mail address to subscribe again to the group. On the other hand, be aware that there are laws against defamation, slander, and stalking.

A study on e-mail states that "e-mail offers users chances to develop positive attitudes but can also offer some undesirable behaviors."[5] What are the positive and negative behaviors and consequences?

POSITIVE ASPECTS OF INTERNET USE

If you are an Internet user and are asked to identify the positive aspects of using e-mail, instant mail, and chat rooms, what would you answer?

LEARNING EXPERIENCE: Interested in identifying what you perceive to be the positive aspects of using the Internet? If so, do Activity 10.3.

As already indicated, people list such factors as receiving pleasure, relaxation, and escape as positive reasons for using the Internet. People advance their careers through online education or conduct school research online. People use **e-commerce**—online business interaction—to look for a job, buy goods they want, gamble online, shape public images of their employers, and more. The rich variety and ease of access to the Internet makes information available to people as never before. Online stock-market trading, for example, enables any consumer to access information previously only available to stock brokers.

The Internet offers enormous flexibility. People can deal with e-communications when they have time to do so. E-mails—for example—can be ignored until a person has a chance to read and respond.

ACTIVITY 10.3
Positive Aspects of Using the Internet

You have been asked to present your views on the positive aspects of using the Internet. Before reading the section of this chapter entitled, "Positive Aspects of Internet Use," make a list of at least five specific ideas you would mention, and be able to explain why each of these is beneficial.

1.

2.

3.

4.

5.

An early scholar in mediated communication who systematically studied how people use personal computers suggested that the computer serves as the "second self,"[6] engaging the individual in intrapersonal communication and self-exploration available in no other way. Blogging, Facebook, and other social network tools are media for self-expression.

E-mail is quick and inexpensive. The average person can open e-mail, type a message, and send it faster than they can place a phone call or walk down the hall to talk to a coworker. The problem is that e-mails are less personal, and because they lack nonverbal communication, have more room for misinterpretation than face-to-face or phone communication.

Some people communicate better in writing than orally. They can write and re-write, choose their words carefully, and not risk mistakes common in the spontaneity of oral communication.

Historically, most employers applauded workers who spent their work day engrossed in such business related activities as reading reports, writing letters, sending faxes, and making contacts. Today, while the same kind of work is being conducted through computer mediated communication, employers may wonder if an employee is playing games, gabbing with friends, or surfing the Net instead of working.

The collegiate environment opens many positives. Today students supplement their face-to-face classes with online course environments such as Blackboard, use discussion boards to talk with peers, conduct online database research of high quality, check for plagiarism through Turnitin, and continue discussions that they started during class. "Seventy to 80% of US university faculty report using electronic messages to communicate with students and colleagues."[7] Sometimes out of fear of negative face-to-face reactions, or cultural patterns which restrict a student from speaking directly to an authority figure, or out of shyness, students don't approach professors. For example, some Asian students have been brought up to avoid losing face, so they will not admit that they don't know information, nor cause others to lose face, as by asking questions of authority figures who may not know the answers. These students often are more comfortable asking for information online.

Online communities—discussion boards, online work groups, course environments, social networking—can create a sense of connection between people which is similar to group or team communication.[8] Some people have turned to chat rooms to supplement their psychological needs. Support groups can aid a person to interact with individuals who have similar problems or issues. People in remote areas can find others who can be of assistance. For example, an isolated gay youth, a woman with breast cancer, a couple who has lost children, can find interactive voices on the Net.

NEGATIVE ASPECTS OF INTERNET USE

In spite of all the positive aspects of the Internet, it has its negative aspects and, therefore, its detractors.

Most people will use the Internet with discretion and experience few if any problems. In fact, research has shown that ninety percent of people get online, do what they need to do, and then get off. It's the other 10 percent that are problem users.[9] There is evidence that an individual can feel socially isolated by becoming so engrossed in Internet activities that their Internet activities interfere with their personal and employment responsibilities and relationships. Even back in 1997, before the Internet use explosion, 13 percent of college students indicated that their computer use interfered with personal functioning.[10]

Some Internet users indicate they have become overwhelmed by the number of e-mails they receive daily. As one businessperson states, "E-mail was a fantastic invention but now, even without spam, it's a nightmare to deal with."[11] Some feel guilty about not being able to answer e-mails immediately, and if they do spend the time to answer, they may find themselves behind in studies or work. One trend is to declare **e-mail bankruptcy**,[12] which is to delete all e-mails not answered within a specific period of time, such as twenty-four hours.[13] Another approach to e-mail overload is to pledge not to go into it for a day or two. Intel Corporation is running "zero-E-mail Fridays," in which no company employee is to send or open an e-mail on Fridays.[14] E-mail-free Fridays already are the norm at cell carrier U.S. Cellular and at order-processing company PBD Worldwide Fulfillment Services.[15] This avoids **e-mail twitching**, reading every new e-mail as it arrives.[16]

Cyber Addiction

Whether it's called computer addiction, impulse control disorder, Internet addictive disorder, or the most commonly used term, **cyber addiction**, it is considered the major negative aspect of Internet usage.[17] It is classified as an addiction since it fits into the Psychological Addiction Cycle,[18] which is *need* leads to *use* which leads to *trouble* which leads to *repeating the action* to satisfy the *need*.

"In the case of the cyber addict, there is a *need* to escape from the real world due to angst, boredom or depression. The *use* is to create the world "I" want which allows the needed escape. The *trouble* that results centers on the time spent which causes missed work or classes, or being constantly tired. The trouble leads to deeper *need*, so the cycle is repeated."[19]

A person who lies about Internet use, won't admit to how much time he or she is spending online, constantly "works" on the computer instead of interacting with others, and/or neglects job or school tasks in order to spend inordinate time on the computer, is in trouble. Such a person is being controlled by the computer instead of controlling the computer.

A cyber addict is controlled by the computer, rather than he controlling the computer.

Obsessive Internet use has caused lost jobs, academic problems, marital problems, mounting debts, broken trust, being caught in lies, and cover-ups.[20]

Excessive computer users tend to be those who have one or more of the feelings of loneliness, isolation, boredom, depression, anger, or frustration. One study indicated that "about 71 percent were diagnosed as suffering from bipolar disorder, commonly called manic depression."[21]

The causes of excessive computer usage are typically short-term and understandable. When a student goes away to college, there is a need to connect with family and friends. When a person gets away from the office for a few days, escalating problems at work may need a little attention in order for the employee to feel relaxed. Or, a shy person may find that making contacts on the Internet can lead to initial personal contacts, thus allowing him to overcome the first fear of introductions and open the possibility of meeting someone later, with whom he is familiar and has established some intimacy.

Cyber addiction might signify a strong psychological need for attention. This need could include satisfying a desire to be popular by setting up situations where a person's e-mail or cell phone is constantly bombarded with in coming messages and texts. This excessive communication gives people an illusion of being well liked and getting lots of attention from cyber "friends." Perhaps what they really want to show is that they are indispensable because others can't survive without them. By constantly checking the cell phone for messages and texts, or the computer for e-mails and twitters, they also are attempting to give the illusion to others that the receiver is well liked and constantly in demand.

The Internet can also be a means for those who suffer from sexual addiction and pedophilia to live their fantasies or make illicit contacts.

LEARNING EXPERIENCE: Interested in finding out if you are cyber addicted? If so, do Activity 10.4.

Even if you are not a computer addict, you may still be overusing electronics. If so, what are some ways to move away from overuse?

- Have an e-communication-free day a week.
- Limit your time or hours when you use e-communication, such as no e-communication after 9 P.M.
- Use a timer to limit your time.
- If you have online access on your phone, leave your cell phone in the car or give it to someone else to hold so that you can't use it to go online.

You might ask yourself what is the bottom line when it comes to communication. "Of what value is sending or receiving this message? Will anyone's life be lost, a calamity avoided, or vital information not be passed on if I don't text or answer the phone or e-mail?"

If you are unable to do any of these on your own, you may want to join a support group for cyber addicts or seek psychological counseling. Despite the irony, even joining one of the many online support groups for cyber addicts may be a way to begin

ELECTRONICALLY MEDIATED COMMUNICATION

ACTIVITY 10.4
Are You a Possible Cyber Addict?

Directions: How many of these describe your tendencies regarding the use of the Internet or texting? Circle every answer that applies to you.

1. Given a choice I would generally choose to go onto the Internet or text than go to a social event.
2. Often, I stay on the Internet or text for longer periods of time than I intend.
3. I have repeated, unsuccessful efforts to control, cut back on, or stop engaging in the use of the Internet or texting.
4. I am restless or irritable when attempting to limit or stop engaging in the use of the Internet or texting.
5. Using the Internet or texting is a way of escaping from problems or relieving feelings such as helplessness, guilt, anxiety, or depression.
6. Returning to the Internet or text in search of a more intense or higher-risk experience.
7. Lying to friends, family members, therapists, or others to conceal your involvement on the Internet or texting.
8. Committing illegal or unethical acts online (e.g., downloading pornography, gambling, hacking, or creating a computer virus or exchanging test or homework answers).
9. Jeopardizing or losing a significant relationship, job, or educational or career opportunity because of online or texting behavior.
10. Incurring significant financial consequences as a result of engaging in online behavior (bidding for items on e-Bay), or text messaging overcharges.
11. While attending classes, I am constantly playing with my cell phone, even if it is off, wondering what text messages I am missing or wanting to text someone.
12. E-bullying, such as spreading gossip, uploading inappropriate pictures of others, flaming.

Scoring guide: "Yes" to three or more of these indicates problematic online or texting behavior.

What did you learn about your Internet and texting behavior from doing this exercise?

Source: Adapted from a workshop presented by Carnes, P. (2004, February 27). *The criteria of problematic online sexual behavior.* Cleveland, OH: Free Clinic.

changing. A growing number of psychologists and counselors have become specialists in cyber addiction.

Negative Social Impact

E-mails lack nonverbal cues. E-communication lacks any subliminal information—facial movement, clothing, appearance, body language, even handwriting. Without normal face-to-face feedback, attachments form quickly. Online, people often move from casual chat to intimacy with startling speed. Much care is needed to avoid disappointment later. What you read in online and what you see face-to-face may be two different things.[22] "People experiment with their identity on-line or in texting, both deliberately and unconsciously. It's not uncommon for someone with an introverted personality to be bolder on-line, or for people to be more playful than they normally would be face-to-face."[23] The idea that a person has a real self and a second self (the online persona) often becomes confused in e-communication.[24] Because of this, people who are naive or trusting often get hurt and disappointed.

Internet users may deal with ideas from a wide array of people, and that may challenge their belief systems and threaten the values by which they live. Individuals may also find it difficult to tolerate the intrapersonal conflict they experience from being exposed to ideas that are not familiar, asked to evaluate long-held beliefs, or are challenged to defend their ideas or values.

The amount of face-to-face interpersonal communication can be depleted as people spend more and more of their time on the Internet or texting. It's often easier to bang out a message online than make physical contact, and spend the same amount of time looking into another individual's face, listening to his or her concerns, and showing concern.

Flaming

Flaming, e-mail or text aggression, happens when people send hostile, insulting, or intimidating messages online or via phone.

Because there is no direct personal contact online, some people feel they can get away with verbally abusing others. There are few consequences for the abuser. Interestingly, the person who has been victimized in face-to-face communication may become a flamer. They may feel powerful in being able to flame, to get away with what they wouldn't do face-to-face. Be aware that there are laws regarding the use of flaming. Threatening someone, spreading ill-truths, and stalking are all against the law and can be punishable with fines and/or jail.

Sexting

"**Sexting** is the sending of nude, semi-nude, or erotic pictures or video via cell phone."[25] It garnered a significant amount of attention following the 2008 suicide of an eighteen-year old girl after her former boyfriend circulated nude pictures of her. After suffering humiliation and abuse from her classmates, she contacted law enforcement for aid. She received no help and, subsequently, committed suicide. This revelation resulted in an increased number of cases sent to law enforcement and district attorneys, resulting in legal convictions for child pornography and other crimes against those who circulated pictures and other materials."[26]

While often perceived to be an activity of teens, a recent study found that 73.5 percent of those ages twenty to twenty-six sexted, while 66 percent of the general population participated in the activity. Many of the sexters were unaware that they were even participating in the act. Few realize that sending or forwarding revealing nude or suggestive pictures (of themselves or others) and certain stories that contain pornographic information could be considered sexting, depending on the legal jurisdiction in which you reside. That includes taking and sending pictures of those in locker rooms or at social gatherings.

Legal actions include a case in Greensburg, Pennsylvania, in January 2009, when six teens were charged with child pornography after three girls sent sexually explicit photographs to male classmates. [27]

In Fort Wayne, Indiana, a teenage boy was indicted on felony obscenity charges, when he allegedly sent a photo of his genitals to several female classmates.[28] Another boy was charged with child pornography in a similar case.[29] Two southwest Ohio teenagers were charged with contributing to the delinquency of a minor, a first-degree misdemeanor, for sending or possessing nude photos on their cell phones of two fifteen-year-old classmates.[30]

What appears to some as "just fun" can turn out to have severe consequences. Besides the legal fines and school expulsions, in some cases those prosecuted were listed as sex offenders,[31] meaning that they are classified the same as pedophiles, rapists, and child molesters. This is often a lifelong identification.

Before sending out pictures on the Internet, ask yourself whether the materials can get you into trouble that could result in fines, jail sentences, a ruined reputation, or being considered a legal pervert for the rest of your life.

Cyber Bullying

Cyber bullying—also known as digital harassment—is mistreatment that takes place using an electronic medium.[32]

Cyber bullying is considered worse than the regular schoolyard kind because it knows no bounds of time, space or geography. A bullied child used to be able to go home to escape. Now, bullying can happen when a child is in his or her own bedroom.[33] Sometimes cyber bullying is more malicious, vindictive, and brutal than face-to-face bullying "because the cyber bullies can often hide their true identities."[34] As one person against sneaky, online confrontation explained, "I'd rather be slapped in the face than stabbed in the back." The bully can use false identifications and, since they can't be identified, they don't have to prove their insinuations. "They are immune from the tears of the bullied and removed from feeling empathy for them."[35]

There have been cases of cyber bullying in which camera phones have been used to take compromising pictures of individuals, head shots have been attached to the bodies of other people to create pornography, and malicious gossip has been spread with no ability to counter the stories. For example, "A heavy set boy, hot and sweaty after his gym class, was getting dressed in what he thought was the privacy of the school's locker room. One of his classmates took a picture of him with a cell phone camera. Within seconds, the picture was flying to the cell phones of the boy's schoolmates through instant-messaging. By the time he was dressed and in his next class, he was the laughing stock of the school."[36]

Some municipalities have made online harassment a crime.[37] A thirteen-year old girl in Missouri read disturbing posts on the Internet after she broke up with her boyfriend. The girl thought her boyfriend said "she was a bad person and the world would be better without her." The girl committed suicide.[38] The "boy," in fact, had been created by the mother of a neighbor girl who had had a falling out with the girl. An FBI investigation followed. The community became outraged when the e-mailing mother received no legal penalty because there were no laws forbidding cyber harassment. They pressured the legislature to pass such regulation with stiff penalties. In California the Megan Meier Cyber Bullying Prevention Act is an effort to impose regulations on the Internet.[39]

How prevalent is cyber bullying? In 2005, nine percent of children ages ten to seventeen said they were abused by "cyber bullies." According to a report from the U.S. Centers for Disease Control and Prevention, there is an increasing trend for college students to be bullied.[40] A study indicates that over 60 percent of students had been cyber-bullied sometime in their academic career.[41]

How can you stop from being cyber bullied or being part of a cyber bullying attack?

- Refuse to pass along cyber bullying messages.
- Block communication from cyber bullies.
- Report cyber bullying to the proper authorities.
- Never post or share your personal information online (this includes your full name, address, telephone number, school name, credit card number, or Social Security number) or your friends' personal information.
- Never share your Internet passwords with anyone.
- Never meet anyone face-to-face whom you only know online unless it is in a public place and you think you are totally safe.

Cyber Stalking

Another negative aspect of the Internet and cell phones is that people may use them for devious means. Cases of rapes, teen runaways, invasion of privacy, harassment, and stalking, which had their basis in e-mail, instant messages, and texting, have been reported. Students have sent bomb threats to schools and universities, and hate mail to teachers and professors thinking that they can get away with these acts because they don't use their real identity.[42] There have been instances of cyber stalking. **Cyber stalking** centers on following and harassing both males and females. In many cases, the cyber stalker and the victim had a prior relationship, and the cyber stalking begins when the victim attempts to break off the relationship. However, there also have been instances of cyber stalking by strangers. "Given the enormous amount of personal information available through the Internet, a cyber stalker can easily locate private information about a potential victim with a few mouse clicks or key strokes."[43]

In order to protect yourself from stalking, you might want to follow these suggestions:

- Create a gender neutral e-mail name, not one about your interests or your gender.
- Remove all gender and personal information from your user profile.
- Make your e-mail signature dull, businesslike, and gender neutral.
- Check your e-mail headers, which may be sending information without your knowledge.
- "If you find yourself being victimized, the classic advice is to ignore the stalker. Even responding to their E-mail to say, 'Leave me alone,' just encourages them. Remember, those of us who are playing with a full deck don't send anonymous and threatening cyber threats. Your best bet is to hope that your cyber stalker will get bored by your lack of response."[44]

Diminishment of Writing Skills

Writing skills can be diminished by using e-mail to correspond, as devotees may exhibit bad writing habits including:

- Dashing off notes without stopping to think about what you're writing or to whom you're writing causing little audience analysis and poor grammatical constructions.
- Using **e-lingo** and **e-bbreviations**—computer or texting shorthand and Internet nonverbal indicators—without concern for whether or not the receiver understands the argot. One of the authors of this book received so many essays with texting e-lingo that he finally had to put a notice in his syllabus that "All assignments must be written or keyboarded in Standard American English. Any use of e-lingo will cause a deduction to your grade."

DEVELOPING PERSONAL RELATIONSHIPS ONLINE

The development of personal relationships is a pivotal issue in the larger debate about human relations in cyberspace. On one side are those who view online relationships as shallow, impersonal, and often hostile. The other side argues that computer-mediated communication liberates interpersonal relations from the confines of physical locality and thus creates opportunities for new, but genuine, personal relationships and communities.

For some people, online relationships are crucial to their well-being. You may know someone who found love or marriage online. For lonely teens, for instance, an online relationship is a place to turn in times of need.[45] Parents of children with disabilities may find support from other parents through an online group. Colleagues may develop relationships online. There are all kinds of acquaintanceship, friendship, emotional support, and even love relationships that develop online, just as there are face-to-face.

Remember, when searching personal advertisements or entering chat rooms, that people may lie because they think they cannot be discovered. They may switch data about their sex, age, locations, and personal appearance. How are you to know? You can't see them! You may not be able to tell whether or not someone is lying, but if the person's posts are longer than normal, use more sense-based words (about taste, smell, touch, sight, sound), and more other-oriented pronouns, those differences may be a tip that the person is lying.[46] Although liars may communicate differently, you probably cannot tell.

Some people talk about both their face-to-face and electronic relationships as their "real" friends. Although the relationships may be different, both are real, but may serve different purposes. Relational research shows that, even though there are exceptions, associations maintained over long distances do not generally provide the kind of support and reciprocity that typically contribute to a sense of psychological security and happiness.[47] Think about it. Why is your best friend your best friend? Probably because he or she is there for you when you need him or her. That person was there to pat you on the shoulder, bring you medicine when you needed it, and acted as a support system. On the other hand, best friends can use e-interactions to enhance a relationship by providing contact between face-to-face meetings.

That person on the Internet, many miles away, isn't immediately with you. Before you break any present-tense relationships, move, fly thousands of miles to meet that "perfect" Cybernet person, heed the advice of a couple who met and "dated" for almost two years on the Internet and who actually decided to get married: "Despite the fact that we had been in steady communication—exploring each other's likes and dislikes and becoming intimate enough to marry—when we finally met face-to-face, we had a lot more exploring and adjusting to do."[48] This was from a success story couple. Though there have been successful Internet relationships developed, most Internet relationships don't wind up this happily.

BEING A BETTER INTERPERSONAL ONLINE COMMUNICATOR

Electronic-mediated interpersonal communication is here to stay. Your desk or laptop computer and/or cell phone is ready and waiting. How can you be a competent interpersonal cyber communicator?

- *Be aware that you may not get a response to your messages.* Many people receive a large volume of mail, may delete days' worth of messages, select "no mail," or be selective about responding when busy. You may have to repeat your message or alter your channel of communication and use the telephone or FAX or snail mail (yes, there are people who still use that method of communication) to make sure the message has arrived and is answered.

- *Be aware that some users become irritated with comments that encourage continued e-mails or texts back needlessly.* Watch for cues that allow you to know that a cor-

An effective on-line communicator realizes that s/he may not get an immediate response to a sent twitter, text, or email.

respondence has reached its climax. Such phrases as, "That about does it for this topic," or "We seem to have concluded this," or "I'll get back to you when I have something more to say," are forecasters of conversational closings.

- *Be considerate.* If you do not have time to answer the message immediately, a short response that you will deal with the matter within a set period of time is often appreciated. If you are going to be gone for a period of time, you might want to let people in your address book know, so they don't expect immediate responses.

- *Be aware that there is no such thing as a private electronic conversation.* Many businesses, for example, use an electronic window, a device which allows managers to monitor e-mail. If you don't want others to know the sites you are visiting or the content of your personal messages, don't use your business computer or a home computer to which others have access.

- *Be aware that software is available that can enable your employer, service provider, a disgruntled colleague, or the legal system to use your computer mediated communication against you.* Programs are available that can break the password of any account. In addition, sources such as spymastertools.com lists hundreds of devices to use to aid in finding you, tracking you, and revealing what and to whom you are communicating.

- *An attachment can contain a virus.* Be careful of what messages you open. Be aware of the latest computer bugs and their message titles.

- *Remember, your computer provides "cookies" to most Internet sites so that companies, law enforcement, and stalkers can track back to you and/or your computer or cell.* You may want to use a program that removes tracking from your computer such as Ad-Aware or Spybot. Do not assume you are anonymous and protected on the Internet or cell. Revelations that the Bush administration's post–September 11 surveillance efforts went beyond the widely publicized warrantless wiretapping program, and encompassed secretive activities that created "unprecedented" spying powers,[49] illustrates how pervasive is the ability to spy on the citizenry.
- *Be aware that if you are using a university or company computer or e-mail system, the organization owns your e-mails, and e-mail messages that are encoded by their computers are being kept on their Internet provider.* A rule of good sense should be, "don't say anything on the Internet that you would be ashamed for your family, boss, or best friend to read."
- *Be aware that harassment charges can be lodged regarding e-mail and twittering.* For example, if you send a private e-mail to a friend which contains gender-centered jokes, or you send racist humor to another person, you can be charged with harassment. Be careful about quickly sending out copies of those "funny jokes" you receive without considering the consequences. Be conscious of what sexual, religious, racial, gender, and sexual-orientation harassment is, and that you can be legally libel for both same- and other-sex harassment. "Two black employees brought a $60 million racial discrimination case against a US investment bank after racist jokes were allegedly circulated on its E-mail system."[50]
- *Be aware that you can't take e-mail back.* Once it is sent, it is sent. Also remember that the receiver might forward the message to other people without your permission. Take your time. If you are angry or upset, don't pound your feelings out on the keyboard. If you do consider whether you want to delete the message once you have vented your frustrations. Stop and think if that's really what you will want to say tomorrow.
- *Be aware that most educational institutions and businesses prohibit chain letters, jokes, and politically oriented e-mails.*
- *Be aware that voyeurs can use electronic devices to record your private moments, then rebroadcast your photos and videos on the Internet.* Ask yourself, when sending photos and videos, whether you are willing for others to view them.
- *Before you flame, you might want to consider extinguishing the message.* You are liable for the abusive, aggressive, or deliberately antisocial e-mail you send.
- *Remember that on the Internet there is no intonation, affect, or facial expression, as e-mails and twitters offer only bare words.* To make your e-mail more expressive, pretend you are writing a novel. Include in the information necessary descriptive information so your receiver can picture what you are talking about and know the feelings being expressed.
- *Be aware that there are those who manipulate.* As with any type of good listening, ask whether what's being said is reasonable, if it makes sense, if the sender is taking responsibility for what is said, and if are there facts and examples that lead you to the conclusion or solution being proposed.

As a sender and receiver of EMC, be a wise and responsible consumer and communicator.

Blogging

"A **blog** is a Website with dated entries, usually by a single author, often accompanied by links to other blogs. Think of a blog as one person's public diary or suggestion list."[51]

Blog is short for "Weblog." Though many students are using social networking sites that act like blogs, the personal Internet blog is still a viable way of sharing information. One web blogger's service has a section called "Blogger Comments" which allows readers of your site from all over the world to give feedback on what you share on your blog.[52] You can choose whether or not you want to allow comments on a post-by-post basis and you can delete anything you don't like. The same service has another section entitled, "Group blogs," which they indicate "can be excellent communication tools for small teams, families, or other groups."[53] A special type of blog is a photo-sharing community. Understandably, an individual's self-expression and relationships online are determined by the type of photos shared.[54] In fact, blogging may have positive effects on a person's feelings of well-being because of the good feelings associated with self-disclosure.[55]

Blogging has found its way into the corporate world. When a work team uses blogging, they can exchange information and provide information to other people in the company. Blogging in business can increase accountability because the project is organized, documented, and visible to others.[56]

Teachers, professors, schools, colleges, and universities are using blogs to communicate with students, archive student work, learn with far-flung collaborators, and manage the knowledge that members of the school community create.[57]

Academic interpersonal blogging opportunities include starting conversations about academic topics, using portals to post and exchange assignments, fielding questions, and opening doors for interactions between students and professors from the same or different institutions, majors, and classes.[58]

As with any interpersonal means of communication, there are certain guidelines that can help you to be competent. In blogging these include:[59]

- Once you have sent a blog in cyberspace you cannot retrieve it. Do not write anything that you don't want the entire global population to know.
- Normally, do not include your address or phone number. Harassment, stalking, and death have resulted from the wrong information in the wrong hands.
- Remember that the laws related to defamation of character and slander are in effect on the Internet.
- It is usually wise to protect the privacy of others by using fictitious names of people, places, schools, and businesses.
- Though blogging is usually considered an informal act, clear idea development, correct grammar, clarity of structure, appropriate language, and correct spelling should be considered a requirement.

- The concepts of ethical communication should be followed.
- Writing something in haste, especially when you have strong emotional feelings, can result in your saying things that you might not want in public view.
- Blogs are generally forever. Do you want this information "out there" in five, ten, or twenty years? People have been compromised and blackmailed by things they have said in the past which they regret having said when looked at with a present-day eye.
- Use encrypted e-mail so that undesirable people cannot easily trace you.
- For security purposes, avoid giving out your social security number.
- Be aware that prospective employers often do a web search to find out about you, so don't put anything on your blog that might give them reason to question your honesty or integrity.

There are several sites that may be particularly useful to those who are bloggers or who wish to join the blogging ranks, including blogger.com, which is a free service, and has a three-step format that takes less than thirty minutes to follow. Another site is Bloglines.com.

Social Networking

If you are a typical college student you spend much time on **social networking** sites, talking online in such communities as Facebook.com, MySpace.com, and/or Twitter.com. These sites allow you to interact with others from down the hall, across the campus, or around the world.

FACEBOOK

Facebook has become so common among students that a frequent comment on some college campuses is, "Facebook me," much as older generations said, "Call me." In fact, the verb *facebooking*,[60] is now in many standard dictionaries, which means to communicate with someone via Facebook.

Research shows that "nearly 80% of students on college campuses visit facbook.com on a daily basis."[61] Because the restriction of having to be a college student has been lifted, it is expanding quickly, and high school students and businesses have invaded the space. Consider these statistics about Facebook:[62]

1 billion photos are uploaded to the site each month.
10 million videos are uploaded each month.
120 million users log on to Facebook at least once each day.
250 million are active users.
30 million users update their statuses at least once each day.
5 billion minutes are spent on Facebook each day (worldwide).
The fastest growing demographic is people thirty-five-years old and older.

Two-thirds of Facebook users are outside of college.

Facebook ranks as the most viewed site on the Internet.[63] More females aged seventeen to twenty-five (69 percent) visit the site than males (56 percent).[64]

There are both positive and negative aspects to the use of Facebook.

Positive Aspects of Facebook

There are many positive aspects to using Facebook. They include:

- People who are shy can create a positive self-image by meeting other people.
- People can create social networks.
- People can reconnect with people they used to know and stay in touch with family, friends, and colleagues.
- Surveys and event listings can be accomplished easily.
- Subscribers can advertise.
- Regional, local, and individual parties and events can be announced.
- People can create a "web-portal" that is easier than designing a webpage.

Negative Aspects of Facebook

Like most social networking services, people's personal information is visible to many people, including potential stalkers, salespeople, and harassers. For example, the week before the 2007 Ohio state high school football championship game, fans of one of the finalists began a poke campaign against the quarterback of their opponents, with the intent of psychologically rattling him.[65]

Other negatives include:

Facebook addiction can be obsessive behavior just like other cyber addiction. "Social networking junkies count the minutes to their next profile fix, checking their computers or cell phones multiple times per day to see how many shout-outs, virtual drinks or new friends they've acquired."[66]

Identification with certain interest groups, inappropriate behavior, and sexually explicit content or photos may lead to negative evaluations by prospective employers, school authorities, or law enforcement. For example:

- Pictures from Facebook were used to cite violators of the university alcohol policy at North Carolina State University. Charges included underage drinking and violations of the dormitory alcohol policy, specifically students holding open bottles of alcoholic beverages in the dorm hallway.[67]
- Four students at Northern Kentucky University were fined for posting pictures of a drinking party on Facebook. The pictures, taken in one of NKU's dormitories, proved that the students were in violation of the university's dry campus policy. The students each received a $50 fine, one year of probation on campus, and were forced to attend a class about the dangers of binge drinking.[68]

- A sophomore was expelled from Fisher College in Boston for comments about a campus police officer made on Facebook. The comments were judged to be in violation of the college's code of conduct.[69]
- At Syracuse University, four students were placed on disciplinary probation after creating a group entitled "Clearly [instructor's first name] doesn't know what she's doing ever." The group featured derogatory and personal attacks aimed at the instructor.[70]

A person can find others who back similar bizarre or dangerous inclinations. For example, a Pennsylvania high school student found an ally in Finland who shared information on how to plot and carry out a school attack. The sharing between the teenage outcasts was discovered when the computer of the Finish teenager who killed eight people and himself in a school rampage was analyzed and communication between the two boys was revealed. A search of his home and computer determined that the Pennsylvania youth was planning to carry through a similar violent act.[71]

Profile and other information can be used to blackmail members. "In 2007, Miss New Jersey Universe posted to her Facebook profile several pictures of herself partying. They were later mailed anonymously to the pageant's executive board, in an alleged smear campaign."[72] An attempt to embarrass 2008 Republican Presidential candidate Rudy Giuliani took place when it was made public that his daughter had "joined a Facebook group supporting Barak Obama."[73]

Users can become more concerned about the quantity of interpersonal relationships than the quality of their relationships. The average Facebook user has 120 friends.[74] Obviously, if a person maintained that many close personal friendships, there would be no time to do anything else.

MY SPACE, TWITTER, YOUTUBE

Other social networks are available to Internet and cell phone users, including My Space, Twitter and YouTube.

MySpace accounts for 4.92 percent of all Internet visits and is an important part of the social network.[75] Since MySpace is used more by junior and senior high school students than Facebook, most college students will have "outgrown" its use.

Twitter is a more direct communication social networking service than Facebook or My Space, as specific sources are selected for message receipt. As their advertisements state, its purpose is "the exchange of quick, frequent answers to one simple question: What are you doing?"[76]

Actually a form of microblogging, Twitter enables its users to send and read messages known as *tweets*. Tweets are text-based posts of up to 140 characters displayed on the author's profile page and delivered to the author's subscribers who are known as *followers*.

Be aware that Twitter collects your personal identity information and shares it with third parties. This means that your identity is not yours, but can be sold and shared. Also be aware that Twitter has displayed a number of security breaches.

YouTube is a video sharing system where users can upload, view, and share video clips. Created in 2005, it was purchased by Google in 2006.[77] Some 100 million videos are available in YouTube, with more than one hundred thousand new videos being uploaded each day.[78] Today, viral videos have become a popular way of spreading ideas, information, and entertainment. *Viral videos* spread like a cold virus, from person to person, as people tell each other about favorite videos. There are millions of videos available on YouTube, the most popular of which have been seen by 50 million or more viewers.[79]

The warning "rules" about personal dangers regarding Facebook apply equally to MySpace and Twitter. The possibility for problems exists and caution must be taken.

PROTECTING YOURSELF ON SOCIAL NETWORKING SITES

There are strategies you can use to protect yourself in social networking sites. You need to use common sense and understand nature of the venue.

Only post information you want everyone to know. If you don't want your mother to be your friend on Facebook because of what she will see, then you may have a problem.

Chose your privacy options carefully. Don't assume that because you are honest, all of those who can access your account will also be good citizens. Use privacy options to restrict who can access your account. Keep private information such as phone numbers, address, your schedule, social plans, and social security numbers to yourself. This will eliminate identity fraud and thwart those who might be interested in stalking you. Unfortunately, "41% of users divulge personal information."[80] Are you one of them?

If you need to hide from a violent ex-partner or a vindictive ex-friend then you will want to stay off social networking sites. Since 2007 anyone who searches the Internet on Google, Yahoo, and Microsoft will have access to Facebook members' names and photos.[81] The move was made to "make it an even more lucrative advertising vehicle."[82] If you are a Facebook user, you are the product that is being advertised!

You can Google yourself to check on what information is out there. Google yourself to see how your name or identity is used. Subscribe to www.pubsub.com or a similar service to keep track of your name and identity on the web.[83]

Assume that once information is on the Internet—an e-mail is sent, a message posted, a photo uploaded—it can be accessed by anyone indefinitely.

Delete inappropriate photos, information, and posts from discussion boards, webpages, and social networking sites months before you hunt for a job. Because materials are typically available for some time after deleted, you will need to start changing content well in advance.

Use security software to block unwanted hacking into your computer. Be aware that Sophos Web Appliances, for example, can be used to control access to websites like Facebook. It also can be used to block malicious **phishing** ("an attempt to criminally and fraudulently acquire sensitive information, such as usernames, passwords, and credit card details, by masquerading as a trustworthy entity in an electronic communication") and virus-infected webpages.[84] Using spyware can help keep unwelcome visitors out of your computer's information.

Some organizations are taking a direct attack on Facebook. The Ohio Education Association, the state's largest teachers' union, sent teachers a memo discouraging them from using MySpace and Facebook. "The union worries that students will create 'imposter' sites, pose as adults and engage in conversations with teachers, or use online communication to make allegations against educators. Teachers who make inappropriate postings on Web sites risk losing their licenses or facing other punishment."[85]

LEARNING EXPERIENCE: Interested in finding out about *your* Facebook awareness? If so, do Activity 10.5.

ACTIVITY 10.5
Facebook Awareness

Circle whether you believe each of these statements is T(rue) or F(alse).

T   F   You should be cautious of friend requests.
T   F   You should adjust your privacy settings to match your level of comfort, and review them often.
T   F   You should be cautious about posting and sharing personal information, especially information that could be used to identify you or locate you offline, such as your address or telephone number.
T   F   You should report users and content that violate the Facebook Terms of Use.
T   F   You should block and report anyone that sends you unwanted or inappropriate communications.
T   F   You should not post your phone number on Facebook.
T   F   Facebook's user interface, the result of its fundamentally collegiate, video gamer sensibility, is not designed to be an effective business tool.
T   F   Facebook developers often spring new features on users without warning.
T   F   Facebook phishing (scamming) is a reality.

All of the statements are True. If you answered False to any statement, you need a refresher course on Facebook awareness.

Text Messaging

Text messaging, or *Short Message Service* (SMS) is communication of very short messages via cell phones. Estimates are that ninety-five percent of sixteen- to twenty-four-year olds use text messaging regularly, and teenagers send nearly one hundred texts per day.[86]

Because texting is immediate and spontaneous, it can be an easy and fast way to connect. Texting allows users to quickly send a short message to someone without the necessity of dialing a phone, waiting for a response, and then talking for an unlimited amount of time. Texting allows people who are not near computers or need privacy to send a quick message. Because texting is silent and discreet, you can text without anyone knowing it and not disturb anyone. Unlike using the Internet, you are not bombarded with messages from strangers. The only people who can text you are those who have your cell number.

Texting has become an important medium of interpersonal communication. Informing people of safety issues and locating someone are all positive aspects of text messaging. Many campuses have set up a texting system for emergency notification. Businesses may encourage employees to keep in touch via texting while traveling. In addition, texting is often used in fun and playful communication.

Texting can cause problems when people are supposed to be focused on something else (when driving, in a meeting, at a family dinner, or in class).

Texting can divert focus. Research indicates that in one recent year *text messaging contributed to nearly one thousand vehicle crashes* involving sixteen- and seventeen-year-old drivers.[87] The same report indicated that:

- Almost 50 percent of all drivers between the ages of eighteen and twenty-four are texting while driving.
- One-fifth of experienced adult drivers in the United States send text messages while driving.
- Over 60 percent of American teens admit to risky driving, and nearly half of those that admit to risky driving also admit to text messaging behind the wheel.
- Over one-third of all young drivers, ages twenty-four and under, are texting on the road.

Laws against driving and texting have been passed in some states and cities.[88]

The Chartered Society of Physiotherapists has warned that the "increase in Text messaging may contribute to a rise in repetitive strain injuries (RSI) which is pain and swelling of the tendons at the base of the thumb and wrist."[89] An effect of RSI is the inability to hold a pen or pencil, which can have severe effects on academic work and future job success.

Texting may be causing a general deterioration of writing skills in other communications. Academically, students may lose their ability to correctly spell words, use correct grammar, and develop a complete thought with a back-up idea. Teachers have found that some students have actually started to turn in assignments in texting format and language. For example, a professor at Syracuse University cites an example of a student who left him this note: "hi prof how are u culd u tell me my sm grade—tim[.]"[90]

There may be a temptation to use texting for cheating in academic settings. Since students can text an outside of class accomplice to look up materials while taking exams, many academic institutions are forbidding students to bring or activate phones during classes.

Texting can be addictive. There are students who are so obsessed with their text messages that they have been determined to have **texting addiction**.[91] They must check their phones constantly, thus not listening attentively in class, not eating properly because of the need to be available for quickly answering messages, and losing sleep because of the need to be instant and present so that you don't miss a message.[92] It is estimated that the average teen sends twenty-three hundred text messages a month.[93] This type of constant texting has the disadvantages of being distracting, preventing teens from having adequate time to think through ideas, problems, and actions. Further, research suggests that texting can make people overly dependent on others because they text friends when trying to make even minor decisions.[94] "Research shows that there has been a big rise in the number of behavioral addictions, and many involve Texting."[95]

Key Terms

Electronically Mediated Communication (EMC)	cyber stalking
e-commerce	e-lingo
e-mail bankruptcy	e-bbreviations
e-mail twitching	blog
cyber addiction	social networking
flaming	Facebook addiction
sexting	phishing
cyber bullying	text messaging
	texting addiction

Competencies Check-Up

Interested in finding out what you learned in this chapter and how you use the information? If so, take this competencies check-up.

Directions: Indicate the extent that each statement applies to you:

1—Never   2—Seldom   3—Sometimes   4—Often   5—Usually

____1. I recognize the values and limitations of electronically mediated communication and adapt my mediated communication accordingly.

____2. I use the Internet in positive ways, such as to gain pleasure, to relax, and to escape from everyday concerns.

____3. If I use the Internet, I use it to nourish my existing relationships.

____4. I recognize the close connection between electtronically mediated communication and development of the self and interpersonal communication.

____5. I use electronically mediated communication in positive ways (such as to create community, to create or enhance effective relationships).

___ 6. I am not obsessive about my electronically mediated communicating. I do not allow the computer or texting or Facebook or twittering to substitute for quality relationships, give me a way to hide from face-to face relationships, or interfere with the relationships I already have.

___ 7. I do not engage in abusive electronically mediated communication by flaming, cyber bullying, cyber stalking.

___ 8. I avoid computer argot and use appropriate and quality writing.

___ 9. I use communication, such as blogs and Facebook for positive purposes, such as knowledge sharing, communication, self-expression, learning, gaining self-awareness, self-marketing, campaigning for social reform, community building, experience tracking, and storytelling.

___10. I am careful about the information and opinions I reveal online, and recognize that I cannot retrieve that information.

___11. Where appropriate, I use online security measures, including encrypted e-mails and digital credentials.

___12. I respond promptly to important e-mails and keep the content of my e-mails brief, appropriate.

___13. I am aware that there is no such thing as a private e-mail conversation.

___14. I am aware that software is available that can enable an employer, service provider, or a disgruntled colleague, or the legal system to use my electronically mediated communication against me.

___15. I don't say anything on the Internet that I would be ashamed for my family, boss, or best friend to read.

Scoring: A total of 45 suggests that you have basic competencies in your computer mediated communication. Even a score over 60, however, suggests you may need to improve in some areas.

I-Can Plan!

Revisit test items in the Competencies Check-Up with a score of less than 5 and create a plan for strengthening your communication skills. Pay particular attention to any items with a score of less than 3 because these areas may need considerable skill improvement. Only you can motivate yourself to become a more effective communicator in group contexts. Motivate yourself to develop and implement a concrete plan. In addition, pledge not to text while driving.

Activities

1. Develop a list of rules for yourself to ensure appropriate self-disclosure online. You can think of the nature of self-disclosure in face-to-face contexts and the unwritten rules in that context, and use the same good judgment online.

2. Here are some topics and questions that you might want to probe. Your instructor will tell you the format for processing your inquiry.

   a. Is it better to convey bad news via the computer rather than on the telephone or face-to-face?
   b. How can one convey nonverbals on the Internet?
   c. What are at least ten guidelines regarding writing style on the Internet?
   d. How does computer-mediated interpersonal communication vary in the workplace from two-way direct communication?
   e. What is the role of computer-mediated interpersonal communication for the college student?
   f. What is the effect of psychological distancing on interpersonal communication?
   g. What are some personal guidelines, beyond those discussed in the text, regarding cyber addiction?
   h. What is an Internet relay chat?
   i. Define and explain the virtual community.
   j. What is the role of information overload on the Internet?
   k. Compare and contrast electronic and traditional mail.
   l. What is computer phobia?
   m. What are techno prisoners?
   n. Read Greenfield, D. (1999). *Virtual addiction: Help for netheads, cyberfreaks, and those who love them*. New Harbinger Publications. Retrieved from www.newharbinger.com. Summarize the advice of the author.
   o. Read Wallace, P. (1999). *The psychology of the Internet*. New York: Cambridge University Press. Retrieved from www.cambridge.edu. Summarize the advice of the author.

CHAPTER 11

Interpersonal Communication Skills

Learning Outcomes

After reading this chapter, you should be able to:

- Use appropriate self-disclosure as you express yourself to others.
- Recognize approval-seeking behavior.
- Manage different points of view by understanding compliance-gaining strategies, power, fair-fighting techniques, handling criticism, and apologizing appropriately.
- Improve your conversational skills by effectively demonstrating conversational listening skills, conversational nonverbal skills, and giving directions.
- Use strategies for probing, making requests, and delivering bad news.
- Tap into your personal reservoir of creativity.

As Abbey was driving to work, she looked out the side window of her car and was both amused and horrified to realize that the man driving next to her was smoking a cigarette, talking on his cell phone, had a newspaper draped over his steering wheel and was attempting to navigate through traffic. She remembered having read a newspaper article that morning about the dangers of talking on a cell phone while driving. When she got to work she checked the paper and found the article. It said, "As people who drive a standard car—or stick shift—know you can drive a car with one hand, because you have one hand on the stick. But when you start talking, it's not the actual holding of the object that's important, it's the planning of the conversation, which takes away resources from attending to the road."[1] Thinking back to this morning's commute she was not surprised that the smoking/cell-talking/newspaper reading driver was maneuvering so erratically.

Being an effective intrapersonal and interpersonal communicator takes skills and understanding of the communication process. Knowing you can't multitask is one of these concepts. Sean realized that he needed to end his relationship with his roommate, but wondered how to do so without being aggressive. Tera's mother stopped by her daughter's house with some upsetting news, but was uncertain of how to share the information. Felicia tried to give her brother directions to navigate the confusing road layout on the way to her new apartment. These specific instances are just a few examples of times that require effective interpersonal communication strategies.

The essential elements of effective interactions include: commitment, equality, trust, respect, and communication skills.[2] People should gain the abilities to use these elements from their significant others (e.g., parents and teachers). Unfortunately, many people do not have the opportunity to learn these abilities with any high degree of competence because most schools don't teach specific oral and nonverbal communication skills and many families don't model these skills very effectively. So, here's your opportunity to hone or polish skills as you are exposed to methods to communicate about yourself, seek approval, manage difficult people, deal with power as it relates to communication, fight fair, handle criticism, apologize, converse, give directions, ask questions, make requests, deliver bad news, use interpersonal technology, and be creative.

The Self and Others

The view you have of yourself, your **self-concept**, guides your communication, as it determines what you will say and to whom you will say it. For example, if you perceive yourself to be a good communicator, you are likely to feel confident in your communication. But if you label yourself as "shy" or "apprehensive," you may find it difficult to express yourself. At the heart of this dynamic process is the premise that if you do not accept yourself, probably no one else will either. Your lack of confidence is easily picked up by those with whom you interact.

Some people worry about appearing too self-confident and being thought a braggart. Confidence and accepting yourself as a worthy person does not necessarily mean you are boasting. Sometimes you have to "blow your own horn" because no one else knows how to play the tune. You know yourself better than other people do because you know more about yourself and your skills and talents. There is a difference, however, between tooting your own horn (e.g., sharing with others your accomplishments) and playing a symphony (e.g., exaggerating your accomplishments).

How well do you like yourself? **Self-love** means accepting yourself as a worthy person because you choose to do so. You can still listen to the input of others and attempt to make changes in yourself, but to be a healthy communicator, you need to accept yourself as a viable human being. Your concern for self does not, of course, permit you to physically, sexually, or psychologically injure others. What are some strategies you can use to reinforce and increase your self-esteem?

Use positive self-talk. Every day you can look in the mirror and through self-talk tell yourself what a good person you are, how you are accomplishing your objectives, and how much you like yourself. **Affirmations**, positive statements intended to guide positive thinking (e.g., "I am a kind person," "I can speak to others in social situations") can be constructive.

Your self-concept guides your communication, as it determines what you will say and to whom you will say it.

MESSAGES THAT COMMUNICATE THE SELF

Self-disclosure involves sharing information about yourself including your history as well as your present emotions and thoughts. It can improve intimacy and rapport in interpersonal communication because, when you share information about yourself, you allow yourself to be "seen."[3] This revealing of the self can be accomplished through verbal or nonverbal messages.

Self-disclosure must be appropriate. Whether or not the atmosphere is supportive influences how vulnerable you will allow yourself to become. The amount and type of disclosure also will be based on the relationship between the people involved. The deepest level of self-disclosure occurs when two people open themselves in such a way that each can be hurt by the other's actions.

Self-disclosure allows others to understand you as well as helping you to understand yourself. When you talk about yourself, you allow the other person into yourself. Not only does the other person learn about you, but you learn about yourself. As you think, organize your thoughts, and verbalize aloud, you can make sense of your perceptions and experiences. One of the activities in psychotherapy, for example, is to get a client to talk about herself or himself in order to bring about self-understanding of the person's thoughts and feelings. The intent is to help the patient learn who she or he really is. This understanding opens the doors to acquiring the skills needed to cope with the person's real or perceived world.

All your communication messages are an expression of your self. To be an effective interpersonal communicator, you can take steps to make sure your messages clearly belong to you. Here are some skills you can apply in sending effective messages.[4]

- *Use personal pronouns—I, my—to indicate that you own the message as your personal perspective.* Your perception belongs to you and should not be voiced as a universal truth. In other words, saying "we" or "you" deflects obligation from yourself, stops you from assuming responsibility and escaping personal accountability. Stating, "I *believe* that the college should include sexual orientation in its civil rights code" illustrates that it is *your* opinion, you own it. Saying, "*Everybody* thinks that prayer should be allowed in public schools," does not indicate your ownership of the proposal.
- *Describe behavior without judgment or evaluation.* Stay away from interpreting and embellishing the truth. Tell exactly what you *saw* (fact), avoiding what you *felt* (emotion). Don't interpret, don't assign meaning to things you don't know to be absolutely true. If you saw a confrontation, say, "I was standing about five feet from Omar when Beth walked up and slapped him." Don't embellish by stating, "Beth looked really mad and her face indicated that she was having a bad day. Then, she let out her feelings by slapping Omar." Unless you are a scholar on nonverbal communication, and maybe not even then, you don't really know what Beth's face indicated (you'd be guessing based on your experiential background) and, unless you know that she said specifically that she was having a "bad day," that is outside of your reporting arena.
- *Describe realistic and specific potential changes in behavior that can improve the quality of the communication.* Rather than saying, "You are always late and you are doing that just to aggravate me," state, "The last two times we were supposed to meet you were more than ten minutes late. Your coming late makes me think that I'm being taken advantage of, so I'd like you to come on time next time."
- *Adapt your message to the knowledge and interests of the other person.* Make sure that you recognize that you may have information that others lack. Ask yourself, "What would I have to know in order to understand what I'm explaining if I didn't know what I now know?" With that information, relate all the necessary details. Also ask yourself if what you want to talk about is of interest to the other person.
- *Describe your personal feelings.* Use **I-statements**—explaining ideas from your perspective rather than your perceived perspective of the other person. Stating, "I get concerned when you tell me that we will meet at one o'clock and you don't get here until one thirty." This is nonaccusatory and is impossible to refute. You are explain-

ing from your perspective, which the other person can't say is "wrong." You know how you feel and think. That is your reality.

- *Use nonverbal messages to support your verbal messages.* Direct eye contact, a firm handshake, keeping an acceptable distance away from another person, appropriate touching, or refraining from touching all add to your message's effectiveness.
- *Make sure the nonverbal and verbal messages agree so your communication is believable.* Our messages can be misunderstood if what we are doing does not parallel what we are saying. Sarcasm is based on a lack of congruency between the verbal and the nonverbal. Saying you have lots of time to talk to someone, as you look at your watch, move slightly away from the person, and turn sideways like you are about to leave, can confuse your conversational partner.
- *Repeat important messages through various channels.* In giving directions, you may present the information face-to-face as you trace the route on a map showing how to get to your apartment for the party, or write out specific directions.
- *Avoid purposeless babbling just to keep a conversation going or allowing you to egospeak.*

Sensitive and clear messages can help you to create positive relationships with family and friends.

LEARNING EXPERIENCE: Are you interested in what characteristics you consider important in a friend as part of your understanding of your self? If so, do Activity 11.1.

SEEKING APPROVAL

Most people want to be liked, supported, and accepted. Although people understandably want the acceptance of their friends and other significant people in their lives, **approval-seeking behaviors** can work against effective relationships. Too often individuals seek approval because they want to please others at the expense of their own needs and feelings of self-worth. Some people are so controlled by others—strangers, relatives, friends, or employers—that they seem immobile. Thus, they find themselves at a standstill and unable to make decisions for themselves. Unfortunately, this behavior turns one's destiny over to other people.

If you want to eliminate approval-seeking behavior as a major need in your life, keep these guidelines in mind:

Speak up. If you think someone else is trying to control you by withholding approval, say so. Use I-statements and assert yourself rather than you-statements, which attack the other person. For example, say, "I think I have the right to go if I accept the responsibility for my actions." Instead of "You can't tell me what to do."

Follow personal goals. When you are faced with disapproval, ask yourself, "If she agreed with me, would I be better off?"

Accept yourself. Accept that some people will never understand you and that this is perfectly acceptable. The odds are, if you have unique ideas, stand up for your beliefs, and don't allow others to intimidate you, you will alienate some people. So what? No one is liked by everyone! This does not mean that you should intentionally alienate

ACTIVITY 11.1
What Do I Believe Constitutes a Friend?

What do you think constitutes a good friend? What do you consider the most important to least important characteristics of a close, personal friend?

Directions: Check each item that you think is vital and necessary for a person to be considered by you to be a good friend.

_____About my same age
_____Frankness
_____Job accomplishments
_____Keeps confidences
_____Personal loyalty
_____Physical attractiveness
_____Sense of humor
_____Similar educational level
_____Similar income
_____Similar occupation
_____Being emotionally supportive
_____Warmth and affection
_____Honesty
_____Other:

Using the information from this activity, write a one- or two-sentence description of the kind of person who has the qualities to be your close, personal friend and what that says about you and your self.

others, but you need to accept yourself and your ideas, and present yourself and your concepts in a communicatively competent way, and let what happens happen.

Believe in yourself. You can refuse to argue or try convincing anyone of the rightness of your stance. You can simply believe it and if someone else doesn't, then that is his or her decision. Not everyone will always agree with what you say, as you don't believe everything that someone else says or believes. You might adopt the mantra, "If they don't like me or what I believe in or say, that's their problem, not mine." Be aware that with that statement, you assume the responsibility to accept the consequences of your actions.

Trust yourself. You can follow your perceptions based on your personal experiences and values as you trust your feelings.

Stop verifying your ideas by having them substantiated by others. You are capable of making your own analyses and decisions, which fit your individual needs and expectations.

Know the difference between your feelings and your thoughts. What you feel is emotional. What you think is logical. The former doesn't need proof or thoughts, the latter does.

Stop apologizing for your beliefs. Work at eliminating the apologies you make when you are not wrong or sorry for what you have said or done. Use of phrases like "This is probably a dumb idea, but . . .," or "Excuse me for even suggesting this, but . . .," or "I'm really not an expert on the subject, so I shouldn't even be suggesting this, but . . .," are degrading what you are saying and diminish both you and the idea.

Do you accept yourself? The **self-fulfilled person**—the person who confidently chooses what to reveal and to whom—holds a positive self-concept and cannot be intimidated into self put-downs. Self-fulfilled individuals understand that all people lack perfection and there will always be problems, frustrations, and failures in life. Self-fulfilled people have learned to adapt and adjust to life's negatives.

LEARNING EXPERIENCE: Interested in finding about your friendship as it relates to your being a self-fulfilled person? If so, do Activity 11.2.

MANAGING DIFFERENT POINTS OF VIEW

Every individual is just that, an individual. We all have different points of view, life experiences, knowledge levels, and influences from family and culture that help create who we and how we think. Your effectiveness in handling yourself in the face of different points of view is an important aspect of interpersonal communication. How effectively can you persuade others? Stand up for yourself in the face of a power imbalance? Fight fairly? Handle criticism? And genuinely apologize for your mistakes?

Gaining Compliance

In your relationships with other people, you often need to gain **compliance**, entice others to do something for you, agree with you, or otherwise engage with you. To that end you need to apply the skills of persuasion to your interpersonal communication. Physicians must work to get patients to follow their recommended treatment plans. Parents rely on persuasive strategies to gain their children's compliance with their wishes. The same is true of professors regarding students.

Research on compliance-gaining strategies reinforces the transactional and give-and-take nature of the process. Some compliance-gaining strategies that have been found to work effectively include:[5]

Pregiving. In *pregiving*, before requesting an action, you give someone something he or she may want in order to aid in convincing them to act as you might want. For example, give your significant other a gift of a new hiking backpack and then request agreement with your plan to go backpacking. This may appear to be a form of bribery. And you are right to classify the strategy as such. Certain kinds of

ACTIVITY 11.2
Keeping Friends

These questions may help you consider whether you are increasing or decreasing the quality of your friendships.

Directions: Answer yes or no to each question as it pertains to you:

Y N   1. Do you enjoy doing favors for people you care about?
Y N   2. Do you publicly find fault with other people?
Y N   3. Can you keep a secret?
Y N   4. When a friend receives public recognition for his or her efforts, do you secretly wish it were you being recognized?
Y N   5. Are you generally cheerful and happy?
Y N   6. Do you see friends only if they will do things you like to do?
Y N   7. Do you feel free to share your reactions and feelings with your friends?
Y N   8. When a friend hurts your feelings, do you decide the person is not really your friend and avoid him or her?
Y N   9. Do you promise to do things and then forget about them?
Y N   10. Do you sometimes tell others things a friend told to you in confidence?
Y N   11. Is it easy to see good qualities in others?
Y N   12. Do you seek out activities and projects that you and your friends can do together?
Y N   13. Are you often depressed and negative?
Y N   14. Do you feel genuinely happy when a friend succeeds?
Y N   15. Do you hide your "true self" from your friends?
Y N   16. When you are angry with a friend, do you sit down with him or her and try to solve the problem?

Answers:
1. Yes 2. No 3. Yes 4. No 5. Yes 6. No 7. Yes 8. No 9. No
10. No 11. Yes 12. Yes 13. No 14. Yes 15. No 16. Yes

Analysis:
14–16 correct answers: You have friends because you are a friend to others. You are open, trustworthy, reliable, supportive, cooperative, committed, and caring, each a true art.
10–13 correct answers: You have friends, but some of them stick with you despite your faults.
5–9 correct answers: You find yourself looking for friends, but unable to find them. Look at yourself carefully and plan some changes.

What did your scores tell you about the quality of your friendships as they relate to your being a self-fulfilled person?

Source: Based on Johnson, D. W. (2000). *Reaching out: Interpersonal effectiveness and self-actualization.* Boston: Allyn and Bacon, pp. 34–35.

bribery make life easier, and if they are not illegal or immoral, may be desirable to get the desired end result.[6]

Liking. In order to assist in the persuasive interpersonal act, try and put the other person in a receptive mood by being friendly to them. For example, offer to help another student with a class project so she will be inclined to have positive feelings toward you and might, therefore, be open to a suggestion that she assist you in studying for the final exam.

Promising. In proposing assistance or conformity to your view you might make a promise. A parent might promise a toy if the six-year-old behaves well at Grandma's house. The promise of a reward can entice people to comply.

Influencing. Influencing is when you include in your proposal the intention to use influence or control over the other person if he or she doesn't conform to your request. For example, when you were a teenager your parents told you that if you failed to return home by curfew, you would be grounded. That is a threat. Of course, the threat would only have been successful if you knew that your parents would enforce their words with actions. Don't threaten unless you are willing to carry out the action proposed and have the power to do so.

Self-feelings. A person may include a statement of guilt in a proposal. A father might tell a daughter that given how hard he works to help pay for tuition, he will feel hurt if she doesn't receive high grades next semester.

Esteem. Because one of our basic needs is pleasure, people often strive for esteem, achieving personal recognition as part of that need satisfaction. Indicating that there is potential recognition or praise may sway the person to your side. For example, as a manager at a business you might indicate to a worker that he could be a candidate for the "Employee of the Month Award," which might inspire him to work harder.

Debt. You may decide to indicate to a person who is indebted to you for a past favor that she "owes you one" in order to get her to comply with your request. For example, asking a friend to drive you to the airport could include the comment that she owes you a return favor since you gave her your Adolescent Psychology class notes when she missed class.

Of course, these strategies can backfire if you aren't careful regarding when and how you use them. You must consider the people involved, the setting, and your purpose when deciding which, if any, of these strategies you will use. Realistically, people might consider any of these tactics to be manipulative, so be ready for a potential rejection. It must also be realized that some people, no matter your good will and intentions, simply are not interested in being helpful or cooperative.

Power

Power is the ability to control what happens—to create things you want to happen and to block things you don't want to happen. Through power you can choose for yourself or control the choices of others. Power is often perceived to be negative. In and of itself, power is not negative. *How the power is used can turn it into a positive or negative factor.*

The perception that power is bad may stem from several causes:

People can abuse power. Power may cause one person to win at the expense of another.

Power contradicts the belief that all humans should be equal. If one person has more power, the other person cannot be equal. In reality, in few if any relationships are the participants equal in all matters.

Power can cause waste. Sometimes there's really no opportunity to gain anything, but a power struggle can waste resources in the process. Putting in time, effort, or finances when there is nothing to gain from it, seems foolish.

Potential problems can result when people fail to exert their power. First, people who feel powerless often lack the ability to make choices about their relationships, such as which to maintain and which to terminate. Second, powerless people may feel that they lack the ability to make choices and, therefore, settle for unsatisfying relationships. In addition, people who feel powerless in one situation often inappropriately take out their frustrations in other situations.

Many Euro-Americans are raised to believe that they have **empowerment**, have great control over their lives and even the lives of others, that they are "masters of their own fate," and that they can "pull themselves up by their bootstraps." Not only do many Euro-Americans want power, and think they deserve it but they also do not want other people to have power over them or power at all.

This belief has a long history. In the 1700s, the Revolutionary War was a power conflict between the British who wanted to keep control and the colonists who wanted self-power. The Civil War was a conflict for elimination of the power of one group over another (e.g., slave owners and slaves). The civil rights movement, when Blacks and their helpmates used boycotts, marches, and the legal system to alter the power position held by others over them, is yet another illustration of action that can result in the shift of power. Unionization, the women's rights movement and the present-day gay rights movement are other illustrations of attempts to give equal power to those who were and are oppressed.

The desire to take control of oneself, of course, is not prominent in all cultures. Most of the world, in fact, believes that an outside source or fate—be it "God," "the gods," "karma," or "nature"—controls their lives. Many Muslims use the phrase, "it is Allah's will," and many Hindus believe that life events are their karma being acted out. In both instances, these followers do not feel powerless, they perceive their mission is not to seek power. Generally, many of these people hold the view that the legitimacy of power is irrelevant.

LEARNING EXPERIENCE: Interested in finding out about your feelings of empowerment? If so, do Activity 11.3.

Fair Fighting

When you find yourself in a power imbalance or a disagreement, do you know how to manage the conflict productively? By learning **fair fighting**, you can work toward an amicable solution to a problem and have **conflict resolution**, solving the problem. More importantly, fair fighting respects the importance of the relationship. This kind of effective conflict management in marriage, for example, is crucial to a stable relationship.[7] Despite disagreements, you must protect your relationship with your relational partner, coworkers, children, parents, and/or friends. Some fair-fighting strategies include:

Get as much information as you can, and adjust to the problem based on this information. Fact, rather than hearsay, speculation, or emotion is essential. The facts may show that the actual cause is different from the supposed cause of the conflict.

Keep arguments in the present tense. Do not argue about what happened in the past; the past can't be changed.

Do not try to make the other person change things that cannot be altered. We cannot trade in our relatives or become totally different people.

Avoid a fight that cannot be finished. Starting a stressful discussion never works when a person is walking out the door on the way to work, on a tight schedule, or when one or both parties are extremely tired.

The setting can affect a conflict. Disagreeing in public or in front of individuals who are not part of the conflict is poor strategy.

A fight can take place only if both parties participate. If the conflict is getting out of hand or has gone on too long, then one party should simply stop participating. The length of a constructive argument is normally about twenty minutes; people get tired and their reasonable intentions break down after that. When the participants start repeating the same arguments, they have run out of concepts regarding the issue and it is not uncommon, at that point, for one of the participants to start verbally or physically attacking the other person rather than dealing with the issue.[8]

Listen to your body. If you are aware of your voice getting louder, your body tightening up, or your hands making fighting fists, you should either physically leave or limit your role to that of a passive listener for a while.

Identify realistically what you need to get out of the transaction. Often we enter into a conflict situation without having identified our goals, which means we have no clarity of purpose and don't even know if the conflict is over.[9]

LEARNING EXPERIENCE: Interested in learning more about your fair fighting skills? If so, then do Activity 11.4.

ACTIVITY 11.3
My Feelings about Empowerment

Think of one of your important relationships and keep it in mind as you respond to the questionnaire. Each item has two alternatives. Your task is to divide 10 points between the two alternatives according to how well each describes you. You may give all 10 points to one alternative and none to the other, split the points evenly, 5 and 5, or assign any other combination of 10 points that seems appropriate.

1. When the other person says something with which I disagree, I
   _____a. assume my position is correct.
   _____b. assume what the other person says is correct.
2. When I get angry at the other person, I
   _____a. ask the other person to stop the behavior that offends me.
   _____b. say little, not knowing quite what to do.
3. When something goes wrong in the relationship, I
   _____a. try to solve the problem.
   _____b. try to find out who's at fault.
4. When I participate in the relationship, it is important that I
   _____a. live up to my own expectations.
   _____b. live up to the expectations of the other person.
5. In general, I try to surround myself with people
   _____a. whom I respect.
   _____b. who respect me.

Scoring:
Add all of your a responses. $a =$ _____
Add all of your b responses. $b =$ _____

The two totals, a and b, indicate how powerful you feel in the relationship you chose. The total number of points is 50, so one score could be 50 and the other zero, although that is unlikely.

If your b score is greater than your a score by 10 or more points, you probably feel somewhat powerless in your relationship because you see the other person's choices as more important than your own.

If your two scores are within 10 points of each other, you are probably unsure of your own power and your potential to influence others.

If your a score is greater than your b score by 10 or more points, you most likely feel quite powerful and in control of the choices you make in the relationship.

Do you exert the type of empowerment you would like to exert?

Yes ___   No ___

If not, which type of empowerment would you prefer to exercise?

What difference would this make in your relationships?

Source: Adapted from Cuming, P. (1981). Empowerment profile. *The power handbook* Boston: CB, pp. 2–5.

ACTIVITY 11.4
Conflict-Resolution

Step 1:
Recall the typical interactions you have with a particular person when the two of you disagree. Use the survey below to improve your conflict-resolution skills by indicating how you behave with the person you have identified. The more honest you can be on the survey, the more valuable it will be to you.

5: Almost always; 4: Often; 3: Sometimes; 2: Infrequently; 1: Rarely; 0: Never

___ 1. When I disagree, I am honest about the fact that I disagree, and why.

___ 2. When proven wrong, I admit it, rather than deny it or try to cover my tracks.

___ 3. In our oral exchanges I let the other person talk first; I don't have to get in my two cents' worth before he or she speaks.

___ 4. Before I respond to the other person's assertions, I ask questions or attempt to paraphrase his or her points to make certain I understand what was said.

___ 5. I stay calm and rational, being careful not to engage in name-calling or to otherwise say anything I'll regret later.

___ 6. When I do allow myself to get angry, I talk about that anger, rather than what the person did to elicit it.

___ 7. I am careful to direct my attacks at issues, not personalities. I condemn this person's claims without condemning him or her for making them.

___ 8. Even as I may disagree with the person's assertions, I recognize the validity of his or her feelings.

___ 9. I direct our attention to *fixing the future* rather than rehashing the past.

(continued)

ACTIVITY 11.4 (*continued*)

__10. I keep the focus on our comparative needs, *not our opposing positions*, so we can search for creative ways to meet both sets of needs and reach a common ground.

__11. I use *we*, *us*, and *our*, rather than I, me, and you, when discussing the problem.

Step 2:
Circle all scores below a 4.
Are these items more a reflection of your relationship with this particular person or more a reflection of your personal conflict-resolution style? One way to answer this question is to complete the survey for other people in your life with whom you have disagreements. Note which items tend to be scored differently (a reflection of the relationship) and which remain unchanged (a reflection of your conflict-resolution style).

What do these scores suggest you do differently the next time you come into conflict with this person or someone else?

Step 3:
Choose the new conflict-resolution behaviors you will try to adopt.
These recommended improvements in problem-solving skills are keyed by number to the items in the survey.

1. Be honest.
2. Admit mistakes.
3. Speak second.
4. Make sure you understand.
5. Bite your tongue.
6. Talk about your anger.
7. Condemn claims, not claimers.
8. Allow for feelings.
9. Fix the future.
10. Meet needs; don't take positions.
11. Favor cooperative pronouns regarding mutual problem-solving.

Source: Deep, S. & Sussman, L. (1998, January). *Power tools: 33 Management inventions you can use today.* New York: Perseus.

Handling Criticism

Criticism is the act of judging someone or something. Like it or not, you are going to be the recipient of criticism. Few people handle criticism well. Most people will attempt to deny or dismiss it. Criticism often triggers internal memories of being corrected by your parents, teachers, coaches, or clergy. Criticism may make you feel inadequate and unacceptable.

To deal with **constructive criticism**, criticism aimed at you with no intention of malice or vengeance on the part of the giver, without feeling the need to justify yourself or to counterattack, you can try these strategies:

When criticized, seek information. If someone accuses you of having done something, ask for specifics. For example, if a friend says that you are arrogant and put down other people, ask for specific examples or the precise instance that prompted the comment. Don't accept generalizations such as "you always act that way." Ask for specific instances, specific examples.

Paraphrase the ideas of the person making the criticism to clarify for both of you. Repeat the accusation and ask if that is what he or she really meant. That way you will be dealing with exactly what has been said. For example, "You said I put you down all the time. What do you mean by that? Give me a specific instance of when I did that."

Listen to the person and, if the criticism is just, accept his or her opinion. Use such techniques as: agreeing with the truth (admit the person is right); agreeing with the odds (if it is a projection into the future, agree with the possibility for its occurrence); agreeing in principle (if the criticism comes in the form of an abstract ideal against which you are being unfavorably compared, you can agree with it in principle without agreeing with the comparison); or agreeing with the critic's perception (accept that the critic has the right to perceive things the way he or she does). For example, if you are accused of spending too much time studying and not enough socializing, and you feel this is true, why not simply agree rather than arguing that you have a right to spend your time as you wish? Or say, "I never thought about it from that perspective," or, "That's an interesting perspective."

In dealing with criticism, recognize that much of it is well intentioned. Family members, friends, or the boss will tell you how to change for what they perceive is "your own good." This criticism does not mean that they are right or wrong or that you have to take their suggestions.

Remember that no one has a crystal ball to see into the future. Your desires, needs, and goals are ultimately your responsibility, and you can do as you wish as long as you also are willing to accept the consequences. You might feel justified and healthy with the attitude: "I am what I am, and I'll be that way no matter what you say!"

Apologizing

Have you ever broken a promise? Have you offended someone by being sarcastic when it was perceived to be serious and not funny? Have you ever acted inappropriately toward someone you really like? If the answer to any of these questions is, "yes," what did you do about it?

We all have said or done things that hurt or offended a personal friend, a significant other, or even a stranger. In the Euro-American culture, one key to getting along with people is knowing when and how to apologize. An **apology** is an earnest expression of regret for inappropriate words or deeds. The way we react to having offended someone has a great deal to do with our background. If you've been brought up to fight for being right, never giving in, or to hold a grudge, you are not likely to consider apologizing. If you've been brought up to believe that relationships are more important to happiness than being right or winning a battle, then an apology is probably your automatic reaction.

Apologies are not about who "won" or who "lost." Remember, relationships are not battles unless you or the other person choose to make war. Stubborn pride often leads to a loss of friends and can result in physical confrontations. "An apology is a tool to affirm the primacy of our connection with others."[10]

Sometimes, even though you may want to apologize, you may not know how. Too often people respond with a simple "sorry," which often has no real meaning to the other person.

A face-to-face apology is often best because you can display your honesty. It can be a humbling experience as you must see the other person's expressions, show yours, and probably hear a verbal and/or nonverbal reply. As one expert stated, the difficulty of a face-to-face apology is worthwhile because "you will be respected by the person you are addressing as well as by yourself more if you are able and willing to make your apology in this manner. Smiles, laughter, hugs, handshakes, and other displays of appreciation and affection are added benefits for both parties that are all possible when apologizing this way!"[11]

Here are some skills for making an effective apology:[12]

Take responsibility. The starting point is that any apology warrants a change of behavior such as self-admission. Admit to yourself that you have offended someone. You may know this right away, the other person's reaction may let you know you have done something hurtful, someone else might alert you to the situation, or you may realize it yourself at a later time. However you find out, you must admit you have done wrong and accept responsibility for your actions or you won't be prone to take action.

Explain. Recognize that your actions caused a problem for the other person. If you can do so, and it is appropriate, explain *why* you acted as you did. For example, if you were angry and blurted out something you regret having said, you might state, "I'm really having a bad day, and what I said wasn't really aimed at you. I'm mad at myself and I took it out on you. I'm sorry." On the other hand, many people have little interest in excuses, and instead want you to focus on how you will change your behavior in the future. For satisfying that need you might add, "I'll try not to take it out on you the next time."

Show your regret. The other person needs to see that you are aware that what you did was wrong. That is, if you think you were wrong say you are sorry or ashamed with a phrase such as "I felt bad the minute I told your secret. You trusted me, I betrayed your trust. I shouldn't have done that." Without earnest verbal and nonverbal regret, the apology will sound phony and, maybe even sarcastic, possibly causing bigger conflicts.

Repair the damage or at least try and lessen the emotional hurt. To be complete, an apology should attempt to correct the injury. If you damaged someone's property, offer to fix it. If the damage is emotional, you might ask, "I'm really sorry. What can I do to make it up to you?" There may be nothing concrete you can do, but a repair offer is often crucial to show your sincerity. You might follow up by stating something appropriate, such as, "I'll try and be more considerate in the future. In the meantime, let me buy you a cup of coffee."

Use good timing. If possible, apologize immediately for little things. For example, if you bump into someone, say you're sorry right away. If you have done something more serious, however, like insult a friend out of anger, you may need some time to figure out what to say. A quick apology might not give you time to realize what you've done, why you did it, and what the ramifications might be.

Choose an appropriate conduit. What's the best conduit for an apology? Letters, e-mail, voice-mail, the phone, face-to-face are all message channels that are available. The first three are impersonal. They may be easier, and save you from facing the person directly, but they are usually not as emotionally effective. Only resort to those if there is no way to get face-to-face. If a person lives far away then there may be no choice. If that's the case, the phone is probably a better alternative than a written presentation. At least hearing the tone of your voice can be a clue to the honesty of your message. If you do it by voice-mail, it is best to plan exactly what you want to say, and keep it between thirty seconds and a minute. Long rambling messages lose their impact.

LEARNING EXPERIENCE: Interested in practicing an effective apology strategy? If so, do Activity 11.5.

The person who has been wronged may reject your apology. That is not your problem. If you offer a sincere apology then you have fulfilled your obligation to the relationship. You have recognized what you did or said was wrong and taken an action to let the other person know that you are remorseful and willing to fix the problem. You can only be responsible for one person's actions, your own. You cannot make another person act as you would like him or her to act. Therefore, their acceptance of your apology is beyond your control.

Conversational Skills

Conversations, verbal interactions between people, usually start with small talk and then move to more in-depth sharing. **Small talk** is an exchange of information with someone on a surface level. Small talk takes place at informal gatherings, parties, bars, and meetings. The information exchange centers on *biographics* (personal information that tells about yourself, such as your name, occupation or college major, hometown, college attended or attending) or slightly more personal information (hobbies, interests, future plans, acquaintances). You can say something positive about the person's appearance, ask for advice, or ask a question. Small talk usually goes on for fifteen minutes, and then in-depth conversation starts. If you are in a work situation the small

ACTIVITY 11.5
Write An Apology

Think of a problem or mistake that you made recently, which deserved an apology. Perhaps you have already apologized, but think about what you might have done using the strategies outlined in this chapter. If you feel wronged by another person, you can write this activity according to the way you wish the other person had apologized!

Write a paragraph explaining what you could say and do in each step. Indicate specific words in quotation marks.

1. Take responsibility.
2. Explain.
3. Show your regret.
4. Repair the damage.
5. Use good timing.

My paragraph:

---

talk may be brief because in business contexts people often go quickly to the point of their interaction due to time constraints and corporate protocol.

People usually like to talk about themselves, their perceptions, and their experiences and are stimulated by various communication techniques. These include questions, which are powerful devices for building conversations.

Questions encourage people to open up by drawing them out (e.g., What university do you go to? What's your major? I've been considering switching my major to communication; do you think that's a good idea?).

Questions aid you in discovering the other's attitudes (e.g., Why did you decide to be a communication major?).

Questions keep the conversation to the topic at hand. Whenever a response is irrelevant, ask a follow-up question that probes for more information about the topic (e.g., What do you feel the future job market is for communication majors?).

Questions can be used to direct the conversation. A question can change the topic, probe for more information, or keep the conversation going.

Questions help you gain information and clarify meanings. If what the person says is not clear, you can ask for definitions or examples or ask for the source or basis of information.

To use questioning most effectively, start with easy questions, ask short questions, and after each question wait for an answer. Let your partner know you are listening by giving nonverbal feedback such as "Uh huh" and "that's interesting," while you are looking at the person.

Nonverbal communication plays an important role in conversation. If you do not think so, pay attention to the facial expressions and postures of the person to whom you are talking. Quick glances away may indicate that the person is anxious to leave and the same may be implied when that person glances repeatedly at a watch, looks around the room, or shifts from one foot to the other, or begins to turn the body away from you. If, however, the person leans forward, is intently looking at you, or is directly facing you, then the interaction is probably positive. Judge whether to continue or end the interaction based on these cues.

One of the biggest problems for people who are nervous about conversations is staying calm and not giving themselves negative messages like, "I'm really messing this up." Periods of silence are all right. Other specific suggestions for conversational continuance include:

Turn the spotlight on the other person. Discover the person's interests. People are usually flattered by your curiosity about them.

Listen closely for a nugget to explore that will interest you both. Follow up with such phrases as, "What did you mean by that?" "Oh, that must have been exciting," or "It sounds like that was tough on you."

Keep it light. Generally stay away from controversial subjects on your first meeting. If you need to voice your opinion, indicate it with a soft phrase such as, "I can see we look at that differently," or "That's an interesting opinion."

Try not to be nonverbally confrontational. How you stand while speaking may have an affect on the conversation. Research shows that Euro-American women, for example, tend to face each other directly when interacting, while males tend to stand side-by-side/hip-to-hip.[13] Men standing face-to-face can indicate conflict. If you are a male and align yourself with a conversational mate, watch his facial reactions and body. If he seems anxious or irritated, change your body alignment. If you are a woman and want to create an inviting position for conversation with another woman, face her directly. Again, be aware of your partner's reactions, and adjust your stance if necessary. The same concept holds true to getting too close to another person, or touching the person during the conversation. Be aware of cultural differences in body closeness and touching.

Remember that some people are difficult to get to know and that there are some people you may not want to get to know any better. The small talk at the start of a conversation can give you and a new acquaintance an opportunity to determine whether a closer relationship merits exploring.

Be aware that culture influences the way people talk conversationally. *(Note that in this discussion, generalizations are presented regarding trends of various cultural groups. These are based, whenever possible, on research findings and expert observations. They are in no way intended to lead to the conclusion that all members of the cultural group noted conform to the generalized patterns.)*

In general, Euro-American conversations are focused, especially between males, getting right to the point. Behind this directness is the assumption that a speaker ought to know explicitly the idea or information he or she wishes to convey. Educated Euro-Americans tend to speak using **analytical thinking** in which thought patterns emphasizing analysis and ideas are backed up with facts and examples. Analytical thinking dissects events and concepts and are linked into chains that lead the listener from the general idea to the conclusion in a sequential way. Analytical thinking is not the typical reasoning process of all cultures.

Holistic thinking, which looks at the big picture instead of dissecting events or concepts, is more typical in many South American, Asian, Arabic, American Indian, and African cultures and people descended from these cultures.[14] Storytelling and the use of parables is common in holistic thinking. Though the stories may be interesting, they sometimes confuse Euro-Americans because the stories fail to answer questions and seldom have direct conclusions and often don't fall into the definition of "proof statements." Much is left to the receiver to interpret.

Unlike many of those in other cultures, Euro-Americans tend to be open to approaching strangers, often start conversations with new people, are responsive to strangers who approach them, and talk about personal issues. Some cultures are less open to invasion of personal space. People from some Asian cultures are more standoffish toward strangers, are more reluctant to approach them, and respond less favorably to conversations initiated by people they do not know,[15] and are sometimes uncomfortable talking about themselves. The same can be said for people from small towns in the United States, where newcomers and strangers are sometimes met with suspicion.

CONVERSATIONAL LISTENING SKILLS

Listening is a crucial part of conversations. People who can converse with strangers effectively are invariably good listeners. To be a good listener, learn how to paraphrase the speaker's ideas, repeat the person's name as you are introduced, continue to use the name during the conversation as it will help you remember it and make the other person feel that you are centering on him or her. You'll want to maintain eye contact and listen both with your eyes and ears for clues for what topics are of interest to the other conversant. Be sure to allow the speaker to finish her or his point before you respond, because interruptions are considered by some to be very annoying, especially to those from mannerly cultures like Japan and the various American Indian tribes. Asking questions is one of the most effective ways of opening and engaging in conversations. For openers, ask for biographic information. Listen to what the other person says and ask follow-up questions that probe more deeply into the topic. More specific suggestions about listening in conversations include the following:

Listen to the concerns of others. Both people should get an opportunity to participate. Often people ask questions only so that they can give their own answers. If you are interested in a real conversation, find out what others think and address their ideas. Nothing is more deadly than a personal monologue which centers on "I"-"I" and "Me"-"Me."

Don't assume. Too often we assume one thing and later find we were mistaken. Because physical and oral first impressions are not always accurate, give the other person a chance to prove he or she is worthy of your conversation or repugnant enough to be cast aside.

Before speaking, ask yourself what message is needed. Many people do not like to participate in small talk because it appears to offer no opportunity for in-depth discussion or because finding out little tidbits about people whom they are not interested in seems a waste of time.

Giving Directions

We often find ourselves giving other people directions. **Direction giving** includes instructions for accomplishing a task, achieving an effect, or getting somewhere. In giving directions, you are wise to include all the necessary details, organize the ideas in a specific order, and use terms that can be clearly understood. Some suggestions for direction giving include:

Give specific details. How many times have you asked someone for directions and been given only a general description that failed to make sense? Don't assume that because you know what you are talking about, the other person does also. Specifics help whether you are giving travel directions, assembly information, or a recipe.

Adapt to the listener's knowledge level. Have you ever attempted to assemble an electronic device that was accompanied by vague directions? Too often the directions are written by the experts who designed the item, and assume you understand more than you do. Adapt your message to the educational, experiential, and linguistic level of the listener. Don't speak down to people, but acknowledge that the important task is understanding, not impressing them with your vocabulary and knowledge. A student was overheard saying to a college economics instructor, "Why don't you teach this class in English?" He was teaching in English, the English of an expert in the field, not the English of a college student who had no experience in the field of economics.

Organize your ideas. Directions are easiest to follow when given in either a chronological or a spatial order. In chronological order, you indicate a step-by-step procedure by telling what is to be done first, second, third, and so on. Chronological organization is a good method to use when explaining how something should be assembled or operated. Spatial order is based on visual imaging which follows a mapping order or specific directions from one place to another (e.g., visual directions on a Garmin GPS is a spatial presentation). You can explain to a new student at your college how to get from the student union building to her next classroom building by using the student union as the starting point and then giving a place-to-place narration on how to get from that spot to the desired building.

Adapt to potentially different processing styles. If you know a person's listening/learning style you can adjust the directions to best fit the person's needs. For a global thinker, you could draw a picture. For example, global thinkers prefer pictures and oral directions with specific landmarks, such as restaurants or gas stations. Linear thinkers prefer maps and written directions. (See Chapter 3 for a discussion of linear and global thinkers/listeners.)

Use understandable terms. If a person cannot understand the directions, the explanation is of no value. The prospect of operating a computer is often more frustrating than it should be because in many instances the operational procedures are written in computer jargon rather than Standard English. No wonder many people have computer phobia!

LEARNING EXPERIENCE: Want to practice giving directions? If so, complete Activity 11.6.

ACTIVITY 11.6
Direction Giving

The members of your class have been divided into study groups. You have been selected to choose a place to meet. Select a place. On a separate sheet of paper, write the directions on how to get there from your communication's classroom. Assume that no one in the group is familiar with the venue. Be sure to organize the directions in a step-by-step spatial order.

After you have finished writing the directions, go to your communication classroom and follow your directions *exactly* as you've written them. Don't make any turns that are not on the map/directions.

How did you do?

Probing

Have you sat in a class confounded by what a professor was saying? Or, have you had someone give you directions, but you can't figure out what to do? The solution may center on asking questions.

The purpose of **probing** is to ask for information that is necessary to ensure that the sender's message is clear and free of noise. Probing is essential to effective communication. If, for example, you receive directions to begin a new procedure at work, you will want to ask questions of the trainer providing the instructions. If you are reluctant to ask for clarification for fear of appearing uninformed, you probably are just creating more problems for yourself. Later, when called on to actually perform the new procedure, you may be unable to do so. The interaction of questioning not only clarifies, but also creates involvement and higher attention in the conversation. Remember, if it is important for you to know, it is important for you to ask.

When you probe for information, word the queries in a way that the listener will know exactly what you need. Asking a specific, well-worded question will often solve your dilemma. If you cannot identify what you do not understand, recognize that confusion usually centers on the need for *restatement, definition,* or *clarification.*

Whether in school, at work, in the home, or talking with friends, your relationships will be enhanced through effective question asking.

Asking for a restatement can help you understand other people. Sometimes in explaining, people state their ideas in such a way that they are unclear. Confusion may be caused by the order in which the ideas were presented. For example, an explanation about assembling a piece of equipment that fails to tell the first step, second step, and so on will probably lead to not being able to complete the assembling. In this case you could ask, "Can you tell me exactly what I should do first, then what is second, and what do I do next?"

Asking for definitions can help you avoid problems associated with vague and overly difficult vocabulary. Asking someone to define his or her terms often clears up a misunderstanding. Terminology is often a problem between physicians and patients as the doctor uses medical terms to explain a patient's illness. Many professionals forget that the average person does not have much expertise in the subject. An explanation appropriate to a layperson's vocabulary is necessary. Ask, "What does [fill in the word] mean?"

Asking for clarification can help you understand the meaning of a message. Sometimes the basic information in a communication message is not enough. Clarification can be achieved through the use of examples, illustrations, and analogies. While listening to a lecture, you will find that the first few sentences dealing with each new concept tell the idea, and the rest of the statements clarify. Sometimes, however, senders forget to give examples, illustrations, or analogies. If the illustrations used are not clear, ask for new or additional ones. Asking for examples is especially helpful if you are a global listener or learner because you need examples to clarify and make abstract ideas concrete. Not asking for clarification could have life-or-death implications for a patient who doesn't ask the doctor if the newly prescribed medicine could cause a potential lethal drug interaction with other medicines the patient is taking.

Requesting information—asking a person to specify the exact nature of the information you need—should include a request in specific language that explains how the request should be answered. If you tell the research librarian that you are "looking for stuff" about Mexico, she is going to be unable to help you unless you give specifics. Are you looking for information on Mexico's connection to the H1N1 Flu (Swine Flu) during the 2009 epidemic, or the policies of the country regarding the drug trade? Whatever your interest, try to be as specific as possible.

If you are not presenting the request in person, indicate how you wish to receive the reply—by phone, e-mail, letter, or in person. If the information must be received by a deadline, be sure to specify the time and date as well. This information concludes the communication so that you and the other person both understand what is wanted and how your request will be processed.

Delivering Bad News

Delivering bad news is often difficult, no matter how strong your interpersonal communication skills. Few people want to be in the position of giving bad news, but you may have to tell someone about a seriously ill friend or loved one, a horrible accident, or the death of someone. When bad news is communicated poorly, it can result in confusion, excessive distress, and resentment. When the bad news is communicated effectively, the individual may be able to understand, accept, and adjust. The same strategies that health-care professionals find most beneficial can be positive strategies for all interpersonal communicators.[16] These include:

- *Provide full information or as much information as possible.*
- *Enlist the help of family and friends because many people receive bad news better when there is more than one person explaining the problem or tragedy.*
- *Take care of the person's immediate needs.*
- *Listen empathically, don't give advice.*
- *Don't diminish the other person's grief or loss by using trite statements such as "Everything will be all right," or "It's okay, it's not that bad," or, "I know how you feel." You* don't know how anyone else feels unless they tell you, and then you can only empathize with them, not feel the same way. You have never had the same experience, under the same conditions.
- *Encourage him/her to display their emotions.* This may be difficult for Euro-American males, who have often been told to control their emotions, or many Asians, who have been encouraged not to show emotions in public.
- *Help the person connect with support groups, training, or other useful professionals.* This may not be appropriate for individuals from non-Euro-American cultures, as worldviews concerning mental help may not be shared.
- *You—as the bearer of bad news—may need special help and support yourself as a way to help you handle your own stress.* (One of the authors of this book is a crisis counselor who sometimes needs an outlet to express his thoughts and feelings after a long period of doing interventions.)

Creativity

Creativity is one of the buzz words of the new millennium. In modern thinking, to be creative is to be valued—even if the creative person may sometimes be labeled as eccentric, nonconformist, or a troublemaker. We often value creativity because it is the ability to create things that are new and different and to think in unusual ways. In the Euro-American culture, the new and the unusual are what make life exciting! In spite of this, creative people may be labeled negatively because they force thinking in different modes, approach typical problem-solving techniques with new perspectives, and, in general, decrease conservative security.

CREATIVE THINKING

Creative thinking is looking for alternatives and ideas and expanding on and diverging from what is discovered. This differs from **usual thinking**, which concerns itself with one alternative or idea at a time and building one thought on the other. Usual thinking, in the Western world, proceeds by selecting a group of solutions that have previously been tried or and then narrowing in on fewer and fewer ideas and alternatives.

Usual thinkers are more comfortable with creating a well-developed plan for solving a problem, understanding how to approach a problem, and conducting an orderly search for information. They often ignore hunches, new and untried actions or ideas, and avoid considering several alternatives simultaneously. They are more secure with "thinking in the box" and using traditional solutions. People like accountants, computer technicians, and engineers often are usual thinkers.

In contrast, creative thinking requires a "looseness" that includes relying on hunches, avoiding overpreparedness, allowing a problem to be redefined as new information arises, and simultaneously looking at a variety of ideas and alternatives. Creativity calls for faith in yourself—faith that you can do what needs to be done by *expanding* how you look at things instead of *narrowing* your focus.Creativity also requires that the creative person must be willing to try and fail and try again if the "out of the ordinary" idea doesn't work.

Creativity offers many benefits, all of which, according to those who use it, can contribute to the quality of solutions and relationships. These include:

Creativity is essential if you hope to solve difficult mutual problems that conventional approaches can't settle. Inventions such as the paper clip, windshield wipers, the GPS, the x-ray machine, the light bulb and cell phones are all examples of items that were created out of the desire to create something that was needed, but hadn't been envisioned before.

Creativity can keep you out of ruts. When you can predict the contents of a dialogue that you and your best friend will have, you may be in a well-worn rut, one that, though probably comfortable, could increase feelings of dissatisfaction and boredom. It is common for couples, after knowing each other for a long time, to avoid certain topics altogether because each knows what both will say and how each will react. The end result can be a stifled, though safe, relationship.

Creativity offers choices. Creativity is important if you hope to discover alternatives that are potentially different and more unique ways of doing things—whether dividing up household chores, deciding where to go on a date, or completing a group assignment.

Creativity can help relationships. Did you know that one of the keys to successful relationships may be to creatively solve problems? Creativity is important if you want to discover new ways for your relationships to develop and different ways to solve problems. Repeating the same patterns, which have not worked before, but have become habitual because you can't think of any other approaches or because they're safe, may lead to stagnation in relationships and business dealings, and can be dangerous. One of the favorite phrases of Dr. Phil McGraw on his syndicated television show is, "How's that working for you?" What he is indicating is that if you are doing something and it isn't working, why are you continuing to do the same thing? It isn't going to fix what is wrong any more this time than it did the last time. If it is working, then there is reason to continue that practice. If not, break the pattern and create a new one.

REMOVING OBSTACLES TO CREATIVITY

Small children are naturally creative, probably because no one has yet told them to "think logically" or to "stay in the lines when you color." A child can think of unique methods of reaching the cookie jar on top of the refrigerator, novel ways of putting unconnected thoughts together (a child the authors of this book know was told to "look at the car being towed," which he converted to "look at the Carbine Toad," a two-gun carrying, ten gallon hat-wearing frog), and poetic ways to use language. Guess the age of the author of this poem who, upon seeing a sunset, declared: "I'd love to go for a ride on the rays and go to bed in sheets made of clouds." It was a four-year-old who said such a unique and creative thing.[17]

Before the age of four, a child spends as much as half the time dreaming, having hundreds of unconnected thoughts. From about three to five years of age, a child spends half the time engaged in poetic thinking, intuitively making associations and using metaphors and similes. From about age four to age six, a child spends half the time inventing, putting the poetic similes to practical use, such as by turning a stool, a drawer, and a counter top into "steps" to climb to some desired cookies.[18]

You may have trouble remembering your own creative acts as a child because of the obstacles that parents and teachers raised in your path—obstacles that said, "don't be creative." Most of us heard dos and don'ts that included, "Don't make a fool of yourself," "Follow the rules," and "That's not the right way to do this." But, in reality, does how to act, how to think, have rules? Do trees have to be colored brown and green? Why can't a cat be named "Woof?" And, why does every family member have to believe the same things?

Obstacles to creativity may be classified as either cultural or personal barriers.

Cultural obstacles stem from the values and attitudes that a culture considers important. For example, whereas the high value that Euro-American culture places on individuality and competition should encourage the risk-taking required for creative problem-solving, the high value placed on logic and practicality may inhibit solutions requiring feelings and imagination. Many adults learn that to be other than serious and humorless—except during specified times—is to risk being perceived as frivolous. Although many teachers may say they like students who are creative, challenging, and assertive, many really seem to prefer students who are pleasant, compliant, and obedient.

Some students who are diagnosed with Attention Deficit Disorder don't have any disorder other than not being compliant and being creative in their approaches to school. Not wanting to sit quietly for long periods of time, doing repetitive work, which they find boring, their minds and bodies want to be free to act creatively.[19] Some of these same diagnosed "ADD kids" can sit and play computer games for hours on end. Where is their attention deficit?

There appear to be three personal obstacles to creativity: (1) habitual ways of doing things, (2) beliefs about how things are done, and (3) fear of failure.

People tend to be guided by their habits. Habits curb the natural urge to be creative. As a brief experiment, try the following: Fold your arms across your chest. Note which arm is on top. Now, put your arms at your side and, once again, fold them across your chest—only this time change which arm is on top. How does this feel? How difficult was it to do? Did it take you several times until you succeeded?

Few people feel comfortable changing their customary ways of doing things, and some people find it difficult to make change at all. What habits determine your interaction when you meet someone for the first time?

Do you always say the same things in the same order, such as, "Hi, how are you?" and expect a response of, "Fine." What happens when the answer to your question is, "I just got out of the hospital"?

Do you automatically stick out your hand to shake someone's hand to whom you are introduced? What if the person was brought up in France and attempts to kiss you on both cheeks or you jab the young man from Japan in the stomach as he attempts to bow? How ingrained is your meeting-new-people habit? How ingrained are your ways of dealing with problems or reacting to stress?

Not all habits are harmful, of course. Most habits, in themselves, are helpful, such as when a task is easily performed or done very often. These tasks do not require reflection or the development of "new and improved ways" of doing them. However, not all tasks can or should be accomplished while on "automatic pilot." When you fail to question the "why" of these habits, you hinder your effectiveness in solving new problems and interacting with people. People often believe that solutions and ideas can be found in comfortable, typical ways of looking at things, and often they fall into the habit of presuming that a problem has only one solution—especially after they have found what they believe is *the* solution.

The first step in overcoming a limited repertoire of actions is to recognize your habits, and the second step is to break away from them, if so desired. To be creative and develop new ideas, you must stop your customary ways of behaving and looking at things. And to change your typical responses, you must reject the comfortable answers that habits automatically provide.

Another obstacle to your creativity may be your beliefs about the world, about how things "are." Although reality is based only on perception, people usually create beliefs about the world around them and then fail to think any further. *The belief becomes the reality.* Do you believe that only men and women should be in a "married" relationship? Or, that only men can be good mechanics? Or, that women should stay at home and take care of the children since men aren't very good nurturers? Or, that children should only be brought up in homes where there are two heterosexual parents present? If you mistake your beliefs for reality, how do you begin to respond to same-sex couples who are in committed relationships, the number of women who are handy with tools, the number of house husbands, or the vast number of children who are being brought up successfully by single parents? Where did you get these beliefs from? Have you ever asked yourself whether there are other points of view that might be valid? Do you habitually follow the beliefs of your parents, a religious organization or leader, or the media without questioning them?

Creativity requires **open-mindedness**, the willingness to receive new information, perspectives, assumptions, beliefs, and opinions. Recognize that your beliefs are merely beliefs—not reality—and you can begin to stimulate your creativity, to think in new and exciting ways.

LEARNING EXPERIENCE: Interested in learning more about your creativity? If so, complete Activity 11.7.

At the root of all these reasons for avoiding sharing creative thoughts is the fear of failure, whether it is failing at being a "strong person" (who is fearless and sane), an "intelligent person" (who is smart and practical), a "good communicator" (who is agreeable and able to put complex ideas into understandable words), or some other type of person. Creativity often takes courage, mainly the courage to possibly be wrong, to go away from the safety of repeating a procedure over and over, to open yourself to the fear of new experiences.

ACTIVITY 11.7
Overcoming Old Beliefs

Part A

Many of the verbal associations people make stem from fixed ways of looking at things that they learned as children and never bothered to change. For example, consider your automatic responses to the following word combinations:

bread and _____

ham and _____

hot and _____

short and _____

If you said "butter," "eggs" or "cheese," "cold," and "tall" or "fat," you made habitual responses. Such associations are made almost by reflex. Now, go back and redo your answers and think outside of your traditional box.

Part B

You are given some forks. You are told that they are *not* to be used for eating. What are five other things you can do with them?

Did you come up with such creative ideas as making a mobile out of them, combing your hair with one, using one or more to stake up plants, using them as Christmas tree ornaments, using one as a shovel to dig in the dirt, using them in place of a bow on a present? In reading the "creative use list," did you think, "That's dumb, a fork is made to eat with?" If so, you are a victim of restrictive thinking. Is that bad? No, but it is limiting in coming up with nontraditional solutions, and may reflect living a life of narrow beliefs.

Doing something the same way over and over again may feel safe, but it is no reason for continuing to do it that way.

LEARNING EXPERIENCE: Interested in finding out the reasons for your creativity or lack of creativity? If so, complete Activity 11.8.

Analytical Breakdown

Analytical breakdown is taking a complex problem and breaking it into its individual components, listing as many alternatives as possible for each component, and then combining the alternatives to create new variations. Using analytical breakdown can increase your creativity. Assume that you wanted to improve staff meetings in your office. This is a complex problem that can be broken down into several key issues. One issue is when to have a meeting, a second is where to have it, a third is who should attend, and a fourth is what to discuss. As you consider the situation, you note that *when* includes before opening, in the morning, at lunchtime, during the afternoon, and after closing; *where* includes in your office, in someone else's office, in the coffee room, at a restaurant, at someone's house, or in a nearby park; *who* includes everyone, managers only, staff only, managers and staff, personnel from one office, and personnel from two or more departments; and *what* includes the discussion of office procedures, how to deal with the public, salary concerns, new personnel issues, scheduling, new-product possibilities, and improving productivity.

ACTIVITY 11.8
Identifying Reasons for
Not Sharing Creative Thoughts

Part 1

Is your creativity crippled by fear of failure? What exactly worries you about using your creative abilities? Check each reason you might have for not sharing one of your creative, imaginative, unique, or novel ideas.

_____I was afraid.
_____It sounded stupid.
_____It seemed impractical.
_____It was too odd.
_____It was too abstract.
_____People would think I was crazy.
_____It was too personal.
_____It was hard to express.
_____It wasn't like other people's ideas.
_____People would make fun of me.
_____I was taught to be seen and not heard.
_____I wanted to agree with what others had to say.
_____It was foolish.
_____Other _____

Part 2

Go back over your checked items and ask yourself: "Must I reevaluate the way I make decisions and think about things because of these beliefs?" If your answer is, "yes," ask, "What's the worst thing that could happen if I altered my present mode of actions?" Yes, there could be some discomfort, but not much else. Breaking your mold will probably not be life threatening, but it could make life a bit more interesting.

By placing one key issue at the top of a column and generating a list of alternatives for each heading, you can begin to see possibilities that you may not have thought of before. When the information is laid out in columns, you can visualize the various combinations that will lead to a variety of potential meeting formats.

Manipulating Details

Another approach to increasing creativity is *manipulating the details* that you notice about an object. For example, you can change something by enlarging it, miniaturizing it, dividing it, rotating it, stretching it, hardening it, softening it, flattening it, flipping it, squeezing it, freezing it, heating it, rearranging it, shortening it, changing it, fluffing it up, and patting it down.

Consider that many items made for travel, such as a travel-sized hair dryer, resulted from applying the verb *to minimize*. Large-print books resulted from applying the verb *enlarge*. Frozen food and other forms of packaging all came from attempts to *manipulate* the details of an object. Even a bed of nails can become a relatively comfortable place on which to sleep if you flip it over!

The only way to be creative is through conscious effort. The more you set aside habitual associations and practice making new connections, the higher the probability that you will be creative in other aspects of your life, including your relationships. The more you try new analytical techniques, take reasonable risks, and open yourself to new experiences—and potential failures—the more you can increase your creative approach to interpersonal communication and the resulting relationships you want to create.

Key Terms

self-concept
self-love
affirmations
self-disclosure
I-statements
approval-seeking behaviors
self-fulfilled person
verbal/sexual harassment
compliance
power
empowerment
fair fighting
conflict resolution
criticism

constructive criticism
apology
conversations
small talk
analytical thinking
holistic thinking
direction giving
probing
creativity
creative thinking
usual thinking
open-mindedness
analytical breakdown

Competencies Check-Up

Interested in finding out what you learned in this chapter and how you use the information? If so, take this competencies check-up.

Directions: Indicate the extent that each statement applies to you:

1—Never   2—Seldom   3—Sometimes   4—Often   5—Usually

____1. I demonstrate commitment, equality, trust, respect, and communication skills in my important relationships at home, work, and social contexts.
____2. I have a strong self-concept and a sense of self-love that serves as a positive foundation for my interpersonal communication.

___ 3. I use positive strategies to improve who I am in relation to others (for example, I use positive self-talk, work to get to know myself, broaden my experiences, reward myself for trying new things, keep a journal, focus on the positive, and seek positive and nourishing people).

___ 4. I use self-disclosure in appropriate ways (to understand myself and others, using personal pronouns, describing behavior without evaluation and judgment, describing realistic and specific potential changes, adapting to the knowledge and interests of the other person, and using "I" strategies).

___ 5. I monitor my interpersonal communication and take steps to eliminate my "approval-seeking behaviors."

___ 6. I carefully monitor my interpersonal communication to avoid sexual harassment, and I respond appropriately when I confront sexually harassing behavior in others.

___ 7. I recognize the sources and uses of power in myself and others and avoid abusive, oppressive, and wasteful interpersonal communication.

___ 8. I insist on fair fighting from myself and the important people in my life.

___ 9. I welcome feedback from others and know how to handle criticism effectively.

___10. I avoid over- or underapologizing and instead use apologies effectively to create and maintain my relationships.

___11. I have excellent conversational speaking and listening skills, including the appropriate use of small talk.

___12. I use effective, multichannel strategies for giving understandable directions.

___13. I know how to request, question, and gain information effectively in my interpersonal communication.

___14. I can deliver bad news so that others can understand, accept, and adjust, while minimizing confusion, excessive distress, or resentment.

___15. I am a creative communicator who consistently monitors the quality of my interpersonal communication and relationships, I have a plan for improving my interpersonal communication skills, and consistently work to improve my interpersonal communication.

Scoring: If your score is above 45, you probably have basic competencies in your relational communication. Carefully contemplate your test results to determine the quality of your interpersonal communication skills.

I-Can Plan!

Whether or not the course is nearly over, you will need to continue your work to improve your interpersonal communication so that you develop positive and constructive relationships you will need in all aspects of your life. Now is a good time to look over the course information in a holistic way—including this chapter's information—to create a long-term plan that can make a difference in the quality of your life. You can work to create the knowledge, values, attitudes, and skills you need to be an effective interpersonal communicator.

Activities

1. The essential elements of effective interactions are: commitment, equality, trust, respect, and communication skills. Define each. Which of these do you think it most important to effective interactions? Explain your choice.

2. Agree or disagree with the statement: Sometimes you have to "blow your own horn" because no one else knows how to play the tune. You know yourself better than other people do because you know more about yourself and your skills and talents. There is a difference, however, between tooting your own horn (e.g., sharing with others your accomplishments) and playing a symphony (e.g., exaggerating your accomplishments).

3. Have you ever used affirmations? If so, what were they, why did you use them, and are/were they of value?

4. What do you find the most difficult aspect of self-disclosing? Why? Where do you think you gained that attitude?

5. Have you ever been a witness in court? If so, describe the experience and indicate whether you think you were a good witness.

6. Write an I statement for each of these situations:
   a. A friend continues to ask you to loan him money and though he has promised to do so, he never has paid you back.
   b. Your roommate brings friends to your room, they bring food and drinks with them, leave all the rubbish behind when they leave, and your roommate does not clean up after the friends left.
   c. Your instructor said you would have a test on Monday. You spend the entire weekend studying. When you get to class the instructor says, "I didn't have time to get the test ready. I guess we'll have to put it off."

7. Do you know anyone who is an egospeaker? Explain specifically what s/he does?

8. Review the list of approval-seeking behaviors listed in the book. Select the one that you tend to do effectively and be ready to state which one it is and give an example of your using that behavior.

9. Find a story of a case of verbal/sexual harassment. It may either be a personal story, an instance that happened to a friend, or one in the news. Explain what the harassment was and what happened as a result of the harassment.

10. Who held the power in your family of origin. How did the person exert the power?

11. The class will break up into groups of two. Use one of these topics to carry on a conversation of five minutes. Following the conversation explain what techniques you used to keep the communication flowing (e.g., asking questions).
    a. Why I liked/disliked high school.
    b. My favorite social activity is _____.
    c. My three biggest pet peeves are _____.
    d. Why can't people (finish the statement)_____.

CHAPTER 12

Interpersonal Communication in the Workplace

Learning Outcomes

After reading this chapter, you should be able to:

- Identify communication patterns in an organization, such as culture, climate, group dynamics.
- Adapt interpersonal communication to the patterns of an organization.
- Explain expectations of professional relationships.
- Identify strategies for rhetorical sensitivity at work.
- Apply rhetorical sensitivity to the workplace context, with communication relevant to such principles as change, deception, and personal boundaries.
- Avoid and respond to sexual harassment.

Marcus asked a coworker to help him. The colleague said that he didn't have time to teach another person how to do the job. Marcus needed guidance and advice, but didn't know where to turn.

Carmen sat in the lobby waiting for the person she hoped would hire her. When the prospective supervisor arrived, Carmen introduced herself, shook hands, and went into the office where the job interview was to be held.

In a work group, Darian became frustrated with the lack of participation by several members. He asked their opinions and encouraged them, but they just didn't seem motivated to do the job.

The world of work requires knowledge of strong interpersonal abilities.

LEARNING EXPERIENCE: Interested in finding out about your interpersonal communication effectiveness at work? If so, do Activity 12.1.

ACTIVITY 12.1
Interpersonal Communication at Work

Directions: Think about your interpersonal communication at work. If you are not currently employed, remember what you did in a previous job or imagine what you might do in a future job. Answer with your first impression about how frequently you use the following communication behaviors at work.

1 = never or almost never, 2 = sometimes, 3 = often,
4 = always or almost always

___ 1. I have trouble understanding and adapting to the organizational culture where I work.

___ 2. Whether my coworkers are helpful or difficult determines whether or not I have anything to do with them.

___ 3. I'm open-minded and able to see the perspective of other people at work.

___ 4. I offer encouragement, respect, and information to others and work well at solving problems.

___ 5. I can quickly figure out whether or not I will like or work well with co-workers and whether they're as talented as I am.

___ 6. I always keep my supervisor informed about what I'm doing, including problems that come up or mistakes I make.

___ 7. Usually when there's a problem at work, it's someone else's fault.

___ 8. I like listening to others. I often ask a supervisor or consult with cowork-ers, and I have developed a network of support for my job.

___ 9. I think roles at work are inappropriate. Just because someone is in a su-pervisory position or has worked there for a while, doesn't mean I need to listen to them or do what they say.

___10. I don't have any power or opportunity for leadership at work.

___11. I listen to others and reflect about situations, but I also try to directly express my thoughts and use clear language.

___12. I'm a positive person. I make an effort to engage others in appropriate conversation, be considerate, and encourage my coworkers. When I'm in an interview, for example, I know how to engage others and make them feel comfortable.

___13. My coworkers always enjoy what I know about others in the way of gos-sip or the latest rumor. In addition, I often forward entertainment e-mails and jokes at work.

___14. I keep private information confidential, and I'm known for my honesty and integrity at work.

___15. I tend to procrastinate. I'm not big on meeting deadlines at work.

___16. I pay attention to my nonverbal communication at work, such as good posture, adequate vocal volume, friendly handshakes, and good eye contact, which builds rapport and respect for my coworkers and supervisors.

___17. In a one-on-one interview or meeting situations—whether formal or not—I know how to plan, stick to time guidelines, and focus on the task. In fact, I make sure I arrive early, present a warm and dynamic image, and engage fully with others.

___18. I'm not so concerned about dressing or behaving professionally at work. I'm not too committed to this job or the people around me.

Scoring and Reflection

Step 1: Put a line through 1, 2, 5, 7, 9, 10, 13, 15, 18, then add your answers from these items.

Step 2: Add your answers from items 3, 4, 6, 8, 11, 12, 14, 16, 17. These items suggest effective interpersonal communication at work.

Your score from step 1 suggests negative interpersonal communication behaviors that may work against your on-the-job effectiveness. Your score from step 2 suggests positive communication that may enhance your successful job performance. We have no normative score, but for effective interpersonal communication at work, your total from step 2 should be higher than your total from step 1 because the score would suggest you use more positive communication behaviors than negative ones.

Go back and notice your negative communication behaviors and consider what you need to improve.

Adapting to Communication Patterns in the Workplace

Effective communication at work depends on expectations at multiple levels: the organization's culture, organizational hierarchy, networking, group collaboration, and interviewing. The communication patterns and skills at these levels are intertwined to determine how people communicate in their places of work.

ORGANIZATIONAL CULTURE

One of the variables affecting interpersonal communication is the organization's culture.[1] The **organizational culture** is the shared personality or character of the organization as a whole. Organizational culture is the overall environment, complete with unwritten rules and expectations about how people communicate and interact.

Culture is not something you can change, but something you need to figure out and adapt to if you want to fit in at your place of work. These written and unwritten rules, company values, and work expectations determine the framework for what is appropriate interpersonal communication at work.

Consider the influences of organizational culture on one student. A summer internship at a long-established Fortune 500 company taught the student that each person has his or her niche in the organization. He became aware that everyone must follow the union's rules and the company's policies. New ideas were appreciated only if they fit within the role of the intern's job description. The intern was expected to be at a desk by 7 A.M., wear professional style clothing, and communicate in proscribed ways. At meetings, the intern was supposed to observe, not speak. On the other hand, the next summer, the student worked at an alternative energy corporation, where the student had to adapt to a completely different organizational culture. The intern met no employees older than age thirty. Appropriate dress and communication were quite informal. To adapt to the city's rush hour traffic patterns, employees were expected to arrive between 7 A.M. and 10 A.M., then work eight hours after their arrival times. At the second company, the culture promoted active engagement of employees and interns and respect for listening to everyone's ideas. He realized that there was nothing inherently right or wrong with any of the written or unwritten rules of either organization environment because they each reflected the nature of each organization's culture. The point is, your interpersonal communication needs to adapt to the organizational culture where you work.

Whatever communication style becomes entrenched, an organization's culture tends to be consistent over time and perpetuated by the rituals and stories that are passed on from group to group and generation to generation. When you begin a new job and hear a joke about the last employee who was fired for lateness and disagreeing with the supervisor, your coworkers are teaching you about the organization's culture and rules.

ORGANIZATIONAL CLIMATE

Organizational climate is the holistic perception of life in the organization, including the emotional or psychological dimensions conveyed through communication.[2] The people within a department, for example, may develop certain expectations about who talks to whom and how they should interact with each other.

Some organizations are warm and friendly, and people feel a strong sense of commitment. Other organizations are less personalized, so workers feel less engaged or committed to the organization.

See Figure 12.1 for a list of supportive and defensive climates at work.

Part of the organizational climate, the design of a work space, and place can affect the way people communicate.[3] The environment is usually structured for certain kinds of activities, such as individual work space, areas to meet customers, rooms for meetings, and technology connections. The lighting, temperature, and seating, for example, may or may not make people comfortable and support effective interpersonal communication. When you consider principles of formal space,[4] a long, narrow

Figure 12.1.   Communication Climates at Work

	Supportive Climate	Defensive Climate
Task Orientation	**Collaboration**, which may include being open-minded, willingness to consider other points of view, equality, using a team approach, information flow, spontaneity, openness, transparency, and empathy.	**Authoritarian**, which may include controlling others, having a "my way or the highway attitude," looking out only for oneself, and acting superior to others.
People Orientation	**Description**, which may include giving information, offering encouragement, paraphrasing, listening, being sensitive to diversity, and seeking to solve problems.	**Manipulation**, which may include using strategies, bullying, back-stabbing, criticizing, and acting superior to others.

Source: Adapted from Forward, G. L., & Czech, K. (2008, November 20). *Why (most) everything you think you know about Gibb's Climate Theory may be wrong and what to do about it.* Paper presented at the annual meeting of the National Communication Association Annual Convention, San Diego, CA.

conference table suggests that the people who sit at the head of the table have more power. A plain, organized space may give the impression of a "get-the-job-done" climate. Formal outdoor landscaping may suggest a formal climate inside too. A more cluttered space where people are located close to each other for easy interaction may suggest a more interactive climate. You can learn about your organization's climate by paying attention to the built environment.

How can you adapt to the organizational climate? In general, accept the organization the way it is.[5] If you come from another job, you may think those ways are better simply because you are used to them. If you don't like the way something operates, ask why it's done that way.

Employees often think that a new job will be great, then after a honeymoon period, they become disillusioned. This period is a good time for employees to focus on the tasks that need to be done, while keeping opinions to themselves, avoiding negativity, and silencing their complaints. Usually as they learn more, the job and the organizational climate make more sense. As employees adapt to a new environment and expectations, they usually come to understand and appreciate the way the organization works.

If your opinion is sought out, offer it. If not, at least at the start of your career, keep your opinions to yourself. Your time to be an agent for change often comes with tenure, after you've proven yourself and earned the respect of your coworkers and supervisors.

ORGANIZATIONAL HIERARCHY

Traditional organizations have been very hierarchical. An **organizational hierarchy** is a system that codifies a company's ladder of command. In most traditional U.S. organizations, it is a *hierarchy of top-down*. The CEO reports to the president, who reports to the vice president, who reports to the supervisors, who report to the workers. Because the channels are adhered to rigidly, the information starts at the top and flows downward.[6]

In a hierarchy, you may need to simply accept that people above you in the hierarchy have more information, and they expect you to follow policies, often without asking for your input or offering a rationale. This process can be very difficult for new employees who come from a college environment where they have been encouraged to express their opinions and challenge the ideas of others. As communicators, these new employees need to understand that in a hierarchy, individual ideas of lower level employees may not seem valued. When employees have years of experience and move up in the hierarchy, they will have more opportunities to affect the organization through their communication.

In contrast to traditional top-down structures, some organizations have a more flattened format. A *flattened organization* has fewer levels of employee status, offers more upward communication, and often uses group collaboration. Even in a flattened organization, however, you will want to be respectful of the chain of command while using appropriate interpersonal style in face-to-face, encounters, texting, e-mail, and other communication. If the CEO says it's okay to make direct contact, but your supervisor doesn't know about your private meeting with the CEO, you may be in serious trouble with the people around you. You'll want to keep your supervisor informed about informal and formal communication with people outside your work group or line of authority.

In the *bottom-up organization*, which is common in Japanese workplaces, the employees are divided into work teams which collectively decide how tasks will be accomplished. Their input is given to the supervisor, who conveys the process to those at higher levels. Recently, some American organizations have started to adopt this procedure. For example, at one company, **work teams**, workers who form a group to pool their knowledge and skills in order to accomplish a task, have been formed and are making suggestions as to how the production line is to operate. This, according to one worker, has "resulted in less errors, better work attendance, and higher quality."[7]

NETWORKING

Networking is the practice of creating a web of support and influence with other professionals. Networking is when you create extended relationships with people beyond your immediate coworkers. You make connections with people in other departments, divisions, corporations, clients, and beyond. Your network is a relationship support system you develop to help you succeed in your job.

In the bottom-up organization, the employees are divided into work teams who collectively decide how tasks will be accomplished.

Effective workers communicate with professionalism, which often includes these practices:[8]

- *Maintain confidentiality* about work, tasks, and employee information.
- *Be honest* with others and show integrity in your work.
- *Set deadlines* and meet deadlines, which includes fulfilling any promises you make.
- *Admit your mistakes*, apologizing when appropriate, and giving credit where it is due.
- *Share relevant experiences* and give rationale during the decision-making process.
- *Demonstrate open-mindedness* toward the culture, beliefs, values, and opinions of others.
- *Use respect* through civil talk, commitment to organizational goals, and respect for others' time.
- *Meet the standards, values, and ethics* of the particular profession you have joined.
- *Learn* the knowledge and skills needed for the profession.

If the idea of networking seems overwhelming, you can divide the process into which small steps you take over time. You can decide to learn something new about one person at each meeting you attend. You might keep a small notebook with names and information so you can ask a more personal "How is Chris?" versus the less personal "How is your family?" Another strategy is to write yourself a note on the back of the person's business card, then put it in a box where you can use the card in your networking. A thank-you note for a business referral, taking a colleague to lunch, or a phone call about a new product's development are examples of communicating to help develop your network.

GROUP COLLABORATION

Group collaboration or teamwork is a commonly used communication pattern in about half of U.S. organizations.[9] In addition, the typical professional spends about five to six hours each week in meetings that require group skills.[10] Unfortunately, research also found that 69% of workers said their meetings weren't productive.[11] The lack of productivity may be because members lack work skills, social skills, motivation, or perseverance to complete the task. Given these potential problems, you may wonder why organizations bother to have their employees work in groups. The reason? When a group works together well, the benefits are increased productivity, creativity, innovation, and work satisfaction.[12]

To communicate effectively in groups or teams requires the same kinds of interpersonal communication skills discussed throughout this book: negotiation, moral responsibility, conflict management, cultural sensitivity, critical thinking, understanding the complexity of the communication process, self-monitoring, understanding roles, developing relationships, knowing how to collaborate, and good persuasive skills.[13] The process of working in groups is a complicated one that may be more appropriately covered in a course or book on group dynamics or team building. Until you have that opportunity, however, you can begin to analyze your areas of interpersonal communication strength and need as a first step in skill development.

LEARNING EXPERIENCE: Interested in finding out about the effectiveness of your interpersonal communication in work groups? If so, do Activity 12.2.

What are the communication skills you need for effective participation in a work team?[14] Listening is probably the most important communication skill. Other important communication skills are asking clear questions, establishing rapport with others, receiving and transmitting information, and effectively presenting information to the group.[15]

Group Leadership

A good leader helps people to be productive, while a bad leader lowers the quality of life of the people involved.[16] Unfortunately, "the majority of people consider their managers the worst part of their job."[17] So, what communication skills do you need to develop so that you can be an effective leader?

ACTIVITY 12.2
Communicating in Work Groups

Directions: When working with a group, which of the following communication behaviors do you typically use?

1 = never or almost never, 2 = sometimes, 3 = often,
4 = always or almost always

____ 1. I find I can persuade the group by withholding what I know, not sharing my skills, or keeping my ideas to myself.

____ 2. When I disagree with the ideas of certain people in the group, I can change their influence on the group through gossip or negative talk behind their backs.

____ 3. I use humor to persuade the group, particularly humor that teases, is sarcastic, or makes fun of people.

____ 4. I have the training and information I need to get the job done, and I help the group determine and meet our goals.

____ 5. I am a good model of effective teamwork, and I strive for good communication with minority and majority opinion holders.

____ 6. I engage in conflict, but I avoid words or a tone that may be interpreted as aggressive or hostile.

____ 7. When people in the group have close or deteriorating friendships that may affect the group, I encourage them to work together for the success of the team.

____ 8. When members of the group are trying to make me hurry or conform, I still make sure my concerns are heard by the group.

____ 9. I persuade people in advance of the meeting so I know I have a coalition of people who agree with me.

____10. Competition is always a great way to get things done.

____11. I strive to include all group members in the decision-making and work process, even if they are located at a distance.

____12. When we have inadequate resources, I figure out creative ways the group can consider as ways to solve problems.

____13. When it comes to group work, I'm not motivated to work as hard as most people.

____14. I'm good at listening, paraphrasing, summarizing what others say, and sharing our collective vision.

____15. When someone undermines my work, I usually can find a way to get even.

____16. I feel irritated when a group member is always upbeat and optimistic about the group's ability.

(continued)

ACTIVITY 12.2 (*continued*)

Step 1: Put a line through 1, 2, 3, 9, 10, 13, 15, 16, then add up your answers
to these items.

Step 2: Add up your answers from items 4, 5, 6, 7, 8, 11, 12, 14. These items
support teamwork communication.

Your score from step 1 suggests negative communication that may work against effective teamwork. Your score from step 2 suggests positive communication that may enhance successful teamwork. For effective team participation and leadership, your total from step 2 should be higher than your total from step 1. Go back and notice the negative communication behaviors you use and write out a plan for how you can change those behaviors. What communication behaviors can you use to improve your teamwork skills?

Source: Based on Seibold, D., Kang, P., Bailliard, B., & John, J. (2008). *Communication that damages teamwork: The dark side of teams.* A paper presented at the annual meeting of the International Communication Association, 2008 Annual Meeting in Quebec, Canada.

The group needs someone to organize the meeting and to keep everybody on track as they move through a process. In organizations, that individual usually will be designated beforehand as a function of her/his supervisory role. If the "titled" person isn't the leader, then leadership may emerge within the group. Some groups are led by a different member each meeting. Even though the individual who assumes this role is recognized as the facilitator, any group member can demonstrate leadership communication to enhance the group's success. Figure 12.2 illustrates what qualities and actions define effective and poor leaders.

Meeting Efficiency

Given that many workers think the majority of meeting time is wasteful, groups may benefit by increasing their efficiency. For swift-moving, high-performance meetings, the group can begin by setting protocols or codes of behavior, such as when, where, and how often they will meet, and for what purpose.[18] Often the group leader will request that group members send in items for the agenda to ensure that important topics will be discussed. To help members prepare, the leader may send the minutes from the last meeting and an agenda to group members (a few days in advance). An e-mail reminder the day of the meeting may be a good idea, with a final agenda and minutes attached, or printed copies of materials for the meeting. A good outline with time segments may be helpful to keep the group focused and on target. Consider this agenda:

Review of minutes from last meeting (5 minutes).
Committee reports (3 minutes each).

Decision topics (10 minutes each).
Discussion topics for future decisions (5 minutes each).
Announcements.

One strategy for efficient meetings is a stand-up meeting. In a **stand-up meeting**, everyone stands and discusses the issues in a short, focused time frame, such as five minutes for the whole meeting. Often the meeting is held in a space where everyone can stand in a small circle. The idea is that if you're standing up, you're not as comfortable, physically, so you will want to stay focused on finishing the task quickly.

A variation of the stand-up meeting is the **popcorn meeting**, where everyone stands in a circle and each person quickly gives an opinion or information about the topic. Each person speaks only once, but all ideas are heard without allowing anyone to respond or dominate. Then each group member can go away and think about the ideas for discussion or decision at a later time. In the cooking popcorn analogy, each kernel pops (each person's idea), then you must quickly remove it from the pan (end the meeting).

The reason for collective communication in groups is for everyone to share ideas, ask questions, complete the tasks, and contribute to the organization. For effective group communication, you have to be willing to set aside your own personal agenda and self-interest for the greater good of the group product.

There is no way to learn what you need to know about effective group communication from a brief explanation. When you enter a job that requires group work, that may be the perfect time to take a course or read a book about effective group communication.

Figure 12.2. Interpersonal Communication of Leaders

Effective Leaders	Poor Leaders
Communicate clearly. Confront others without offending them. Establish relationships. Work well with the majority of coworkers. Keep confidential information secret. Keep promises. Show objectivity and sensitivity to others. Participate as a vital part of what needs to be done. Use perspective-taking (being able to see things from the point of view of others). Take responsibility for their own actions. Understand human dynamics and processes. Work well with others despite disagreements.	Are arrogant. Attempt to dominate or defeat others. Blame others for their errors. Act cold and uncaring. Exploit, manipulate, and deceive others to reach their own goals. Fail to admit mistakes. Fail to recognize the perspectives of other people. Lack empathy. Use poor interpersonal skills. See life as a competition where there is only one winner. Seek to keep others from participating in decision-making. Are stubborn. Take unwarranted credit for what other people do.

Source: Blair, C. A., Hoffman, B. J., & Helland, K. R. (2008). Narcissism in organizations: A multisource appraisal reflects different perspectives. *Human Performance, 21*(3), 254–276.

INTERVIEWING

Your first full-time job after college is an important selection because it can set your path and dictate opportunities for the future.[19] Finding that job may take months or years. To give you some ideas about that process, here are some practical tips for the job-hunting process.[20]

You can change cities, which allows you to shed local obligations and open job-market choices.

Create a network for your search. Networking and research can be the keys to obtaining a job.[21] If you haven't developed a network of connections, you can start that today. Interpersonal, face-to-face networking through friends and colleagues may be the most effective way of finding employment.[22]

Ignore some advice from well-meaning family and friends and take responsibility for yourself in this process. Sometimes the process is challenging, requiring you to show considerable initiative. If you send several e-mails about a job and hear nothing, obviously, you're using the wrong approach. Use the telephone, send information via regular mail, and seek face-to-face interaction.

Work on your appearance—update your sense of fashion, weight, hair-style, and attitude projected by your facial expression—because how you look matters. You need to look "open, friendly, energetic, and thoughtful. Consider your posture, your breathing, your smile"[23] everywhere you go. Most organizations operate at a certain level of professional clothing style, and you would want to be consistent with that style.

Take any job, so you have contact with others and maintain your skills, because it's easier to move from one job to another, than from unemployment to work.

Find a way to mitigate your frustration, stay calm, and be positive. Obtaining a job interview may be a job in itself. No matter how many jobs seem to be available, you only need one job, and you want it to be a good fit for you and your employer.

Since most jobs are obtained through the interviewing process, you have to be successful in an **employment interview**, a process by which organizations select their employees, in order to be hired for the position in the organization.

Many organizations use a multilayer interview process when hiring new employees.

The initial screening may happen through a computer application, large group interview, personality test, or Human Resources review.

A second stage may be a phone interview.

A third stage may be a face-to-face interview with a supervisor or a group of coworkers.

An additional stage may be a trial work situation, where you solve a problem or complete a task.

Planning for the Job Interview

You will want to start early—probably a year before graduation—in working with your college career placement office in learning how to prepare an effective job application, cover letter, resume, letters of reference, and portfolio of work. Mock interviews

If you're going on a job interview, be prepared to answer questions about your knowledge, values, experiences, and beliefs.

through the placement office can be an excellent help. Also part of your planning and research is finding out about companies or organizations.

If you're going on a job interview be prepared to answer questions about your knowledge, values, experiences, and beliefs. Commonly asked questions include:

What was your favorite area of study in college?
What hobbies or interests do you have?
What work experiences have you had relevant to this job?

You may also be asked to give examples that illustrate what you would do in certain situations. In advance, you might want to plan to illustrate your answers with stories and examples to explain your values and work ethic if you were asked these questions:

Tell me about a time when you and your supervisor disagreed.
Give me an example of a problem you had with a coworker and how you resolved it.
If you thought your supervisor was making a mistake, how would you handle it?

Planning for a Performance Appraisal Interview

Although there may be many types of interviews during employment, probably the most important after you've been hired is the performance appraisal interview. A **performance appraisal interview** is designed to evaluate your work success, set goals for the next employment period, and give you feedback about strengths and needs. Often your supervisor will give you a written assessment of how you have done on the job and what you need to do for the next employment period. Usually you will then be given an opportunity to respond with your perceptions of your work, what you've done well and what you can do to improve.[24]

Make sure the performance report is in synchronization with your goals and the organization's expectations. Setting your performance target has been found to be a useful means for making performance appraisal interviews more productive and purposeful.[25] Even if your supervisor is an excellent guide in this process, you need to take responsibility for making your appraisal interview a positive one, then implementing needed changes in your work during the next employment period.

USING INFORMAL COMMUNICATION

Informal communication channels can profoundly affect an organization through such interaction as corridor chatter, rumor mills, doing lunch, instant messaging, instant message chat, texting, and the grapevine.[26] Of particular concern is how to use e-mail effectively.[27] Here are some suggestions:

Avoid sensitive content in e-mail. Anyone—either intentionally, innocently, or accidently—can forward your e-mail to anyone inside or outside the organization.

Avoid forwarding other people's e-mails. If they wanted other people to receive the e-mail, they would be copied on the e-mail you received. You can get yourself and others in trouble by forwarding inappropriately.

Keep your e-mails about a year. Figure out an organizational system you can use to save e-mails. You may need to rename documents when you save them so you can find them again easily. There may be times when you need to look up information, and e-mails can provide a helpful record.

Avoid humor because it can be too easily misinterpreted.

Be careful about the Reply to All function. If you are copying something to keep others informed, a better approach than a mass e-mailing may be to write a summary to that person.

Be careful about whom you copy. If you are sending an e-mail to someone and copying someone else because you have a complaint or want someone to look bad, don't do it. If you have a problem or complaint, speak directly to the appropriate person (face-to face or on the phone if the person is at a distance).

You may want to cut earlier e-mails from your replies. This editing eliminates other people's e-mails, e-mails they may not want forwarded to someone else.

Keep e-mails short.

Know your employer's policies about e-mails. The organization's policies may be very specific about who is allowed to send e-mails to whom and what kinds of approvals are needed for e-mails. Your employer may prohibit forwarding fun e-mails, playing in football pools, and using IM or Facebook,[28] because the activities waste company time and resources.

Besides electronic communication, be aware of written and unwritten procedures about informal communication. As a new employee, you can talk to experienced workers to find out about the regulations and precedents in informal interactions. Gossip around the water cooler, for example, can be a negative communication form. If someone tells you something negative about another coworker, it is probably not advisable to repeat the information. If you gossip about other people in the organization, that behavior can have a negative effect on your credibility and trust.[29]

If falsehoods are spread about you, you have the challenge of using denial to stop a rumor.[30] Sometimes additional information or explanation of the correct information is helpful because the rumor may be fueled by uncertainty. You can confirm the truth and ignore the rest. You might involve a supervisor to help you because higher level employees have more credibility. Denial and gossip are two communication problems at work that require careful communication.[31]

Rhetorical Sensitivity in the Workplace

Rhetorical sensitivity is a learned skill, where a person uses words and nonverbal communication to adapt with flexibility to the people and context at hand. Many factors affect your ability to be sensitive in your interpersonal communication, including your personality traits, social and emotional functioning, life experiences, values, attitudes, and self-concept.[32] Effective communicators are highly accommodating because they can see other people's perspectives and recognize that how people communicate is part of their personal choices.[33] Being open and flexible means that if something doesn't work, they find another way. Rhetorically sensitive communicators consult with others, figure out a different method, listen to the suggestions of others, or ask a supervisor for advice.

You may have to "pay your dues" and prove yourself through effective task completion, being on time to work, and being helpful rather than a hindrance before your coworkers are willing to listen to you. Effective communicators focus on the present interpersonal interaction, through various types of communication:[34]

Expressiveness, such as saying what you think or feel, articulating your position, and talking fluently.
Language precision, such as using clear and direct language.
Niceness, such as being kind, considerate, encouraging, and positive toward another person.
Reflection, such as consideration, contemplation, and deliberation.
Supportiveness, including being a good listener, having an open mind, and encouraging the other individual.

Effective employees are more than good communicators; they also complete tasks, meet deadlines, pay attention to details, and keep careful records. In other chapters, you've learned about how communication can be risky, which is an important point to remember when you have low status at work or when you begin a new job. Take time to think before you speak or send an e-mail. Listen to the people around you. Respect the points of view of people at different levels. When conflicts arise, use communication strategies that will help everyone win. Make sure your communication behavior does not make you vulnerable at work, but instead contributes to your work success.

Rhetorically sensitive people have a better chance for success in the work environment. Even if you do not feel naturally inclined to be adaptive in your language and nonverbal communication, you can learn skills and choose to be adaptive.

What are the work variables needing communication sensitivity? Included are such factors as impression management, positive communication, time, power, change, boundaries, deception, competition and disagreement, adapting to a diverse workplace, and leaving a job without burning bridges.

IMPRESSION MANAGEMENT

Impression management is a skill where individuals pay attention to how they come across to others so that they make a good impression or impact. Impression management is accomplished through both the words you speak and what your behavior communicates to others. Remembering that your nonverbal communication speaks volumes, pay attention to the details that will make you look like a professional. Depending on your work environment, you might consider these suggestions:[35]

- *Keep your desk or work space clean.* You want people to see that you're getting the job done in an organized and professional way. If there is no janitorial staff to empty wastebaskets or dust, for example, do it yourself.
- *Keep your car clean and gas in the tank.* You never know when a colleague or supervisor will ask you to drive someplace.
- *Carry cash in addition to your credit card.* Particularly at work events, you never know when you will be asked to do something that requires cash, such as paying for parking.
- *Dress for the job you'd like to have, provided it's appropriate.* If you dress like a supervisor, for example, that may enhance the impression you make on others. If you don't know much about clothing styles, many stores have personal shoppers or fashion consultants who are aware of various business environments' clothing requirements to help you.
- *Make sure your body odor is appropriate.* U.S. Americans expect others to have a clean odor. Before important meetings, you may want to avoid garlic and onions at lunch. Many people are allergic to perfume or cologne or find such smells offensive. Know that heavy drinking or smoking the night before may be on your breath the next morning.

- *Carry a pen and small notebook.* No matter where you are, you may want to take notes or write down a phone number.
- *Clean out your bag.* You want to make a professional appearance when you open a purse or computer bag.
- *Always knock before entering.* When you enter anyone's workspace, you should respect the person's privacy. If the door is open, you can knock on the door jam—which is difficult to do—or announce yourself by saying something like "Excuse me," before you go into their space.
- *Program your supervisor's telephone numbers into your cell phone.* You should be able to call immediately any time there is a problem or emergency.
- *Know how to work the office alarm.* Sooner or later you may need to arrive early or leave late. If you accidently set off the alarm, you need to have the code memorized so you can cancel the alarm immediately.
- *Keep business cards handy.* Keep business cards in your wallet, purse, computer bag, or car, so you are never caught without them. If your organization does not supply you with cards, you can have personal business cards printed by an Internet company that offers "free" cards for the cost of shipping.

NONVERBAL IMMEDIACY

You can create a sense of caring and engagement with coworkers through nonverbal immediacy. *Nonverbal immediacy* is the use of nonword communication to generate a sense of interest and caring about the other person.[36] In a business context, you walk up to the person with confidence (or stand if you are already seated). You look the person in the eye, offer a firm handshake (or bow slightly in some cultural contexts), and wait for the person in power to suggest you sit down. Then, with good posture and engaged eye contact, you can begin to build rapport.

Nonverbal immediacy behaviors include using hand-shaking, consistent eye contact, and animated facial expression, smiling, and hand gestures.

LEARNING EXPERIENCE: Interested in finding out about your nonverbal communication effectiveness? If so, do Activity 12.3.

TIME

Two aspects of the use of time seem particularly relevant to the workplace: monochronic time and taking time to think.

The first consideration is the way people use time in an organization: usually a monochronic approach in the United States.[37] In a ***monochronic time culture***, people adhere to schedules, arrive on time (or early), and care about segmenting and organizing according to time units. United States, German, Canadian, Japanese, and Scandinavian businesses tend to use monochronic time. Employees who are consistently late

ACTIVITY 12.3
Nonverbal Immediacy Scale-Self Report (NIS-S)

Directions: The following statements describe the ways some people behave while talking with or to others. Please indicate in the space at the left of each item the degree to which you believe the statement applies *TO YOU*. Please use the following 5-point scale:

1 = Never; 2 = Rarely; 3 = Occasionally; 4 = Often; 5 = Very Often

_____ 1. I use my hands and arms to gesture while talking to people.
_____ 2. I touch others on the shoulder or arm while talking to them.
_____ 3. I use a monotone or dull voice while talking to people.
_____ 4. I look over or away from others while talking to them.
_____ 5. I move away from others when they touch me while we are talking.
_____ 6. I have a relaxed body position when I talk to people.
_____ 7. I frown while talking to people.
_____ 8. I avoid eye contact while talking to people.
_____ 9. I have a tense body position while talking to people.
_____10. I sit close or stand close to people while talking with them.
_____11. I speak quietly and am not enthusiastic when I speak.
_____12. I use a variety of vocal expressions when I talk to people.
_____13. I gesture when I talk to people.
_____14. I am animated when I talk to people.
_____15. I have a bland facial expression when I talk to people.
_____16. I move closer to people when I talk to them.
_____17. I look directly at people while talking to them.
_____18. I am stiff when I talk to people.
_____19. I have a lot of vocal variety when I talk to people.
_____20. I avoid gesturing while I am talking to people.
_____21. I lean toward people when I talk to them.
_____22. I maintain eye contact with people when I talk to them.
_____23. I try not to sit or stand close to people when I talk with them.
_____24. I lean away from people when I talk to them.
_____25. I smile when I talk to people.
_____26. I avoid touching people when I talk to them.

Scoring:
Step 1. Add the scores from the following items: 1, 2, 6, 10, 12, 13, 14, 16, 17, 19, 21, 22, and 25.
Step 2. Add the scores from the following items: 3, 4, 5, 7, 8, 9, 11, 15, 18, 20, 23, 24, and 26.

Total Score = Start with the number 78, add to that score your total from Step 1, and then subtract your total from Step 2.

78 + _____ = _____ – _____ = _____
  (step 1 score)   (step 2 score)   (total)

Norms:
Females High = >112 (more nonverbal immediacy); Mean = 102.0 S.D. = 10.9; Low = <92
Males High = >104 (more nonverbal immediacy); Mean = 93.8 S.D. = 10.8; Low <83

Interpretation: The higher your score, the more you have nonverbal immediacy. This means you are more dynamic, engaging, and captivating as a speaker. The higher the score the more likely it is that you will grab and hold a listener's attention. If you are a female and your score is 92 or a male who has a score of 83 and below go back over the list and try to ascertain why your nonverbal immediacy is low. You might want to work with a speech therapist or communication consultant to increase your nonverbal immediacy or make a conscious effort to speak more dynamically, and look directly at and align your body with the person to whom you are speaking.

Source: Richmond, V. P., McCroskey, J. C., & Johnson, A. D. (2003). Development of the Nonverbal Immediacy Scale (NIS): Measures of self- and other-perceived nonverbal immediacy. *Communication Quarterly, 51,* 502–515.

to work or for meetings may be seen as rude, wasteful, or self-centered, and may be fired if they can't conform to the time demands of the organization.

In *polychronic time cultures*, the use of time is more fluid, with less emphasis on a certain time being absolute or strict adherence to a schedule. Cultures of Africa, Latin America, and the Middle East tend to be polychronic. In business contexts, employees need to adapt to potential differences in the perception of time. One U.S. American was shocked when she had to wait days before seeing a government official in Madagascar, for example, even though she had an appointment. The American thought the official was stalling and being uncooperative, when in fact, the official turned out to be accommodating during the meeting and allowed her to accomplish her goals just as she hoped. The conflict was in both parties not taking into consideration the time culture patterns of the other.

The second consideration is taking time to think. Decide tomorrow instead of today.[38] We are not suggesting that you procrastinate, but that you take time to reflect. Have you noticed how often effective leaders wait before taking action? Sometimes with a little time, the problem will resolve itself, give people a chance to calm down, or provide an opportunity to think of a better solution. When your supervisor tells you "I need it yesterday," then the task must take top priority for completion. In many instances, however, if you can wait to decide, you should delay. Communication mistakes are common when you rush to clear up loose ends for the day, feel hurried, decide without considering alternatives, make a comment off the top of your head, or send an e-mail that you wrote when in a strong emotional state. Instead, take measured action through analytical thinking. Probably the decision can wait a day, so if you delay, you have more assessment time to ensure good judgment. That way you can avoid "What was I thinking?!?" consequences.

Of course, you probably have met someone who can never make a decision, so the course of events takes on a life of its own without the individual's input. Instead, we are suggesting that your decision-making show patience and wisdom, while meeting deadlines.

POWER

No matter what your job is, remember who is in power, and as a new employee that's probably not you.[39] Even chief executive officers (CEOs) must report to boards and stockholders. The roles that people assume in organizations perpetuate the power structure of the workplace, and this power structure can have a significant impact on the interpersonal communication of the organization.

Power is the ability of one person to influence another to do something. This power can come from various sources.[40] **Legitimate power**, for example, is ascribed to people as a result of the status and prestige of their positions. **Referent power** emerges from perceptions that people have or give to a person because of being liked or having good character. **Expert power** comes from a person's knowledge and skills.

You cannot always tell a person's power by the status of the work position. People who have been at your company a long time have tenure and status you may not recognize because you are an outsider or new employee. A person with a long tenure is a survivor. People with a long work history at your company have figured out how to obtain information, they have heard organizational stories, they have learned to adapt, and they have communication flexibility. Administrative assistants or secretaries, for example, might not seem to be powerful people. In fact, the assistant who has watched people come and go over twenty years may actually exert more influence than the person being assisted. Older people, for example, are sometimes inappropriately treated as invisible by younger employees and ignored as unimportant.[41] In fact, these work veterans may exert real power in the system. Cross them or dismiss them, and you may end up dismissed yourself, or miss out on a valuable resource for information and advice.

Part of your sense of empowerment comes from your self (self-efficacy), and part of your sense of empowerment comes from the organization. Employees may feel frustrated when they know they have the desire and skills to complete a task but don't have the right resources or authority to finish the task. Thus, you can motivate yourself and seek influences from the organization that can help you feel empowered at work. These empowerment strategies include self-efficacy (feeling you can do it), active attainment (taking steps to achieve), verbal persuasion, vicarious experience (enjoying the success of others), and emotional arousal (having a passion for your work).[42] In addition, you can increase your workplace power through effective interpersonal relationships.

People who are well connected, who know others and are known by others, operate from power positions through their interpersonal communication.[43] Along the same lines, you also can increase your power by being a trustworthy, dynamic, knowledgeable, and credible communicator.

COMMUNICATION BOUNDARIES

What topics should you discuss at work? How much should you talk at work? To what extent should work be done at home? Should you conduct personal business in the workplace? There are four general areas of **communication boundaries**, descriptions of what can and cannot be spoken about as well as how they should be discussed, regarding your job: appropriate communication content, appropriate communication style, appropriate communication methods, and appropriate communication time.

Talk about appropriate content. Sometimes at work, a colleague will tell you about a personal problem. As a friend, you may want to listen. As a coworker, you may need to tread carefully in this area. A coworker may have a grievance against another worker, for example. Don't necessarily share it with your coworkers. A better choice may be to involve a supervisor or a representative from human resources to talk to the individual needing help. If it's a serious psychological or physical issue, your coworker needs the help of a specialist, and that probably isn't you. As well-meaning as you are, you might do more harm than good.

Use an appropriate communication style. Not everyone is comfortable in casual conversations with other people at the office. A first consideration is whether or not the conversation is appropriate for the work context. Employees need to be careful about talking too much about their personal lives while at work. Many workers and supervisors may see such personal talk as a waste of company time. Some workers prefer to keep some distance between their personal and work lives. The breadth and depth of self-disclosure at work is something that requires good judgment. There is considerable difference in the tolerance people have for individuals who disclose an excess of personal information.[44]

You also will want to be careful that you don't talk too much. Research suggests that some people are so verbose they can be considered "talkaholics."[45] A **talkaholic** is someone who talks too much about inappropriate topics and thus can be perceived negatively by others.

LEARNING EXPERIENCE: Interested in learning if you are a talkaholic? If so, do Activity 12.4.

DECEPTION

Lying may be a normal part of social interaction, and not something particularly unusual or unique.[46] Your coworkers may smile and say "good idea" because you are enthusiastic about something, even if they don't totally agree because they don't want to hurt your feelings. You may say "Hi friend," to be welcoming at work to someone you don't really consider a friend. These kinds of little white lies are probably not a

ACTIVITY 12.4
Talkaholic Scale

Directions: Read the following questions and select the answer that corresponds with what you would do in most situations. Do not be concerned if some of the items appear similar. Please use the scale below to rate the degree to which each statement applies to you. Use the following responses:

Strongly Disagree = 1; Disagree = 2; Neutral = 3; Agree = 4; Strongly Agree = 5

_____ 1. Often I keep quiet when I should talk
_____ 2. I talk more than I should sometimes
_____ 3. Often, I talk when I know I should keep quiet
_____ 4. Sometimes I keep quiet when I know it would be to my advantage to talk
_____ 5. I am a "talkaholic"
_____ 6. Sometimes I feel compelled to keep quiet
_____ 7. In general, I talk more than I should
_____ 8. I am a compulsive talker
_____ 9. I am not a talker; rarely do I talk in communication situations
_____10. Quite a few people have said I talk too much
_____11. I just can't stop talking too much
_____12. In general, I talk less than I should
_____13. I am not a "talkaholic"
_____14. Sometimes I talk when I know it would be to my advantage to keep quiet
_____15. I talk less than I should sometimes
_____16. I am not a compulsive talker

Scoring: To determine the score on the Talkaholic Scale, complete the following steps:

Step 1: Add the scores for items 2, 3, 5, 7, 8, 10, 11, and 14.
Step 2: Add the scores for items 13 and 16.
Step 3: Complete the following formula: Total Score = 12 + Total from Step 1 – Total from Step 2.

Note: Items 1, 4, 6, 9, 12, and 15 are filler items and are not scored.

The score should be between 10 and 50. Most people score below 30.

People who score between 30 and 39 are borderline talkaholics, and are able to control their talking most of the time, but sometimes they find themselves in situations where it is difficult to be quiet, even if it would be very much to their advantage not to talk.

People with scores above 40 are talkaholics. They are truly compulsive communicators.

If your Talkaholic Scale score is between 30 and 38, you fall into the norm area. As you contemplate your score, consider how effectively you genuinely listen to others, balancing your amount of speaking and listening.

If your score is high, what do you need to do to be a more sensitive communicator?

Source: McCroskey, J. C., & Richmond, V. P. (1993). Identifying compulsive communicators: The talkaholic scale. *Communication Research Reports, 11,* 39–52. Used with permission of the authors.

problem because they are designed simply to help the social process. But **deception**, self-serving communication that is dishonest or unethical, can be problematic. Examples of deception include saying something that is not true, telling a partial truth, falsifying information, and omitting key information.

Not telling the truth often results in problems. Consider the example of a new employee who contacted Information Technology (IT) to say there was something wrong with his computer because the laptop was requiring new security questions beyond the finger swipe system. The IT person asked if the employee downloaded some software or made any changes in the computer's bios. Although the employee had downloaded software, he said, "No, I didn't do anything." By not admitting what he did, the employee made the IT trouble-shooter's job more difficult, and the IT person discovered the illegal software anyway. When the employee's supervisor asked the IT person how the new employee's computer was working, and was told of the deception, the results were not pleasant.

People tend to lie for two reasons: for the benefit of others or for the benefit of themselves.[47] People may lie to avoid disapproval of others, avoid embarrassment, to protect something or someone, or gain advantage over others.[48] Although it may be difficult to predict when someone will intentionally be unethical, the kinds of factors that may be present are whether or not someone believes the behavior is okay, the extent to which one feels a lack of control over the situation, whether the person feels pressured by others, the extent of the benefit, and whether or not they will be accepted by their peers.[49]

Failure to take responsibility for your actions may be considered a sign of being immature or untrustworthy. A person who is dishonest about something will make others wonder if trust can ever be warranted in other circumstances.

There may be a relationship between power and deception in the workplace, influencing the type of deception and reason for the lie.[50] Leaders tend to lie to maintain their power, which can be highly dangerous when they are found out because they can lose credibility and damage their reputation and their ability to lead.[51] Examples of this include the leadership of Enron and the bank and stock firms that helped cause the economic crash of 2008. These leaders and institutions have put the spotlight on lying in organizations.

Consider these research findings about lying at work:[52]

- The majority of job interviewees think it's okay to lie to get a job.
- Many managers suspect their sales staff may lie to customers in order to make sales.
- Under everyday circumstances, people lie from zero to fifty times a day.
- Most people cannot tell when another person is lying.

Although most people believe they can tell by a person's nonverbal communication when they are lying, in fact, nearly all of us are quite poor at detecting lies. Probably you should assume—like other people—that you cannot accurately detect when someone is lying.[53] Poor eye contact, giving too much detail, foot tapping and hesitancy during speech may seem like indicators of lying, but they are also consistent with nervousness. Nervousness can be common when anyone is being questioned or perceives judgment by another. There are also vast differences in various cultures regarding lying.

If you think someone has lied to you about something that may affect your ability to work, you may want to check information with a third party. There's no need to suggest that you are trying to catch a person in a lie, but you are simply seeking information so you know how to do your work appropriately. Although deception may in some ways be pervasive, lying at work can have serious consequences for both supervisors and subordinates.

DISAGREEMENTS IN THE WORKPLACE

People and departments in an organization may feel competitive with each other, which can lead to disagreements. Competition at work can motivate some people to behave in ways that may seem dishonest, unethical, or disagreeable to others. Some organizations rank the performance of each employee each year, and set a bottom percentage of people who will be automatically fired.[54] When people are scared about losing their jobs, they may work in self-protective ways.

You may disagree with a coworker's values, dislike the coworker's personality, or find the coworker to be untrustworthy, lazy, or two-faced. But the question is still: How will you work through disagreements? You can still choose to treat the person positively and with respect. There is nothing inherently wrong with disagreement. Usually the problem comes when you don't listen to the other's point of view or when you disagree because you want to get your own way.

To gain insight into how well you tolerate disagreement, take the Tolerance for Disagreement Scale.

LEARNING EXPERIENCE: Interested in learning how well you tolerate disagreement? If so, do Activity 12.5.

ACTIVITY 12.5
Tolerance for Disagreement Scale (TFD)

Instructions: This questionnaire involves people's feelings and orientations. Hence, there are no right or wrong answers. We just want you to indicate your reaction to each item. All responses are to reflect the degree to which you believe the item applies to you. Please use the following system to indicate the degree to which you agree that the item describes you:

5 = Strongly Agree, 4 = Agree, 3 = Undecided, 2 = Disagree, 1 = Strongly Disagree

____ 1. It is more fun to be involved in a discussion where there is a lot of disagreement.
____ 2. I enjoy talking to people with points of view different from mine.
____ 3. I don't like to be in situations where people are in disagreement.
____ 4. I prefer being in groups where everyone's beliefs are the same as mine.
____ 5. Disagreements are generally helpful.
____ 6. I prefer to change the topic of discussion when disagreement occurs.
____ 7. I tend to create disagreements in conversations because it serves a useful purpose.
____ 8. I enjoy arguing with other people about things on which we disagree.
____ 9. I would prefer to work independently rather than to work with other people and have disagreements.
____10. I would prefer joining a group where no disagreements occur.
____11. I don't like to disagree with other people.
____12. Given a choice, I would leave a conversation rather than continue a disagreement.
____13. I avoid talking with people who I think will disagree with me.
____14. I enjoy disagreeing with others.
____15. Disagreement stimulates a conversation and causes me to communicate more.

Scoring:
Step 1. Add the scores for the following items: 1, 2, 5, 7, 8, 14, and 15.
Step 2. Add the scores for the following items: 3, 4, 6, 9, 10, 11, 12, and 13.
Step 3. Complete the following formula: TFD = 48 + total of Step 1 − total of Step 2.

Scores above 46 indicate High TFD. Scores below 32 indicate Low TFD. Scores between 32 and 46 indicate moderate TFD.

(continued)

ACTIVITY 12.5 (continued)

Note, the higher your score, the better chance you face conflict with effective interpersonal communication skills. You may want to reexamine questions 1, 2, 5, 7, 8, 14, and 15 and think about how you can incorporate those kinds of behaviors into your interpersonal communication style.

Source: Teven, J. J., Richmond, V. P., & McCroskey, J. C. (1998). Measuring tolerance for disagreement. *Communication Research Reports, 15,* 209–217; Richmond, V. P. & McCroskey, J. C. (2001). *Organizational communication for survival: Making work, work* (2nd ed.). Needham Heights, MA: Allyn & Bacon, Chapter 14.

The authors of the Tolerance for Disagreement Scale believe that avoiding destructive interpersonal conflict is partly about how much you like the other person and partly about your willingness to tolerate disagreement.[55]

Effective interpersonal communicators tend to be tolerant of uncertainty and disagreement. Remember, the organization can survive without you.[56] No matter how intelligent, hard-working, talented, and helpful you are, you can be swapped for someone new.

If you start feeling or acting like you are irreplaceable, you may be surprised to find yourself looking for a job. In a time of leaner organizations, people who are disagreeable, can't get along, or create problems may be shed quickly. An organization doesn't need a reason for replacing you beyond the fact that you are incompatible.

ADAPTING TO A DIVERSE WORKPLACE

Today's workplace has people of various ages, ethnicities, cultural backgrounds, languages, gender, urban and rural perspectives, and sexual orientations. You are likely to encounter a wider diversity of people at work than you have in your home or perhaps even college contexts. In this section, we want to emphasize adapting to people of diverse cultures and to people of the opposite gender.

Rhetorical sensitivity is particularly important in adapting to people of other cultures.[57] The main problem in the workplace is ethnocentrism. **Ethnocentrism** occurs when a person thinks his or her group is the best and all other people should be measured against that group. Probably everyone has some ethnocentrism. The problem comes when ethnocentrism creates poor judgment, causes people to think of themselves as superior, more honest, more qualified, or more well-trained than people belonging to other groups.

In the workplace, ethnocentrism is "negatively and significantly correlated with perceptions of social attraction, competence, character, and hiring recommendations."[58] This means that people tend to hire people like themselves and consider similar coworkers to be more attractive and competent. Similar results were found regarding the supervisor-subordinate relationship. For the person who is ethnocentric, managers who are of the same ethnicity are seen as having more physical, social, and task attraction and competence.[59] Workers need to be extremely careful when working with people of other groups so they avoid inappropriate assumptions about people who are different from themselves.

GENDER IN THE WORKPLACE

Understanding the differences between the way men and women tend to communicate is critical in the workplace because it often determines salaries, promotions, and power.[60]

Though the concepts are generalizations, research in gender and organizations indicates that "men go to work as if they're going to battle, whereas women go to work as if they're going to the village square."[61] "Men don't like to ask questions, because they've been traditionally brought up and conditioned to think that their job as a man is to have all the answers. For women, asking questions is a very valid way of getting information that works well for them. But men look at a woman and think, 'She must not know enough to do her job.'"[62] "Men communicate to share what they know; women communicate to establish relationships."[63] Another difference is that "women don't want to focus on the solution until they've finished venting, and men don't want to hear all the details."[64] Recognizing these differences and working to accommodate the styles of each gender can facilitate communication.

All of these findings aid in understanding why, in the workplace environment, when males and females communicate, they may be perceived differently.

As indicated in Figure 12.3, there are challenges for both men and women in the workplace.

Figure 12.3.   Gender Challenges at Work

Women	Men
Feeling dismissed, ignored, excluded, talked down to, or avoided. Being continually tested regarding knowledge and competence. Needing to "act like a man" to be taken seriously. Questioning one's self because of negative coworker treatment. Hearing that "she only got the job because she's a woman" (tokenism).	Confused about ground rules of appropriate behavior toward women coworkers. Avoiding women because at some point accused of sexual harassment. Believing there is reverse discrimination or overcompensation for women or minorities, which makes it harder for men in general. Seeing women who don't support other women, so being hesitant to push for support of women coworkers. Being afraid that support of women will be perceived as something more than it is. Fearing spontaneity and authenticity with women at work because of possible misinterpretation or sexist charges.

Source: Adapted from Annis, B. (2004). Gender differences in the workplace. WITI careers. Retrieved from www.witi.com/careers/2004/genderdiffs.php.

So what can be done about these differences? "For men, some of the things they need to do is to become more considerate, caring, trusting—basically to become good communicators. Give women enough time to finish their ideas. Avoid interrupting them, finishing their sentences or being sarcastic and condescending."[65]

"A more balanced workplace would include allowing both genders to display emotion and accept that display as healthy. We don't want a passionless workplace."[66]

It must be recognized that over the last twenty or so years there has been a general shift in the roles played by men and women. There are more women in the professions and in the workforce, in general. Some men have been brought up by parents who have taught them to be more caring and sharing, and who broke many of the traditional roles. Some women have been raised by parents who have taught them competition, teamwork, and direct communication. The result is that many men and women are more effective interpersonal communicators at work because of their adaptive styles.

LEAVING A JOB WITHOUT BURNING BRIDGES

At some point, you may leave that first key job. There are many possible reasons for leaving a job, such as not being able to work effectively with the supervisor, seeking new opportunities, or being fired or laid off.

Flexible workers are open to new job possibilities. By maintaining the best possible relationship with your supervisor and coworkers, you may actually find out about new job opportunities within your current organization or other organizations. For example, a coworker may be job hunting and notice an excellent opportunity at another organization, which is the perfect fit for you. Many supervisors want to see their successful subordinates advance within the organization or to better their position outside the organization.

If you approach the process carefully, never speak ill of your current supervisor or coworkers, and maintain contact after you leave the organization, you should be able to maximize your networking and relational success. Leaving jobs without burning bridges can be important because a large percentage of today's jobs will not exist in thirty years.[67] You may need your former coworkers for networking and references.

Everyone understands that with today's changing workplace, people change jobs often. Although past generations tended to stay in the same job for a long time, the predictions are that today's college graduate will have many jobs over his or her lifetime. The average U.S. American worker has been in the current position for a median of four years.[68] In the computer land of Silicon Valley, the average employee "will have worked in 10 different jobs by the time they are 45."[69] By making an effort to maintain good communication with current and past coworkers, the long term career outlook may be more promising.

When you leave an organization, you may receive an exit interview. At that time, your employer may ask you for information about your supervisor, coworkers, and the organization. You will want to project a positive, engaged image as you leave. Be careful not to complain about people or conditions. If you're asked for suggestions for how the organization might do better, offer your ideas with a positive and tactful perspective.

Violence and Harassment in the Workplace

Although people want to feel safe at home and at work, they may not be safe. More than 1.5 million cases of workplace violence happen each year, including about one thousand murders. In fact, the leading cause of death of women at work is not caused by unsafe working condition, but homicide.[70] At Yale University, for example, a lab technician murdered a coworker. New Haven Police Chief James Lewis said: "It is important to note that this is not about urban crime, university crime, domestic crime but an issue of workplace violence, which is becoming a growing concern around the country."[71] Remembering that communicators usually cannot tell when another person is lying, so, without being paranoid, a bit of skepticism about coworkers may be wise.[72]

Think of the adage "sticks and stones can break my bones, but names will never hurt me." It is wrong! Words can hurt, abuse, and violate. Violence in the workplace not only includes physical violence, but psychological violence as well. The effect of sexual harassment as a communicative event was clarified during an acceptance speech for the Nobel Prize for literature when the speaker explained, "Oppressive language does more than violence . . . it is violence."[73]

Words carry meanings; meanings can hurt, degrade, take away rights, retract actions, demean. Repeating over and over to a coworker, "You're stupid" may convince the person that he is not intelligent, creating a pattern or negative self-perception and negative self-fulfilling prophecies. Telling a coworker that she can't "add," "write," or "give a speech," may convince her she is incompetent, with the resulting negative self-attitudes.

Verbal/sexual harassment is gender-based unwelcome words or actions. Sexual harassment includes sexist remarks or behaviors that are inappropriate and offensive, as well as sex-linked behavior that promises rewards. Harassment can take place in your home, at work, or in educational environments. Girls may find themselves belittled or violated by members of their family or their family's circle of friends. In corporate life, harassment can be a serious and pervasive problem, with both the targets and those accused (falsely or not) suffering personal anguish.[74]

Harassment is more prevalent than many believe. In 2008, the U.S. Equal Opportunity Commission received 13,867 charges of sexual harassment. Of those charges, 15.9 percent were filed by males. EEOC resolved 11,731 sexual harassment charges and recovered $47.4 million in monetary benefits for charging parties and other aggrieved individuals.[75] Even the U.S. army's first female three star general filed a harassment complaint against another general who inappropriately touched her[76] (a nonverbal act of aggression). Among college women it is estimated that one out of six are sexually assaulted while in college.[77]

Men can also be recipients of sexual harassment. One out of every five to eight men will be sexually assaulted during his lifetime.[78] Men may face the secondary trauma of a lack of understanding from the people around them who think that guys should simply enjoy sexual advances and even assault.[79]

In contrast to popular belief, men can be and are harassed and sexually abused.[80] Harassers can be men or women.[81] The harasser may see himself or herself as intending to exercise power over others, protect professional turf, enhance self-image, or even demonstrate friendliness and helpfulness.

Verbal/sexual harassment has not changed over the years, but "people are more willing to talk about it, and people are more angry about it."[82] Part of the reason for this change in attitude and reporting is that it is only in recent years that sexual harassment has been given a name and identified as an unacceptable act. Until 1964, when the first federal regulation regarding sexual harassment was enacted, there was no official name for the action. Language creates our reality, so without a way of identifying it, the action was, in reality, not perceived as a reality. Interestingly, it was not until 1997 that the "Final Amendment Guidelines on Discrimination Because of Sex" was added to the regulations of the United States Equal Employment Opportunity Commission's Guidelines.[83]

The harassed may want to stop the harassment; deter future incidents; preserve her or his reputation; avoid retaliation; maintain rapport; and preserve self-respect, physical safety, and psychological well-being, but may not know how to do it or realize that he or she has the right to be treated with dignity and respect.

RESPONDING TO VERBAL OR SEXUAL HARASSMENT

"What should I do if I'm a recipient of unwelcome behavior?" If you question a person's actions as being inappropriate you can use the following responses:[84]

Trust your instincts. If something feels wrong to you, then it is wrong for you.

Don't blame yourself. You are the person being wronged, not the perpetrator. A common ploy by harassers is to suggest that the victim is at fault because she or he encouraged the harassment by the type of clothing she or he wore, the way the person looked at them, or the type of language the person used. This ploy is an attempt to turn the innocent person into the guilty party.

Get emotional support. Turn to a mental health professional, an expert in harassment, or a support telephone hotline that deals with harassment.

Say "no" clearly and early to the individual whose behavior or comments make you uncomfortable. Stop the other person; don't allow the person to continue with the harassing actions or verbalizations. Confront the perpetrator. Call a halt to harassment immediately by saying emphatically, "No. Stop. I will not allow you to . . . (*speak to me like that; threaten me; attempt to humiliate me; or touch me*)."

Document every incident in detail. Keep a record. Immediately write down everything that happened including exactly what was said or done, with dates and times, and any other supporting evidence. Share the information with another person to verify the acts have taken place. If possible, get a witness to attest to the action(s).

Find a way to speak out. Make a statement to a counselor at your college, the human resources department of your organization, your supervisor. Seek out institutional and company channels and use them. The harassment probably has happened before to someone else or—if left unchecked—will happen again to someone else.

Seek out supportive individuals. Find a safe zone, which can be a person or department responsible for providing resources for persons who perceive that they have been harassed. Without a safe zone, you may want to talk to another manager, whom you think may be helpful.

File a charge with a local, state, or federal antidiscrimination agency if necessary. As with any legal action, it will be your responsibility to prove the harassing actions or verbalizations. Be sure you can document the accusations and be aware that this process can be difficult financially and emotionally on the person making the charges.

Be a good listener to someone who has been harassed. If a friend or coworker shares that he or she has been or is being harassed, you should:

- *Listen without judging.*
- *Validate that harassment is wrong.*
- *Offer to help explore resources and support the recipient's efforts to seek help.*
- *Be prepared for displaced anger as the recipient may not be able to channel it appropriately.* In some instances, when a person is feeling stressed, she or he will attack the nearest source. So, don't be surprised if the victim turns her or his wrath on you, even if you are trying to be helpful. The person is not really attacking you, just acting out of frustration.
- *Offer affirmation to the recipient that whatever feelings are being expressed are his or her right to have.* Victims sometimes are confused and don't trust their own judgment. They need affirmation as to their rights and responsibilities.
- *Reassure the recipient that you care and are there to be supportive.* Offer to be of assistance in whatever way you can, but be aware that you are not the person who was harassed.
- *Do not take matters into your own hands but, rather, help the individual to find the appropriate channels either inside or outside of the organization.* Unless you are a lawyer or a mental health professional, be aware of your limitations.

Key Terms

organizational culture	monochronic time culture
organizational climate	polychronic time cultures
organizational hierarchy	power
work teams	legitimate power
networking	referent power
group collaboration	expert power
stand-up meeting	communication boundaries
popcorn meeting	talkaholic
employment interview	deception
performance appraisal interview	ethnocentrism
rhetorical sensitivity	verbal/sexual harassment
impression management	

Competencies Check-Up

Interested in finding out what you learned in this chapter and how you use the information? If so, take this competencies check-up.

Directions: Indicate the extent that each statement applies to you:

1—Never   2—Seldom   3—Sometimes   4—Often   5—Usually

____ 1. I am aware of the need to analyze the corporate culture to ascertain the communication actions accepted and expected of me in a work environment.

____ 2. I'm open-minded and able to see the perspectives of other people at work.

____ 3. I keep private information confidential, and I'm known for my honesty and integrity at work.

____ 4. I understand the time concepts in my work environment and follow them.

____ 5. I know and follow the dress requirements at work.

____ 6. I realize, if I am a new employee, that my ideas may not be solicited until I have earned the respect of my coworkers and supervisor.

____ 7. I am aware of the differences between a supportive and defensive climate in the work environment.

____ 8. Though I may perceive that the work climate needs adjusting, I am willing to accept the organization as it is until I am either asked for input or rise to the place in the hierarchy where I can affect the climate.

____ 9. I am aware of the operational differences between hierarchies that are top-down, flat, or bottom-up.

____10. I am aware of the value of networking and how it can provide me a support system.

____11. I am aware of the use of groups as part of organizational business and know why groups are used.

____12. I appreciate the need for group cohesion.

____13. I know the basic reasons why some leaders are effective, while others are ineffective.

____14. I know the basic concepts of interviewing techniques and follow them when I am interviewed.

____15. I know the dangers of gossiping at work and avoid doing it.

____16. I know the basic principles of impression management and try to follow them.

____17. I am aware of the role of power in organizations and respect the differences between legitimate, referent, and expert power.

____18. I understand the concept of deception and realize the potential negative impact of lying in the organizational setting.

____19. I am aware of my own ethnocentrism and take it into consideration when interacting in the organizational setting.

____20. I realize that there is sometimes a difference in communication by women and men and take that into consideration when communicating in the organizational setting.

____21. I can define verbal and sexual harassment and know not to participate in it.

Scoring: A total of 63 suggests you have minimum interpersonal communication competencies in the workplace. Carefully examine your answers and needed areas of change.

I-Can Plan!

Whether you are in a job you want to keep or thinking about the one you'd like to have, now is a good time to take stock of your strengths and needs regarding interpersonal communication in the workplace. How effectively you communicate with the diverse people you encounter in the workplace will affect every aspect of your life. As one attorney told a potential client, "As soon as you get things straightened out at work, I'll handle your divorce." The attorney knew that when work was going smoothly, so would the man's marriage. At work you will need to figure out how to get along with people of the opposite sex, different sexual orientations, different ethnicity, a variety of ages, a range of work experiences, and more. Rhetorical sensitivity can be a way of adapting language and nonverbal communication appropriately regarding effective communication with people of a different gender or sexual orientation.[85] As you start out your career and for some years to come, virtually everyone will have more experience, knowledge, status, and power than you do. Now is a good time to write down a plan for your goals and figure out what skills you need to develop so you can negotiate your career effectively.

Activities

1. Create your own interpersonal communication workplace profile. Write down what you would like to *continue* doing as a communicator; what you would like to *start* doing as a communicator, and what you would like to *stop* doing as a communicator. Be sure to begin your list with what you want to continue. Communicators need to recognize what they do well so they'll reinforce those behaviors.
2. Arrange an interview with someone in your professional field of interest. Set up a series of questions concerning what you would like to know about interpersonal communication in this field. How central is communication in the field? Do you spend the majority of your time listening or speaking? What is the role of computer mediated communication? What suggestions would you offer for being an effective interpersonal communicator in the field?
3. Look at some of the popular books in the business section of your local library or bookstore. What do the authors have to say about the role of communication in managing an organization? The role of communication in leading an organization? Are there some useful recommendations that would enhance good interpersonal communication in the workplace?
4. Conduct a case study on interpersonal communication in an organization. Obtain permission to do your research. Ideally, you should interview some people in the organization, do some observations during a typical work week, and conduct a

questionnaire survey. Your case study should report your research results. Does the organization have good interpersonal communication? Why or why not? What characterizes the communication in this workplace? What channels are used? What is the communication climate? Is good communication supported at all levels in the organization? What can be learned about communication in the workplace from this organization? What are benchmarks for effective interpersonal communication in the workplace?

5. Identify an experience you've had at your job which could have been improved by more effective communication. Based on what you learned in this book, what could you have done differently?

6. Your instructor will divide the class into small groups of three to five students. Discuss one of these questions:

    a. How should you adapt your work communication in this, a global society?

    b. What are the problems created by diversity in the workplace?

    c. What are your major concerns about job interviews?

    Based on your discussion, indicate how effectively your group operated. What were the group's strengths and weaknesses? How could the group have worked more effectively?

Notes

Chapter 1: Foundations of Interpersonal Communication

1. College graduates aren't ready for the real world. (2005, February 18). *The Chronicle of Higher Education*, p. B11.

2. This classic theory was developed by David Berlo and first presented in Berlo, D. K. (1960). *The process of communication: An introduction to theory and practice.* New York: Holt, Rinehart and Winston.

3. Factors that cause communication difficulties are sometimes called *interference.* In this textbook, these factors are referred to as *noise.* The identifiers of the noise factors are arbitrary and are not necessarily limited to these identifiers.

4. For an investigation of the topic, use a search engine such as Google or Yahoo under the topic "Ethnography of Communication."

5. The theory presented is based on a synthesis of concepts about ethnography as they relate to communication. The general idea was conceived as a student project of Roy Berko, as part of a graduate seminar under the direction of Gerald Phillips, at Pennsylvania State University, and has been developed through personal observation and informal testing.

6. Greenspan, P. (2007, November 19). *The home court advantage.* Swans. Retrieved from www.swans.com/library/art13/pgreen125.html.

7. The theory of interpersonal communication is credited to various sources. The discussion of interpersonal communication that is the basis of much of this text was first introduced to the lead author of this book by Dr. Gerald Phillips, Pennsylvania State University, in a 1969 course, Interpersonal Communication.

8. For a discussion of communication needs of employees, see Marchant, V. (1999, June 28). Listen up! *Time,* p. 72; Grubb, J. (2002, Fall). Get that job. *Young Money,* p. 11; Bartoo, H., & Sias, P. M. (2004). When enough is too much: Communication apprehension and employee information experiences. *Communication Quarterly, 52*(1), 15–26.

9. Samovar, L., Porter, R., & McDaniel, E. (2009). *Intercultural communication: A reader* (12th ed.). Boston, MA: Wadsworth Cengage Learning, p. 10.

10. *Whites to be minority in US by 2020: Study.* (2008, February 11). Retrieved from News.yahoo.com/s/afp/2008

11. Ibid.

12. Andersen, P., & Wange, H. (2009). Beyond language: Nonverbal communication across cultures. In Samovar, Porter, & McDaniel, pp. 264–277. For other perspectives about culture and nonverbal communication, see Pell, M., Monetta, L., Paulmann, S., & Kotz, S. (2009*)*. Recognizing emotions in a foreign language. *Journal of Nonverbal Behavior, 33*(2), 107–120; or Young-Ok Lee (2009). Perceptions of time in Korean and English. *Human Communication, 12*(1), 119–138.

13. Rhine, R. D. (1989, Spring). William Graham Sumner's concept of ethnocentrism: Some implications for intercultural communication. *World Communication, 18*(2). For an additional definition and discussion on ethnocentrism see Barger, K. (2004). *Anthropology.* Indiana University Indianapolis. Retrieved from www.iupui.edu/~anthkb/ethnocen.htm.

14. Johannesen, R. L. (2001). *Ethics in human communication* (4th ed.). Prospect Heights, IL: Waveland Press, p. 2.

15. Ibid.

16. Bauder, D. (2003, July 7). MSNBC fires Savage on anti-gay remarks. Associated Press. As cited in *The Miami Herald.* Retrieved from www.miamiherald.com/

17. Ibid.

18. MSNBC spokesman Jeremy Gaines, as cited in Bauder, 2003.

19. Banned by U.K., Savage hits back. (2009). *WorldNetDaily.* Retrieved from www.wnd.com/index.php?fa=PAGE.view&pageId=97127.

20. Satter, R. G. (2009, May 5). Michael Savage banned from entering UK: Country publishes list of people not allowed. *Huffington Post.* Retrieved from www.huffingtonpost.com/2009/05/05/michael-savage-banned-fro_n_196631.html.

21. Cathy Renna, GLAAD spokeswoman, as cited in Bauder.

22. Berko, R., Wolvin, A., & Wolvin, D. (2004). *Communication: A social and career focus* (9th ed.). Boston, MA: Houghton Mifflin, p. 30.

23. Nilsen, T. (1966). *Ethics in speech communication.* Indianapolis: Bobbs-Merrill, p. 139.

24. Adapted from Nilsen.

25. Newton, I. (1687). *The principia.* Retrieved from www.archive.org/details/newtonspmathema00newtrich.

26. A concept expressed on her nationally syndicated radio program by Dr. Joy Browne. See Browne, J. (2009), www.drjoy.com/.

27. Ibid.

Chapter 2: The Self and Communication

1. Pamela Butler, as noted in McGarvey, R. (1990, March). Talk yourself up. *USAir Magazine*, 90. For more information on self-talk go to: more-selfesteem.com.

2. Ibid.

3. The concept of vultures was originally presented in Simon, S. B. (1977). *Vulture: A modern allegory on the art of putting oneself down.* Niles, IL: Argus Communications.

4. A concept developed by Joan Aitken based on the ideas of Sidney Simon.

5. David Grant, as noted in McGarvey, p. 90.

6. Bernie Zilbergeld, as noted in McGarvey, p. 94.

7. Robertson, S. (2002). *Learning and the brain.* Tempe, AZ: Rio Salado. Retrieved from www.rioo.Maricopa edu/classes/edu/edu270/020402/.

8. A concept presented in Festinger, L. (1957). *A theory of cognitive dissonance.* Evanston, IL: Row, Peterson.

9. A concept presented in Wahlross, S. (1974). *Family communication*. New York: Macmillan, p. xi. For more information on self-concept see: www.eruptingmind.com/self-concept-self-esteem/.

10. Bernie Zilbergeld, as noted in McGarvey, p. 94.

11. Based on the theories of William Glasser. For more on Glasser, see: www.wglasser.com/.

12. Lockett, C. T., & Harrell, J. P. (2003). Racial identity, self-esteem, and academic achievement: Too much interpretation, too little supporting data. *Journal of Black Psychology*, *29*, 325–336.

13. Crocker, J., & Luhtanen, R. K. (2003). Level of self-esteem and contingencies of self-worth: Unique effects on academic, social, and financial problems in college students. *Personality and Social Psychology Bulletin*, *29*, 701–712.

14. Chang, V. Y., Bendel, T. L., Koopman, C., McGarvey, E. L., & Canterbury, R. J. (2003). Delinquents' safe sex attitudes: Relationships with demographics, resilience factors, and substance use. *Criminal Justice and Behavior*, *30*, 210–229.

15. Isnard, P., Michel, G., Frelut, M. L., Vila, G., Falissard, B., Naja, W., Navarro, J., & Mouren-Simeoni, M. C. (2003). Binge eating and psychopathology in severely obese adolescents. *The International Journal of Eating Disorders*, *34*, 235–243. Retrieved from www.ncbi.nlm.nih.gov.

16. Theory of Dr. Joy Brown, media psychologist, as expressed on her syndicated talk-radio show.

17. Maasen, T., & Sandfort, T. Counselling unsafe sex problems of young gay men. gatteway.nim.nih.gov/MeetingAbstracts/ma?f+102206876.html.

18. Based on theories presented in Fromm, E. (1955). *The sane society*. New York: Rinehart.

19. Theory of Dr. Joy Brown, media psychologist, as expressed on her syndicated talk-radio show.

20. Wyle, R. C. (1979). *The self-concept*. Lincoln: University of Nebraska Press, p. 9.

21. The verb *to be* provides us with our basic label of our *self*. Native Americans and those from some other cultures, such as West Africans, may have difficulty understanding and applying this concept because of linguistic and cultural differences. Most European Americans, however, should find it an understandable concept.

22. The concept of the Johari window was first explained in Luft, J. A. (1963). *Group process: An introduction to group dynamics*. Palo Alto, CA: National Press, ch. 3.

23. Based on Rosenfeld, L. Relational disclosure and feedback. Unpublished paper developed by Lawrence Rosenfeld, Department of Communication, University of North Carolina, Chapel Hill, and printed in Berko, R., Rosenfeld, L., & Samovar, L. (1997). *Connecting: A culture-sensitive approach to interpersonal communication competency*. Forth Worth, TX: Harcourt Brace College Publishers, pp. 304–311.

24. Schrof, J. M., & Schultz, S. (1999, July 21). Social anxiety. *U.S. News and World Report*, 50.

25. Based on early research of Zimbardo, P. (1977). *Shyness: What it is; What to do about it*. Reading, MA: Addison Wesley, 13–14. These statistics have been confirmed by various other researchers.

26. Azar, B. (1995, November). Shy people have inaccurate self-concepts. *American Psychological Association Monitor*, 24.

27. Ibid.

28. Ayres, J., & Hopf, T. (1993). *Coping with speech anxiety*. Norwood, NJ: Ablex Publishing, p. 4.

29. Gilbert, R. (2001). *Shy is everywhere, shy/socially phobic celebrities and everyday people*. Retrieved from www.shakeyourshyness.com/shypeople.htm.

30. Based on information supplied by James McCroskey; also see Richmond & McCroskey.

31. In 1998 Jerome Kagan reported that shyness had a biological base, as indicated in Newman, S. (2008, November 14). Shyness: A mental disorder or personality quirk? *Psychology Today*.

32. Schwartz, C. (2004). *Born shy, always shy?* American Association for the Advancement of Science (AAAS). Retrieved from www.scienceblog.com.

33. Ibid.

34. Ibid.

35. Wheeless, L. R. (1975, September). An investigation of receiver apprehension and social context dimensions of communication apprehension. *Speech Teacher, 24,* 261–268. For more information on listening apprehension see: Wheeless, L. R., & Schrodt, P. (2001). *Communication research reports, 18*(1), 1–10.

36. For an extensive discussion of the effects of communication anxiety, see www.jamesc mccroskey.com/.

37. Chesebro, J. W., et al. (1992). Communication apprehension and self-perceived communication competence of at-risk student. *Communication Education, 41,* 345–360.

38. Based on an unpublished investigation of speech reticence conducted by Doug Pederson, Pennsylvania State University, 1971.

39. Daly, J., & McCroskey, J. (Eds.). (1997). *Avoiding communication: Shyness, reticence, and communication apprehension* (2nd ed.). Cresskill, NJ: Hampton Press.

40. Richmond & McCroskey.

41. Ibid.

42. Ibid.

43. MedicineNet.com. (2000, April 10). *Is shyness a mental disorder?* Retrieved from www .medicinenet.com/script/main/art.asp?articlekey=50793.

44. Ibid.

45. Based on anecdotal evidence collected by Roy Berko, crisis counselor, from working with groups of both clients self-identified and individuals who scored highly on the CAGC questionnaire.

46. Richmond & McCroskey.

47. Ibid.

48. Ibid.

49. Schrof, J. M., & Schultz, S. (1999, July 21). Social anxiety. *U.S. News and World Report,* 50.

50. Ibid; Raghunathan, A. (1999, May 18). Drug firms work on treatment for extreme forms of shyness. *Cleveland Plain Dealer,* 8A. Paxil was the first selective serotonin reuptake inhibitor to win approval by the Food and Drug Administration for treatment of debilitating shyness. In addition, the drugs Zoloft and Prozac may be of some value. A new form of Paxil, Paxil CR, was introduced in 2004.

51. A theory proposed by Roy Berko, crisis counselor, and proven through anecdotal evidence to be successful with communicatively anxious and phobic clients in his counseling practice.

Chapter 3: Listening as an Interpersonal Skill

1. Oldsenburg, D. (1984). Sometimes people only hear what they really want to hear. *Washington Post*, as reprinted in *Cleveland Plain Dealer* (1987, March 18), p. G1, using materials developed by Montgomery, R. (1984). *Listening made easy*. New York: Amacom.

2. Based on materials developed by Robert Montgomery as they appear in Berko, R., Rosenfeld, L., & Samovar, L. (1997). *Connecting: A culture-sensitive approach to interpersonal communication competency* (2nd ed.). Fort Worth, TX: Harcourt Brace College Publishers, p. 100.

3. Friedman, T. (2005, January 27). Read my ears. *New York Times.*

4. Buckley, M. F. (1992). Focus on research: We listen a book a day; we speak a book a week: Learning from Walter Loban. *Language Arts, 69,* 622–626.

5. For information on listening, see the International Association of Listening: www.listen.org/.

6. Lloyd, R. (2009, June 24). *Most people prefer right ear for listening.* Based on studies by Luca Tommasi and Daniele Marzoli. Retrieved from www.livescience.com/health/090624-right-ear.html.

7. Ibid.

8. *How many deaf people are there in the USA?* Retrieved from www.signgenius.com/sign-language/how-many-deaf-people-in-usa.shtml.

9. Marcia Warren, CCC-A, licensed audiologist, interviewed, July 10, 2009.

10. For a discussion of short-term memory see: psychology.wikia.com/wiki/Short-term_memory; and *Human memory: Can short-term memory and long-term memory be improved?,* www.audiblox.com/human_memory.htm.

11. *The negative effects of television.* Retrieved from Raw-Food-Health.net based on Johnson et al. (2002, March). Television viewing and aggressive behavior during adolescence and adulthood. *Science, 29.* Early release of selected estimates based on data from the January–June 2007 *National Health Interview Survey* (2007, December). CDC NCHS, 2007–11–19. Retrieved from www.cdc.gov/nchs/data/nhis/earlyrelease/200712_06.pdf.

12. *Video games to treat ADD?* (2005, November 5). Retrieved from About.com: Mental Health.

13. Ibid.

14. *Quick and easy effective tips for speaking rate; or: How to pace your words for maximum effectiveness.* (2009). Write-out-loud.com. Retrieved from www.write-out-loud.com.

15. Zachmeier, A. (2007). Time-compressed speech. In B. Hoffman (Ed.) *Encyclopedia of educational technology.* Retrieved from coe.sdsu.edu/eet/articles/fast_speech/start.htm.

16. For a discussion of right/global and left/linear brain theory see *Right brain vs. left brain.* Funderstanding. Retrieved from www.funderstanding.com/content/right-brain-vs-left-brain; Anderson, D. (1998). *Brain differences, creativity and the right side of the brain.* Retrieved from tolearn.net/hypertext/brain.htm; and Cutter, R. (1994). *When opposites attract: Right brain/left brain relationships and how to make them work.* New York: Dutton; and Connell, D. (2009). *Left brian/right brain.* Retrieved from www2.scholastic.com/browse/article.jsp?id=3629; and Springer, S. P., & Deutsch, G. (2001). *Left brain, right brain: Perspectives from cognitive neuroscience* (5th ed.) (Series of books in psychology). Cranbury, NJ: W. H. Freeman and Company/Worth Publishers.

17. Theory first reported in Rogers, C. R., & Roethlisberger, F. J. (1952, July–August). Barriers and gateways to communication. *Harvard Business Review, 30,* 46–52.

18. An analysis developed by Andrew Wolvin and Carolyn Gwynn Coakley.

19. Based on a training program for help-line volunteers developed by Roy Berko, crisis counselor, Whitman Walker Clinic, Washington, DC, in 1995 and updated in 2009.

20. *What is compassionate listening?* Berman Healing Arts. Retrieved from www.bermanhealingarts.com/3_compassion/index.htm.

21. The teachings of Thich Nhat Hanh as expressed in his concept of Three Steps of Peace, as cited in Monroe, C. (n.d.) *Compassionate listening.* Retrieved from www.newconversations.net/compassion/cl_chap5.htm.

22. Weingarten, R. U. (2006, November 12). Communication with compassion: The art of listening. A report of the Bikur Cholim Conference. *Turn to me: Faces and phases of Bikur Cholim.* New York, p. 4.

23. Borysenko, J. (2006, November 12). Guilt is the teacher, love is the lesson, p. 78, as cited in Weingarten.

24. Weingarten, p. 10.

25. For a teaching guide to compassionate listening, see suggestions for compassionate listening. *The seven challenges workbook.* Retrieved from www.NewConversations.net; also of interest is Rehling, D. L. (2008). Compassionate listening: A framework for listening to the seriously ill. *International Journal of Listening, 22*(1), 83–89.

26. Early principles of active listening styles were stated by William E. Arnold and Michael Beatty; also see *Active listening, hear what people are really saying.* (2009). Mind Tools, Ltd. Retrieved from www.mindtools.com/CommSkll/ActiveListening.htm; and Cichon, E. J. (2001). Practicing active listening. *Communication Teacher, 16*(1), 11–14.

27. Based on research by Deborah Tannen and reported in Tannen, D. (1990). *You just don't understand: Women and men in conversation.* New York: William Morrow.

28. Beall, M. (2007). Perspectives on intercultural listening. In P. Cooper, C. Calloway-Thomas, & C. J. Simonds (Eds.), *Intercultural communication: A text with readings.* Boston: Pearson, p. 156.

29. Ibid., p. 157.

30. Ibid., p. 158.

31. Thomlison, T. D. (1996). Intercultural listening, in M. Purdy & D. Borissof (Eds.). *Listening in everyday life.* University Press of America, Chapter 4, p. 89.

32. Ishii, S., & Bruneau, T. (1991). Silence and silences in cross-cultural perspective: Japan and the United States. In L. A. Samovar, & R. E. Porter (Eds.). *Intercultural communication: A reader* (7th ed.). Belmont, CA: Wadsworth, p. 125.

33. A concept set forth in Hall, E. T., & Hall, M. R. (1989). *Understanding cultural differences.* Yarmouth, ME: Intercultural Press. For an in-depth discussion of high/low contexts, see Lustig, M., & Kioester, J. (2010). *Intercultural competence, interpersonal communication across cultures.* Boston, MA: Pearson, pp. 112–113.

34. Atwater, D. (1989). *Issues facing minorities in speech communication education: Moving from the melting pot to a tossed salad.* Proceedings from the Future of Speech Communication Education, Speech Communication Association Flagstaff Conference Report. Annandale, VA: Speech Communication Association, p. 41.

35. Ibid.

36. Ibid.

37. A concept developed by Lawrence R. Wheeless, first reported in Wheeless, L. R. (1975, September). An investigation of receiver apprehension and social context dimensions of communication apprehension. *Speech Teacher 24,* p. 263. For a follow-up discussion, see Wilcox, A. K. (2002, November). *Receiver apprehension and college students, An examination of remediation via interactive skills training.* Retrieved from www.lcsc.edu/humanities/Wilcox-paper.htm.

38. Ayres, J., Keereetaweep, T., Chen, P., & Edwards, P. A. (1998, January). Communication apprehension and employment interviews. *Communication Education, 47*(1), 1–17.

39. A concept first discussed in Addeo, E., & Burger, R. (1974). *Egospeak.* New York: Bantam Books, p. xiv.

Chapter 4: Verbal Language

1. For details on language development, see *Language development in children*. Retrieved from www.childdevelopmentinfo.com/development/language_development.shtml; and Gleason, J. B., & Ratner, N. B. (2008). *The development of language* (7th ed.). Boston: Allyn Bacon Pearson.

2. *Civil marriage v. civil union, what's the difference?* (n.d.). Boston, MA: Gay & Lesbian Advocates & Defenders. Retrieved from www.massequality.org/ourwork/marriage/marriagevscivilunions.pdf

3. *Civil unions for gays favored, polls show.* (2009). MSNBC. Retrieved from www.msnbc.msn.com/id/4496265/.

4. Definitions of language. (2009). *The American heritage dictionary*. Retrieved from dictionary.reference.com/browse/language.

5. Ministère de l'Éducation de la Saskatchewan. (n.d.). Canada. Retrieved from www.sasked.gov.sk.ca/docs/francais/frcore/sec/inst2.html. According to Janusik and Wovlin, people spend most of their time (48%) communicating with their friends, followed by time in school, at work, and with families. Students spend 24% of their time listening, 20% speaking, 13% using the Internet, 9% writing, and 8% reading. See Janusik, L., & Wolvin, A. (2009). 24 hours in a day: A listening update to the time studies. *International Journal of Listening, 23*(2), 104–120. doi:10.1080/10904010903014442.

6. Eakin, E. (2002, May 18). Before the word, perhaps the wink? Some language experts think humans spoke first with gestures. *New York Times*, Section B, p. 7, Column 5, based on Corballis, M. C. (2002). *From hand to mouth: The origins of language*. Princeton, NJ: Princeton University Press.

7. Ibid.

8. Ibid.

9. Corballis; also see Gillis, J. (2002, August 15). Gene mutations linked to language development. *Washington Post*, p. A13. Retrieved from www.washingtonpost.com/ac2/wp-dyn?pagename=article&node=&contentId=A17863-2002Aug14&notFound=true.

10. See Littlejohn, S. W. (2004). *Theories of human communication* (7th ed.). Belmont, CA: Wadsworth, chapter 9.

11. Eakin.

12. Ibid.

13. Ibid.

14. Ibid.

15. *Hypermiling is latest automotive term added to Oxford English Dictionary.* (2008, November 14). Retrieved from automotive.com.

16. Ibid.

17. *Stroke.* (1999–2007). American Speech-Language-Hearing Association. Retrieved from www.asha.org/public/speech/disorders/Stroke.htm.

18. In square breathing, breathe in through the nose to a count of four (four seconds), maintain the air in your lungs for four seconds, breathe out through your mouth to a count of four, repeat the process as many times as necessary. For alternative breathing techniques see www.phospheniis.com.

19. A concept developed by George Herbert Mead and presented in his book Mead, G. H. (1934). *Mind, self, and society*. Chicago: University of Chicago Press.

20. A concept proposed by Steven Pinker and presented in Pinker, S. (1994). *The language instinct*. New York: William Morrow.

21. A theory proposed by Paul Madaule and presented in his book Madaule, P. (1994). *When listening comes alive*. Norval, Ontario: Moulin.

22. For an explanation of the Blank Slate Theory, see discussion of Steven Pinker in Jochnowitz, G. (2002). *The blank slate: The modern denial of human nature*. New York: Viking. Retrieved from www.jochnowitz.net/Essays/BlankSlate.html; also of interest is Jones, M. G., & Brader-Araje, L. (2002, Spring). The impact of constructivism on education: Language, discourse, and meaning. *American Communication Journal, 5*(3), p. 1. Retrieved from acjournal.org/holdings/vol5/iss3/special/jones.htm.

23. Littlejohn.

24. A concept developed by Benjamin Whorf and discussed in J. B. Carroll (Ed.) (1997) [1956]. *Language, thought, and reality: Selected writings of Benjamin Lee Whorf*. Cambridge, MA: Technology Press of Massachusetts Institute of Technology; for a discussion of the Sapir-Whorf Hypothesis, see Badhesha, R. S. (2002, Spring). *Sapir-Whorf Hypothesis*. Retrieved from zimmer.csufresno.edu/~johnca/spch100/4-9-sapir.htm.

25. For a discussion of whether Eskimo people really do have a large vocabulary for snow, see Martin, L., & Pullum, G. (1991). *The great Eskimo vocabulary hoax*. Chicago: University of Chicago Press.

26. For a discussion of the issues raised in this section, see Trenholm, S. (1986). The problem of signification. *Human communication theory*. Englewood Cliffs, NJ: Prentice-Hall, pp. 68–96.

27. For a discussion of gayspeak, see Sims, A. (2004). Gayspeak. *GLBTQ: An encyclopedia of gay, lesbian, bisexual, transgender, and queer culture*. Retrieved from www.glbtq.com/socialsciences/gayspeak.html; or for a historical perspective of gayspeak, see Chesebro, J. (Ed.). (1981). *Gayspeak: Gay male and lesbian communication*. New York: The Pilgrim Press; and Ringer, R. J. (Ed.). (1994). *Queer words, queer images*. New York: New York University Press.

28. For a discussion of African American argot and Ebonics see Ebonics. (2006). *Urban dictionary*. Retrieved from www.urbandictionary.com/define.php?term=ebonics; also see Kretzschmar, W. A. (2008). Public and academic understandings about language: The intellectual history of Ebonics. *English World-Wide, 29*(1), 70–95.

29. Ibid.

30. Ibid.

31. Hartman, C. (2005). *Government seeking to preserve dying languages*. Associated Press.

32. Bruce Cole, chairperson of the National Endowment for the Humanities, quoted in Hartman.

33. For a discussion of Yiddish, see www.answers.com/topic/yiddish-language.

34. Schmid, R. (2007, September 18). *Researchers say many languages are dying*. Retrieved from www.huffingtonpost.com/huff-wires/20070918/endangered-languages/.

35. This classic study was first reported in Hayakawa, S. I. (1978). *Language in thought and action* (4th ed.). New York: Harcourt Brace.

36. The concept of doublespeak was first written about in Lutz, W. (1990). *Doublespeak*. New York: Harper & Row; to read about the concept related to listening, see Bosik, M. (2004). Listening to doublespeak. *Listening Professional, 3*(1), 13–19.

37. Koehli, H. (2006, November 24). *Psycho-Babel: A ponerological approach to modern doublespeak and the distortion of language*. Signs of the Times Forum. Retrieved from Support SOTT.net.

38. Ibid.

39. Classic theory on dialects proposed by Howard Mims. His views on Black dialect can be found in Mims, H. A. (1979, August 31). On Black English: A language with rules. *Cleveland Plain Dealer*, p. A-21.

40. Ibid.

41. Ibid.

42. Alford, R. L., & Strother, J. (1992). A Southern opinion of regional accents. *The Florida Communication Journal, 21*, p. 51.

43. Payack, Paul, president of Language Monitor, as cited in *The English language: 900,000 words, and counting.* (2006, February 1). NPR. Retrieved from www.npr.org.

44. For a creative view of slang, see www.slanguage.com/.

45. Erard, M. *Um*. New York: Pantheon Books, as cited in Walton, D. (2007, August 26). Um, pardon me while I figure out what I'm saying. *(Cleveland) Plain Dealer*, p. M4.

46. Ibid.

47. An idea expressed by Howard Mims. Publicly recorded in Henry, R. (1987, July 26). "Black English" causes confusion in the classroom—An interview with Dr. Howard Mims, associate professor of speech and hearing, Cleveland State University. *Elyria (Ohio) Chronicle-Telegram*, p. G-2.

48. For a discussion on Black English/Ebonics/Ebony English, see Jackson, R. A. (2004). *African American communication and identities: Essential readings.* Newbury Park, CA: Sage; and Hecht, M. L., Collier, M. J., & Ribeau, S. (1993). *African American communication: Ethnic identity and cultural interpretations.* Newbury Park, CA: Sage.

49. Ibid.

50. *Teaching Standard English: A sociological approach.* (n.d.). Unpublished manuscript based on the syllabus for the Basic Communicating Strategies course at LaGuardia Community College, New York; also of interest is Corbett, J. (2003). *An intercultural approach to English language teaching.* Tonawanda, NY: Multilingual Matters.

51. Teaching Standard English, with reference to Major, C. (1971). *Dictionary of Afro-American slang.* New York: International Publishers; also of interest is Mufwene, S. S., & Condon, N. (1993). *Africanisms in Afro-American language varieties.* Athens: University of Georgia Press.

52. Labov, W. (1980, March 31). Allow Black English in schools? Yes—the most important thing is to encourage children to talk freely. *U.S. News & World Report*, 63–64; for additional investigation, see Rickford, J. R. (2000). *Spoken soul: The story of Black English.* Hoboken, NJ: Wiley.

53. Hecht, et al.

54. Ibid.

55. Teaching Standard English, with reference to Miller, R. (2006). *Dictionary of African American slang.* Working Title Publishing.

56. Ibid.

57. Akbar, N. (2004). Cultural expressions of African personality. *Akbar papers in African psychology.* Tallahassee, FL: Mind Productions, pp. 116–120.

58. Ibid.

59. Ibid.

60. Ibid., based on the theories of Carl Jung.

61. Ibid.

62. Ibid.

63. The theory of Sheila Mayers, as cited in Oubré, A. (1997). *Black English vernacular (Ebonics) and educability: A cross-cultural perspective on language, cognition, and schooling.* Retrieved from www.aawc.com/ebonicsarticle.html.

64. Ibid.

65. Hecht, et al., p. 87.

66. Ibid., p. 88.

67. For a description of Spanglish and its usage see *Spanglish—A new American language.* (2003, September 23). NPR. Retrieved from www.npr.org/templates/story/story.php?storyId=1438900; or Neuliep, J. W. (2009). *Intercultural communication: A contextual approach* (4th ed.). Thousand Oaks, CA: Sage, pp. 92–93; also of interest are Chavez, C. (2006). *Spanglish in persuasive communications: A study of code-mixing and linguistic preference in advertising.* A paper presented at the annual meeting of the International Communication Association, Dresden, Germany; and Rothman, J., & Rell, A. B. (2005). A linguistic analysis of Spanglish: Relating language to identity. *Linguistics & the Human Sciences, 1*(3), 515–536.

68. *Spanglish—A new American language.* (2003, September 23). NPR. Retrieved from www.npr.org/templates/story/story.php?storyId=1438900.

69. Ibid.

70. Stavans, I. (2004). *Spanglish: The making of a new American language.* New York: Rayo Publishing, as broadcast on the PBS NewsHour, an interview with Ray Suarez. Retrieved from www.pbs.org/speak/seatosea/americanvarieties/spanglish/book/.

71. Carmen Silva-Corvalan, University of Southern California, as cited in Castro, J. (1988, July 11). Spanglish spoken here. *Time,* p. 53.

72. Adapted from *Asian-American experience.* (2009, July 16). Office of the Deputy Chief of Staff for Personnel, Directorate of Human Resources. Retrieved from www.gordon.army.mil/eoo/asian.htm.

73. Ibid.

74. Ibid.

75. Ibid.

76. Ibid.

77. Althen, G. (1992, Fall). The Americans have to say everything. *Communication Quarterly, 40,* p. 414.

78. Ibid.

79. Native languages of the Americas: Preserving and promoting American Indian languages. (1998–2009). Retrieved from www.native-languages.org/; also see Mithun, M. (2001). *The languages of native North America:* Cambridge Language Surveys. New York: Cambridge University Press.

80. Pratt, S. B. (1994, April). Razzing: Ritualized uses of humor as a form of identification among American Indians. Paper presented at the annual meeting of Central States Speech Association, Oklahoma City, OK; and Mokros, H. B. (Ed.), *Interaction and identity: Information and behavior: Vol. 5.* New Brunswick, NJ: Transactions, p. 4.

81. Philipsen, G. (1972, June). Navaho world view and culture patterns of speech: A case study in ethnorhetoric. *Speech Monographs,* p. 134.

82. Ibid., p. 135.

83. Pratt, p. 2.

84. Ibid.

85. Ohlemacher, S. (2007, September 12). *20 percent of people living in the U.S. speak a language other than English at home.* Associated Press. Retrieved from www.postandcourier.com/news/2007/sep/12/language15626/.

86. *English only.* American Civil Liberties Union of Florida. www.aclufl.org/take_action/download_resources/info_papers/6.cfm.

87. English-only laws. *Law Encyclopedia.* www.answers.com/topic/english-only-laws.

88. *English First.* englishfirst.org/englishstates/.

89. Fausset, R. (2009, January 24). Relief over a defeat of "English only." (*Cleveland*) *Plain Dealer*, p. A6.

90. Based on research by Sandra Terrell and Francis Terrell.

91. Ibid.

92. See for example, the American Speech-Language-Hearing Association www.asha .org/publications/journals/submissions/person_first.htm; *Disability is natural*, www.disabilityis natural.com/images/PDF/pfl09.pdf.

93. Raymond, E. B. (2004). *Learners with mild disabilities: Characteristics approach*. (2nd ed.) Boston: Pearson.

94. Smith, S. (2000, September/October). Words that sting, *Psychology Today*, p. 24; for techniques to stop verbal abuse at work, see Saunders, R. M. (1999, December). Fighting back: Ten ways to end verbal abuse. *Harvard Management Communication Letter, 2*(12), 8.

95. Ibid.

96. Ibid.

97. Tannen, D. (1990). *You just don't understand*. New York: Morrow, p. 14.

98. Crenson, C. (2005, February 28). *Summers' remarks supported by some exports*. Yahoo! Associated Press News.

99. Neuropsychiatrist Brizendine, L. (2007). *The female brain*. New York: Random House; as cited in Tyre, P., & Scelfo, J. (2006, July 31). What girls will be girls. *Newsweek*. p. 46.

100. Ibid., p. 7.

101. Ibid.

102. Dr. Nancy C. Andreasen, a psychiatrist and neuroimaging expert, as cited in Tyre & Scelfo.

103. Goldsmith, D. J., & Fulfs, P. A. (1999). "You just don't have the evidence": An analysis of claims and evidence in Deborah Tannen's *You just don't understand*. In M. E. Roloff (Ed.), *Communication Yearbook, 22* (pp. 1–49). Thousand Oaks, CA: Sage, as cited in Hot type. (June 18, 1999). *Chronicle of High Education*, p. A22.

104. Ibid.

105. For a preliminary discussion on early writings concerning the differences between male and female communication, see Arliss, L. P., & Borisoff, D. J. (1993). *Women and men communicating: Challenge and changes*. Ft. Worth: Harcourt Brace; Tannen, D. (1990). *You just don't understand*. New York: Morrow; Gray, J. (1992). *Men are from Mars, women are from Venus: A practical guide for improving communication and getting what you want in your relationships*. New York: HarperCollins; and Wood, J. T. (1994). *Gendered lives: Communication, gender, and culture*. Belmont, CA: Wadsworth; and Stewart, L., Cooper, P., Stewart, A., & Friedley, S. (2003). *Communication and gender* (4th ed.). Boston: Pearson Education.

106. Arliss & Borisoff, p. 3. For further investigation, see Gamble, T. K., & Gamble, M. W. (2002). *The gender communication connection*. Boston: Houghton Mifflin; and Ivy, D. K., & Backlund, P. (2007). *GenderSpeak: Personal effectiveness in gender communication* (4th ed.). Upper Saddle River, NJ: Allyn & Bacon.

107. Moir, A., & Jessel, D. (1991, May 5). Sex and cerebellum: Thinking about the real difference between men and woman. *Washington Post*, p. K3.

108. Ibid.

109. Mathias, B. (1993). Male identity crisis. *Washington Post*, p. C5.

110. Gray, p. 16.

111. Mathias, p. C5.

112. Burleson, B., Dindia, K., & Condit, C. (1997). *Gender communication: Different cultural perspectives*. Paper presented at the annual meeting of the National Communication Association Conference, Chicago.

113. What's in a word? A job, Hood senior's study says. (1991, June 6). *Washington Post,* p. MD8.

114. Tannen, pp. 43–44.

115. Mehl, M., Vazire, S., Ramirez-Esparza, N., Slatcher, R., & Pennebaker, J. (2006, July). Are women really more talkative than men? *Science, 317*(5834), 82. Details on methods and analysis are available on *Science* online. Retrieved from www.sciencemag.org/cgi/content/abstract/317/5834/82

116. For a discussion on interruptions, see Stewart, Cooper, Stewart, & Friedley, p. 54; and Wood, pp. 31, 144.

117. Based on the research of H. G. Whittington, James P. Smith, Leonard Kriegel, Lillian Glass, and Hilary Lips.

118. Ibid.

119. Gray, p. 26.

120. Ibid., p. 25.

121. Ibid., p. 15.

122. Fanning, P., & McKay, M. (1993). *Being a man: A guide to the new masculinity.* Oakland, CA: New Harbinger, p. 13.

123. Zinczenko, D. (2007, December 17). Why men don't talk. *Men's Health.* Retrieved from health.yahoo.com/experts/menlovesex/73762/why-men-dont-talk; additional material on this subject is discussed in Zinczenko, D. (2006, November). *Men, love and sex: The complete user's guide for women.* Old Saybrook, CT: Tantor Media.

124. Ibid.

125. Gray, pp. 11–13.

Chapter 5: Nonverbal Communication

1. Knapp, M., & Hall, J. (2006). *Nonverbal communication in human interaction* (6th ed.). Belmont, CA: Thomson Wadsworth, p. 56.

2. Ibid., p. 5.

3. Burgoon, J. K., Buller, D. B., & Woodall, W. G. (1996). *Nonverbal communication: The unspoken dialogue* (2nd ed.). New York: McGraw-Hill, p. 136.

4. Ibid.

5. Ibid.

6. Ibid.

7. Ibid.

8. Levine, D. R., & Adelman, M. B. (1993). *Beyond language.* Upper Saddle River, NJ: Prentice Hall. www.rpi.edu/dept/advising/american_culture/social_skills/nonverbal_communication/reading_exercise.htm.

9. Ibid.

10. Edward Hall, as cited in Freedman, K. (1979, August). Learning the Arabs' silent language, *Psychology Today, 13,* p. 53.

11. For an extensive discussion of international gestures, see Axtell, R. E. (2007). *The complete guide to international business and leisure travel.* Hoboken, NJ: John Wiley and Sons.

12. Samovar, L., Porter, R., & McDaniel, E. (2007). *Communication between cultures.* Belmont, CA: Thomson Higher Education, p. 199.

13. American Psychological Association (2008). *The truth about lie detectors (aka polygraph tests).* APA Online. Retrieved from www.psychologymatters.org/polygraphs.html.

14. Schmid, R. (2002, October 9). Lie detectors called too inaccurate for national security. *(Cleveland) Plain Dealer*, p. A10.

15. Temple-Raston, D. (2009, July 1). *Neuroscientist uses brain scan to see lies form.* Based on the research of Daniel Langleben. NPR.

16. A concept proposed by Edward Hall and described in Hall, E. T. (1976). *Beyond culture.* New York: Anchor Books.

17. Samovar, Porter, & McDaniel, p. 210.

18. No specific identifying channels of nonverbal communication have been universally defined. The names used here are a compilation of those that have appeared in various textbooks on nonverbal communication.

19. Jordan, N. (1986, January). The face of feeling. *Psychology Today,* p. 8; for an extensive discussion on the face and its effects on human communication, see Knapp & Hall, Chapter 9; for additional reading, see Heisel, M. J., & Mongrain, M. (2004). Facial expressions and ambivalence: Looking for conflict in all the right faces. *Journal of Nonverbal Behavior,* 28(1), 35–52.

20. Knapp & Hall, pp. 43–45.

21. Furman, M. E., & Gallo, F. P. (2000). *The neurophysics of human behavior: Explorations at the interface of brain, mind, behavior, and information,* as referred to in Warren, P. (n.d.). *Emotional freedom is in your hands with emotional freedom processes (EFP).* Delta Life Skills, p. 2, Retrieved from www.rebprotocol.net.

22. Based on a research study conducted by Joe Teece, Boston College, neuropsychologist. See Fields, S. (2008, February 7). *Wellesley's Joe Teece predicts presidential electability in blink of an eye.* Retrieved from www.wickedlocal.com/wellesley/homepage/x1973322880.

23. Westover, B. (2006, July 25). *The science behind non-verbal expression via dilation of the pupils.* Discussing the research of J. M. Pott and E. H. Hess. Retrieved from www.associated content.com/article/45165/the_science_behind_nonverbal_expression.html?cat=4.

24. Knapp, M., & Hall, J. A. (1997). *Nonverbal communication in human interaction* (4th ed.). Forth Worth, TX: Harcourt Brace, pp. 386–390.

25. The Navajo tradition of the evil eye is discussed in much of the traditional literature; for instance, see Cardinal, F. (2001, November 18). *Navajo Skinwalkers.* Suite 101.com. Retrieved from www.suite101.com/article.cfm/mysterious_creatures/84997.

26. *How to use eye contact effectively in conversation.* (2005, September 15). Searchwarp.com. Retrieved from searchwarp.com/swa17401.htm.

27. Burgoon, p. 41.

28. Wright, C. (1989). *NLP workbook, introductory level: Books 1 & 2.* Portland, OR: Metamorphous Press.

29. *The Pegasus mind-body newsletter.* (2002, January 4). Issue 9; for more information on NLP Eye Accessing Cues, see Pegasus NLP Trainings. Retrieved from www.nlpnow.co.uk/.

30. Wright, C. (1989). *NLP workbook, introductory level: Books 1 & 2.* Metamorphous Press: Portland, OR.

31. Ibid., p. 4.

32. Ibid.

33. Ibid.

34. For a further discussion of thinking and eye movement, see Adler, E. (1998, November 26). Speak to me with thine eyes (and head and arms). *Washington Post,* p. C5.

35. Pescovitz, D. (2009, May 19). *Gesturing helps you think.* Boingboing. Retrieved from boingboing.net/2009/05/19/gesturing-helps-you.html.

36. Howe, H. (1999, March 1). Show me what you're thinking. *Psychology Today.* Cited from research by psychologists Jana Iverson and Susan Goldin-Meadow. Retrieved from www.psychologytoday.com/articles/199903/show-me-what-youre-thinking.

37. For a discussion on speech-independent gestures, see Knapp & Hall, 2006, pp. 225–236.

38. For a discussion of speech-related gestures, see Knapp & Hall, 2006, pp. 225, 236–241.

39. For a discussion on affect displays, see Knapp & Hall, 2006, pp. 20, 37, 437, 466.

40. For a discussion of emblems, see Knapp & Hall, 2006, pp. 226–236.

41. Yenchkel, J. T. (1991, October 20). Fearless traveler: Sorting through the chaos of culture. *Washington Post*, p. E10.

42. For a discussion of illustrators see Knapp & Hall, 2006, pp. 236–254.

43. Ackerman, D. (1990, March 25). The power of touch. *Parade Magazine*, p. 3.

44. Concept used in counseling rape survivors (Cleveland Rape Crisis Center training) and espoused by Roy Berko, in his role as crisis counselor.

45. Yenckel, p. E10.

46. Burgoon, p. 224, based on the work of S. M. Jourard & N. M. Genley; also see Anderson, P., & Guerrero, L. (2008). *Haptic behavior in social interaction*. New York: Birkhauser Basel/Springer. Retrieved from www.authormapper.com/.

47. Roese, N., Olson, J., Borenstein, M. B., Martin, A., & Shores, A. (1992, Winter). Same-sex touching behavior: The moderating role of homophobic attitudes. *Journal of Nonverbal Behavior, 16*(2), 249–259. Citation from p. 250.

48. Ibid.

49. Anderson, P. (1999). *Nonverbal communication: Forms and functions.* Mountain View, CA: Mayfield Publishing, p. 47.

50. Ibid.

51. Ibid.

52. Jones, S. (1994). *The right touch.* Cresskill, NJ: Hampton Press, Inc., p. 26.

53. Classic study reported in Ekman, P., & Friesen, W. (1969). The repertoire of nonverbal behavior: Categories, origins, usage, and codings. *Semiotica, 1*, 49–98.

54. *Firm handshakes help land jobs.* (2008, May 7). LiveScience.com. Retrieved from www.livescience.com/health/080507-firm-handshake.html.

55. Ibid.

56. For a discussion on posture, walk, and stance see Knapp & Hall, 2006, pp. 225–254.

57. Johnson, K. (2007). UCLA as cited by PsychOrg.com. Retrieved from www.physorg.com/news108047183.html.

58. Ibid.

59. Steinhauer, J. (1995, April 2). It's "The Gap" once you're hired, but job hunters must spiff it up. *The New York Times*, p. F13; for a discussion of clothing for the job interview, see Epand, V. (2008, March 16). *Do you have a job interview?* Articlesbase. Retrieved from www.articlesbase.com/careers-articles/do-you-have-a-job-interview-360809.html; Alexander, R. (2007, August 23). *Ten recommendations for women's interview attire: What's appropriate attire for a job interview?* Lifescript. Retrieved from www.lifescript.com/Life/Money/Work/10_Recommendations_For_Womens_Interview_Attire.

60. Doyle, A. (2009). *How to dress for a job interview.* About.com: Job Searching. Retrieved from jobsearch.about.com/od/interviewattire/a/interviewdress.htm.

61. Lilly, C. (n.d.). *Casual dress craze affects business.* Retrieved from homepages.ius.edu/Horizon/Web_Files/HArchives/022601-caual.html.

62. Ting-Toomey, S., & Chung, L. C. (2005). *Understanding intercultural communication.* New York: Oxford University Press, p. 203.

63. Ibid., p. 204.

64. Washington, R. (1996, June 18). Culture weighs body image. *Cleveland Plain Dealer*, pp. 1E, 4E; also reported in *Black bodies.* (1999, April 19). 20/20 ABC News. ABCNews Home Videos, #T990419.

65. Ibid.

66. The classic theory was described in The eyes have it. (1973, December 3). *Newsweek*, p. 85.

67. Ibid.

68. Biel, J. (2009, July 1). *Being hot "really is a problem."* Retrieved from http://omg!.yahoo .com.

69. Roy Berko recounting examples given by clients in his counseling practice who were discussing their relational/dating issues.

70. Sherr, L. (1996, December 27). *Short men.* 20/20, ABC-TV.

71. Ibid.

72. *Tom Cruise biography.* (2009). Retrieved from www.who2.com/ask/tomcruise.html.

73. Frankel, E. (2006–2009). National Organization of Short Statured Adults, Inc. Retrieved from www.nossaonline.org/heightism.html.

74. Ibid.

75. Ibid.

76. Ibid.

77. Yunkman, T. (2008, April 24). No matter who's elected president, they'll be no. 1 in some category. *The Bay City Times.* Retrieved from blog.mlive.com/bcopinion/2008/04/ no_matter_whos_elected_preside.html.

78. Ibid.

79. Knapp, M. (1978). *Nonverbal communication in human interaction* (2nd ed.). Fort Worth: Harcourt Brace, pp. 166–167. For a further discussion on height see Knapp and Hall, 2006, p. 194.

80. Burgoon, p. 224 referring to research by Edward Hall.

81. Knapp & Hall, 2006, pp. 151, 357, 462–463, information based on the findings of Edward Hall.

82. These factors are reported as they relate to Euro-Americans.

83. *Communication patterns in circular seating versus straight row in the classroom.* Unpublished study conducted by Roy Berko, Notre Dame College of Ohio.

84. Knapp & Hall, 2006, pp. 105–106.

85. For a discussion on vocal cues and persuasion, see Knapp & Hall, 2006, pp. 390–391.

86. Samovar, Porter, & McDaniel, p. 25.

87. Ibid.

88. Ibid.

89. Ibid.

90. Ibid., p. 226.

91. Ibid., p. 227.

92. Ibid.

93. For a discussion of time as a nonverbal communicator see Knapp & Hall, 2006, pp. 108–110.

94. For a discussion on the causes for procrastination, see *The boomerang effect, What are the causes and effects of procrastination?* (2009). (in)action. Retrieved from overcoming -procrastination.com/action/causes-and-effects-of-procrastination.html; *Eliminating procrastination.* (2006). Self improvement gym. Retrieved from www.selfimprovement-gym.com/cause_ for_procrastination.html; for a procrastination measure, see Choi, J. N., & Moran, S. V. (2009). Why not procrastinate? Development and validation of a new active procrastination scale. *Journal of Social Psychology, 49*(2), 195–212.

95. Andrews, L. (2007, November/December). The hidden force of fragrance. *Psychology Today*, p. 57.

96. Ito, S. (2000). *Smell and memory.* Retrieved from serendip.brynmawr.edu/bb/neuro/neuro00/web2/Ito.html; examples of current research on the topic include Scalco, M. Z., Streiner, D. L., Rewilak, D., Castel, S., & Van Reekum, R. (2009). Smell test predicts performance on delayed recall memory test in elderly with depression. *International Journal of Geriatric Psychiatry, 24*(4), 376–381; and Wen Li, Moallem, I., Paller, K. A., & Gottfried, J. A. (2007). Subliminal smells can guide social preferences. *Psychological Science, 18*(12), 1044–1049.

97. *The human sense of smell.* (2009). Social Issues Research Centre. Retrieved from www.sirc.org/publik/smell_human.html.

98. Andrews, p. 57.

99. *The business of business music, environmental music.* (1989). Muzak Limited Partnership; Reid, A. (1989). *Unoriginal sound tracks.* (1998, January). *Washington Post,* p. B 1; Milliman, R. (1982). The effects of slow tempo background music on the behavior of supermarket shoppers. *Journal of Marketing, 46,* as reported by Muzak.

100. Bridgewater, C. A. (1983, January). Slow music sells. *Psychology Today, 17,* p. 56.

101. McCormick, P. (1979, January 12). Rock music can weaken muscles. Elyria (Ohio) *Chronicle-Telegram,* Encore, p. 15.

102. Ibid.

103. Reid; Milliman; Muzak Limited Partnership.

104. Britt, R. R. (2005, May 18). *Red outfits give athletes advantage.* Live Science. Retrieved from www.livescience.com/health/050518_red_wins.html.

105. For a discussion of Gustorics (the study of taste communication), see Hickson, M. III, Stacks, D. W., & Moore, N. (2004). *Nonverbal communication: Studies and applications* (4th ed.). Los Angeles, CA: Roxbury Publishing, pp. 294–295.

Chapter 6: The Principles of Relational Communication

1. This is an account of an actual event. The song was Stephen Schwartz's "With You" from the musical *Pippin.*

2. A concept discussed by Dr. Joy Browne on her syndicated radio show, August 20, 2009; see www.drjoy.com/.

3. Gudykunst, W. B., Ting-Toomey, S., Sudweeks, S., & Steward, L. P. (1995). *Building bridges: Interpersonal skills for a changing world.* Boston: Houghton Mifflin, p. 358.

4. Skow, L., & Samovar, L. A. (1991). Cultural patterns of the Maasai. In L. A. Samovar & R. R. Porter (Eds.), *Intercultural communication: A reader* (3rd ed.). Belmont, CA: Wadsworth, p. 93; for additional discussion about communication and cultures, see Samovar, L. A., Porter, R. E., & McDaniel, E. R. (2010). *Communication between cultures* (7th ed.). Belmont, CA: Wadsworth.

5. Proposed by Dr. Sonya Friedman, author and media psychologist, www.drsonyafriedman.com/.

6. Theory of Dr. Joy Browne, media psychologist, www.drjoy.com/.

7. Ibid.

8. Baxter, L. (2004). A tale of two voices: Relational dialectics theory. *The Journal of Family Communication, 4*(3–4), 181–192.

9. *Divorce statistics.* (2004). Retrieved from www.divorcestatistics.org/.

10. Ibid.

11. A concept explained by Dr. Joy Browne, media psychologist, 2009. For additional information about Dr. Browne and her theories, see www.drjoy.com/; for a discussion of relationships, see Solomon, D. H., Knobloch, L. K., & Fitzpatrick, M. A. (2004). Relational

power, marital schema, and decisions to withhold complaints: An investigation of the chilling effect on confrontation in marriage. *Communication Studies, 55*(1), 146–167; or a foundational work: Williamson, R. N., & Fitzpatrick, M. A. (1985). Two approaches to marital interaction: Relational control patterns in marital types. *Communication Monographs, 52*(3), 236.

12. Based on a compilation of various psychologists and researchers. For a specific list see Luv, K. (2007, April 24). *Relationships—10 rules that never change.* Scribd. Retrieved from www.scribd.com/doc/31606/Relationships-10-Rules-That-Never-Change.

13. Zinner, C. D. (1988, Spring). Beyond Hall: Variables in the use of personal space. *The Howard Journal of Communication, 1,* 28–29; also see Ting-Toomey, S., & Chung, L. (2005). *Understanding intercultural communication.* New York: Oxford University Press, pp. 214–218.

14. Flora, C. (2009, August). Patterns of pursuit. *Psychology Today,* p. 81. For additional information see Bennett, J. (2009). *The last word on commitment phobia.* Retrieved from www.doctorlovecoach.com/name-News-article-sid-199.html.

15. Ibid.

16. For a discussion about runaway brides, see Stritof, S., & Stritof, B. (2009). *Runaway brides, an extreme form of disengagement.* Retrieved from marriage.about.com/od/proposing beingengaged/a/runawaybrides.htm.

17. A concept developed by Roy Berko, crisis counselor.

18. For a further discussion of intimacy and revealing/nonrevealing cultures, see Ting-Toomey & Chung, pp. 194, 293, 295, 299.

19. Ibid.

20. Ibid.

21. Wood, D. (2000–2003). *The truth about women.* Retrieved from lifecoachingsoucrce .com; and Sachs, M. A. (2004). *Male/female communication styles HYG 5280–9.* Ohio State University Extension face sheet. Family and Consumer Sciences. Retrieved from ohioline .ag.ohio-state.edu.

22. Reissman, C. K. (1990). *Divorce talk: Women and men make sense of personal relation-ships.* New Brunswick, NJ: Rutgers University Press.

23. Berko, R., Wolvin, A., & Wolvin, D. (2010). *Communicating: A social, career and cul-tural approach* (11th ed.). Boston, MA: Allyn Bacon Pearson, p. 167.

Chapter 7: Beginning, Maintaining, and Ending Relationships

1. For a discussion of primarily task-oriented, friendship-oriented, or intimate-oriented rela-tionships, see Nussbaum, J. F., Pecchioni, L. L., Robinson, J. D., & Thompson, T. L. (2000). *Communication and aging* (2nd ed.). Mahwah, NJ: Lawrence Erlbaum; also see Borchers, T. (1999). *Relationship development.* Retrieved from www.abacon.com/commstudies/interper sonal/indevelop.html.

2. For an extensive discussion on the role of attractiveness, see Knapp, M., & Hall, J. (2006). *Nonverbal communication in human interaction* (6th ed.). Belmont, CA: Thomson Wadsworth. For dating and marriage and physical attraction, see pp. 175–178.

3. For a discussion on mate selection, see Alvarez, L., & Jaffe, K. (2004). Narcissism guides mate selection: Humans mate assertively, as revealed by facial resemblance, following an algorithm of "self seeking like." (2004). *Evolutionary Psychology, 2,* 177–194. Retrieved from www.epjournal.net/filestore/ep02177194.pdf; also, see Mathews, M. (2006, June 12). *Mate selection.* Associated Content. Retrieved from www.associatedcontent.com/article/ 35397/mate_selection.html?cat=41.

4. *The US dating services industry.* (2009, March). Marketdata Enterprises. MarketResearch.com. Retrieved from www.marketdataenterprises.com/DatingMarch2009TOC.pdf.

5. Hanson, D. (2004, February). Net Zero or dating hero. *Cleveland Magazine*, pp. 60–63, 80; *10 tips for online dating safety.* Retrieved from UniquePersonals.net; *8 tips for safe online dating.* Retrieved from freedating-services.net.

6. *Ad writing tips.* (n.d.). Dreampal.com. Retrieved from www.dreampal.com/guests/ads.htm.

7. For a discussion on sexting, see CBS News. Retrieved from www.cbsnews.com/stories/2009/01/15/national/main4723161.shtml.

8. See www.eharmony.com.

9. See www.matchmaker.com.

10. See www.great-expectations.net/.

11. See www.eharmony.com.

12. Richard Sides, *Solo Lifestyles Magazine*, as cited on www.singlesearch.com.

13. See www.matchmaker.com.

14. See McGraw, P. (2001). *Relationship rescue: A seven-step strategy for reconnecting with your partner.* New York: Hyperion Press, as cited on www.successbroker.com.

15. Ibid.

16. A concept proposed by Lawrence Rosenfeld and written about in Rosenfeld, L., & Kendrick, W. L. (1984). Choosing to be open: Subjective reasons for self-disclosing. *Western Journal of Speech Communication, 48,* 326–343.

17. For a discussion on compliance gaining, see Canary, D., Cody, M., & Manusov, V. (2008). *Interpersonal communication: A goals-based approach* (4th ed.). Boston, MA: Bedford/St. Martins, Chapter 12.

18. Grant, J. A., King, P. E., & Behnke, R. R. (1994). Compliance-gaining strategies: Communication satisfaction and willingness to comply. *Communication Reports, 7,* 99–108.

19. Cutter, R. (1994). *Right brain/left brain relationships and how to make them work.* New York: Penguin Books, p. xiii.

20. Ibid., p. xvi.

21. Ibid., p. xiii.

22. Ibid., p. 44.

23. Ibid., p. 21.

24. Ibid., p. 19.

25. Ibid., p. 38.

26. Ibid., p. 21.

27. Ibid., p. 43.

28. Ibid., p. xv.

29. The information in this section is based on Knapp, M. (2008). *Interpersonal communication and human relationships* (5th ed.). Boston: Allyn and Bacon, as cited on The Allyn and Bacon Home Website, Communication Studies. Allyn and Bacon.

30. Yew, C. (1997). A language of their own. *Porcelain and a language of their own: Two plays.* New York: Grove Press.

Chapter 8: Conflict Resolution

1. Berko, R., Wolvin, A., & Wolvin, D. (2010). *Communicating: A social, career and cultural focus* (11th ed.). Boston, MA: Houghton Mifflin, p. 191.

2. Donohue, W. A., & Kolt, R. (1992). *Managing interpersonal conflict.* Newbury Park, CA: Sage, p. 2.

3. Ibid.

4. Ting-Toomey, S., Leeva C., & Chung, L. C. (2005). *Understanding intercultural communication*. New York: Oxford University Press, p. 276.

5. Ibid., p. 276.

6. Rowland, D. (1985). *Japanese business etiquette*. New York: Warner Books, p. 5; also see Lustig, M., & Koester, J. (2010). *Intercultural competence: Interpersonal communication across cultures* (6th ed.). Boston: Pearson, pp. 269–270.

7. For a discussion on Asian American and Native American conflict styles, see Ting-Toomey, S., & Chung, L. (2005). *Understanding intercultural communication*. New York: Oxford University Press, pp. 277–279.

8. Ting-Toomey & Chung, pp. 277–278.

9. Ibid.

10. A classic explanation of anger can be found in Lerner, H. G. (1985). *The dance of anger*. New York: Perennial Library, p. 1.

11. Carnevale, F. (2009, August 7). *Rush: Health care logo like Nazi image*. My Fox National/My Fox Tampa Bay. Retrieved from www.myfoxtampabay.com/dpp/news/dpgo _Limbaugh_Obama_Health_Care_Logo_fc_20090807_2883243; Limbaugh, R. (2009, February 9). *The march to socialized medicine starts in Obama's Pokulus Bill*. Retrieved from www .rushlimbaugh.com/home/daily/site_020909/content/01125111.guest.html; *Rush Limbaugh on Obama health care logo*. Rant Rave. Retrieved from rantrave.com/Rant/Rush-Limbaugh -On-Obama-Health-Care-Logo.aspx.

12. Parry, R. (2009, August, 11). Palin's "death panel" and GOP lying. *Baltimore Chronicle & Sentinel*, as originally published on ConsortiumNews.com. Retrieved from www.baltimore chronicle.com/2009/081209Parry.shtml.

13. Michael Levittan, as cited in Lovley, E. (2009, August 12). *Town hallers scream way to therapy*. Politico. Yahoo News. Retrieved from news.yahoo.com/s/politico/26039.

14. Ibid.

15. Steven Stosney, as cited in Lovley.

16. Ibid.

17. Jacqueline Whitmore, as cited in Lovley.

18. Missouri Senator Claire McCaskill, as cited in Lovley.

19. Dave Schwartz, Americans for Prosperity Maryland, as cited in Lovley.

20. Based on the concepts of Marlene Arthur Penkstaff.

21. The principles are based on the theories of Susan Forward on her call-in show on ABC Talk Radio. Retrieved from www.susanforward.com/.

22. Ibid.

23. The principles are based on the theories of Sonya Friedman. Retrieved from www. drsonyafriedman.com/.

24. Berko, R. (2004). *Dealing with stress*. Unpublished manuscript presented in a workshop to the counseling staff at the Social Service Agency, Alexandria, VA.

25. This is a principle of Gestalt therapy, as explained by Les Wyman, Gestalt Institute, Cleveland, OH.

26. Trujillo, M. A., & Miller, L. (1999, February 19). *Activity 1. Responding to conflict around issues of difference workshop*. Unpublished manuscript. National Conference for Community and Justice, Northern Ohio Region, Cleveland, OH.

27. Ibid.

28. Ibid.

29. Maiese, M. (2003, October). Negotiation. In G. Burgess & H. Burgess (Eds.). *Beyond intractability*. Conflict Research Consortium, University of Colorado, Boulder. Retrieved from www.beyondintractability.org/essay/negotiation/.

Chapter 9: Interpersonal Relationships in the Family

1. Berko, R. (n.d.). *Iv posed to be: A collection of family tales.* Unpublished manuscript.

2. Goldberg, J. (n.d.). *Family communication.* Unpublished syllabus. Arapahoe Community College, Littleton, CO.

3. Turner, L. H., & West, R. (1998). *Perspectives on family communication.* Mountain View, CA: Mayfield Publishing, pp. 2–3. Also see 3rd. ed., 2006.

4. Judith Plaskow, as cited in Banks, A. M. (2000, April 2). Feud over definition of family. *The Plain Dealer*, p. 2L.

5. Ibid.

6. Turner & West, p. 25.

7. Ibid., p. 27.

8. Ibid., p. 21.

9. Smith, D., & Gates. G. (2009). *Gay and lesbian families in the United States.* Urban Institute. Retrieved from www.urban.org/url.cfm?ID=1000491.

10. Mary Stewart Van Leeuwen, as cited in Banks, A. M. (2000, April 2). Feud over definition of family. *The Plain Dealer*, p. 2L.

11. Puente, M. (2004, March 9). Language lags behind the flurry of gay marriages. *USA Today*, p. 1D.

12. Ibid.

13. Turner & West, p. 5.

14. Ibid., p. 125.

15. Ibid.

16. Ibid., p. 270.

17. Tannen. D. (1990). *You just don't understand: Men and women in conversation.* New York: William Morrow, p. 44.

18. Turner & West, p. 194.

19. Ibid., pp. 204–206.

20. Marks, S. R. (1989). Toward a systems theory of marital quality. *Journal of Marriage and the Family, 51*(1), 15–26; also see *Family theory and systems theory.* (2002, June 10). Retrieved from www.geocities.com/a_lonely0us/publications/systems_theory.htm.

21. Forward. S. (1989). *Toxic parents.* New York: Bantam Press, cover.

22. Ibid., p. 136.

23. Ibid.

24. Ibid.

25. Ibid., pp. 6–7.

26. Turner & West, p. 134.

27. Ibid., p. 136.

28. Ibid., p. 159.

29. Chandler, T. (1988, April). *Perceptions of verbal and physical aggression in interpersonal violence.* Paper presented at the annual meeting of the Eastern Communication Association, Baltimore, MD; also see *Family Violence Research Program.* Family Research Laboratory, funded by the National Institute of Mental Health. University of New Hampshire, Durham, NH. Retrieved from www.unh.edu/frl/frlbroch.htm.

30. O'Leary, K. D. (1999, April). Tailoring interventions to meet the needs of partner and abuse clients. *Joining Forces, 3*(3), p. 1.

31. For up-to-date statistics and information, see www.childwelfare.gov, www.abanet.org, and www.nlm.nih.gov.

32. Ibid.

33. Ibid.

34. Ibid.

35. Ibid.

36. Popkin, M. (n.d.). *Active parenting now* [Multimedia program]. Active Parenting Publishers. Retrieved from www.activeparenting.com/xapn.htm.

37. There are many local, as well as national organizations that offer families help. Calling a local social service agency, a mental health facility, city mental health department, or consulting the yellow pages of a telephone book can lead to discovering resources. College campus student counseling centers, as well as hotlines and online searches, can be used to unearth additional resources.

38. http://ids.org.

Chapter 10: Electronically Mediated Interpersonal Communication

1. Fatal wreck spurs cell phone fight. (2003, January 10). *Pittsburgh Tribune-Review.* Retrieved from www.pittsburghlive.com, based on research by the Center for Cognitive Brain Imagery, Carnegie Mellon University.

2. Cell phone use laws lawyers. (1999–2009). Legal match. Retrieved from www.legalmatch.com/law-library/article/cell-phone-use-laws.html.

3. Adapted from *Courtesy month: Five basic cell phone rules.* (2003, July 1). NokiaCell phone. Retrieved from www.classbrain.com; Proper cell phone etiquette. (n.d.). Retrieved from cellphonecarriers.com; and Toft, M. (2004). *Cell phone etiquette.* Retrieved from www.staples.com.

4. Based on the work of psychiatrist Nathan Andrew Sahpira's study on obsessive Internet use. See Davis, J. L. (2003, August 7). *Internet addiction: Ruining lives?* WebMD. Retrieved from www.webmd.com/; also see Beranuy, M., Oberst, U., Carbonell, X., & Chamarro, A. (2009). Problematic Internet and mobile phone use and clinical symptoms in college students. *Computers in Human Behavior, 25*(5), 1182–1187.

5. Tao, L. (2005). *What do we know about e-mail—An existing and emerging literacy vehicle?* Retrieved from ERIC database. (ED399530).

6. Turkle, S. (1984). *The second self: Computers and the human spirit.* Cambridge, MA: The MIT Press.

7. Tolson, J. (1999, March 22). The life of the mind goes digital. *U.S. News and World Report,* 58–59; for articles on the nature of discussion on the Internet, see Shedletsky, L. J., & Aitken, J. E. (Eds.) (2010). *Cases on online discussion and interaction: Experiences and outcomes.* Hershey, PA: IGI Global.

8. Shedletsky, L. J., & Aitken, J. E. (2010). *Cases on online discussion and interaction.* Hershey, PA: IGI Global.

9. Schultz, C. (1999, July 4). Internet addiction is not a way-out malady; experts say overuse of computers can be as damaging as other obsessions. *The Plain Dealer,* p. 1A; and see Yellowlees, P. M., & Marks, S. (2007). Problematic Internet use or Internet addiction? *Computers in Human Behavior, 23*(3), 1447–1453.

10. Sherer, K. (1997, November–December). College life on-line: Healthy and unhealthy Internet use. *Journal of College Student Development*, *38*(6), 655–665. For a more recent discussion about interpersonal relationships and media use, see Baym, N. K., Yan Bing Zhang; Kunkel, A., Ledbetter, A., & Mei-Chen Lin. (2007). Relational quality and media use in interpersonal relationships. *New Media & Society*, *9*(5), 735–752.

11. Harlow, J. (2007, October 29). You've got e-mail. *Johannesburg, South Africa Sunday Times*, p. 12.

12. Ibid.

13. Ibid.

14. Kessler, M. (2007, October 5). Fridays go from casual to e-mail-free. *USA Today*. Retrieved from www.usatoday.com/tech/techinvestor/corporatenews/2007-10-04-no-email_N.htm?csp=34; also see Parcell, G. (2005, October). "Learning to fly" in a world of information overload. *Bulletin of the World Health Organization*, *83*(10), 727–729.

15. Kessler.

16. Ibid.

17. Carnes, P. (2004, February 27). The criteria of problematic online sexual behavior. Unpublished manuscript presented at the Free Clinic of Cleveland; also see Delmonico, D. L., & Griffin, E. J. (2008). Cybersex and the e-teen: What marriage and family therapists should know. *Journal of Marital & Family Therapy*, *34*(4), 431–444.

18. Carnes.

19. Ibid.

20. Schultz.

21. Ibid.

22. The concepts of sociologist Sherry Turkle, author of *Life on the Screen* and psychiatrist Esther Gwinnell, author of *Online Seductions*, as cited in Herbert, W. (1999, March 22). Getting close, but not too close. *U.S. News and World Report*, 56–57.

23. Ibid.

24. Ibid.

25. Locker, S. (2008, December 6). *Sexting definition*. Retrieved from sarilocker.com/blog/2008/12/06/sexting-definition/.

26. Cyberbullying.us. (2009, March 10). Retrieved from cyberbullying.us/blog/sexting-the-jesse-logan-case-and-what-schools-can-do.html.

27. *Pennsylvania teens charged with cell phone "sexting."* (2009, January 13). FoxNews.com. Retrieved from www.foxnews.com/story/0,2933,479803,00.html.

28. Wiehe, J. (2009, January 11). Racy "sexting" photos piquing police interest: 2 juveniles at local schools facing charges. *The Journal Gazette*. Retrieved from www.journalgazette.net/apps/pbcs.dll/article?AID=/20090111/LOCAL/901110389/1002/LOCAL.

29. Fisher, K. (2009, February 11). *Porn charges for "sexting?* Strollerderby. Retrieved from www.babble.com/CS/blogs/strollerderby/archive/2009/02/11/porn-charges-for-sexting.aspx.

30. *Sexting: Parenting education.* (n.d.). Love Our Children USA. Retrieved from www.loveourchildrenusa.org/parent_sexting.php.

31. *"Sexting" lands teen on sex offender list.* (2009, April 8). CNN.com/crime. Retrieved from www.cnn.com/2009/CRIME/04/07/sexting.busts/index.html.

32. Mitchell, A. (2004, January 24). *Bullied by the click of a mouse.* www.globeandmail.com/servlet/story/RTGAM.20040124.wbully0124/BNStory/.

33. Chapman, G. (2007, December 2). *Online bullying a growing part of the US teen Internet life.* AFP News Report, p. 2. Retrieved from news.yahoo.com/s/afp/20071202/tc_afp/lifestyle usitInternetyouthschool; also see Mesch, G. S. (2009). Parental mediation, online activities, and cyberbullying. *CyberPsychology & Behavior*, *12*(4), 387–339.

34. Chapman.

35. Ibid.

36. www.cyberbullying.us/, July 12, 2009. Also see Chapman.

37. Huffstutter, P. J. (2007, November 23). Fatal cyber-bullying hits home. *Los Angles Times*, as cited in *Cleveland Plain Dealer*, p. A12.

38. Ibid.

39. Cyberbullying Research Center. (2009, July 12). Retrieved from www.cyberbullying.us/.

40. Chapman, G. (2007, December 2). *Online bullying a growing part of the US teen Internet life*. AFP News Report. Retrieved from news.yahoo.com/s/afp/20071202/tc_afp/lifestyleusit Internetyouthschool; Cassidy, W., Jackson, M., & Brown, K. N. (2009). Sticks and stones can break my bones, but how can pixels hurt me?: Students' experiences with cyber-bullying. *School Psychology International, 30*(4), 383–402.

41. Heimowitz, D. (n.d.). Stanford Research and I-Safe.org. Retrieved from www.i-safe.org/.

42. Silver, M. (1999, March 22). Hooked on instant messages. *U.S. News and World Report*, p. 57.

43. *1999 Report on cyber stalking*. Retrieved from www.usdoj.gov/criminal/cybercrime/cyberstalking.htm.

44. Ibid.

45. Subrahmanyam, K., & Lin, G. (2007, Winter). Adolescents on the Net: Internet use and well-being. *Adolescence. 42*(168).

46. Hancock, J. T., & Curry, L. E., Goorha, S., & Woodworth, M. (2008). On lying and being lied to: A linguistic analysis of deception in computer-mediated communication. *Discourse Processes, 45*, 1–23.

47. Harmon, A. (1998, August 30). Sad, lonely world discovered. *New York Times* reporting about *Homenet*, a $1.5 million project sponsored by Intel Corporation, Hewlett Packard, AT&T Research, Apple Computer and The National Science Foundation.

48. Wray, Herbert. (1999, March 22). Getting close, but not too close. *U.S. News and World Report*, 56.

49. Meyer, J. (2009). Report: Bush-era surveillance went beyond wiretaps. *Chicago Tribune*. Retrieved from Chicagotribune.com.

50. Corbett, M., & Thatcher, M. (1997, June 26). People management. *Personal Publications, 13*(3), 26.

51. Siemens, G. (2002, December 1). *The art of blogging—part 1: Overview, definitions, uses and implications*, p. 2. Retrieved from www.elearnspace.org/Articles/blogging_part_1.htm.

52. www.blogger.com.

53. *Publish your thoughts.* (1999–2004). Google. Retrieved from www.blogger.com.

54. Suler, J. (2008). Image, word, action: Interpersonal dynamics in a photo-sharing community. *CyberPsychology, 11*(5), 555.

55. Ko, H., & Feng-Yang, K. (2009). Can blogging enhance subjective well-being through self-disclosure? *CyberPsychology & Behavior, 12*(1).

56. Dickerson, C. (2004, May 24). Blogging to ourselves. *InfoWorld, 26*(21), p. 34.

57. Richardson, W. (2004, January). *Blogging and RSS—The "what's it?" and "how to" of powerful new web tools for educators*. Retrieved from www.infotoday.com/MMSchools/jan04/richardson.shtml.

58. Ibid.

59. For a detailed discussion about blogging skills, see Doctorow, C., Dornfest, R., Johnson, J. S., Powers, S., Trott, B., & Trott, M. G. (2002). *Essential blogging*. Sebastopol, CA: O'Reilly.

60. McDonald, S. N. (2005, July 5). *Facebook frenzy*. The Associated Press.

61. Bugeja, M. (2006). Facing the Facebook. *The Chronicle of Higher Education*. Retrieved from chronicle.com/jobs/news/2006/01/2006012301c/careers.html.

62. Facebook Press Room. (2009). Retrieved from www.facebook.com/press/info.php?statistics.

63. Ibid.

64. Ibid.

65. St. Xavier gets pokes in, but fails to rattle Tanski. (2007, December 1). *Cleveland Plain Dealer*, p. D1.

66. Tancer, B. (2007, October 24). My Space v. Facebook: Competing addictions. *Time*. Retrieved from www.time.com/time/printout/0,8816,1675244,00.html.

67. *NCSU students face underage drinking charges due to online photos.* (2005, October 29). Retrieved from web.archive.org/web/20051031084848/www.wral.com/news/5204275/detail.html.

68. Facebook postings, photos incriminate dorm party-goers. (2009, January 7). *The Northerner*. Retrieved from www.thenortherner.com/2.9399/facebook-postings-photos-incriminate-dorm-party-goers-1.1281445.

69. Schweitzer, S. (2005, October 6). Fisher College expels student over website entries. *The Boston Globe*. Retrieved from www.boston.com/news/local/articles/2005/10/06/fisher_college_expels_student_over_website_entries/.

70. Pepitone, J. (2006. February 8). Kicked in the face: Freshmen claim Judicial Affairs threatened expulsion for creation of Facebook group critical of TA. *The Daily Orange*. Retrieved from www.dailyorange.com/media/paper522/news/2006/02/08/News/Kicked.In.The.Face.Freshmen.Claim.Judicial.Affairs.Threatened.Expulsion.For.Crea-1603618.shtml?norewrite.

71. Waler, P. (2007, November 13). Teen accused of school plot in Pa. linked to fatal shooter in Finland. *Cleveland Plain Dealer*, p. A5.

72. Levy, S. (2007, August 20/27). Facebook grows up. *Newsweek*, p. 41.

73. Ibid.

74. www.facebook.com/press/info.php?statistics.

75. Tancer.

76. twitter.com/.

77. Surprise! There's a third YouTube co-founder. (2006, October 11). *USA Today*. Retrieved from www.usatoday.com/tech/news/2006-10-11.

78. *YouTube statistics.* (2008, March 18). Retrieved from mediatedcultures.net/ksudigg/?p=163.

79. MacManus, R. (2007, August 21). *Top 10 YouTube videos of all time.* Retrieved from www.readwriteweb.com/archives/top_10_youtube_videos_of_all_time.php.

80. *Facebook, the privacy and productivity challenge.* (1997–2009). Sophos. Retrieved from www.sophos.com/security/topic/facebook.html.

81. Swartz, J. (2007, September 12). Soon millions of Facebookers won't be incognito. *USA TODAY*, p. 3B.

82. Ibid.

83. *What you need to know about Facebook.* (n.d.). Office of Career Services, University of Central Missouri. Adapted from materials developed by Kathleen McCabe, Director of Peer Education at Creighton University.

84. Facebook, the privacy and productivity challenge. *SOPHOS*. sophos.com.

85. Levy, p. 42.

86. Sherry Turkle, MIT, as cited in "Did you know that . . ." (2009). *Bottom Line*, 30 (15), 7.

87. *Car accident cell phone statistics.* (2002–2009). Edgar Snyder and Associates. Retrieved from www.edgarsnyder.com/auto-accident/auto/cell/statistics.html.

88. *Arizona may ban vehicular text-messaging.* (2007, December 15). United Press International. Retrieved from www.upi.com/NewsTrack/Top_News/2007/08/15/arizona_may_ban_vehicular_textmessaging/2863; also see *Cleveland, Albany say no to texting.* (2009, April 19). Retrieved from handsfreeinfo.com/cleveland-albany-say-no-to-texting.

89. Bronwyn Clifford/Association of Chartered Physiotherapists in Occupational Health and Ergonomics. (2005). *The Times of India.* Retrieved from www.acpohe.org.uk/.

90. Jeff Stanton, associate professor of information sciences, as cited in Friedman, T. L. (2007). *The world is flat.* New York: Picador/Farrrar, Straus and Girous, p. 522.

91. Ravindhran, S. (2008, March 26). *Is text messaging a mental illness?* KABC-TV/DT. Retrieved from abclocal.go.com/kabc/story?section=news/health&id=6043089; also see Rutland, J. B., Sheets, T., & Young, T. (2007). Development of a scale to measure problem use of short message service: The SMS Problem Use Diagnostic Questionnaire. *CyberPsychology & Behavior, 10*(6), 841–844.

92. *Pitfalls of child text messaging.* (2007, October 5). Retrieved from MSN.com.

93. Turkle, 2009.

94. Ibid.

95. *All about texting, SMS, and MMS.* (2003). Textually.org. Retrieved from www.textually.org/textually/archives/2003/10/001845.htm; also see Faulkner, X., & Culwin, F. (2005). When fingers do the talking: A study of text messaging. *Interacting with computers, 17*(2), 167–185.

Chapter 11: Interpersonal Communication Skills

1. Based on a study conducted by Atchely, P. (2001, July 12). University of Kansas, Department of Psychology. Lawrence, KS. Retrieved from www.ur.ku.edu/News/01N/July12/cellular.html.

2. Bluebanning, M., Summers, J. A., Frankland, H. C., Nelson, L. L., & Beegle, G. (2004, Winter). Dimensions of family and professional partnerships: Constructive guidelines. *Exceptional Children, 70*(2), 167–184.

3. Bacal, R. (2009). *Self-disclosure as a communication tool.* Retrieved from www.work911.com/communication/skillselfdisclosure.htm.

4. Johnson, D. W. (2000). *Reaching out: Interpersonal effectiveness and self-actualization.* Boston, MA: Allyn and Bacon, pp. 132–134.

5. The list of strategies are updated, but were based on Kellerman, K., & Cole, T. (1994). Classifying compliance gaining messages: Taxonomic disorder and strategic confusion. *Communication Theory, 4,* 3–60; for further investigation, see Boster, F. J., Shaw, A. S., Hughes, M., Kotowski, M. R., Strom, R. E., & Deatrick, L. M. (2009, July/August). Dump-and-chase: The effectiveness of persistence as a sequential request compliance-gaining strategy. *Communication Studies, 60*(3), 219–234; and Kellermann, K. (2004, August). A goal-directed approach to gaining compliance. *Communication Research, 31*(4), 397–445.

6. A concept referred to by Dr. Joy Browne, media psychologist on her nationally syndicated radio show. For additional information, see www.drjoy.com/.

7. Burchard, G. A., Yarhouse, M. A., Kilian, M. K., Worthington, E. L. Jr., Berry, J., & Canter, D. E. (2003, Fall). A study of two marital enrichment programs and couples' quality of life. *Journal of Psychology & Theology, 31*(3), 240–253.

8. Berko, R. (1993, December). Dealing with stress. Unpublished paper presented in a workshop to the counseling staff at the Social Service Agency, Alexandria, VA.

9. A principle of Gestalt Psychology, as explained by Les Wyman, Gestalt Institute, Cleveland, OH.

10. Zander, R. S. (2001, July 29). The power of an apology. *Parade*, p. 8.

11. Tesdell, D. R. (1997). *The top 10 ways to apologize to someone you have hurt or offended.* Lifecoach@coachdt.com. Retrieved from topten.org/content/tt.BN30.htm.

12. *When and how to apologize.* (n.a.). The University of Nebraska Cooperative Extension and the Nebraska Health and Human Services System; for a perspective on apology in negotiation and business contexts, see Regain your counterpart's trust with an apology. (2009, February). *Negotiation*, 6.

13. Reported by Dr. Susan Forward, media psychologist. See www.susanforward.com/therapist.htm.

14. For a discussion of universe and nature, see Kim, Y. Y. (2009). Toward intercultural personhood: An integration of Eastern and Western perspectives. In L. Samovar, R. Porter, & E. McDaniel (Eds.), *Intercultural communication: A reader* (12th ed.). Boston, MA: Wadsworth Cengage Learning, p. 436.

15. For a discussion of direct and indirect verbal styles see Ting-Toomey, T., & Chung, L. (2005). *Understanding intercultural communication.* New York: Oxford Press, pp. 175–182.

16. Fallowfield, L., & Jenkins, V. (2004, January 24). Communicating sad, bad, and difficult news in medicine. *The Lancet*, *363*(9405), 312–320.

17. The other examples in this paragraph were said by Eric Berko during his childhood years.

18. Lehane, S. (1979). *The creative child.* Englewood Cliffs, NJ: Prentice-Hall; for a position paper on child creativity, see Jalongo, M. R. (2003). *The child's right to creative thought and expression.* Association for Childhood Education International. Retrieved from www.acei .org/creativepp.htm.

19. A concept proposed by Roy Berko, a certified school counselor, speaking about the misdiagnosis of ADD by primary care physicians.

Chapter 12: Interpersonal Communication in the Workplace

1. Varner, I., & Beamer, L. (1995). *Intercultural communication in the global workplace.* Chicago: Irwin.

2. There are various publications that elaborate on the concepts of culture and climate. See, for example, Ashkanasy, N. M., Wilderom, C., & Peterson, M. F. (2000). *Handbook of organizational culture and climate.* Thousand Oaks, CA: Sage.

3. Neuliep, J. W. (2009). *Intercultural communication: A contextual approach* (4th ed.). Los Angeles: Sage, pp. 124–127.

4. Hall, E. T. (1966). *The hidden dimension.* New York: Doubleday.

5. Richmond, V. P., McCroskey, J. C., & McCroskey, L. L. (2005). *Organizational communication for survival: Making work, work.* (3rd ed.) Boston: Pearson, pp. 10–14.

6. For an interesting review of the research on communication flow in organizations, see Papa, M. J., Daniels, T. D., & Spiker, B. K. (2008). *Organizational communication perspectives and trends.* Los Angeles: Sage, pp. 51–60.

7. A worker at the Avon Lake, Ohio, Ford Motor Company plant. Name withheld by request.

8. For a discussion of professionalism, look up the code of ethics and behavior for the national organization for your intended career field.

9. Seibold, D., Kang, P. Bailliard, B., & John, J. (2008). *Communication that damages teamwork: The dark side of teams.* A paper presented at the annual meeting of the International Communication Association, Montreal, Canada.

10. Ibid.

11. *Survey finds workers average only three productive days per week.* (2005). Redmond, WA: Microsoft. Retrieved from www.microsoft.com/presspass/press/2005.

12. O'Toole, J., & Lawler, E. E., III. *The new American workplace.* New York: Palgrave. As cited in Seibold, Kang, Bailliard, & John.

13. Cockburn-Wooton, C., Holmes, P., & Simpson, M. (2008). Teaching teamwork in business communication/management programs. *Business Communication Quarterly, 71*(4), 417–420.

14. Hawkins, K. W., & Bryant P., & Fillion, B. P. (1999). Perceived communication skill needs for work groups. *Communication Research Reports, 16*(2), 167–174.

15. Ibid.

16. Blair, C. A., Hoffman, B. J., & Helland, K. R. (2008). Narcissism in organizations: A multisource appraisal reflects different perspectives. *Human Performance, 21*(3), 254–276.

17. Ibid.

18. Guttman, H. M. (2009, July). Leading meetings 101. *Leadership Excellence, 26*(7), p. 18.

19. Chambers, E. (2008, April 15). Tips on adjusting to your first job after graduation. *Wall Street Journal, 251*(88), p. D6.

20. Quoted or closely adapted from Wolgemuth, L. The inside job: 7 lessons from a successful job search. (2009, July 8). *US News and World Report.* Retrieved from www.usnews.com/money/blogs/the-inside-job/2009/7/8/7-lessons-from-a-successful-job-search.html.

21. Kerr, L. (2007, October 3). Networking and research can help find that first job. *Nursing Standard, 22*(4), p. 33.

22. Get face to face to land a job. (2009, March 1). *The Herald-Sun–McClatchy-Tribune.* Retrieved from www.tmcnet.com/usubmit/2009/03/01/4022073.htm.

23. Wolgemuth, The inside job.

24. See Kikoski, J. F. (1999, Summer). Effective communication in the performance appraisal interview. *Public Personnel Management, 28,* 301–322.

25. Silverman, S. B., & Wexley, K. N. (1984). Reaction of employees to performance appraisal interviews as a function of their participation in rating scale development. *Personnel Psychology,* 703–710.

26. Galpin, T. (1995, April). Pruning the grapevine. *Training and Development Journal, 49,* 28–33.

27. *Adapted from Top 10 workplace email tips.* (2008). Speedbrake Publishing. Retrieved from www.speedbrake.com/atwork/workmail.htm; Smith, S. (1996–2009). *Email in the workplace: Avoiding legal landmines.* Mediate.com Solomon International Dispute Resolution Institute. Retrieved from www.mediate.com/articles/smith.cfm.

28. Madge, C., Meek, J., Wellens, J., & Hooley, T. (2009, June). Facebook, social integration and informal learning at university: 'It is more for socialising and talking to friends about work than for actually doing work'. *Learning, Media, & Technology, 34*(2), 141–155.

29. Pawlik-Kienlen, L. (2007, August 28). *Gossiping at work: Talking about your coworkers makes you look bad.* Retrieved from psychology.suite101.com/article.cfm/gossip_at_work#izzORTnVWQHF.

30. McIntosh, J. (2007, November 19). Stop rumors at work: Respond to rumors and lies on the job with effective communication. Retrieved from businessmanagement.suite101.com/article.cfm/stop_rumors_at_work#ixzz0RTooScUd.

31. van Iterson, A., & Clegg, S. R. (2008, August). The politics of gossip and denial in interorganizational relations. *Human Relations, 61*(8), 1117–1137.

32. Hall, J., Andrzejewski, S., & Yopchick, J. (2009). Psychosocial correlates of interpersonal sensitivity: A meta-analysis. *Journal of Nonverbal Behavior, 33*(3), 149–180.

33. Richmond, V. P., McCroskey, J. C., & McCroskey, L. L. (2005). *Organizational communication for survival: Making work, work.* (3rd ed.) Boston: Pearson, pp. 10–14.

34. de Vries, Reinout E., Bakker-Pieper, A., Siberg, R. A., van Gameren, K., & Vlug, M. (2009). The content and dimensionality of communication styles. *Communication Research, 36*(2), 178–206.

35. Papinchak, K. (2007, April). Things I wish I'd known before I showed up on the job: A student's practical guide to surviving the first few weeks (and beyond) of your first job. *Public Relations Tactics, 14*(4), p. 19.

36. Goodboy, A. K., McCroskey, J. C. (2008). Toward a theoretical model of the role of organizational orientations and Machiavellianism on Nonverbal Immediacy Behavior and job satisfaction. *Human Communication, 11*(3), 293–307.

37. Neuliep, pp. 140–144.

38. Richmond, McCroskey, & McCroskey, pp. 10–14.

39. Ibid.

40. A classic work on power is French, J. R. P., & Raven, B. (1959). The bases of social power. In D. Cartwright (Ed.), *Studies in social power.* Ann Arbor, MI: University of Michigan Press.

41. Broderick, P. C., & Blewitt, P. (2006). *The life span: Human development for helping professionals* (2nd ed.). Boston: Pearson, Chapter 15.

42. Chiles, A. M., & Zorn, T. E. (1995). Empowerment in organizations: employees' perceptions of the influences on empowerment. *Journal of Applied Communication Research, 23*(1), 1–25.

43. Conrad, C., & Poole, M. P. (1998). *Strategic organizational communication,* Fort Worth, TX: Harcourt Brace, Chapter 7.

44. Weisel, J. J., & King, P. E. (2007). Involvement in a conversation and attributions concerning excessive self-disclosure. *Southern Communication Journal, 72*(4), 345–354.

45. McCroskey, J. C., & Richmond, V. P. (1993). Identifying compulsive communicators: The Talkaholic Scale, *Communication Research Reports, 11,* 39–52; McCroskey, J. C., & Richmond, V. P. (1995). Correlates of compulsive communication: Quantitative and qualitative characteristics. *Communication Quarterly, 43,* 39–52.

46. Kashy, D. A., & DePaulo, B. M. (1996). Who lies? *Journal of Personality and Social Psychology, 70,* 1037–1051.

47. Lindsey, L., Dunbar, N., & Russell, J. (2008). *Risky business or managed event? Power and deception in the workplace.* A paper presented at the annual meeting of the International Communication Association, Montreal, Canada.

48. For an extensive discussion of deceptive communication, see Vrij. A. (2000). *Detecting lies and deceit: The psychology of lying and the implications for professionals.* Chichester, England: Wiley.

49. Wilson, B. A. (2008). Predicting intended unethical behavior of business students. *Journal of Education for Business, 83*(4), 187–195.

50. Lindsey, Dunbar, & Russell.

51. Schweitzer, M. E., Hershey, J. C., & Bradlow, E. T. (2006). Promises and lies: Restoring violated trust. *Organizational Behavior and Human Decision Processes, 101,* 1–19.

52. As cited in Lindsey, Dunbar, & Russell.

53. For a meta-analysis of research on the topic, see Bond C. F., & DePaulo, B. M. (2008). Accuracy in deception judgments. *Personality and Social Psychology Review, 10,* 214–234.

54. Hymowitz, C. (2009). Can ranking employees do more harm than good? *The Wall Street Journal Online.* Retrieved from 208.144.115.170/columnists/inthelead/20010516-inthe lead.html.

55. Teven, J. J., Richmond, V. P., & McCroskey, J. C. (1998). Measuring tolerance for disagreement. *Communication Research Reports, 15,* 209–217.

56. Richmond, McCroskey, & McCroskey.

57. Yen, J. Y., Knutson, T. J.& Posirisuk, S. (2006). Thai relational development and rhetorical sensitivity as potential contributors to intercultural communication effectiveness. *Journal of Intercultural Communication Research, 35*(3), 205–217.

58. As cited in Neuliep. For additional explanation, see pp. 175–176.

59. Ibid.

60. Cho, J. (2008, June 28). The great divide: Learning to talk so the other sex hears you is more complicated than you think. *Cleveland Plain Dealer,* p. E1.

61. Ibid.

62. Ibid., p. E2.

63. Ibid.

64. Ibid.

65. Annis, B. (2004). *Gender differences in the workplace.* WITI careers. Retrieved from www.witi.com/careers/2004/genderdiffs.php.

66. Ibid.

67. *USA Today Magazine.* (1996, May). *124*(2612), 9–10.

68. Hoffman, E. (2006, February 10). Changing jobs, changing benefits. *BusinessWeek,* p 5.

69. Ream, R. (2000). Changing jobs? It's a changing market. *Information Today,* 17(2), 18–21.

70. *Intimate partner violence statistics.* (n.d.). Yale University Mental Health & Counseling. Retrieved from www.yale.edu/uhs/med_services/share/violence-statistics.html; also see *Safety and health topics workplace violence.* United States Department of Labor (2007). Retrieved from www.osha.gov/SLTC/workplaceviolence/.

71. *Lab technician held in Yale student's slaying.* (2009, September 17). MSNBC. Retrieved from www.msnbc.msn.com/id/32890245/ns/us_news-crime_and_courts/.

72. For additional reading, see *Occupational violence.* (2009, May 28). National Institute for Occupational Safety and Health (NIOSH) Division of Safety Research. www.cdc.gov/niosh/topics/violence/; *Violence in the workplace.* Canadian Centre for Occupational Health and Safety. (2008). www.oshcanada.com/oshanswers/psychosocial/violence.html.

73. Morrison, T. (1993). *Nobel Prize for Literature acceptance speech.* As reported on National Public Radio. NobelPrize.org. Retrieved from nobelprize.org/nobel_prizes/literature/laureates/1993/morrison-lecture.html.

74. For a discussion of sexual harassment, see *Sexual harassment.* (2009, March 11). U.S. Equal Employment Opportunity Commission. Retrieved from www.eeoc.gov/types/sexual_harassment.html; for a perspective on the topic, see O'Leary-Kelly, A. M., Bowes-Sperry, L., Bates, C. A., & Lean, E. R. (2009, June). Sexual harassment at work: A decade (plus) of progress. *Journal of Management, 35*(3), 503–536.

75. *Sexual harassment.* (2009, March 11). U.S. Equal Employment Opportunity Commission. Retrieved from www.eeoc.gov/types/sexual_harassment.html.

76. Schindehette, S., Sellinger, M., & Margery, B. K. (2000, April 17). Tarnished brass. *People, 53*(15), 75–77.

77. Nayak, M. B., Byrne, C. A., Martin, M. K., & Abraham, A. G. (2003, October). Attitudes toward violence against women: A cross-nation study. *Sex Roles, 49*(7/8), 333–343.

78. *Male survivors of sexual violence.* (n.d.). Michigan Resource Center on Domestic and Sexual Violence. Retrieved from www.michigan.gov/documents/datingviolence/DHS-Dating Violence-MaleSurvivors_198439_7.pdf.

79. Rentoul, L., & Appleboom, N. (2003). Understanding the psychological impact of rape and serious sexual assault of men: A literature review. *Journal of Psychiatric and Mental Health Nursing, 4*(4), 267–274.

80. *Male victims of sexual abuse, rape, incest, and sex-base offenses.* (2007, January 22). Aardvarc. Retrieved from www.aardvarc.org/rape/about/men.shtml.

81. Ibid.

82. Morin, R. (1992). Harassment consensus grows. *Washington Post,* p. A–22.

83. *Title VII of the Civil Rights Act of 1964.* (2009, February 17). *The U.S. Equal Employment Opportunity Commission.* Retrieved from eeoc.gov/policy/vii.html.

84. Based on the writings of Rebecca L. Ray. See for example, Ray, R. L. (1993, January). *Bridging both worlds: The communication consultant in corporate America.* Lanham, MD: University Press of America.

85. House, A., Dallinger, J. M., & Kilgallen, D. (1998). Androgyny and rhetorical sensitivity: The connection of gender and communicator style. *Communication Reports, 11*(1), 11–20.

Index

About the Authors

Dr. Roy Berko is the former Associate Director of the National Communication Association. He has authored or coauthored over twenty-five communication textbooks and numerous professional articles and studies. His academic work in both the fields of communication and counseling offer a unique perspective on interpersonal communication. He has been a professor (Lorain County Community College, Towson University, George Washington University, University of Maryland, and Notre Dame College of Ohio), a mental health counselor in private practice, a crisis counselor, and a communication trainer.

Dr. Joan E. Aitken is a professor of communication at Park University. Her research has focused on communication and technology. She has taught at the University of Missouri, Kansas City; University of Louisiana, Lafayette; and University of Arkansas, Fayetteville. A former editor of the National Communication Association's *Communication Teacher*, Aitken has published seven books and more than fifty articles and book chapters.

Dr. Andrew Wolvin, a professor of communication at the University of Maryland, is an internationally recognized expert in listening behavior. Identified as one of the top-ranked active researchers in communication, he has published widely in the field. Director of the basic communication course at Maryland, he also has extensive experience as a listening and communication consultant in federal agencies and private corporations.